MANAGING WORLD ECONOMIC CHANGE: INTERNATIONAL POLITICAL ECONOMY

Robert A. Isaak

Pace University

PRENTICE HALL, UPPER SADDLE RIVER, NEW JERSEY 07458

Library of Congress Cataloging-in-Publication Data

ISAAK, ROBERT A.
    Managing world economic change: international political economy/
Robert A. Isaak.—3rd ed.
        p.   cm.
    Includes bibliographical references and index.
    ISBN 0-13-011775-7
    I. International economic relations.   I. Title.   II. Title:
International political economy.
HF1411.I76   1999
337—dc21   99-39016
                                                       CIP

Editorial director: Charlyce Jones Owen
Editor in chief: Nancy Roberts
Senior acquisitions editor: Beth Gillett Mejia
Editorial assistant: Brian Prybella
Marketing manager: Christopher DeJohn
Editorial/production supervision: Kari Callaghan Mazzola
Electronic page makeup: Kari Callaghan Mazzola
Electronic art creation: John P. Mazzola
Interior design: John P. Mazzola
Cover director: Jayne Conte
Cover design: Bruce Kenselaar
Buyer: Ben Smith

This book was set in 10/12 Novarese by Big Sky Composition
and was printed and bound by Courier Companies, Inc.
The cover was printed by Phoenix Color Corp.

Printed in the United States of America
10   9   8   7   6   5   4   3   2   1

ISBN   0-13-011775-7

PRENTICE-HALL INTERNATIONAL (UK) LIMITED, London
PRENTICE-HALL OF AUSTRALIA PTY. LIMITED, Sydney
PRENTICE-HALL CANADA INC., Toronto
PRENTICE-HALL HISPANOAMERICANA, S.A., Mexico
PRENTICE-HALL OF INDIA PRIVATE LIMITED, New Delhi
PRENTICE-HALL OF JAPAN, INC., Tokyo
PEARSON EDUCATION ASIA PTE. LTD., Singapore
EDITORA PRENTICE-HALL DO BRASIL, LTDA., Rio de Janeiro

To Gudrun, Sonya, and Andrew,
who light up my life

CONTENTS

PREFACE

Our sin is a lack of transparency.

—Charles Wright, *Disjecta Membra* (1997)

CHANGE IN THE GLOBAL ECONOMY HAS SO INCREASED IN VELOCITY BY THE DAWN OF THE twenty-first century that by the time a word hits the page to describe it, the word is history.

The key question since the first edition of this book was published as *International Political Economy* in 1991 thus becomes: Which principles of the past help to explain the politics of international economic relations and how are they managed in the present for individual and group interests? The book, in short, is a summary of historical principles, key concepts, and persistent trends set in the context of a collective learning framework of adapting to global change without losing cultural integrity.

Writer Donald Barthelme put the same thing differently in his short story "The Rise of Capitalism": "Smoke, rain, abulia. What can the concerned citizen do to fight the rise of capitalism in his own community? Study of the tides of conflict and power in a system in which there is a structural inequality is an important task." Power and wealth come together in the management of global change and no one claims that the playing field is level: The objective is to understand the nature of world economic inequalities in a strategic manner that gives one the courage and knowledge to act to better the life chances of one's self, one's group, and one's people.

The world economy seems to reinvent itself daily. In October 1998, for example, President Bill Clinton rallied the Group of 7 industrialized nations to create a special credit line for the International Monetary Fund to give "preemptive" credit to nations threatened with the international contagion of financial meltdown due to speculators—such as Brazil. What is important in this example is not the event itself but understanding the concepts, institutions, and relationships that make the event possible: Why can only the president of the United States rally the richest countries? Who are the G-7? What does the International Monetary Fund do and how is it changing? What caused the global financial meltdown and why is it "contagious"? What role do capitalistic speculators play and why did Brazil come under siege? How did Alan Greenspan of the U.S. Federal Reserve Bank become the surrogate world central banker who loosened global money in order to stem the threat of global deflation? These are the kinds of questions we will seek to understand, if not to answer.

This edition has been significantly restructured. A new chapter focuses on business cycles and capital flows and suggests some of the persistent trends no one can get around, whether rich or poor. A look at the fashionable mode of "globalization" may help one to cope and perhaps to defend one's culture. There are new sections on the speeding up processes of the development of "virtual organizations" and the making of national economic miracles over the past fifty years. But there are also slowing down principles and developments introduced, dealing with environmental policies and efforts at resistance for the sake of cultural integrity and political and economic independence—including international environmental agreements and the elaboration of trade blocs. The ordering of the chapters has been recast to be more natural in terms of what is most important: Money and trade have been moved up to the front.

A glossary has been added, as well as numerous figures. A test item manual of both multiple choice and essay questions is available from Prentice Hall, which is unusual for a book of this kind but which helps to make the learning process more transparent.

Books are colored by what "the reporter" has experienced. As a Europeanist who has spent part of each year of the past three decades in Europe, I often use European examples in my writing. Yet since beginning my studies of international relations at Stanford University in the 1960s, I have sought to understand the depth of the American experience (in, for example, *American Political Thinking*, 1994), and the global context, particularly in terms of the relations between the economies of developed and developing countries. My work with German economist Wilhelm Hankel while we were both teaching at the Johns Hopkins University SAIS Center in Bologna, Italy, focused on this North-South interaction (*Modern Inflation*, 1983). Most recently, on a Fulbright grant at the Alfred Weber Institute of the University of Heidelberg, I deepened my knowledge of environmental economics and management: Both the rich and the poor will suffer more ecological change than they might imagine. We have an obligation to regard everywhere on the earth as "home" rather than passively accepting the placelessness that globalization stimulates (research summed up in *Green Logic: Ecopreneurship, Theory, and Ethics*).

My consulting for Prudential Intercultural has added a cross-cultural dimension to the management of change added here, introducing yet another growing source of literature that helps us to understand why peoples of different cultures solve problems and approach dilemmas of change uniquely: I now know why the Italians tried to persuade me to declare poverty and let the state pay a hospital bill like 90 percent of the others; why a Spanish plumber used the palm of his hand to unstop a bathtub instead of a plumber's helper; why the Swiss chose to stay out of the European Union while adjusting their currency to the Euro; why the Russians often prefer to take wage payments in potatoes; and why a typical American investor does not even begin to ask what lies behind the companies in his or her pension stock portfolio.

As for debts of gratitude, I could round up the usual suspects—my colleagues at Pace University, New York, and the Alfred Weber Institute in Heidelberg; others in Potsdam, Berlin, Leipzig, Aix-en-Provence, Benissa, Rome, Tokyo, Singapore, and Sheffield, and at Prentice Hall (particularly my editor, Beth Gillett Mejia); but the number of credits would be too numerous. However, the staff help under deadline pressures at Pace University by Lucille Kenney, Janet Picolo, Gail Pietrangolare, Mary O'Conner, Anna Peroux, Vicci Hottenrott (who contributed a great deal to the text), Yanlin Li, and Jackie Womack was out of the ordinary and merits special thanks. I would also like to thank Juliann Allison of the University of California at Riverside, who reviewed the manuscript, and Kari Callaghan Mazzola and John P. Mazzola, who were responsible for the production of the book. Let us leave with the sin of the lack of transparency undone: My family holds together because of modifications I refused to take the time to make. Each of us, in our own small way, must discover how to buffer ourselves and the integrity of our small cultural unit against the insatiable demands of global change. Meanwhile, our fingers are still itching with thoughts that have not yet landed in a written text.

Robert A. Isaak

INTRODUCTION

Ill fares the land with the great deal of velocity where wealth accumulates and there ain't any reciprocity.

—O. Henry, "Supply and Demand"

O. HENRY'S SHORT STORY "SUPPLY AND DEMAND" IS THE TALE OF A BIG WHITE MAN WHO GOES down to "Gaudymala" and uses force and his wits to turn an Indian tribe into slaves. The white man, Patrick Shane, sets himself up as king. He takes the biggest house in the village for himself, and has the natives wash the streams for gold dust that they bring only to him. To keep this colonized political economy going, King Shane, or the "Grand Yacuma," gives the Indians a weekly sermon in the council-house (He is the council) on the law of supply and demand: He praises supply and knocks demand; he teaches them not to desire anything beyond their simplest needs. They bring him all the gold and remain contented on a bit of mutton, cocoa, and fruit, even making their own clothes.

All goes well until a capitalist laden down with artificial jewelry and mirrors comes into the village on a mule and tempts the local population with Western luxuries in order to get at the gold that is rumored to be in the village. Enlightened by the marketing of the foreign salesman, the natives revolt against their ruler. The king and the capitalist flee for their lives, taking their trinkets with them, but leaving behind the gold, which is not worth much if there are no goods to be traded for it.

O. Henry's tale illustrates key elements involved when managing change in the international political economy. Some people have more than others to start with. They use their advantageous position to speed things up, accumulating even more wealth and further increasing the gap between themselves and the poor. The rich, in short, are better positioned and better able to use speed to their advantage. Noting this, they continue to speed things up to increase their holdings. Wealth does not seem to buy happiness, however. The hectic velocity of materialism combined with the lack of reciprocity (equitable give and take) in the community leads to a sense of meanness in the quality of life. Leisure becomes hectic and time-starved. There is hardly a moment left for "others." Ultimately, if the gap between the rich and the poor is perceived to be too great, or too "unfair," those in power may see their power base begin to crumble. The political recipe of pushing supply and knocking demand works only as long as the community can be isolated from the infinite variety of goods and services available to consumers on the global market. As the majority of people gain information and goods from markets external to the community, a process of collective learning is stimulated. The people suddenly want more than they have and they know what they want. As their leaders adopt the ways of foreign elites who bring new knowledge, goods, and opportunities into the community, this process of collective learning accelerates.

The same impulse that leads the wealthy elites to speed up social and economic processes to maximize their own short-term interests forces those down the social scale to accelerate their learning curves in order to adapt and survive in the emerging economy. As the scarcity of resources appears to become less scarce to the general population, they demand more, buy more, and learn faster. **International political economy** is the study of the politics behind the economic relations among peoples and nations in order to assess their relative wealth and power.

What is striking in O. Henry's tale is not so much the inequality between the foreign elite and the natives—which is the nature of the world—but rather the specific ways in which this asymmetrical status quo is at first preserved and then eventually undermined. Nor are the natives necessarily better off when the foreigners leave, despite their freedom. Like Adam and Eve, they have bitten knowledge of the world and can never return to ignorant bliss. International political economy is a process of continual disenchantment. But by examining the collective learning patterns of other peoples as they cope with the conditions and rules of the global political economy, individuals can perhaps understand their own disenchantment as a fruitful learning process for themselves and their people. For there are strategies and tactics in this ceaseless struggle of the strong to keep what they have in conflict with the weak who seek to change the international system in their favor. Perhaps, as Antonio Gramsci suggested, one can learn to train the individual will to be optimistic despite the pessimism of the intellect when it is applied to the outcome of the collective behavior of human beings.

Ever since the Industrial Revolution, the gap between industrialized and developing countries has become a central preoccupation of the study of international political economy. Some define international political economy as the interplay between international politics and international economics or business. Others stress the process of international wealth acquisition and transfer. But the key question concerns the essential dynamics that give rise to unequal distributions: Who gets what, when, and how among different players in the global economy?

Because unequal distributions are not immutable or frozen, the most fruitful focus is on managing change for the sake of specific collective interests. By stressing ongoing collective learning and positioning processes, one can understand how managers of nation-states, multinational corporations, and international organizations are able to outmaneuver each other and how they can see the consequences for different peoples. It is particularly important to pay attention to nations or multinational companies that make innovative breakthroughs, or alternatively, undergo severe economic crises.

For example, the seven "superstars" of East Asia (excluding Japan)—South Korea, Taiwan, Singapore, Hong Kong, Indonesia, Malaysia, and Thailand—increased their income per person between 5 and 6 percent per year from 1965 through 1996. The dark side of the excesses of this growth, which resulted in the banking and stock market crisis in these countries in 1997–1998, initiating a global financial crisis, does not wipe out this amazing thirty-year record. The financial crisis served as a warning to those who speculate on growth without concerning themselves with political corruption, arbitrary banking regulations, and building social capital without democratic legitimacy. The positive "collective learning" contagion of miracle growth transformed itself into the negative "collective learning" contagion of financial panic—when the hot money from abroad could no longer be properly digested.

To understand these collective excesses—euphoria followed by mass panic—one must probe beneath for the perceptions and cultural values that steer "collective learning" across cultures and drives it to extremes when the legitimacy of limits is thought to be either nonexistent or to be totally undermined.

Are these extreme examples an outgrowth of something uniquely Asian? Which factors permitted the development of such collective capacity for learning or adaptation in the global economy on the part of states or multinational organizations? Are neo-Confucian societies superior in their ability to learn quickly to adapt collectively to global transformations? What caused the financial meltdown in these "miracle" emerging economies? Which factors of leadership and legitimacy limited the damage to some of them more than others?

On the level of multinational firms, which breakthrough models of organization of the end of the twentieth century are most worthy of emulation: the complacent Big Blue IBM that almost went under while clinging to its mainframe computer ideology in the mid-1980s, or the decentralized IBM of hit-team consumer targeting, which began with giving a creative group the autonomy to develop the PC (personal computer) without bureaucratic hurdles to jump? Which structures block such innovative learning or adaptation, and why? What are the social costs?

The old IBM took care of its employees and had a reputation for keeping them for a lifetime. The new IBM turns people over fast, gives few employees the expectation they will be there very long, cycles them through depersonalized virtual offices, and gives them few opportunities to build up any communal ties with others in the firm. How, in short, can we collectively learn to pick up competitive learnings of others swiftly enough to satisfy the social and economic needs of our own communities without losing the quality of life and stability of culture that used to give us a sense of social meaning and belonging?

The focus in this book upon collective learning and positioning of unequal actors in the global economy and upon strategies for managing change will be contrasted with other, more conventional approaches or schools of thought. The assumptions of Western liberalism and its stress upon markets will be contrasted and what will be termed "postliberalism"—"interventionist" reactions to liberalism stemming from older visions such as Marxism, economic nationalism, structuralism, or from newer communitarian visions seeking to transcend liberalism for the sake of the integrity of an existing culture or community. As one observes how these various perspectives illuminate the explanation of major phenomena in the global economy—such as the world trade and monetary systems—one also senses what has been left out or left in the dark. The observer can only wear one set of glasses at a time, and each set only permits the wearer to see what the lenses were designed to see. International political economy is a war of disciplines and ideologies over the same worldly turf.

Yet the turf remains to be explained in some sort of universal and verifiable way—namely, the human use and abuse of the earth and the way people learn to position themselves to improve their collective life chances upon it. And in this process the picture of the whole earth or global context cannot be lost without ignoring the dominant revolutionary transformation of our times: the evolution of one global market or economy that will be managed one way or another by managers with transnational perspectives—whether they be managers of governmental institutions, multinational corporations, unions, or international organizations. This integration of finance, markets, technology, information flows, transportation, institutions, and product standardization throughout the world is referred to as **globalization**.

POLITICS VERSUS ECONOMICS OR LIBERALISM VERSUS POSTLIBERALISM

The "whole earth" approach to political economy—a world view—remains the exception and not the rule.[1] Economists note that their discipline was traditionally called "political economy," the queen of the social sciences dating back at least to Adam Smith's *Wealth of Nations*, published in 1776. Smith's classical laissez-faire view was based on a Western society of small shopkeepers, anticipating the Industrial Revolution but hardly the global consequences of the multinational corporation or the nuclear superpower state. Nevertheless, Smith's classical tenets of economic liberalism—that minimal state interference in the economy and maximum reliance upon the market result in business productivity and social wealth—still predominate in Anglo-American cultures today.

The sacrosanct value of individual freedom in the United States, for example, originally depended on the assumption that economics and politics could be kept separated; that the state should be kept out of people's private "business" lives as much as possible. "That government is best which governs least." But in the twentieth century, this "negative" view of the state was modified by a "positive" view of the state intervening to save the private sector from itself in times of potential economic depression and to create equal opportunities for access to the market for the disadvantaged. Nevertheless, the guiding rule of even "positive state" American liberalism was to rely on the markets as much as possible and to preserve the stability of individual freedom above all else, even collective competitiveness.[2] Americans, what historian David Potter called "the people of plenty," have been reluctant to accept that there are no clear boundaries between politics and economics within their own society, not to mention in American attempts to impose their liberal ideology upon other societies. But politics and economics always overlap; they are logical spheres that can never be totally separated.[3]

One of the most influential critiques of the assumption that politics and economics can be separated was offered by the continental theorist Karl Marx in *Das Kapital*, published in 1867. Perhaps a third of the world's population have been taught that Marx's massive critique of laissez-faire capitalism—focusing on class struggle as the prime mover—is "the economic truth." As American political economist Charles Lindblom noted in *Politics and Markets*: "Except for the distinction between despotic and libertarian governments, the greatest difference between one government and another is the extent to which market replaces government or government replaces market." Adam Smith understood this. So did Karl Marx.[4] Neither planned (or "control") economic systems, based on Marx, Lenin, and Stalin, nor market economies, based on Smith and Ricardo, can avoid key questions of governmental-market relations where politics and economics overlap. If the United States traditionally attempted to embody the ideology of Smith's market economy, the Soviet Union and the People's Republic of China sought to adapt Marx's economic vision to their own distinctive ideological purposes. The relationship between politics and economics thus became the ideological basis for cold wars between would-be superpowers.

Ideology involves falling in love with ideas that further a certain group's concrete interests. Such action-oriented nests of ideas or worldviews serve to shore up the legitimacy of elites in power. The pragmatic individualism and empiricism of Anglo-Saxon thought served as the backdrop of the birth of the Industrial Revolution in the nineteenth century. Adam Smith's classical liberal doctrine of maximizing self-interest was a precondition for the emergence of the Industrial Revolution in Britain.

Students of international political economy often ask about the origins of the Industrial Revolution: Why Europe first? Why England? Conditions other than economic ideology are necessary for a sufficient explanation. But historical developments suggest that individual self-interest and organizational efforts to optimize what already exists are ideas without which no adequate explanation is possible. The notion of "industrial society" is an ideological objective of Western modernization rooted in ideas of individual and group self-interest, accumulation, and autonomy.[5]

Another basis of the Industrial Revolution underlying the British development was the birth of modern technology itself, which dates at least back to the first half of the eighteenth century. **Technology** derives from the Greek word *techne*, meaning skill or craft, combined with "ology"—organized, systematic, purposeful knowledge. By applying knowledge in systematic ways, the Industrial Revolution demystified the secrecy of the craft guilds where access was limited and "skill" was assumed to be based on experience. Apprenticeship schools of applied knowledge emerged in Germany. In the last half of the eighteenth century, Britain shifted its patent system from monopolies for those favored by the monarchy to a system of rewards for inventors applying their work to tools and production processes. Collective learning thus became applied learning. The diffusion of technology throughout the population made capitalism the dominant form of political economy in the West.

The Americans consolidated the economic power of the British by following their Industrial Revolution with a "productivity revolution," stimulated by the influence of Frederick Winslow Taylor (1856–1915). Taylor applied knowledge to the analysis of work, inventing "scientific management." While the British gentleman was schooled to look down on mere work, Americans celebrated the independence and wealth it promised. Taylor attacked the mythology of "skilled work," arguing that there was no "skilled work," just "work," which could be analyzed in the same way through "task studies." Task studies reduced redundant movements and sought out the most efficient tools for the job. Taylor's method enabled the Americans to organize their military machine quickly in order to win World War II. It also permitted the Japanese to mobilize their workforce in order to succeed in the "cold-war peace" economically.[6]

The influence of Anglo-Saxon ideas upon the world economy deepened with the impact of John Maynard Keynes' *The General Theory of Employment, Interest and Money* (1936), emerging as a therapy for the Great Depression that began in 1929.

A father of the "mixed economy," Keynes focused upon the role of capital investment in providing for national economic growth and stability. In bad times, the government was to intervene in the economy by increasing the money supply and government spending to stimulate the demand for production, which in turn would increase employment. In boom times government was to cool down the economy by intervening to tighten up the money supply, thus reducing demand to assure stable growth. Since government spending is more popular with democratic populations than are government austerity measures, Keynesian policy prescriptions, which have predominated in Western industrialized countries, have had an inflationary, debt-creating bias upon the structure of the world economy.

Anglo-American ideology has "structured" much of world economy since the British Empire dominated it in the nineteenth century and the American regime in the twentieth century. *Pax Britannica* was followed by *pax Americana*.

The compatibility of President Ronald Reagan and Prime Minister Margaret Thatcher on political economy was the cultural outcome of a traditional "special relationship."

The majority of the world's nations and peoples are not of the Anglo-Saxon culture—yet they find themselves asked to play by its rules of the economic game and to speak its language. British hegemony—or power domination—was replaced by American hegemony after World War II, epitomized by the system of Western monetary and trade agreements emerging in 1944 in Bretton Woods, New Hampshire. To the victors went the spoils. Only the United States had the military and financial power to enforce its economic will and to attempt to impose its classical liberal vision upon the world economy. As Louis Hartz noted in *The Liberal Tradition in America* (1955), the United States skipped the feudal stage of history and the revolutionary reaction against feudalism. Since Americans basically know only what they have experienced, they could never really understand the leftwing rebellion against feudalism (**socialism**) nor the right-wing reaction to socialism (fascism). Rugged individualistic liberalism based upon Anglo-Saxon roots was all Americans knew. Their liberal ideology was rigid and dogmatic. Any form of socialist thought, much less fascist thought, was simply incomprehensible. Americans tended to see the world in terms of black-and-white categories of laissez-faire capitalism versus state-controlled, socialist communism.[7]

THE MORAL DILEMMA OF LIBERALISM: THE THICK, THE THIN, AND THE VIRTUAL

When the Berlin Wall collapsed in 1989, so did the simplistic black-and-white categories of the cold war that served to define the ideology of American liberalism. American liberals confronted a moral dilemma: If the self-maximizing principles of democratic liberal markets had "won," what community limits to this self-aggrandizement could there be? What could become the basis of social ethics to limit freedom with responsibility?

Political philosopher Michael Sandel argued in *Liberalism and the Limits of Justice* (1982) that American liberalism involves a notion of the "thin self," or minimal self, "free" to satisfy basic needs or lowest common denominator views of what is "good." For, while the ideal vision of liberalism assumes that "justice" or "duty to do the right thing" is more important than what any one person believes is "good" personally, this notion of justice is too abstract to serve as a practical standard in everyday life. As a consequence, people in liberal societies tend to forget about "justice" and to maximize their own views of what is "good"—often defined in terms of their own selfish interests in the short run. Truly ethical human beings of "character," on the other hand, are "thickly constituted selves" with a sense of duty to a specific community, friends, and long-term commitments.[8] Feminists, such as Carol Gilligan (in *In a Different Voice*), suggest that the problem is a male-dominated world in which males perceive justice in terms of an abstract standard, whereas women tend to perceive justice in terms of caring community relationships.[9]

American theorists who stress the priority of thickly constituted selves loyal to specific communities are usually referred to as "communitarians." The communitarian vision is reinforced by political philosopher Michael Walzer, who sees the world as a collection of unique "thick" moral cultures. In *Thick and Thin* (1994), Walzer points out that all domestic cultures have socially distinctive moral frameworks "thick" with intricate symbols and rich meanings. However, societies throughout the world share a set of "thin" moral values, "morality close to the bone," which usually takes the form of negative injunctions against what is universally perceived to be immoral—murder, torture, oppression, tyranny, and deceit. This moral "minimalism" or set of "thin" moral principles serves as a basis for solidarity, sympathy, and joint action across cultures. As Walzer puts it: "Minimalism leaves room for thickness elsewhere; indeed, it presupposes thickness elsewhere." In other words, if you do not understand what "truth" and "justice" mean in their thick meanings of your culture at home, you won't have the ability to empathize with the oppression of these values in the "thin" form in which they appear to you in other cultures.[10]

But those thick with moral virtue who are determined to be true to their own unique moral cultures of their local communities are threatened with being swept away by a liberal American economy seeking to speed up individual productivity and corporate interest over everything else for the sake of economic competitiveness. Mobility and quick adaptation are the qualities rewarded in the economy of the "virtual corporation," where society demands instant consumer satisfaction from companies. Virtual organizations are collective learning networks that can almost instantaneously produce and deliver products or services at any time, in any place, and in any variety to satisfy a specific customer. Like the polaroid camera, they promise instant gratification with just-in-time service. Virtual corporations foster a mobile workforce of thin selves willing to be available anywhere around the clock to follow-through on the latest orders.[11] In contrast, individuals who cling to local communities, friends, and long-term commitments in a specific place risk poverty as the price for their ethical stance. Just consider the example of the barely surviving independent farmer in rural areas of the world.

GLOBALIZATION VERSUS COMMUNITY IDENTITY

The moral dilemma of liberalism is becoming a global moral dilemma in the post-cold-war era. The spread of free market capitalism has speeded up and become more diffuse as formerly "socialist" states have attempted to privatize industries or institutions in an effort to attract foreign investment and to stimulate economic growth. However, this global logic of world markets is countered by other trends. Regional blocs are being formed. At the same time, we see movements of local ethnic groups and community resistance to change for the sake of preserving collective identity and cultural traditions. This book focuses on the ways in which communities, organizations, regions, and states use collective learning processes to adapt to the global logic of capitalism, while struggling to preserve their ethical and cultural integrity and environmental sustainability.

One could not blame the majority of the world's nations and peoples if they were to perceive the hegemony or domination of the Anglo-American culture and its incorporation in American economic liberalism to be self-serving. They look back to the nineteenth century and see colonial expansion by established Western nations, a time when mobility of labor and capital over state boundaries was much more taken for granted, and they discover unfair advantages seized by Western states in building up national wealth and power. By the time many of the world's nations became politically independent after World War II, most of the earth's prime real estate in terms of resources was already occupied, and legal boundaries that had been erected between states regulated and slowed down the flow of labor and capital among them.[12] The doctrine of classical economic liberalism focused on the more efficient use of the status quo allocation of existing resources, not upon their redistribution or radical restructuring for the sake of the disadvantaged. International law was defined as stable reciprocity in terms of protecting existing ownership and contracts. The world economy would become more prosperous and peaceful if each nation used its existing stakes or "comparative advantages" more efficiently. This ideology did not provide for any redistribution of shares among peoples, more or less guaranteeing a widening gap between the wealthy, established nations and the poor, developing countries.

By the end of 1995 the inequality of income worldwide was striking: Sixteen percent of the world's population earned more per week ($475) than 56 percent of the world's population earned per year ($430)! Specifically, of 209 countries, 63 countries had an annual average income of $430 per person, 65 countries an average of $1,670 per person, 30 countries an average of $4,260 per person, and 51 countries an average of $24,930 per person. In 1997, the per capita GNP was $28,740 in the United States versus $590 in Burundi.[13]

The inequality among nations and peoples has become more pronounced in the globalized world economy. Technological development and socioeconomic change have accelerated the tempo. The gap between the haves and have-nots has grown. As the logic of time sped up, the logic of space contracted with international communications, transportation, and financial flows.

The **postmodern sensibility of globalization** is one of no-nonsense disenchantment in which actors from the state, market, and cultural spheres are caught playing a permanent game of catch-up, pushing their businesses across national borders ever faster, only to undermine more systematically the integrity of their home communities. Postmodernism is postindustrialism never achieved, narcissism gone sour, socialism in bankruptcy, and capitalism shifted into high speed throughout the globe. Hot private money replaces public finance, accelerating the socioeconomic tempo to the disproportionate advantage of the haves, only to undermine even their stability with the global impact of foreign currency devaluations and deflation in the aftermath of speculative euphoria.

Quality of life is the postmodern preoccupation: Money is the means, a trophy, an indicator—not the end in itself. Postmodern language is that of "apolitical management"—transforming political and economic issues into technical or administrative black humor. A status job is more important than money, a safe home or maintenance base the prerequisite to entrepreneurial, existential risk-taking and world travel. The world is seen as a whole in postmodern eyes, but the differentiation between parts is more important than the wholeness.

There are social systems that are less than global but that may not be coterminous with the nation-state—the European Union, for example. Moreover, there are social systems of various sorts within nation-states—the Amish Mennonite community in the United States, for instance. And the anticipation of social change within discrete social systems within nation-states on the one hand, and within regional organizations on the other, is the critical task for those who would manage global economic change.

The fundamental problem of liberalism and globalism is ethically and politically the same: There is no commitment to any particular here and now or local community; all is macro, abstract, future-oriented process. But the content and character of our lives and our community are always here and now. Our life chances are grounded at one point in time.

The grounding of life chances at different places on the globe is made clear when considering that in 1995 about 56 percent of the world's population lived in economies where the Gross National Product (GNP) per capital was less than $765. Of the 5.6 billion people in the world, more than half live on less than $2 per day! Not surprisingly, the people who live in developed countries with average GNP per capita of $25,000 have the longest life expectancy at birth (75 years or more), whereas those countries with the lowest GNP have the lowest life expectancy at birth (people in most of the sub-Saharan countries, for example, have a life expectancy of less than 55 years). And as knowledge spreads, infant mortality falls.[14] To maximize your life chances, you must be born into a rich country.

But how can one picture in one's mind the extreme economic differences between the richest and poorest nations when there are more than two hundred countries? One way is to group them.

TIERS

In economic terms, the world can be divided into a number of tiers or layers:

1. OECD Nations: members of the Organization for Economic Cooperation and Development (OECD), sometimes referred to as "the rich men's club": The United States, Japan, West Germany, France, and other members of the European Union (EU), Switzerland, the Scandinavian countries, Canada, Australia, and New Zealand.

2. Newly Industrializing Countries (NICs): Hong Kong, the Republic of Korea, Singapore, and Taiwan. These are the most upwardly mobile of the developing

countries and they are characterized by economic growth rates that are often higher than those of the more established rich countries of the first tier.

3. *Developing Oil-Exporting Nations*: a nonhomogeneous group like the others ranging from Saudi Arabia (with the largest oil reserves in the world) to Nigeria and Venezuela.

4. *Non-Oil-Producing Developing Nations*: numbering about 100.

5. *"Socialist" Nations*: a heterogeneous mix declining in number with the end of the cold war: North Korea, China, and Cuba.

Since the 1930s, about two-thirds of world trade has taken place within the first tier.[15] In 1995 developed countries supplied almost two-thirds of world exports, selling more than 70 percent to other developed countries. The developing countries accounted for 29 percent of the world total (50 percent of which originated from South and East Asia) and "economies in transition" (from socialism to free-market capitalism) provided the remainder of about 4 percent. In many of the developing countries and the economies in transition the dollar value of exports and imports decreased (showed negative growth rates) by up to 14 percent up until the beginning of the 1990s. Since then, however, their trade volume and value have risen significantly and their share of world trade as compared to the developed countries has grown.[16]

The first tier of the wealthy OECD countries is where the majority of the world's trade and investment takes place: The majority of foreign direct investment (that is, multinational companies setting up manufacturing facilities abroad) occurs in this arena. And the radical transformation in the world economy toward the importance of financial instruments and away from manufacturing—toward the internationalization of capital—has been initiated by the OECD group. Not withstanding the rise in manufactured goods originating in the second tier, the oil revenues in the third tier, and the growth in direct bank lending to the fourth tier, the changes most responsible for the present global disequilibrium have come within the first tier in the past several decades.[17]

MANAGING CHANGE, ENTREPRENEURIAL RISK, AND SOCIAL CONSEQUENCES

The world political economy is dominated by global capitalism, which, in turn, is made up of constantly changing demand and supply—the markets. Markets are not just inevitable processes, but are socially constituted. That is, markets are made and people make them.[18] However, as government elites of economies in transition from centrally controlled to free market rules found out quickly in the 1990s, markets cannot be ignored. Effective management of change means listening to markets and anticipating their direction. Only then can managers adapt their organizations or economies to global trends early enough to maximize their economic interests in a way that simultaneously protects their cultural integrity and the life chances of their people. And the more dependent a country is on dominant market trends—as in the case of the poorest nations in the world—the more managers or elites seek control and stability—the equilibrium that keeps them in power and makes their domestic economy appear predictable enough to attract foreign aid and investment.[19] For instability stimulates the decisive economic fear of the end of the twentieth century: capital flight. Private investors can make a country like Thailand a miracle one day through massive investment, only to break it the next day by withdrawing capital overnight if they become disappointed or alarmed—as in the fall of 1997.

In contrast with poor or "emerging" economies, wealthier countries and multinational firms can more easily take equilibrium for granted. They can use this base of stability to take risks for entrepreneurship and technological innovation. Their managers can concern themselves with strategies of dynamic equilibrium in coordination with the dominant trends of globalization. They can speed up their learning curves and raise their economic productivity. And they have the surplus capital and sense of security that permits them to concern themselves with sustaining the natural environment for their grandchildren.

Many of the wealthy, however, fail to take advantage of the dynamic management potential and ability to manage the earth for long-term sustainability inherent in their privileged position. They prefer instead to minimize their risks for the sake of preserving a status quo that is friendly to their interests. They fail to save or invest enough or to envision how they could make the earth a better place. Thus, there is an understandable conservative bias on the part of both rich and poor alike to seek out stability and to optimize the existing equilibrium. Their risks are neither high enough in the short-run, nor their visions sustainable and concrete enough in the long-run, to adapt effectively to the global political economy for the sake of the integrity of their own culture and people. Inherited structures may shape our choices, but as human beings we are also agents who can shape new structures, make socially responsible markets, and satisfy our needs in ways that will sustain the life chances of future generations.[20]

HOW THIS BOOK WORKS

This book is made up of four parts: Part I, "Concepts for Managing Change"; Part II, "The Global Environment"; Part III, "Domestic Sources of National Economic Behavior"; and Part IV, "Cycles, Trends, Conclusions." Contrasting theories and perspectives of international economic change are illustrated without imposing any one systematic theory. The notions of collective learning and system maintenance merely provide the reader with two ways among others of understanding how global change is "managed," if that is the intention. Clearly, there are many world economic outcomes that occur independently of any effort to manage them: a draught, for instance. And there are theories that appear to be deterministic regardless of human will. But by casting the spotlight on collective learning processes, the complex nature of the world economy becomes more transparent from the viewpoint of organizations or groups who would influence global economic outcomes to their advantage.

Part I introduces concepts for managing change and different theories or points of departure used in explaining the world political economy. A basic tension emerges between classical liberal and Keynesian macroeconomic principles, on the one hand, and local and regional efforts to protect cultural and ethnic identity, on the other.

Part II focuses on global factors without which world economic change cannot be understood. Beginning with the development of the two most important, the world monetary system and the world trade system, Part II then takes up the emergence and contemporary significance of multinational corporations, the north-south system, multinational strategy, direct investment, and technology.

Part III deals with domestic sources of national economic behavior. The transition from comparative political economy to international political economy is but a step in a global era in which domestic policy often determines foreign policy. Part III begins with the concepts of life chances, class, education, and culture, proceeding naturally to state strategy, industrial policy, the prerequisites for so-called "economic miracles," environmental consequences, and green growth strategies. The last section deals with the origins and development of post-cold-war transitional economies, including Russia, Poland, and China, and with possible strategies for helping local communities that are threatened by the creative destruction of globalization to survive in a sustainable manner.

Part IV summarizes cycles, trends, and conclusions. Two themes predominate: (1) business cycles and capital flows in a time of contagious movements in financial markets and mergers, and the factors making up globalization, and (2) resistance to these rootless, placeless, insatiably innovative phenomena.

An underlying assumption of the book is that human beings can learn collectively to manage economic change by establishing a limited, efficient, risk-reducing maintenance base (or "home base") from which they are able to launch targeted, sustainable risk-taking in the form of entrepreneurship and creative endeavors.

QUESTIONS FOR THOUGHT

1. Why does the increase in the speed of globalization matter in the relationship between the rich and the poor? Define "international political economy" in comparison with "international relations," "political science," or "economics."

2. What did Adam Smith mean by "liberalism" and what conditions have changed the meaning of this concept today? What are the ethical morals of liberalism? Compare the views of Sandel, Gilligan, and Walzer. Why might cultures

outside the Anglo-American tradition not understand the importance of these ethical tensions of liberalism?

3. How would John Maynard Keynes manage the global economy in a time of deep recession? Of economic boom? In the world economic circumstances of today?

4. What does *technology* mean and how did Frederick Taylor apply it to management? How does technology relate to (a) how fast people learn? (b) average per capita income in different countries?

5. How are your "post-modern sensibility" and view of environmental responsibility apt to be effected by which "tier" you belong to in terms of the country where you live?

NOTES

1. Notable among the recent exceptions that do take a global view of political economy are: World Resources Institute, United Nations Environment Program, and United Nations Development Program, *World Resources 1998–99: A Guide to the Global Environment* (New York: Oxford University Press, 1999); World Bank, *Global Development Finance* (Washington, D.C.: World Bank, 1998); United Nations, *World Economic and Social Survey 1998* (New York: United Nations, 1998); Peter Dicken, *Global Shift: The Internationalization of Economic Activity* (New York: The Guilford Press, 1992); Francois Chesnais, *La Modernisation du Capital* (Paris: Syros, 1994); Jean Vickers, *Women and the World Economic Crisis* (London: Zed Books, 1991); Kenichi Ohmae, *The Borderless World: Power and Strategy in the Interlinked Economy* (New York: HarperCollins, 1991); Wilhelm Hankel, *Weltwirtschaft* (Wien: Econ Verlag, 1977); W. Arthur Lewis, *The Evolution of the International Economic Order* (Princeton, NJ: Princeton University Press, 1977); Charles Kindleberger, *The International Economic Order* (Cambridge, MA: MIT Press, 1989); Immanuel Wallerstein, *The Capitalist World-Economy* (Cambridge, MA: Cambridge University Press, 1979); Independent Commission on International Development Issues (Brandt Commission), *North-South: A Program for Survival: Cooperation for World Recovery* (Cambridge, MA: MIT Press, 1983); Harold K. Jacobson and Susan Sidjanski, eds., *The Emerging International Economic Order* (Beverly Hills, CA: Sage Publications, 1982); Johan Galtung, *The True Worlds: A Transnational Perspective* (New York: Free Press, 1980); Garret Hardin and J. Raden, eds., *Managing the Commons* (San Francisco, CA: W. H. Freeman & Co., 1977); Thom Kuels, *Beyond Sovereign Territory: The Space of Ecopolitics* (Minneapolis, MN: University of Minnesota Press, 1996); James Mittelman, ed. *Globalization: Critical Reflections* (Boulder, CO: Lynne Rienner, 1996); and Robert Boyer and Daniel Drache, eds., *States Against Markets: The Limits of Globalization* (London: Routledge, 1996).

2. See R. Isaak, "The Conservative Tradition of American Liberalism," Introduction to *American Political Thinking: Readings from the Origins to the 21st Century* (Fort Worth, TX: Harcourt Brace, 1994).

3. See, for example, Charles E. Lindblom, *Politics and Markets: The World's Political Economic Systems* (New York: Basic Books, 1977).

4. Ibid., p. ix.

5. See Richard J. Badham, *Theories of Industrial Society* (New York: St. Martin's Press, 1986).

6. Although "productivity" was not used as a concept in Frederick Taylor's era, his *Scientific Management* (Westport, CT: Greenwood Press, 1972) aims at the same thing. On Taylor's neglected significance and the impact of his ideas on the world economy, see Peter Drucker, *Post-Capitalist Society* (New York: HarperCollins, 1993), pp. 32–40. For the

need to transcend "Taylorism" in the twenty-first century, see Yuji Masuda, ed., *Human-Centered Systems in the Global Economy* (London: Springer-Veriag, 1992).

7. Hartz's continuing relevance is demonstrated in Robert A. Packenham, *Liberal America and the Third World* (Princeton, NJ: Princeton University Press, 1973).

8. Michael Sandel, *Liberalism and the Limits of Justice* (Cambridge, MA: Cambridge University Press, 1982).

9. Carol Gilligan, *In A Different Voice* (Cambridge, MA: Harvard University Press, 1982).

10. Michael Walzer, *Thick and Thin: Moral Argument at Home and Abroad* (Notre Dame, IN:University of Notre Dame Press, 1994), p. 19.

11. See William H. Davidow and Michael S. Malone, *The Virtual Corporation: Structuring and Revitalizing the Corporation for the 21st Century* (New York: HarperCollins, 1992); and R. Isaak, "Virtual Organizations: From Entrepreneurial Networks to Strategic Alliances," a paper presented at the International Symposium on A Networking of Human Relations and Technology at Tokyo Keizai University, October 25, 1993, Tokyo, and revised for presentation at the International Seminar, A Training for Change, at the Institut d'Administration des Enterprises, at Aix-en-Provence, May 5, 1994.

12. See, for example, Mahbub ul Haq, *The Poverty Curtain: Choices for the Third World* (New York: Columbia University Press, 1976).

13. Statistics from *The World Bank Atlas 1997* (Washington, D.C.: The World Bank, 1997), p. 30; and *World Development Report: Knowledge for Development* (New York: Oxford University Press, 1999), pp. 190–191.

14. *The World Bank Atlas 1997*, pp. 30, 12; and *World Development Report* (1999).

15. Andre Frank, *Crisis in the World Economy* (New York: Holmes and Meier, 1980), p. 4.

16. Statistics from *World Economic Survey 1996: Trends and Policies in the World Economy* (New York: United Nations, 1996), pp. 55–62, 318–323. For example, the trade share of GDP (percent) for low and middle income countries went from 40 percent to 52 percent between 1980 and 1996 (*World Development Report*, 1999, p. 229).

17. James M. Cypher, "A Global Disequilibrium: The Instability of Interdependent Accumulation," *Economic Forum* 11 (winter 1980–81): 23.

18. See Kurt Burch and Robert A. Denemark, eds., "Constituting International Political Economy," *International Political Economy Yearbook* 10 (Boulder, CO: Lynne Reinner Publishers, 1997). Here, Nicholas Onuf summarizes the essence of this "constructivist" perspective: "The co-constitution of people and society is a continuous process. General, prescriptive statements, hereafter called rules, are always implicated in this process. Rules make people active participants, or agents, in society, and they form agents' relations into the stable arrangements, or institutions, that give society a recognizable pattern, or structure. Any change in a society's rules redefines agents, institutions, and their relation to each other; any such change also changes the rules, including those rules agents use to effectuate or inhibit changes in society (p. 7). Or, as Robert Isaak and Ralph Hummel put it in a forerunner of this perspective, *Politics for Human Beings* (North Scituate, MA: Duxbury Press, 1975): "Politics is social action to satisfy human needs using social facts." And "A social relationship that lasts is made an institution by the perceptions of the many." (p. 3).

19. See Stephen D. Krasner, *Structural Conflict: The Third World Against Global Liberalism* (Berkeley, CA: University of California Press, 1985). On how states try to use international economic institutions to maximize their national interests, see Nicholas Boyle, "What Governments Want from International Economic Institutions and How They Get It," *Government and Opposition* 31, no. 3 (1997): 361–379.

20. See R. Isaak, *Green Logic: Ecopreneurship, Theory and Ethics* (West Hartford, CT: Kumarian, 1999; Sheffield: Greenleaf, 1998).

THEORIES

In the knowledge economy, imperfect competition seems to be inherent in the economy itself. Initial advantages gained through early application and exploitation of knowledge (that is, through what has come to be known as the "learning curve") become permanent and irreversible.

—Peter Drucker

Knowledge is the orderly loss of information.

—Kenneth Boulding

THE POSTMODERN WORLD ECONOMY IS CHARACTERIZED BY TOO MUCH INFORMATION TO DIGEST. "To know" has come to mean to lose as much of this information overload as possible in a systematic way in order to have a few basic principles or categories left over. The managers of the World Bank, IBM, or the U.S. Federal Reserve attempt to cut the quick from the dead in this thicket of data: "News" is some breakpoint in an expected trend or an habitual image of how things usually work. Significant news is often decked over by the superfluous. When it became apparent in the early 1980s that the nine largest U.S. banks had lent three times the amount they held in equity to developing countries, which had become incapable of paying back the interest on the loans, the *New York Times* published this sensitive news in a small article buried in its least-read Saturday edition. "Knowledge" that suggests "the sky is falling" could send financial markets into a downward spiral and undermine the Western financial system. For the same reason of global stability, in 1998 the Federal Reserve sponsored the coordination of a $3.5 billion bail-out of Long-Term Capital Management, a hedge fund for the well-to-do, by fourteen banks and brokerage firms out of fear that if the hedge fund failed it could have over a trillion dollars in ripple effects, causing investors who were already spooked by the Asian crisis to panic.

This view of knowledge, however, has a conservative bias. Like Adam Smith's classical notion of capitalism, the motive behind it appears to be to understand the existing equilibrium, to optimize what already exists. In the unequal international political economy, such viewpoints appear to further the interests of the minority of the rich rather than the interests of the majority of the poor: Optimizing what exists implies an inevitability in the status quo. Knowledge is limited to how things are. Classical liberal capitalism is concerned with the growth of existing things and maintaining them more efficiently, productively, and effectively. What could exist, be created, or developed is buried from the view of knowledge as systematically sifted left-over information or from a narrow vision of Adam Smith's stress upon optimization.[1]

That the classical **economic liberalism** of Adam Smith is always on the side of "progress" is an illusion. The private pursuit of self-interest is a powerful motivator, leading individuals and groups to accumulate great stores of private wealth through individual efficiency, rationalization, and productivity. But wealth, unlike the capital that fuels capitalism, is not dynamic. Eventually a point is reached in a capitalist society where so many people have succeeded in creating plump private nest eggs that their interest shifts from efficient productivity to risk-reducing maintenance of that which they have already accumulated. The state of rugged individualism becomes the complacent welfare state; risk-taking for future gains is overwhelmed by risk-reducing insurance against possible losses. Or, as economist Joseph Schumpeter suggested, capitalist societies succeed only to do themselves in: The very wealth and leisure that their economic success makes possible provide the means for counterculture lifestyles and motives that undermine the work ethic and efficient rationality that led to the economic success in the first place.[2] In such societies a conflict emerges between the public (read governmental) and private (read economic) sectors for capital. The focus shifts to deficit-reduction and inflation-fighting, investment for health, education, and other infrastructures for the public good. Global privatization pushes out public funding, led by the mythical assumption that too much public investment squeezes out necessary private investment. Old rich (OECD) capitalist societies attempt to preserve their past gains, steering private capital into the best short-term returns for private investors and pension funds. The upcoming minority of "new rich" newly industrializing countries (NICS) strive to attract this private capital. The majority of poor, developing countries find private investors scarce or fickle and public aid agencies with over-extended budgets. The basic theme of this study is the conflict between efficiently maintaining the old versus effectively creating the new with cultural integrity in order to adapt to global economic change.

COLLECTIVE LEARNING AND THE MAINTENANCE MODEL

The argument here is that the only way individuals, economic organizations, and states can cope effectively with global economic change is through a process of collective learning and structural positioning. Effective collective learning breaks beyond status quo-conditioned maintenance models to initiate targeted, innovative, strategic risk taking and adaptation.

In order to create strategies, an organization or nation must first know what it wants to preserve of its cultural tradition and what it is willing to risk for the sake of adaptation, growth, and development. Collective learning is based on a distinction between the organizational maintenance base and entrepreneurial risk. The **maintenance base** maximizes efficiency, stability, and risk reduction inside the organization. **Entrepreneurial risk**, in contrast, stresses effectiveness, risk taking, export growth, and customer and niche creation in the external arena of domestic and global markets.

The maintenance model of management then is based upon the distinction between a boundaried maintenance base oriented toward internal stability and security "inside" the organization or collective system versus "outside" entrepreneurship oriented toward risky adaptation to global market innovation. The chief maintenance concern is for increasing efficiency or security and reducing risk within the home base or headquarters rather than with entrepreneurial effectiveness and risk taking to adjust to changing outside markets and conditions (see Figure 1-1).

The maintenance model has explanatory power at different levels of analysis and at various stages of development. At the individual level, for example, the maintenance base in the traditional culture of France is the *foyer*, the family circle or quasi-sacred basis of French civilization. The duty of the head of the French household is to use his wits to take entrepreneurial risks outside the family in order to bring home the goods, much like the hunter brings back his catch to his cave. In the process the Frenchman is traditionally supposed to keep clear of emotional extremes or entangling alliances that could undermine his will or render him vulnerable.[3]

At the state level, mercantilism—the philosophy of centrally steered economic nationalism—traditionally permits the French president to view France (or, even more accurately, Paris) as the maintenance base from which to take entrepreneurial risks elsewhere for the sake of maximizing French national interests. For example, the French government subsidized the French company launching the Arian rocket abroad so as to help maximize French market share in the highly competitive commercial satellite launching business.

Figure 1-1   The Maintenance Model

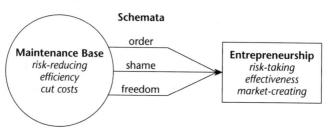

President Bill Clinton learned from mercantilist states such as France and Japan. He asked the government of Saudi Arabia to buy American jets from Boeing to help out the U.S. airline industry.

Effective collective learning from the perspective of the maintenance model focuses upon the entrepreneurial "breakpoints" or developmental "takeoff" points in corporations or states that result in improved competitive positions in the world economy. **Economic miracles** are assumed not to be miracles; they are, rather, effective collective responses to change.

Take the cases of West Germany and Japan after World War II. They were "tight ships in a storm." The efficient reconstruction of the maintenance base of their political economies was combined with targeted external policies of entrepreneurship and export-oriented growth to create "economic miracles." It is significant that the global environment was friendly. The United States bankrolled the world monetary system with dollar credits and the 1950s and 1960s were marked with dynamic global economic growth. That West Germany and Japan received a privileged opportunity from their domineering "godfather," the United States (which took care of their military security), does not distract from their effective collective use of this opportunity. Hegemony means domination. A **hegemon** is a state or organization that dominates others in its region or in the world. To the extent that Germany and Japan have become hegemons in their regions, if not at times in the global economy, it is more fruitful to focus on the preconditions of hegemony that led to their prosperous condition rather than lamenting the injustice involved in the creation of such superior economic positions.

The United States maintenance base functions differently from that of West Germany and Japan. The ordered chaos of the largest domestic market in the world provides economic opportunities and new consumption choices through continuous restructuring within this entrepreneurial, newly rich society: The turbulence of outside markets is brought home to create jobs through flexible investment opportunities and corporate reorganizations for both American and global markets. The government serves as the gatekeeper and as a major customer, insuring the heavy debt structure of the society to keep up the cash flow. Dogmatic classical economic liberalism is the basis for the rugged individualism of the American political economy: It may be all the United States knows (as Louis Hartz suggests). But unlike all other societies, given the wealthy endowment of natural resources, it may be all the United States thinks it needs.

However, classical laissez-faire liberalism may be a wasteful, experimental approach to economic problem-solving in a technocratic global economy, with resource scarcity and payoffs for tightly structured teamwork. The American assumption that each individual learns mainly from his or her own experience (what can be called "learning by burning") implies a multitude of duplicate learning experiences and a host of failures in an uncoordinated trial-by-error approach. The question is the extent to which the rest of the world can afford to continue to subsidize the wasteful individualism that is part and parcel of American liberalism. In

The Waste of Nations (1989), economist Douglas Dowd documents U.S. consumer, military, industrial, agricultural, and human waste and characterizes the style of American hegemony as "an impulsive boyish recklessness."

* * *

Collective learning is a social learning process of distinguishing legitimate patterns of adaptive behavior within an organization in order to manage environmental change without losing cultural integrity. Albert Bandura defined **social learning theory** as the result of reciprocal interactions among person (or cognition), behavior, and the environmental situations.[4] This is a stimulus-organism-response theory. It assumes that individuals can learn from others vicariously—that is, by modeling their own behavior after others whom they have observed.[5] I might, for example, learn by watching a famous tennis player on television always to hit the ball to my opponent's weakest side or backhand. In other words, "learning by burning"—or from one's own experience alone—is not always necessary. It is often cheaper and wiser to learn from others to avoid making the same mistakes oneself. One can learn to manage well by watching other excellent managers in action, and so forth.

Collective learning theory is distinguished from social learning: It is social learning within a specific organizational context and cultural tradition. This cultural tradition is a pattern (or gestalt) made up of indigenous **schemata**; that is, prototypes of meaning in a specific culture used for processing information and "branding" it with particular interpretations.[6] To learn within such a cultural tradition involves cognitive change that brings about reframing that eventually can result in new schemata. Such learning can be stimulated from outside the culture, provided that the stimulus is transparent and comprehensible from the viewpoint of the natives within. Such a cultural collectivity or organization has boundaries that are marked not by an enveloping membrane but by a behavioral design.[7] Such a behavioral design is characterized by many interacting habits of behavior in conformity to modes of action prescribed by the design. (For example, German habits include cleanliness at home, keeping their place in line, and maintaining closed office doors—all patterns of the behavioral design of "order.")

Schemata for the culture of the United States include a pattern of perceiving that stamps all rugged, individualistic actions representing "one-against-the-world" self-sufficiency as "good" and anything else as a form of moral compromise (symbolized by actors John Wayne or Clint Eastwood). However, the stimulus of winning teamwork on the part of Germany and Japan might lead to learning that results in a new schema—the individual as most respectable as a leader of a winning team (symbolized by Michael Maccoby's *The Gamesman*, showing that the true corporate winners of the 1970s in the United States were leaders of winning teams.)[8] A further new schema may eventually be introduced encouraging all members of the team to think of themselves as potential leaders, thereby making the team less dependent upon any one person. The sooner all members see themselves as important stakeholders in a group, the more effective the collective learning of the team will be.

Learning how to learn is thus a social process structured by organizational relationships between individuals and colored by common cultural assumptions. The cultural tradition or pattern framing the collective learning in Japan, for example, is characterized by a "tight" neo-Confucian hierarchical pattern in which lifelong education represents a dynamic receptivity by the people to new learning, setting them up continually for collective cultural and economic development.[9] The cultural pattern of the German culture is a "work-oriented" socialization process in which the majority of teenagers become involved in hands-on vocational training in targeted apprenticeship programs sponsored by corporate-union-government partnership. Compare the German and Japanese patterns, or networks, of schemata with the U.S. cultural tradition of "loose" laissez-faire individualism, in which the "socialization" of immigrants and young people into American values and civic legal arrangements is the focus of the educational system rather than either hands-on work training or a commitment to lifelong learning for its own sake.[10]

Thus, collective learning in a particular culture legitimates certain models of learning and excludes others. It involves comparing how different groups of people learn how to learn—what anthropologist Gregory Bateson called **deutero-learning**. Bateson observed that democratic societies are based on specific learning contexts or meta-learning patterns. People learn to decide in democratic ways, picking it up as if by osmosis from the structure of the culture in which they live.[11] If the dominant learning models of such cultures become "split" or "polarized," political economic effectiveness breaks down.[12] For example, the elites of highly developed societies (such as England) may come to look down upon mere wealth creation or moneymaking, free-riding upon its "bourgeois" industrial base. Simultaneously, such snobs undermine the authority of hands-on management by declassing its status, legitimacy, and motivation.[13] "High policy" learning models and lifestyles become split off from "low policy" entrepreneurial and maintenance management functions critical for creating economic wealth.

When the wealth of the upper class aristocracy declines and this group is declassed by socioeconomic change, as in the case of the downward mobility of the Balinese aristocracy or the samurai of Japan, aristocrats from a feudal tradition often resurrect their entrepreneurial capacities, turning to business to recover their sense of purpose, to create new wealth, and to reverse their decline in status.[14] Thus collective learning involves the shifting legitimacy of various learning modes or models over generations or even centuries with direct economic consequences for the life chances of those in the communities involved. Such generational waves of collective learning or adaptation transcend contemporary ideological movements. They also transcend Western dichotomies such as the politics of productivity versus the politics of redistribution, which were used to characterize shifts in developed political economies during the last half of the twentieth century.[15]

Two things come together to provide the context in which collective learning takes place in the world economy: global capitalism and the nation-state system. Hegemony or competitive dominance in this context is conditioned by both economic and political structures inherited from the past. Economic development, however, is often the measure of breaking beyond these intimidating structures.

CREATIVE DESTRUCTION AND GLOBAL ECONOMIC DEVELOPMENT

Joseph Schumpeter characterized capitalism as a process of creative destruction in which the new incessantly drives out the old. Technological innovation or development led by the dynamism of the entrepreneur is the engine driving this vision of capitalism. **Development** is defined as spontaneous economic change within a nation not forced upon it from without. Development goes beyond mere growth (or the optimization and expansion of what already exists): It implies that something new and distinctive is being produced by spontaneous design or planning that makes a nation (or organization) less dependent upon others. Producers are the agents that usually initiate development—private entrepreneurs in capitalist systems or apparatchik managers in socialist systems.[16] The dynamic for development emerges from some domestic or national base or other, not from the international system as a whole. Power is homemade. (And goods, accordingly, should be "homespun," with capital remaining at home to benefit the nation and the nation's working class, argued John Maynard Keynes during the Great Depression.) However, the economic effectiveness of that power abroad depends on how national development is managed to fit the markets of the capitalist world economy.

In 1979 Johan Galtung noted: "Capitalism is not down and out. There is no crisis in capitalism. There is a profound crisis in the Western [read United States and Western Europe] position inside capitalism."[17] While the rising dominance of the Orient that Galtung predicted still appears to be premature (despite the rise of Japan, the Asian tigers, and, eventually, China), his forecast of a new, capitalist globalization of the economy was on the mark. The British prepared the way for world capitalism with their Industrial Revolution and **pax Britannica**. The United States consolidated the heritage of Anglo-Saxon economic thought, institutionalizing global capitalism at the peak of American hegemony with the Bretton Woods system and **pax Americana**. Some scholars have been surprised that the institutional framework of Bretton Woods has survived as American power has passed its peak, possibly because they have focused too much on "institutional inertia" from an American perspective rather than looking at the universal dynamism of capitalism from a global perspective.[18]

Human beings are overwhelmed by future shock and a sense of loss—from the microelectronic revolution to the decay of Western status-order systems that gave hierarchical meaning to the economic world. Perhaps preoccupied with a perception of decline in global status of their own nation since its historical peak following World War II, American students of international political economy often focused upon what they called "hegemonic stability theory" in the 1980s to explain what was happening to them.

HEGEMONIC STABILITY AND IDEOLOGY

Hegemonic stability theory emerged from an interpretation of the Great Depression beginning in 1929 that attributed its width and depth to the absence of a leading country willing and able to bear a disproportionate share of the costs to discharge the responsibilities of a stabilizer. Or, to put the theory positively: A stable world economic system requires the existence of a single great power state or hegemon willing and able to furnish an outlet for distress goods, maintain the flow of capital to would-be borrowers, serve as lender of last resort in financial crises, maintain a structure of exchange rates, and coordinate macroeconomic policies. The father of this theory, economist Charles P. Kindleberger, called the key stabilizer nation a "leader," not a "hegemon." He noted that "Political science has now transmuted the concept of leadership into 'hegemony,' a word that makes me uncomfortable because of its overtones of force, threat, pressure."[19] The clearest modern examples of such leaders or hegemons are Great Britain in the nineteenth century and the United States after World War II (the historical example *par excellence*).[20]

The hegemon provides stability by disproportionately subsidizing collective or public goods in the world political economy, such as an open market economy based upon an open liberal-trading regime—or a stable international currency or an international security system. A **public or collective good** is one that is not reduced for use by other potential consumers even after consumption by an individual, household, company, or state (a road, sidewalk, or ocean, for example). In addition to paying more than its share of the costs, the hegemon has to try to manage the **free-rider** problem, namely, the dilemma of so-called cheaters who free-ride upon collective or public goods without paying their "fair share." Thus, U.S. managers push their allies for "burden sharing" or picking up more of the economic and security costs of maintaining the global political economic system. From the perspective of collective learning, however, the free-rider strategy is a rational, collective mode of behavior that individuals, companies, states, and international organizations utilize in historical situations where they have few other options. The poor, for example, often have little choice about being free riders. In an era of great mobility and economic uncertainty, the free-rider strategy may even appear to be the optimum mode of managing economic change for a majority of people.

However, theorists of hegemonic stability have been surprised by recent history. Since the 1944 Bretton Woods agreement establishing the **International Monetary Fund (IMF)** and (later) the General Agreement on Tariffs and Trade (GATT) for trade cooperation, American hegemony seemed to decline. And yet the world economy continued to remain basically stable and the institutions emerging from Bretton Woods continued to perform their stabilizing functions. This nest of American-driven institutional arrangements has been referred to as **regimes**—or "principles, norms, and decision making procedures around which actor expectations converge."[21] And the continuation or residue of these regimes, despite the perceived decline in power of the U.S. hegemon, provided the puzzle that preoccupied American students of international political economy in the 1980s. That such a preoccupation may be ethnocentric or premature, or may understate the actual American economic and military power position was at that time a neglected point of view.[22]

From the standpoint of theory, the hegemonic stability focus seems to be an unproven historical examination of one exceptional case before the story is over. No other nation will ever be likely to possess the nuclear monopoly enjoyed by the United States after World War II, nor have the abundance of resources and large domestic market of the Americans. Yet the conservative bias of this perspective is unmistakable: Global information is being eliminated in an orderly manner in order to sort out the big fish (the U.S. hegemon) from the little ones (the other some two hundred countries and territories for which the annual World Bank Atlas lists statistics), even if the big fish should turn out to be as rare as Moby Dick.

The word *hegemony* originated with the founder of the Italian Communist Party, Antonio Gramsci. Gramsci defined **hegemony** as a form of consciousness in which other social classes or the population as a whole accept an order in which one social class is dominant.[23] The "embedded" liberal economic order embodied in the institutions, rules, and habits of the Bretton Woods system dominated by the United States is the case in point. The thrust for openness of classical liberalism became "embedded" in the Bretton Woods hegemony of institutions because of the ongoing compromises this liberalism made with domestic state demands for social stability and full employment.[24]

Hegemony is usually associated with conservative habits or a "right-wing" ideology. Philosopher Silva Tomkins defined right-wing ideology or conservatism as the belief that human beings realize themselves only through struggle toward, participation in, and conformity to a norm, a measure, or an ideal essence basically independent of human beings. "Left-wing" ideology, or liberalism, in contrast considers a human being as "an end in himself, an active, creative, thinking, desiring, loving force in nature."[25] Accordingly, those who believe in sources of value outside of human beings—whether they be members of the "club" of U.S. elite universities, the French Communist Party, or the Catholic Church qualify as "conservatives."

Thus, hegemony has conservative implications when identified as the legitimate ideology of elite classes in the international system. The classic example is the balance-of-power ideology of the dominant European nations—the *ancien régime*—preceding the French Revolution. This balance-of-power hegemony broke down when the ideological elite of the *ancien régime* could no longer communicate with the counter hegemony ideology of Napoleon.[26] Napoleon's drafting of all male citizens and all-or-nothing objectives in war were incomprehensible ideas for established balance-of-power elites who relied upon mercenary soldiers and limited rules of warfare.

The rigidity of both these ideologies—anchoring value in standards outside human individuals in abstract ideals or rules—precipitated the breakdown of the equilibrium of the international system. Similarly, the cold war ideologies of neo-conservative *pax Americana* elites and the counter hegemony of the neo-Marxist socialist bloc threatened the stability of the twentieth-century international system until Gorbachev's reforms initiated the breakdown of the socialist bloc (see Chapter 10). On the global economic level, this ideological conflict was embodied in the defense of the Bretton Woods regime by the developed countries against counterhegemony demands of developing nations for a New International Economic Order (see Chapter 5).

The ideological extremes of Western capitalism and of Marxism-Leninism constitute different varieties of economic determinism. The former argues that material self-interest is the engine of economic growth and progress, the latter that class structures and conflicts determine social life. These competing cold war ideologies served as legitimizing dogmas for established elites and often functioned as top-down deterministic rules, outside of human individuals, used to mobilize more efficiency in the existing social equilibrium of the state, not as bottom-up instigators of grass-roots individualism and risk-loving dissent. Or, as sociologist Ralf Dahrendorf warns, liberty is at risk when economic values begin to dominate politics: "The new economism of capitalists is no less illiberal than the old one of Marxists."[27]

Gorbachev attempted to break through the stalemate of the cold war logic of hegemony-counter hegemony. He tried to position himself ideologically on the side of change and of the future through his "**new thinking**," leaving the defense of the old to his opponents at home and abroad. Ideologies are born radical, mature into pragmatism, and turn self-righteously inflexible in old age, as those who are heavily invested in them weigh the psychic and material costs of change—the **sunk costs**. Gorbachev attempted to symbolize the collective learning he knew his people would have to undertake to restructure their economy to compete in the twenty-first century. But his policies of reform and his reluctance to use force had the effect of dissolving not only the Eastern socialist bloc but the Soviet Union itself. Gorbachev's reforms stimulated the spontaneous collective learning of the peoples of Poland, Hungary, Czechoslovakia, East Germany, Rumania, and Bulgaria as a domino series of democratic movements spread in 1989, leading to radical political and economic change. At home, Gorbachev soon found himself outflanked ideologically both on his right and on his left as he desperately tried to seize the center and hold the Soviet Union together. He failed, setting the stage for the break-away radical reforms of Boris Yeltsin, who established autonomy for Russia from the other Soviet republics—republics that also sought independence but with less political and financial capital. Each of these emergent nations sought to exploit the regional collective learning dynamism to maximize its own cultural integrity and autonomy, but, many fell back into ideological blinders of the past. And widespread chaos in both economic and political circumstances further undermined their efforts.

ECONOMIC NATIONALISM, LIBERALISM, AND MARXISM

The predominant ideologies that often functioned as blinders in the world economy of the late twentieth century were economic nationalism (or neomercantilism), liberalism, and Marxism. Each of these three ideologies or systematic worldviews represents a total belief system concerning human nature and society, which is not easily changed in the minds of true believers by logic or contrary evidence. While each of these ideologies or paradigms sheds some light on the workings of the world economy, all of them are inherently incapable of being disproven empirically—such as the "truth" of the statement: "Chocolate ice cream is best because I like it best." The collective learning approach used here attempts to transcend these ideological camps to focus on which patterns or gestalts of human cultural organization have worked best to foster a harmony of dynamic economic growth on the one hand, and social equity on the other.

The collective learning perspective need not be biased toward successes and breakthroughs: It can be used to analyze panics, contagions, and groupthink in overreacting to global economic crises, for example. And the approach is indifferent as to whether these effective or maladaptive collective behaviors are uncovered in nation-states, multinational corporations, or international organizations.

Each of these three predominant ideologies is a reified or frozen set of beliefs used as a basis for political action in the world economy. Each is like a spotlight in a dark amphitheater, illuminating a limited part of the reality while inadvertently leaving other parts blacked out in the process.

Economic nationalism, otherwise known as mercantilism, statism, and protectionism, spotlights the economic and power interests of a single nation-state in competition with all others, viewing the world economy as a zero-sum game in which that not gained by the state will necessarily be lost to other competitive states. The modern nation-state system emerged from the breakdown of the unity of medieval Christendom and was first officially recognized as the European multistate system with the Peace of Westphalia in 1648 and the Treaty of Utrecht in 1713. The European conception of the sovereign state was one with a concentration of political power that possessed a monopoly on the use of force within its borders.

Following the Industrial Revolution, this consolidation of political power normally corresponded with growing economic power. Economic nationalists are preoccupied with national security and the primacy of military power of the state in the international system, viewing political and economic power as a way to secure national survival. For nationalists or mercantilists, a favorable balance of trade is a prerequisite to national security, and a hard currency is a political weapon in the ceaseless struggle for status and advantage among states. Self-sufficiency, not economic interdependence, is their motto. If every economic system must rest on a secure political base, then in the terms of collective learning, economic nationalists are preoccupied with the viability and security of this "maintenance base" defined in geographical and cultural terms. This search by the extreme realist for national unity is epitomized in a negative way by Machiavelli's observation that Italy is not a state but a mere geographical expression.

The lamp that shines from the ideology of **liberalism** looks for the maximization of individual interest and freedom, as often as not expressed in the form of economic profit. Rather than focusing upon the state, the liberal stresses the market. Critical of the zero-sum, conflictual stance of the economic nationalist, which can ultimately culminate in war, the liberal stresses the mutual gain that can come from international cooperation and interdependence: the creation of more economic pie for all through incentives for economic growth, rather than becoming bogged down in the distributional struggle for the pie that already exists (as besets the economic nationalists). The liberal position is critical of the amassing of both military and other forms of power, which can undermine economic efficiency. But the liberal preoccupation with economic success leads to a lopsided focus on rational, economic individuals in free markets with full information to make their maximizing decisions. Social contexts, "irrational" cultural traditions, collective habits, hierarchical markets, and the normal absence of full information all become "exogenous" variables too easily left out of the equations of liberal economists. The state is understated, the market overmarketed.

Marxism spotlights the contradictions in the capitalist system that emerge from individuals rationally maximizing their personal interests without regard for the overall consequences for social equity and community well-being. Individual interest maximization leads to overproduction and subsequent economic contraction and unemployment, according to the Marxist thesis. Workers become impoverished and the growing gap between the bourgeois classes and proletariat or working classes will ultimately trigger a revolution and the overthrow of capitalism by a classless, socialist society of equity and solidarity. When he noted that workers within capitalist societies did not become poorer, Lenin argued in 1917 that the fault was in failing to view capitalism as a global phenomenon in which imperialism was the ultimate stage of capitalism. Financial capital in the core developed countries dominated industrial capital, and the law of uneven development ensured that the capitalist, colonizing states reap the benefits of economic development, exploiting cheap labor and resources from the developing countries at the periphery of market interactions.

Modern World System theory (represented by Paul Baran, Andre Gunder Frank, and Immanual Wallerstein) extends the Leninist interpretation of Marxism. It assumes that the modern world can only be understood as a global system with a single division of labor and multiple cultural systems forming an international hierarchy in the ceaseless struggle of states and classes: the advanced, dominant core; the newly industrializing semiperiphery; the dependent, underdeveloped periphery (made up of most of the world's people).

Modern World System theorists view state and market as epiphenomena of deeper social and economic forces that drive the world economy to integrate the core and periphery, so that the "metropolitan" core systematically underdevelops the dependent periphery areas. The (Marxist) World System view, however, is often blind to political and strategic factors that can be as important in interstate relations as economic determinants.

RATIONAL CHOICE AND OLIGOPOLIES

Another theory with something of the flavor of the realist or national interest school is the **rational choice perspective**. This framework assumes that individuals will use all information to maximize their own interests rationally, minimizing their costs in contributing to public goods from which all benefit (like roads, cartels, or national security alliances).[28]

A classic example of rational choice theory is the thesis of economist Mancur Olson in *The Logic of Collective Action* (1971), asserting that without outside sanctions or intervention, rational, self-interested individuals in an organization will maximize their own interests or those of their small group and not act to achieve the common or group interests of the larger organization. For example, a union-worker with hungry children would rationally be tempted to cross the picket line to go to work unless he had reason to fear a brick flying through his window at home if he did so. Olson applied this logic of collective action to alliances like NATO, arguing that the only reason NATO functioned is that the United States is willing to assume a disproportionate share of the burden, letting small countries like Belgium more or less free ride upon the security provided by the United States. Moreover, this free-riding behavior was totally rational on the part of Belgium in terms of Belgian national interests, as was the willingness of the superpower to put in excessive chips for extra American influence over NATO policy. Olson demonstrates that because of the collective logic involved and the inability to pass on proportionate burdens of a public good to small groups, there is a systematic tendency for "exploitation" of the great by the small. Over time, parochial cartels and lobbies tend to accumulate in any human society until they start to sap a nation's economic vitality. It usually takes a war or some other catastrophe to wipe out the choking undergrowth of pressure groups, bring in new elites, and return the country to dynamic economic growth. What is striking is that the "free-rider," whether in an organization or alliance, is not "immoral" but merely a rational actor pursuing individual or national interests in the most cost-effective manner.

From the viewpoint of a rational choice perspective, in industry one should ideally aim for a monopoly market structure with a single seller of a commodity or for a service dealing with such a large group of buyers that entry by competitors is more or less closed off. Contemporary examples might be Microsoft or Intel, who each have held up to 80 percent of the world market in their key products and who use expensive technological innovation, price-cutting, and law suits to head off any serious competitors. Rationally maximizing self-interest in the world economy often leads to the formation of an *oligopoly*—a market structure in which a few firms dominate an industry. The "Seven Sisters" or oil multinationals in the 1960s are an example. This structure evolved into an effort to create a commodity cartel, **OPEC—the Organization for Petroleum Exporting Countries**. Here free-rider rationality is often in evidence as the organization agrees to a certain limit on oil production quotas in order to keep prices up and stable, while some individual member countries "cheat" by producing more than their quota, thus "free-riding" on the public good of the production agreement. Olson argued that the larger the group, the less it will further its common interests. This, in turn, leads to a basic principle of oligopolies, which is to form *minimum winning coalitions* (that is, the fewest number of allies or club members required to succeed), since the greater the number of participants, the smaller the share of the economic pie for any one individual or group.

OLIGOPOLIES AND NEOMERCANTILISM

American hegemony was unquestioned in the world system until roughly 1960. During this post-World War II period, smaller states could pursue **neomercantilist** policies of export-oriented growth in order to increase their trade surpluses, free-riding upon the security structure and economic stability provided by the *pax Americana*, or the maintenance base of the American hegemon.[29] Indeed, following defeat of the Axis in World War II, the United States initially prohibited Germany and Japan from rearming, even writing into the Japanese Constitution that not more than 1 percent of that country's gross national product could be spent on defense. While the Americans reaped many commercial and political benefits from the "public good" of international stability that they provided, when American hegemony began to be questioned the Americans found themselves ill-prepared for a more competitive, interdependent environment. Moreover, other leading industrial countries—West Germany, Switzerland, and Japan—were ill-disposed toward picking up the costs of the "public good" of international stability. The Japanese wanted nothing to do with nuclear weapons on their soil. And the West Germans and Swiss resisted having their currencies become international reserve currencies to supplement the dollar, for fear they would lose domestic control over their own "money constitutions." This fear was justified by the increasing anarchy of the global monetary system, stimulated by the expansion of the "stateless" Eurodollar market (see Chapter 2).

The decline of American economic domination was marked by a shift from a **hegemonic (unipolar) global system** dominated by one power to an **oligopolistic (or multipolar) system** steered by an oligopoly or a system controlled by a few major powers. But it became problematic when all the major states making up the oligopoly focused upon neomercantilist policies or export-oriented trade surpluses at the same time. Someone, after all, has to import what the others export—or to accept trade deficits to permit others to have trade surpluses in the global system. In the 1980s, the hegemonic role of the United States was radically transformed from surrogate world banker—providing international credit and liquidity—to major world debtor and borrower and carrier of trade deficits that the borrowing helped to finance. In the process, the legitimacy of the dollar as the world's key reserve currency was undermined. Country elites scrambled to create their own exclusive buffer zones against the resulting international instability—from the OPEC cartel of oil-producing developing countries to the 1979 creation of the **European Monetary System (EMS)** (or European float against the dollar). Multinational companies formed mergers and bought out competitors. Corporate executives of major firms demanded "Golden Parachute" clauses (giving them luxurious pension benefits in case they were fired in the creative destruction caused by merger buy-outs). Leaders of indebted developing countries threatened with instability (President Jose Lopez Portillo of Mexico, Ferdinand Marcos of the Philippines, President Suharto of Indonesia, and so on) built up private mansions and Swiss bank accounts with money borrowed from the International Monetary Fund. Human activity was focused on shoring up the maintenance base of vested interests threatened by the inflation and uncertainty of the 1970s, then by the disinflation, deregulation, recession, and privatization trends of the 1980s, and the currency devaluations and capital flights of the 1990s.

The shift away from multilateral to bilateral agreements between nations illustrates the rational choice thesis that the payoff is greater and clearer for two partners than for more than two. And it is tempting to explain crises of cooperation in the OPEC (over oil prices) and European Union (over agricultural subsidies) cartels on the basis of numbers alone: These clubs have too many members with too many diffuse interests to easily achieve the consensus needed within the organization for effective bargaining with the outside world.

Each of these four ideologies or spotlights of consciousness—the state (economic nationalism), the market (liberalism), the economic struggle between the haves and the have-nots (Marxism), and the rational maximization of interests (rational choice)—constitutes a different worldview of the same anarchical world. Historically, the anarchy of the international system has always been sufficient to undermine any particular oligarchy or imperial power group that sought to impose its will upon the system.

The world has remained anarchical and oligarchical: anarchical given the absence of a monopoly of legitimate violence; oligarchical—or hierarchic—since without civil society, right depends mainly upon might. The dominant oligarchy (or hegemon) is cast in a conservative and defensive role of trying to shore up its power and influence and to maintain the system's equilibrium against inevitable disintegration or entropy. Those outside the oligarchy attempt to change the asymmetrical system—in their favor—and to keep what autonomy they can. Or as Thucydides observed in ancient Greece: The powerful exact what they can, and the weak grant what they must.

An **oligarchy** is a system of government in which power is invested in a few, whether one is speaking of a domestic or international system of government. The asymmetry or inequality between powerful oligarchies and weak, dependent peoples has become more pronounced since World War II. The logic of space has become global, or a question of shares of the world market. The logic of time has speeded up due to global changes in technology, finance, communication, and socioeconomic fashions of modeling behavior after the most successful. Most of the advantages of the increasing tempo of technological and financial development have accrued to those best positioned to take advantage of these innovations. Positioning is the name of the game in political economy: Rich countries (or people) seek to hold their position while the poor attempt to position themselves more favorably (by joining the European Union, for example). The initial starting position carries profound importance in an anarchical world where physical and economic security are scarce commodities, not to mention the freedom of individual choice.

In the emerging "knowledge" economy, the old assumption of "perfect competition" as the basis for the allocation of resources has become obsolete. Imperfect competition has become inherent in the economy itself. Those who gain early access to knowledge and can apply it and monopolize its distribution create what seem to be permanent and irreversible advantages: They shorten their collective learning curves and are able to accrue the first hold on profits in newly emerging technology and knowledge-based service industries.[30] A secure base is needed, however.

THE CHANGING NATURE OF INSECURITY

Although the cold war has ended, the primacy of insecurity—of the infinite striving for security—has not. Where military security prevails, such as in most industrialized democracies, there has merely been a shift in the form of insecurity to the economic or psychological realms (in addition to terrorism), as nations seek to increase economic competitiveness and to reduce unemployment. The continuing primacy of insecurity as a concern makes the global perspective of political economy inevitably conservative. As the simple "balance of terror" between two blocs has fragmented into many countries and factors, the first human task appears to be to order them into a system that can be stabilized in order to prevent breakdown in the forms of either world war or global economic depression. From the perspective of the American hegemon, the primary new threats are spreading nuclear proliferation and terrorism. Clearly, the nuclear powers and the wealthy, developed countries are cast in a conservative role, since they have the most to lose in the event of a breakdown of the world system.

Organizations or individuals representing these countries can hardly escape the dominant conservative logic of this maintenance function of preserving the status quo. The United States, as the only remaining military superpower, finds itself specialized in the role of world stabilizer whether the American people like it or not. Toward the end of the twentieth century, public opinion polls indicated that the majority of Americans were against committing significant resources to defend U.S. allies, to protect small countries against aggression, to promote human rights and democracy, or to support social and economic development in the Third World.[31] A gap emerged between views of the general public, who are interested in immigration and trade negotiation issues that could affect their jobs, global warming, nuclear proliferation, cross-border health threats, drug trafficking, crime, and supporting the United Nations versus opinions of "the experts" or foreign policy elite concerned with NATO, and foreign political and security issues.

But American public opinion cannot dictate to the leaders of the only superpower state what they will or will not do, particularly in areas that can be related even indirectly to "national security." **Security** ultimately means aiming for "unconditional viability"—that is, a party, organization, or nation is considered to be secure if it cannot be absorbed as an independent source of decisions.[32] That this ideal of absolute independence, freedom, or sovereignty can no longer be achieved in a nuclear age of international economic interdependence does not mean it is not sought.

National security or domestic security issues are also useful for elites to solidify their domestic power bases. **Elites**, or those in superior social or political positions ("Those who get the most of what there is to get," according to Harold Lasswell), have an inherent interest in broadcasting the insecurity of the nation in order to make themselves appear indispensable. And next to national security issues, the stability of the national currency and money supply is perceived as an issue to be managed by technocratic elites in most democratic states—one of "vital national interest." To understand why this is so, we must turn in the next chapter to the world's monetary system.

QUESTIONS FOR THOUGHT

1. In what way does Adam Smith's classical economic liberalism stress the optimization of that which already exists? To what extent does creative entrepreneurship involve the negation of that which exists?

2. A recipe for wealth and economic growth: Cut your daily spending in half in order to make your maintenance base more efficient, then invest all the savings immediately in over-the-counter stocks in order to create a nest egg. Why is this recipe so rarely followed?

3. To what extent does national (or global) hegemony color the collective learning of a society and steer its schemata? (Consider the example of privatization as a policy recipe used by the U.S. hegemon to color the collective learning of other societies in the post-cold-war process of globalization.)

4. What are the implications for democracy of Mancur Olson's thesis that without outside sanctions or intervention, rational self-interested individuals in an organization will maximize their own interest or those of their small group and not act to achieve the common or group interests of the larger organization.?

NOTES

1. This conservative view of knowledge is derived from systems theory. See Kenneth Boulding's lucid, understated interpretation: *The Image: Knowledge in Life and Society* (Ann Arbor, MI: University of Michigan Press, 1956). The associated view of Adam Smith's classical economic liberalism as an optimization of what exists goes back, of course, to Jean-Baptiste Say, only to be picked up in 1911 by Joseph Schumpeter in *Die Theorie der Wirtschaftlichen Entwicklung (The Theory of Economic Dynamics)*, and contrasted with entrepreneurial innovation in Peter Drucker's *Innovation and Entrepreneurship* (London: Heinemann, 1985). On the "problem-solving" view of knowledge, see Robert Cox, "Social Forces, States and World Orders: Beyond I.R. Theory," in *Neorealism and Its Critics*, Robert Keohane (New York: Columbia University Press, 1986), pp. 208–210.
2. See Joseph Schumpeter, *Capitalism, Socialism and Democracy* (New York: Harper & Row, 1950) and Daniel Bell's recasting of the same thesis in *The Cultural Contradictions of Capitalism* (New York: Basic Books, 1976). What Bell sees as cause for conservative concern—system breakdown due to cultural and technological subversion—Jean-Francois Lyotard finds a cause for celebration in his *La Condition Postmoderne* (Paris: Les Editions de Minuit, 1979): Paradoxical, cultural language games can lead to imaginative breakthroughs and innovative reconstructions. Compare Lyotard with the less euphoric *Legitimations Probleme in Spät Kapitalismus* of Jürgen Habermas.
3. Substantiated in R. Metraux et al., *Some Hypotheses About French Culture* (New York: Research in Contemporary Cultures, Columbia University, 1950). Also underscored in David C. McClelland, "French National Character and the Life and Works of André Gide," in *Roots of Consciousness* (New York: D. Van Nostrand, 1964) and R. Isaak, "France: An Administrative Economy of Cultural Supremacy," Ch. 3 of *European Politics: Political Economy and Policy Making in Western Democracies* (New York: St. Martin's Press, 1980), pp. 63–98.
4. Albert Bandura, *Social Learning Theory* (Englewood Cliffs, NJ: Prentice Hall, 1977), p. 194. "Reciprocal" here is used to mean mutual action between events rather than referring to its narrower sense of similar or opposite counteractions.
5. Ibid., pp. 16–53. Also see A. Bandura, "Influence of Models' Reinforcement Contingencies on the Acquisition of Imitative Responses," *Journal of Personality and Social Psychology* 1 (1965): 589–595.
6. See David Rumelhart, "*Schemata*: The Building Blocks of Cognition," in *Theoretical Issues in Reading Comprehension*, ed. R. Spiro et al. (Hillsdale, NJ: Lawrence Erlbaum Associates, 1980), pp. 33–58.
7. See Edgar Dunn, *Economic and Social Development: A Process of Social Learning* (Baltimore, MD: The Johns Hopkins Press, 1971), p. 189.
8. Michael Maccoby, *The Gamesman: The New Corporate Leaders* (New York: Simon & Schuster, 1976).
9. See William Theodore de Bary and John W. Chaffee, eds., *Neo-Confucian Education: The Formative Stage* (Berkeley, CA: University of California Press, 1989). The common Confucian culture of China, Japan, Korea, and overseas Chinese communities (and particularly the influence of "progressive" Chu Hsi, whose Sung learning principles were supported by the state) represents a dynamic force in the receptivity of the East

Asian people to new learning and their collective capacity for cultural and economic development.

10. See Thomas Janoski, *The Political Economy of Unemployment: Active Labor Market Policy in West Germany and the United States* (Berkeley, CA: University of California Press, 1990).

11. Gregory Bateson, *Steps to an Ecology of Mind* (London: Paladin, 1976), essay on *Deutero-learning.*

12. Ibid., See essay on "National Character."

13. See Charles Hampden-Turner, *Gentlemen and Tradesmen: The Values of Economic Catastrophe* (London: Routledge & Kegan Paul, 1983) and C. Hampden-Turner and Alfons Trompenaars, *The Seven Cultures of Capitalism* (New York: Currency/Doubleday, 1993).

14. For the case of the samurai, see Everett Hagan, *On the Theory of Social Change* (London: Tavistock Publications, 1964), Chapter 14. For the Balinese, see Clifford Gertz, *Peddlers and Princes: Social Development and Economies in Two Indonesian Towns* (Chicago, IL: University of Chicago Press, 1963).

15. For an example of an interpretation of developed Western economies in terms of the politics of productivity versus the politics of redistribution, see R. Isaak, *European Politics: Political Economy and Policy Making in Western Democracies* (New York: St. Martin's Press, 1980).

16. Some identify Schumpeter as a neoclassical economist, others as a neoMarxist—evidence of his objectivity. He devotes a chapter to the concept of "creative destruction" in *Capitalism, Socialism and Democracy,* while his conception of development is detailed in *The Theory of Economic Development,* translated from the German by Redvers Opie (Cambridge, MA: Harvard University Press, 1934), pp. 63–65.

17. Johan Galtung made this comment at a conference in Ojai, California, in November 1979: transcribed in W. L. Hollist, "Continuity and Change in the World System," paper presented at the convention of the International Studies Association, Los Angeles, CA, 1980.

18. An influential example of this American preoccupation is found in Robert O. Keohane, *After Hegemony: Cooperation and Discord in the World Political System* (Princeton, NJ: Princeton University Press, 1984).

19. Charles P. Kindleberger, "Hierarchy versus Inertial Cooperation," *International Organization* 40 (autumn 1986): 841. This article expands the responsibilities of the would-be world stabilizer or "hegemon" initially set out in Kindleberger's *The World in Depression, 1929–1939* (Berkeley, CA: University of California Press, 1973), Chapter 14. Kindleberger's concept of leadership is derived from Frohlich and Oppenheimer who argue that public goods will be underproduced (because of free-riders) unless a leader agrees to bear a disproportionate share of their costs. See Norman Frohlich and Joe A. Oppenheimer, "I Get Along with a Little Help from My Friends," *World Politics* 23 (October 1970): 20, 104. See also Helen V. Milner, "International Political Economy: Beyond Hegemonic Stability," *Foreign Policy* (spring 1998): 112–123 and T. L. Friedman, "A Manifesto for the Fast World," *The New York Times Magazine,* March 28, 1999, 40–97.

20. The limitations to interpreting British leadership in the nineteenth century in terms of the hegemony stability thesis, particularly in regard to predicting tariff levels in international trade, are demonstrated in Timothy J. McKeown, "Tariffs and Hegemonic Stability Theory," *International Organization* 37 (winter 1983): 73–91.

21. This is Stephen Krasner's definition in his "Structural Causes and Regime Consequences: Regimes as Intervening Variables," *International Organization* 36 (spring 1982): 185.

22. The ethnocentrism implicit in the American fear of international instability due to

the decline of U.S. hegemony is noted in Susan Strange, "Cave! Hic Dragones: A Critique of Regime Analysis," *International Organization* 36 (spring 1982): 299–324. While team-teaching with the late international relations theorist Hedley Bull at the Johns Hopkins Bologna Center in 1980, he told me he thought American economic hegemony was being vastly underestimated. Others who find more continuity than decline in American power include Bruce Russett (Cf. his "The Mysterious Case of Vanishing Hegemony; or, Is Mark Twain Really Dead?" *International Organization* 39 [spring 1985]: 207–231) and Susan Strange (Cf. her "Still an Extraordinary Power: America's Role in a Global Monetary System," in *Political Economy of International and Domestic Monetary Relations*, ed. Raymond E. Lombra and William E. Witte [Ames, IA: Iowa State University Press, 1982]). For a future forecast along these lines, see Mortimer Zuckerman, "A Second American Century," *Foreign Affairs* 77, no. 3 (May/June 1998) 18–35. And note the response in the same issue: Paul Krugman, "America the Boastful," pp. 32–45.

23. A. Gramsci, *Quademi del carere* (Turin: Instituto Gramsci, 1975). For an application of Gramsci's notion of hegemony to the international political economy, see Robert W. Cox, "Production and Hegemony: Toward a Political Economy of World Order," in *The Emerging International Economic Order*, ed. H. K. Jacobson and D. Sidjanski (Beverly Hills, CA: Sage Publications, 1982), pp. 37–58. Cox, in turn, was applied in James H. Mittelman, "Transforming the International Political Economy: A Crisis of Hegemony in the Third World," paper presented at the International Studies Association, Atlanta, Georgia, March 1984.

24. John G. Ruggie, "International Regimes, Transactions and Change: Embedded Liberalism in the Postwar Economic Order," *International Organization* 36, no. 2 (spring 1982): 413.

25. Silvan Tompkins, "Left and Right: A Basic Dimension of Ideology," in *The Study of Lives*, ed. Robert W. White (Chicago, IL: Aldine-Atherton, 1971), pp. 391–392. For the origins of "embedded liberalism," see John Ruggie, "International Regimes, Transactions, and Change," *International Organization* 36, no. 2 (spring 1982): 379–415.

26. See Kyung-Won Kim, *Revolution and International System* (New York: New York University Press, 1970).

27. See Ralf Dahrendorf, *After 1989: Morals, Revolution and Civil Society* (New York: St. Martin's Press, 1997).

28. For an introduction to the rational choice perspective, see Bruno Frey, *International Political Economies* (New York: Basil Blackwell, 1984) and two classic works by Mancur Olson: *The Logic of Collective Action* (Cambridge, MA: Harvard University Press, 1971) and *The Rise and Decline of Nations* (New Haven, CT: Yale University Press, 1982). For a comparison with the other school of thought, see George Crane and Abla Amawi, *The Theoretical Evolution of International Political Economy* (New York: Oxford University Press, 1997).

29. See Paolo Guerrieri and Pier Carlo Padoan, "Neomercantilism and International Economic Stability," *International Organization* 40 (winter 1986): 29–42.

30. See Peter Drucker, *The Post-Capitalist Society* (New York: Harper-Collins, 1993).

31. Opinion data from fall 1998 polls of Pew Center for the People and the Press in Washington, D.C., and of the University of Maryland's Program on International Policy Attitudes. See Barbara Crossette, "On Foreign Affairs, U.S. Public Is Nontraditional: Gap with Experts Continues to Grow," *New York Times*, Dec. 28, 1997.

32. This is Kenneth Boulding's definition of security in his *Conflict and Defense: A General Theory* (New York: Harper & Row, 1963), p. 58. See also Robert Tucker, *The Inequality of Nations* (New York: Basic Books, 1977) and Daniel Philpott, "Sovereignty: An Introduction and Brief History," *Journal of International Affairs* 48, no. 2 (winter 1995): 353–368.

2

THE WORLD MONETARY SYSTEM

Money has a life of its own which it properly should not have.

—Lionel Trilling

The status quo is no streetcar named desire.

—Wilhelm Hankel

MONEY OR CURRENCY (BARGELD IN GERMAN) IS A FORM OF **LIQUIDITY** OR LIFEBLOOD THAT keeps the pieces of the world economy moving. Like a motor without oil, an economic system without sufficient liquidity slows down until it reaches an ultimate break-point—entropy. But although money was once a commodity like gold or potatoes, it has become a fiat object of desire—a mysterious subjective phenomenon: The value of one national form of money or currency relative to another is literally changing every minute. The key question of the world's monetary system is whose currency carries the most weight, why, and for how long relative to other currencies and reserve assets (that is, gold)?

The asymmetry between the rich and poor nations of the world is reflected in their currencies: The rich are usually **hard** (appreciation-tending) **currency** countries, the poor are normally **soft** or "weak" (depreciation-tending) **currency** countries. The richest of the rich—the United States—had the hardest of the hard currencies at its peak moment of hegemony following World War II. At this most sovereign moment of military and economic power, policymakers in the United States, in collaboration with those of the *pax Britannica* power structure whom they were replacing, symbolized the hardness of the dollar by guaranteeing that anyone who wanted to cash it in could do so for gold—at the 1934 rate of $35 an ounce. The dollar was declared as good as gold. It became the world's chief **reserve currency**, meaning that individuals and foreign governments were willing to hold dollars rather than cash them in for gold held in the U.S. Treasury. As long as the emperor (or hegemon) was clothed in untouchable power and could maintain the legitimacy imposed in victory, the credibility of the paper dollar I.O.U.s he printed remained intact.

Led by the United States, the hard-currency countries since World War II have pursued a maintenance strategy of preserving equilibrium among the world's currencies before all else. Generally, stability has been promoted over economic growth, and the containment of inflation over the creation of credit. It is as if Western managers were overawed by Lenin's declaration that the best way to destroy the capitalistic system was to debauch the currency.[1] The stability of the world's money system makes great sense to those who happen to have money—hard money. That this priority should have predominated in the economic settlement at Bretton Woods in 1944 (as World War II was about to end) should come as little surprise in the conservative atmosphere inevitably generated by military chaos and its aftermath. The longing for peace and order included the desire for some fixed and stable source of value.

ORIGINS

The history of money is the story of an evolution from commodity money—shells and gold—to credit (or fiduciary) money—paper currency and credit cards. This evolution was marked by the increasing demystification of money through the secularization of culture. For example, in the West African monarchy of Dahomey, cowrie shell money was considered a sacred currency lending divinity to the king. When Dahomey was conquered by the French, the franc replaced the cowrie shell in the African money market, and the shells lost their sacred aura with the secularization of the society.[2]

Financial innovation transformed barter transactions to paper credit transactions with the creation of letters of credit and, following the invention of the printing press, paper money. As credit money expanded, the status imbued in the possessor of money was democratized: Suddenly one could be rich without owning land, and entrepreneurs could start enterprises on credit, not having a penny of their own to put down on the project. As the technical means to create credit exploded—epitomized today by plastic credit cards and quiet ticks in computer banking systems—the inflationary effects undermining the class status of commodity ownership by the "old rich" nobility surfaced. The established naturally began to resist the inflationary financing and the taxing of old rich estates, which created large numbers of "new rich" competitors. By this time the new rich of the developed countries had accumulated assets of their own to protect against the loss of value, and a stability-over-growth savers' mentality became widespread.[3] This conservative maintenance preoccupation was further stimulated by the inflation following World War I and by the stock market crash and Great Depression that began in 1929. In the United States, between 1929 and 1933 the GNP dropped from $103 billion to $56 billion, resulting in hardship, bankruptcies, bank failures, and political unrest. Stability was sought over all else. And those framing the post-World War II settlement remembered this. From 1945 to 1950, the United States gave Western Europe $20 billion in grants and loans—the Marshall Plan, or what we will call *the first redistribution*. Beyond this the Americans worked to stabilize postwar economic chaos with the Bretton Woods Exchange-Rate System, the International Monetary Fund, and the International Bank for Reconstruction and Development.

THE BRETTON WOODS SYSTEM

The Bretton Woods system refers to the charter negotiated in July 1944 at Bretton Woods, New Hampshire that established the **International Monetary Fund** (IMT) as well as the fund's sister institution, the **International Bank for Reconstruction and Development (IBRD)**, or **World Bank**. This monetary system was fundamentally aimed at avoiding the competitive exchange rate devaluations and "beggar-thy-neighbor" policies that led to the breakdown of the international monetary system in the 1930s following the Great Depression. The system was preoccupied with equilibrium or system maintenance, deriving from Anglo-American hegemony, heavily weighted toward the American position.

American Secretary of State Cordell Hull set the stage for American predominance in the negotiations with Britain by using the Lend-Lease Act of 1941 to break the back of the British financial empire. Desperate for war materials with which to fight the Germans, the British agreed to the loan conditions, which Hull knew would put the British in a structural position of financial dependence after the war: an example *par excellence* of **positioning** as the critical activity of international political economy.

The U.S. plan for the postwar economic order originated, however, not in the State Department but in the Treasury Department, under the supervision of Harry Dexter White.[4] An ambitious man with foresight, White produced a plan for the postwar international monetary system that was to bear his name before the end of 1941. Initially, the White plan aimed to prevent the disruption of foreign exchanges and collapse of monetary and credit systems, to assure the restoration of foreign trade, and to supply the large volume of capital needed throughout the world for reconstruction, relief, and economic recovery. These tasks were to be performed by a stabilization institution (the IMF) and an international bank for reconstruction (the IBRD, or World Bank).

White's plan went boldly against the predominant American public opinion trends of isolation and financial orthodoxy. The Stabilization Fund was to be made up of at least $5 billion (from contributions of member countries in gold, local currency, and government securities). This money would be used to help member countries overcome short-term balance-of-payments difficulties. The World Bank was to have twice as much capital stock as the Stabilization Fund in order to provide the liquidity needed for reconstruction, relief, and economic recovery for the "united" nations. It was to do this by making long-term loans at very low interest rates. However, in 1942 White's group in the U.S. Treasury made the Stabilization Fund the priority, letting plans for the World Bank languish—a decisive preference that was stimulated by the emerging conservative political milieu in the United States.

The British were represented at Bretton Woods by economist John Maynard Keynes, for whom White had great respect. By late 1941 Keynes had developed a plan for an International Clearing Union based upon the centralization of exchange transactions through central banks in contrast to White's stress upon the restoration of competitive exchange markets with limited interventions by central markets to influence the exchange rate. The Keynes plan called for the creation of a new reserve asset, *bancor* (the forerunner of SDRs, or Special Drawing Rights, later adopted by the IMF), while White's design maintained the gold-exchange standard reinforced by a Stabilization Fund (the IMF). Keynes pushed for the symmetry in adjustment of exchange rate imbalances so that the creditor or surplus countries would share the burden with the debtor or deficit countries.

Anticipating a deflationary environment with a scarcity in demand after the war (a false prognosis as it turned out), the Keynes plan provided for overdraft rights of $26 billion, meaning that the potential U.S. liability could have amounted to as much as $23 billion—some $20 billion more than the final version of the White plan (calling for $5.2 billion with a U.S. contribution of $3.2 billion). And access to the credit under Keynes's plan was automatic, whereas White's plan called for strict lending conditions. Ultimately, the articles of the IMF reflected White's proposals rather than those of Keynes—a foregone conclusion given U.S. hegemony in 1944.

The Bretton Woods system, dominated as it was by the maintenance or stabilization bias of the IMF articles *a la* White, is perhaps most accurately seen as a system of macroeconomic management and microeconomic liberalism.[5] Paradoxically, this macromanagement, microliberalism mix was the intellectual position of Keynes preceding World War II—a position so influential that it had become the consensus epitomized by White at Bretton Woods. Keynes, meanwhile, had gone on to more farsighted ideas of creating techniques of credit and liquidity that would assist the countries most devastated by the war with the least capability of helping themselves. This would be achieved by soft, long-term interest terms. Believing that U.S. policies would predominate over all others, Keynes successfully negotiated for a passive IMF role in economic adjustment against the American internationalist, interventionist position. This was consistent with the primacy of national sovereignty. It also squared with Keynes's interwar intellectual position (reflected in his *General Theory*) that exchange rates should be chosen with a view toward supporting domestic policy rather than using international exchange rates as a straitjacket to which domestic policy must conform.

Keynes's position at Bretton Woods was not based merely on a short-term forecast of how he expected the world economy to go (into deflation). Rather, his economic perspective had an ethical base. Having studied the theory of probability under the influence of philosopher G. E. Moore's ethical system, Keynes was inspired by the obligation so to act as to produce by causal connection the most probable maximum amount of eventual good through the entire procession of future ages (as recorded in his *Two Memoirs*).[6] Keynes's long-term preoccupation was with the human suffering of unemployment. He was determined to fight for sufficient international liquidity to stimulate demand in critical situations in order to bring depressed countries back on their feet, providing work through economic growth. As Lord Keynes put it in an address to the House of Lords to win British support for the Bretton Woods charter: "Sometimes almost alone, in popular articles in the press, in pamphlets, in dozens of letters to the *Times*, in text books, in enormous and obscure treatises I have spent my strength to persuade my countrymen and the world at large to change their traditional doctrines and, by taking better thought, to remove the curse of unemployment."[7] The IMF, Keynes claimed, would help check unemployment by supporting three key Keynesian principles:

1. Domestic policies should primarily determine the external value of a country's currency, not the other way around.
2. Domestic policy should have control over domestic rates of interest to keep them as low as suits the national purpose, without interference from the ebb and flow of international capital movements or flights of "hot money."
3. While countries should aim to prevent inflation at home, they should not accept deflation dictated by outside influences.

Naturally, Keynes argued these principles in terms of British national interests, the "dictates from outside" presumably being American influences.

The United States opposed the larger amount of liquidity Keynes proposed. It wanted to limit its potential liability as the world's largest creditor nation in the postwar order and feared that unmanageable inflation would be generated. Similarly, the Americans did not want as much flexibility in exchange rates as the British sought. Finally, the United States lightened the potential sanction on surplus nations to get them to move toward balance-of-payments equilibrium, leaving the weight of the burden for adjustment heavily on the debtor nations. By limiting the amount of liquidity that could be lent by the IMF and by establishing strict conditions (or *conditionality*) for such loans, American diplomats sought to win over a skeptical, conservative U.S. Congress that must ultimately approve how government money is spent. In sum, the Americans succeeded in establishing a blueprint for noninflationary, economic growth aimed at full employment and restoring competitive exchange rates at Bretton Woods. The fatal flaw, which was later to bring down the system, was that everything was based on the assumption that the dollar could forever be converted freely into gold. This flaw was natural for a hegemonic power at its peak when both its dominance and legitimacy as reflected in the strength of its currency were taken for granted.

THE IMF

The International Monetary Fund officially came into being when representatives of forty-four nations signed the Articles of Agreement stemming from the Anglo-American negotiations in July 1944 in Bretton Woods, New Hampshire.[8] By the end of 1945 the critical number of countries had ratified the agreement. The Board of Governors first met in March 1946, adopting by-laws and deciding to locate the IMF's headquarters in Washington, D.C. A year later the IMF began exchange operations. Its objectives were to secure international monetary cooperation, stabilize exchange rates, and expand international liquidity for the sake of international trade and full employment.

To achieve its aims, the IMF initially tried to maintain fixed exchange values of currencies (linked to the given dollar-gold rate) and to eliminate exchange controls. To ease the transition to the new system, a one-time adjustment of up to 10 percent in the initial value of each currency was permitted. However, once the designated *par value* of a currency had been established, a member country could only make major changes with the fund's approval. Such approval depended upon whether or not the country's balance of payments was in "fundamental disequilibrium." The key criterion of the IMF in terms of exchange rates is the *maintenance of stability*, or the recovery of equilibrium in the case of countries with deficits. Stability was assumed to be a prerequisite for economic growth and investment.

Upon joining the IMF, a country's position in the world economy is measured by its volume of international trade, national and international income, and international reserve holdings, and it is assigned a quota depending upon its position. The quota assigned to the country governs the size of its cash subscriptions, its voting power, and its drawing rights. Each member nation pays a quarter of its quota in SDRs and the remainder in its own currency. When a member country runs into balance-of-payments difficulties (that is, if more payments by domestic residents have been paid out than received from foreigners), it can automatically buy foreign currencies equal in value to a quarter of its quota— the equivalent of its gold subscription. Beyond this limit, the country must receive specific approval from the fund based on significant policy changes aimed to solve the balance-of-payments problems. Typically this means striving to control domestic inflation. The IMF is uniquely positioned to influence national policies of countries threatened with balance-of payments deficits, for much of the time a needy country will have to borrow more than the first "gold *tranche*" or quarter of its quota. Countries borrowing from the fund must repurchase their own currency (or repay the loan) within five years. The IMF is geared to service short-term balance-of-payments adjustments, not long-term structural adjustments—the role of the World Bank.

The head of the IMF is the managing director who leads the meetings and negotiations. At Bretton Woods the parties agreed that the head of the IMF should always be a European, whereas the head of the World Bank should be an American. Given the shift of world liquidity to Japan in the late twentieth century, it would not be surprising if eventually a Japanese was made head of the IMF.

Formally, the IMF is governed by two bodies: the Board of Governors and the Executive Board. The Board of Governors is made up of one governor for each nation with voting power proportional to subscription quotas. That is, each member is given 250 votes plus one vote for each $100,000 deposited, ensuring that the major subscribers maintain a dominant role. Initially the dominant countries numbered ten: the United States, the United Kingdom, Canada, France, West Germany, Italy, the Netherlands, Belgium, Sweden, and Japan. Saudi Arabia later joined this group, following the OPEC oil price hikes of the 1970s. The Board of Governors deals with changes in the Articles of Agreement, with the admission of new members, and, with the election of the managing director.

The other body, the Executive Board, is composed of appointed and elected directors. Those appointed are nominated by the five members with the largest quotas, while those elected are nominated by particular groups of member countries. The votes of these directors cannot be split and must be cast as a unit. The Executive Board is permanently in session and handles the everyday operations of the IMF.

The initial quotas assigned to member countries were found to be inadequate. They have been repeatedly increased to provide liquidity to cope with the increasing volume of transactions. Financial crises in the 1960s created a demand for additional reserves to be used in the settlement of international balances. In 1969 a new form of liquidity was introduced: **Special Drawing Rights (SDRs)** are artificial units of account that can be transferred between the IMF and national central banks to help resolve balance-of-payments problems. The unit value of the SDRs is based on a basket of currencies and was sometimes called "paper gold." SDRs permit countries temporarily in deficit to draw supplies of foreign currencies according to predetermined quotas.

The use of SDRs is not subject to negotiations or conditions, does not lead to repayment obligations if a member uses less than 70 percent of its SDR quota, and is accepted in final discharge of debts without being translated into any particular currency.

The first allocation of SDRs to IMF members in 1970 of $9.5 billion over three years represented the triumph of an American proliquidity policy over French resistance. American experts at the time argued that Keynes had been right after all at Bretton Woods: The initial IMF system did not provide enough international liquidity. During the era of dollar scarcity after World War II, the dollar had been forced into the role of key international reserve currency. The Americans moved to shift the international monetary system away from this overexposure by devising a new source of nonnational liquidity. Economist Robert Mundell later referred to the SDRs as "dollars in disguise." The French, on the other hand, wanted less than the $3 billion to $5 billion in SDR annual liquidity advocated by the United States. They demanded strict reconstitution obligations and that

American deficits be put to an end before the SDR system went into operation. It was another instance of the recurrent classic debate of the need for expanded liquidity versus the need for IMF credibility and conditionality.

THE DECLINE OF BRETTON WOODS

The Bretton Woods system serviced economic growth throughout the world for two decades after its founding, less because of its design than because of the ability and willingness of the Americans to play the role of a world central bank, printing dollars to provide liquidity. The American balance-of-payments deficit allowed others to run surpluses, which was convenient. As long as the Americans provided stable, responsible leadership in international economic policy and as long as the dollar was accepted abroad as a "legitimate" substitute for gold, the system seemed to work. Yet Bretton Woods never functioned as Americans and others had planned. After all, it was not the United States that was supposed to perform the role of a world bank but the International Monetary Fund and International Bank for Reconstruction and Development. This illusion had already dissolved by 1947 when the Americans realized how thoroughly World War II had destroyed the European economic system. The European system was based largely on trade that could not work with the sources of Europe's foreign earnings gone and with heavy European balance-of-payments deficits. So from 1947 until about 1960 the United States stepped in. The Americans assumed unilateral management of the international monetary system, appearing to use Bretton Woods as a veil of legitimacy for the liquidity provided by the outflow of American dollars.

However, the constant outflow of dollars from the United States undermined the very monetary system that it serviced.[9] In 1947 the United States held 70 percent of the world's official monetary gold stocks. Between the end of 1948 and the end of 1959 American gold holdings fell by 20 percent. In 1960 foreign dollar holdings exceeded American gold reserves for the first time. Many perceived the U.S. balance-of-payments deficit, which reached $3.7 billion in 1960, to be getting out of control. The weakness of the British pound and the speculative problems associated with European currency convertibility further weakened confidence in the world monetary system. It was no longer possible for the United States to manage the international management system alone. An informal multilateral form of international management emerged, with the United States still predominant but with less clout.

As Europe and Japan recovered and prospered with American support, their bargaining power relative to the United States in international economic policy increased: They lost the war militarily to win the peace economically. European Common Market countries became more independent. In 1958 only 29.6 percent of imports and 30.1 percent of exports by Common Market members came from other member nations. But by 1970, imports reached 48.4 percent and exports 48.9 percent.

In 1961 the most important finance ministers and their deputies in the IMF created the Group of Ten. This was a club within a club that served, together with the central bankers in the Bank of International Settlements of Basel, Switzerland, to help manage the international monetary system throughout the 1960s. Working Party Three of the Organization for Economic Cooperation and Development also assisted in this *ad hoc*, multilateral form of crisis management. As previously noted, Special Drawing Rights (SDRs), or artificial international reserve units to be used among central banks outside the control of the United States and managed by the Group of Ten, were created as a new form of liquidity in the 1960s. Because the Europeans had a veto power on the creation of new SDRs they came to represent a dilution of American financial power mirrored by the rise of European influence. American financial power was further diluted with the rise of the **Euromoney** or **offshore banking system** that originated after 1917, when the Soviets wanted to protect their dollars from being seized by the United States and put them in "friendly" European banks. These offshore dollars started to grow in volume in the 1960s and multiplied immensely after the 1973 OPEC oil crisis, reaching into the trillions by the 1980s.

The greatest crisis in the confidence of the United States came in the late 1960s when President Lyndon Johnson decided to wage war on Vietnam abroad and war on poverty at home without raising taxes. This destabilizing, inflationary decision made the breakdown of the Bretton Woods framework imminent. The breakdown was marked by three major currency turbulences—the pound in late 1967, the dollar in March 1968, and the French franc and German mark in November 1968. French President Charles de Gaulle did what Frenchmen typically do in times of international crisis—buy gold. Already at his press conference of February 4, 1965, de Gaulle had argued passionately for "the supreme law, the golden rule": "Yes, gold, which does not change in nature, which can be made into bars, ingots, or coins, which has no nationality, which is considered in all places and at all times, the immutable and fiduciary value *par excellence*. Furthermore ... it is a fact that even today no currency has any value except by direct or indirect relation to gold, real or supposed." So much for the French confidence in the dollar or acceptance of the legitimacy of American domination. The American government intervened, asking the German and British governments to buy up the dollars being sold off, temporarily stemming the crisis of confidence. But the Bretton Woods system, based on a dollar fixed to gold (at $35 an ounce), was set up for self-destruction. It was only a matter of time.

FROM GOLD TO FLOATING

The shift from the fixed exchange-rate system, based on the dollar's convertibility to gold, to the floating exchange-rate system can be highlighted by tracing three permanent redistributions of wealth from Americans to others: the Marshall Plan of 1947, the OPEC oil price hike of 1973, and commercial bank lending in the late 1970s.

Because of the Marshall Plan (the first redistribution), American defense spending abroad, foreign aid, tourism, and foreign investment, a dollar scarcity following World War II was transformed into a dollar glut. Americans continued to spend more overseas than they earned from abroad. The United States shifted from being the world's principal short-term creditor to being its main short-term debtor. The willingness of the United States to run large deficits and thereby to provide the international liquidity to permit other countries to run surpluses undermined the discipline the Bretton Woods arrangement was supposed to instill, making the agreement increasingly irrelevant. The United States functioned as a world central bank in promoting expansion by pumping up the world's money supply. Developed Western countries were able to maintain currency convertibility without much domestic discipline, tight exchange controls, or protectionism. World trade and investment flourished. But the Achilles heel of the Bretton Woods system was the assumption that the dollar was convertible to gold.

For a while this weakness was successfully covered up. American experts advocated Special Drawing Rights—or "dollars in disguise" as a new source of non-national liquidity to supplement the dollar. Arguing that John Maynard Keynes had been right after all at the Bretton Woods Conference in saying that the initial IMF system did not provide adequate sources of international liquidity, this shift by American advisors seemed to have an altruistic ring. But, in fact, it was consistent with the so-called *policy of benign neglect* (letting things go along as they are).

This policy took politicians off the hook of having to decide whether to promote domestic recession on the one hand, or to restrict tourist, business, or military spending abroad on the other, so as to bring America's balance of payments back in line. *The dollar's position as the key reserve currency allowed the United States to run deficits to finance "global responsibilities" without having to cut back on private outflow.* Many American and European experts honestly believed that SDRs could become the basis of a multilateral reserve system that might eventually replace the domination of the dollar. But the short-term effect was to provide another distraction from the problem of American deficits.

Observing that the United States had only a third enough gold to cover the outstanding dollars and facing the certainty of another dollar devaluation, on August 15, 1971, President Richard Nixon did what perhaps any American president in that position might have been forced to do: Overnight he indefinitely suspended the dollar's official convertibility into either gold or foreign currencies. To put the best face possible on this move, Nixon called it his "New Economic Policy," simultaneously imposing a temporary surcharge of 10 percent on dutiable imports and freezing domestic wages, prices, and rents for ninety days while cutting both federal taxes and expenditures. Using the outspoken Secretary of the Treasury, John Connally, as a lightning rod, Nixon managed to make the dollar's retreat appear to be an aggressive thrust to improve the U.S. trade balance. Within twenty-four hours one person was able to shift the world economy from **fixed exchange rates** (the dollar fixed to the 1934 price of gold at $35 an ounce) to **floating exchange rates** (which officially emerged in 1973, signifying that any one country's currency is worth whatever people think it is worth at a particular moment). Nixon told no one of his intentions, including America's closest allies, thus deterring speculators and using the element of surprise to give drama to his decision.

In the short transitional period between the fixed and flexible exchange rates in the early 1970s, Connally engaged in hard bargaining to ensure that America's European allies and Japan would accept the change. An understanding was reached in the Azores, which resulted in the Smithsonian Agreement of the International Monetary Fund in December 1971. However, the Europeans and the Japanese were "reluctant allies." As an émigré from Nazi Germany, Secretary of State Henry Kissinger was wary of the Europeans and argued that they and the Japanese had become free-riders on the American security system, accepting the economic benefits of the postwar Western system without bearing their share of the burden. So Kissinger gave a cold shoulder to the Europeans, believing (probably correctly) that there was nothing to be gotten out of them. However, this "de Gaulle snubbing tactic" on Kissinger's part was to prove expensive later when the Americans found it increasingly difficult to obtain European cooperation for American objectives in the late 1970s. In the 1970s and 1980s American policymakers, increasingly concerned with the U.S. trade deficit, desired to bring down the price of the over-valued dollar to increase the competitiveness of American exports abroad without losing American status. They used hard bargaining tactics in trade and security negotiations with the Western Europeans and the Japanese, making use of the "free-ridership" argument and protectionist threats, and they shifted the flavor of American policy toward a nationalistic mercantilism with the predictable strains in American-Japanese and American-European relations. Tough, nationalist U.S. bargaining continued in the Clinton era.

Alas, in human affairs, throwing all of one's energies to win in one arena often guarantees losing in another. In their total preoccupation with the chess games going on in the strategic triangle (among the United States, Soviet Union, and People's Republic of China) and in the trilateral trade triangle (among the United States, Western Europe, and Japan), Nixon and Kissinger neglected the "North-South triangle" (among the oil-producing developing countries, the non-oil-producing developing countries, and the developed countries).[10] Nixon and Kissinger appeared to be blinded to the consequences of the 1973 oil price hike due to their preoccupation with the strategic stakes in the Arab-Israeli war on the one hand, and with trilateral trade competition on the other. These "maintenance men'" failed to appreciate the main fulcrum of historical change, so absorbed were they in the *ancien régime* mentality of shoring up the status quo.

THE RISE OF OPEC: THE SECOND REDISTRIBUTION

The quadrupling of oil prices by the OPEC oil cartel in 1973 was facilitated by the rise in the price of gold, gold reserves, and foreign-exchange holdings due to the shift to floating exchange rates. For under the floating system, which officially went into effect in 1973, no mechanism existed for the international control over the quantity of international reserves. The international monetary system float-ed around the dollar, but the dollar no longer possessed the discipline of gold con-vertibility. Countries could simply buy reserves if they wanted them, and there was no check on the inflationary production of liquidity in the system. Paper gold became "paper paper" and commodities in the ground and tangible goods ap-preciated steeply in value with the widespread global inflation in the 1970s. The **Eurodollar** (dollars outside the United States) and credit markets—that "state-less money" that was the international banker's vehicle for expansion throughout the 1970s—financed national exchange rate and interest rate volatility after 1973 but at the cost of uncontrollable price rises.[11] Faced with this "inflation machine" and motivated to unite by the Arab-Israeli war, the oil-producing Arab nations used an oil embargo to jack up their prices.

OPEC could only get away with its huge price hike by (correctly) assuming that the United States would choose to do nothing about it. Given the American de-bacle in Vietnam and U.S. domestic political difficulties at home, it was accu-rately assessed that America lacked the national will to support an invasion and occupation of Arab oil fields at the risk of a major confrontation with the USSR. The OPEC nations shrewdly guessed what price increase their rich customers would bear and launched what some called "the Arab decade."

Leaders of OPEC preferred to view the oil price hikes of 1973 and 1979 as eq-uitable "adjustments," not "revolution." They argued that up until 1973 the major oil companies largely dictated prices, even though oil was the critical develop-mental resource for many oil-producing countries. After 1973 governments as well as oil companies had a hand in the price-setting. From the viewpoint of oil producers, the first oil shock of 1973 was a "revolution." From the viewpoint of con-sumers it was a crisis. And from the viewpoint of most developing nations in the world, the OPEC "coup" was a symbolic victory for Third-World unity, demon-strating that cartel power could lead to a redistribution of wealth from the rich to the poor countries and could help to create a "New International Economic Order."[12] The OPEC oil price escalation (beginning in 1973) was to have revolu-tionary implications for the structure of national economies in the world system that were slow to be fully appreciated. Many advanced Western economies, and particularly the United States, had built cheap energy assumptions into their eco-nomic and industrial calculations. When energy costs skyrocketed in the 1970s—complemented by the inflation stimulated by global food shortages, a flood of international liquidity, and increasing labor costs—many basic industries in ad-vanced Western countries became less and less competitive on world markets. After the 1973 oil price rises, the major industrial nations of the West overreact-ed with deflationary policies, thus helping to prolong the recession of 1974–1975. Old Western policymakers overreacted to international change with stop-go eco-nomic policies—putting on the monetary brakes too heavily all at once, rather like a nervous driver trying to descend a steep hill in an old car, only to speed up too quickly at the bottom out of fear of losing momentum. They used deflationary policies, recycling the $30-billion deficit they acquired from the OPEC price rises to the poor, developing countries of the Third World. Then they expressed surprise in 1975 when these developing countries mobilized the "Group of 77" in the United Nations to demand economic justice.

THE DEBT TRAP: THE THIRD REDISTRIBUTION

The global economic crisis in the 1980s shifted from the inflationary liquidity surplus of the 1970s to a deflationary liquidity shortage and global recession. Private, commercial multinational banks were the institutions of adjustment in the 1970s. They outbid each other to lend money to developing countries at high interest rates, believing that if worst came to worst they might not get back their principal but they could at least survive on the interest. There was little regulation of this international banking activity. The leaders of advanced industrial nations, which were themselves beset with economic and political problems, seemed relieved to have the private sector pick up the increasing burdens of international financial assistance. But both the developing debtor nations and the international banks falsely counted on the global inflation rate continuing at a level high enough to make the debts ever-cheaper from the perspective of the borrowers and to assure the repayment of the interest from the viewpoint of the banks. Conventional wisdom projected that oil prices would continue to rise, not fall. (See also Chapter 5 under "The Debt Crisis" and "The Mexican Case.")

But in the early 1980s oil prices did fall. OPEC's share of the world market dropped below 40 percent and its cartel clout dissipated accordingly. Oil-producing developing countries suddenly found they could no longer pay back the interest on their debts. By January 1, 1983, the gross external debt of eight Latin American countries made up about 55 percent of the $550 billion that fifty developing countries owed to foreign creditors. And the debt of Argentina, Mexico, and Brazil alone amounted to more than $200 billion. The international banks and their Third World clients discovered they had fallen into a **debt trap**: A third redistribution had taken place, not through a Marshall Plan or oil price hikes, but this time through indefinitely extended credit. Wealthy countries attempted to stem the crisis by increasing the resources of the IMF by almost 50 percent and by pressuring their major banks to continue lending to the deficit countries. But the world debt crisis, compounding the scarcity of liquidity so badly needed to stimulate a world economic recovery, appeared to be more than conventional government and private-sector strategies could cope with. It was not a time for the maintenance of the old as much as it was for reform and risk-taking to create new structures and strategies. The early 1980s tight-money, high-interest-rate policy of the U.S. Federal Reserve Bank—anti-inflation-over-everything-else—was part of the problem, driving up variable interest rates of foreign debts.

By the 1990s, the role of the IMF had changed significantly. Growing to 179 members, the organization faced overwhelming strains caused by globalization and the growth of capital markets. The IMF expanded its responsibilities to include general financial and technical assistance, introducing new lending instruments such as the extended Fund facilities to serve medium term needs for structural adjustment. The original intention of J. M. Keynes to provide more liquidity was coming back in new guises. The SDRs continue to be an important substitute for international private capital, to which the poorest countries in particular do not have sufficient access. The 1990 increase in SDRs to $183.4 billion (from the original $7.4 billion) was not nearly enough to cope with the world debt problem. However, the IMF indirectly supports the access of countries to credit by playing the role of "insurer," influencing the risk assessment of investors and thereby lowering interest rates.

But in terms of collective learning, the "signal" the IMF would give to investors is mixed, since conventional IMF policy usually calls for governments receiving loans to raise taxes and devalue currencies. On the one hand, some investors are persuaded that the IMF may bail them out of bad investments (what is called the "moral hazard" problem—see Chapter 11). On the other hand, dropping currencies and the popular political protests that usually follow IMF tax-increases and austerity measures do not give investors confidence in the short-term. Of course the critics are sometimes surprised. The unprecedented $48 billion the IMF lent to Mexico in the (deflationary) peso crisis of 1994 (under U.S. pressure) was a signal to investors that worked: Only half of the money had to be used. However, the much more expensive Asian crisis of 1997 pushed the small resources of the IMF to the limit and resulted in resistance from the U.S. Congress.

When the IMF said it needed $90 billion in order to help resolve the financial crisis spreading from Asia to Russia to Latin America, the Senate passed the full $18 billion requested by the Clinton administration for the IMF but the Republicans in the House of Representatives agreed only to $3.5 billion: The rest would depend upon strict lending conditions. "The IMF has the Midas Touch in reverse—virtually every country it tried to help has become worse off from the experience," said Republican representative Richard Armey of Texas, the House majority leader: "Full funding of an unreformed IMF would be recklessly irresponsible."[13] The "reform conditions" suggested were to reduce secrecy in IMF lending decisions, to end below-market loans to foreign governments, and to demand shorter repayment terms (of perhaps one year). The Clinton administration opposed these "reform" conditions, saying that it is improper for the United States to attempt to dictate policy to a multinational agency such as the IMF. Meanwhile, at the annual meeting of the IMF and World Bank in 1998, the French followed up, proposing a plan to give the developing nations and the European Union more authority over the IMF, a suggestion that appeared aimed at diminishing U.S. domination. The Clinton administration turned down the plan and proposed that the IMF change its strategy in order to inoculate countries that were basically healthy from economic contagion with preemptive aid packages. The reactions from the 182 member countries attending the IMF meeting suggested that the United States come up with more cash before offering more ideas on how to spend it. But within the month the G-7 had adopted Clinton's proposal, opened a special emergency credit line for the IMF to cover the $90 billion needed, and targeted the funds for preventing possible contagion bringing down otherwise "healthy" economies. Brazil was the first recipient of support, having just reelected its reformist president, who then rammed through reforms to meet the IMF conditions.[14]

By the end of 1998, the Clinton administration coordinated a $30 billion international loan plan for Brazil to try to ward off the global financial contagion from Asia, using Clinton's new strategy of "preemptive defense." Neither the Germans nor the Japanese were keen on contributing to the Brazil "inoculation." In addition to having limited IMF resources available, the U.S. administration, under pressures of mid-term elections, managed to avoid tapping the Exchange Stabilization Fund created during the Roosevelt administration to help stabilize the dollar. (The money in this fund is under the secretary of Treasury's control; the president can spring it loose without congressional approval—but this resulted in objections from Congress when the Fund was used in the 1994 Mexican bailout.)[15]

Not trusting in the stability of the U.S. dollar, in U.S. financial support, or in the certainty of IMF effectiveness, some regions have created their own zones of monetary stability. The prime example is Europe.

THE EUROPEAN MONETARY SYSTEM AND THE EURO

The economic recovery of Western Europe and Japan after World War II coincided with the dilution of American hegemony, shifting the fulcrum of managing Western monetary affairs. The creation of the Common Market, or **European Economic Community (EEC)**, in 1958, symbolized the rise of Western Europe as a trading bloc. But coordination of regional monetary matters did not follow suit until the breakdown of the system of fixed exchange rates and Smithsonian Agreement in 1971. At the beginning of 1972, the six members of the EEC, soon joined by the United Kingdom, Ireland, Denmark, and Norway, created the "Snake"—an exchange rate regime that obliged its members to keep their currencies within a relatively wide "tunnel." Each currency was assigned a bilateral central rate with every other currency involved and each member government was required to keep its currency within a 2.25 percent margin either way of this rate, thus limiting the range of exchange-rate fluctuation. While only reluctantly joining the Snake—for fear of the Bundesbank's loss of control over domestic economic stability—West Germany quickly came to dominate the Snake as the strongest currency. Indeed, some referred to the arrangement as the "DMZ"— not "demilitarized zone" but "Deutschmark zone." Weaker currencies—the pound, lira, and Norwegian krone—soon left the system, given speculation against the dollar and pound in the new floating exchange-rate system. By 1974 the French franc, too, pulled out of the Snake.

The uncertainty of the mid-1970s was marked by the dollar devaluations of 1971 and 1973, the quadrupling of oil prices, and the escalation of grain prices drained purchasing power from most nations in the world, resulting in a deflationary impact. Nevertheless, the advanced industrial countries reacted with anti-inflationary policies. Their leaders anticipated a global inflation fueled by the rise in oil prices, the expansion of world liquidity, and the absence of external restraint implied by the shift from fixed to floating exchange rates. This anti-inflation policy was based on an understanding among the United States, Japan, and West Germany, which broke down in the 1974–1975 recession—partly due to those deflationary policies. As the German mark rose 30 percent against the currencies of the Federal Republic's twenty-three major trading partners between 1972 and 1977, the pressure increased on the German authorities to permit the mark to be used as an international reserve currency. This pressure was strongly resisted by the Bundesbank, which feared losing control over domestic money markets. So while the Germans favored a moderately rising or revalued mark as a means to keep inflation out of Germany (provided that the mark did not rise too high and threaten the competitiveness of German exports), they were open to some external restraint or system to take the pressure of adjustment from their shoulders.

Meanwhile, at EEC headquarters in Brussels, President Roy Jenkins of the European Commission perceived the European economies to be overwhelmed, leading inevitably to disintegration in the European Community unless some way could be found to stem the crisis. So he picked up the theory of **European Monetary Union (EMU)** and promoted European unity as an "adventurous idea," which might help to make up for the threats posed by the expansion of the Common Market (enlarged in 1973 to include Britain, Ireland, and Denmark) and general economic uncertainty. In his Monnet Lecture at the European University Institute in Florence in October 1977, Jenkins spelled out five economic reasons for monetary union: It would (1) stimulate efficient rationalization of industry; (2) provide the European Community with the advantages accruing to "the issuer of a world currency" (buffering the Europeans somewhat against dollar instability); (3) contribute to the struggle against inflation; (4) help reduce unemployment; and (5) reinforce policies aimed at leveling out regional differences within the EEC.

Roy Jenkins, a skilled politician, initiated his European Monetary Union strategy on two levels—at the "lower table" of public negotiations with others in the European Community bureaucracy and at the "higher table" of private talks with the leaders of key European currency countries—particularly West Germany, France, and Britain. At the lower table Jenkins, a British subject, had to confront his predecessor, F. X. Ortoli, a bureaucrat who had positioned himself well in the Central Bank Governors Committee with his typical strategy of small steps. Persuasion and co-optation were not in themselves sufficient means for Jenkins to sell his "wild idea" to Ortoli, who believed in achieving success by setting limited objectives. So Jenkins turned to the "high table" in 1977 to persuade the leaders of Germany, France, and Britain to join his monetary crusade for the sake of European unity.

West Germany's Chancellor Helmut Schmidt came out strongly for European Monetary Union in early 1978. His dislike for both President Jimmy Carter and

America's volatile economic policies led him to the conclusion that it was vital for Europe to have a grand design to buffer the impact of U.S. economic inconsistency upon the economies of the European Community. Schmidt was particularly critical of the **locomotive theory** of the Americans, according to which the West Germans and Japanese were pressured to stimulate demand in their domestic economies, thus acting as locomotives for world economic growth to counter the slowdown of the U.S. economy.

French President Valéry Giscard d'Estaing stayed out of the controversial European monetary idea—until he safely steered his center right coalition to election victory against a disunited left in the March 1978 French elections. Then Giscard D'Estaing, a former finance minister (as was his friend, Helmut Schmidt), jumped on the German bandwagon, negotiating with Schmidt behind the scenes in order to announce the European Monetary System as a joint German-French plan. The French wanted to give the appearance that France was as influential as West Germany, and were also concerned about monetary discipline, hoping that the European Monetary System (EMS) could substitute for a return to the system of fixed exchange rates.[16]

The West Germans and the French proposed the "parity grid" system of exchange rates, expanding the Snake in which each country was bound to every other currency. While elastic, the parity grid system allowed currencies to move only 2.25 percent either above or below the bilateral par value. Then the central banks of both the (over) high and (over) low currencies involved were required to act to bring their currencies back to the bandwidth permitted. The Germans liked this system, for the responsibility for exchange-rate adjustment fell equally upon both the strong currency (usually the mark) and weak currency involved. The weak currency countries—particularly Britain and Italy—objected that it was unfair to put as much responsibility upon the weak as upon the strong.[17]

The weak currency countries supported an alternative "basket system" based on a weighted average of all the EEC currencies: This was initially called the European unit of account for central banks or "ECU." This unit of account functioned as a reserve asset replacing part of the excessive dollar reserves. When elites in the European Union decided to create a common currency, the ECU came to be called the Euro.

The debate between the parity grid and basket system proposals was resolved with a Belgian compromise that combined the two systems: The basket system would serve as an indicator of divergence ("the rattlesnake") within the parity grid system. It would signal central banks to start intervening at 75 percent of the 2.25 percent (x 1—the percent of national currency in the basket) limit of flexibility allowed on either side of the central rate. West Germany, France, Denmark, the Netherlands, Belgium, and Luxembourg agreed to this system in late 1978. The ECU was approved for settling accounts among European partners as well as a $35 billion financial cooperation fund for stabilizing currencies. Italy and Ireland joined the EMS agreement by the time it went into effect in 1979 after receiving informal financial concessions (including a 6 percent range of flexibility rather than the normal 2.5 percent). While Britain agreed to have the pound in the basket indicator system, the English did not join the system, given the high rate of the pound and domestic political opposition to further integration with Europe.

In the early years of the European Monetary System (EMS), when the dollar was on a steady uptrend or downtrend and inflation was the primary concern of the eight member nations, participants were more or less content to go along with West Germany's dominant role as disciplinarian and paymaster. The Socialist government of France even reversed its Keynesian policy of public spending, pursued from 1981–1983, to adjust to EMS discipline rather than quitting the EMS. But by 1987, when the dollar's rate became volatile, European countries were more concerned with slow growth and unemployment than with inflation. The anti-inflation austerity of the Bundesbank and its power to crimp the national sovereignty of the non-German members became unbearable. As Jean-Pierre Chevènement, a leader of the left wing of the French Socialist Party, put it: "We cannot accept forever that the EMS be no more than the camouflage of a mark zone." The non-German members received two concessions from the Germans: (1) West Germany would contribute more money earlier in necessary interventions for exchange-rate stability with fewer conditions and (2) West Germany would coordinate policies more frequently with other member nations (implying less autonomy for the German Bundesbank). Germany became discontented as the other members made their own economic policies while Germany footed most of the bill for exchange-rate adjustments. But, initially, the EMS provided for a tighter exchange rate system than the global one and a basis for the Common Market to work its way out of what political scientist Stanley Hoffmann called the European Community's "dark age" (1973 to 1984).

The success of the European Monetary System depended on the predictability of the dollar, the world's key reserve currency, in the background. At first the dollar was predictable in appreciating in the early 1980s, as the U.S. tight-money, high-interest rate policy sought to lower the American rate of inflation. However, as the value of the dollar went up, so did the price of U.S. exports. Finally, the trade imbalance of imports over exports became so great that on September 22, 1985, the Americans called a meeting of the Group of Five major industrial nations' finance ministers at the Plaza Hotel in New York City. There the five (the United States, Germany, Japan, France, and Britain) agreed to a plan for the "orderly appreciation" of the other currencies against the dollar to give American exports some relief. The Americans, in turn, promised to cut back on government spending. A year later, the **Group of Seven (G-7)**—the Group of Five plus Canada and Italy—decided that the dollar had fallen far enough in value. At a meeting at the Louvre in Paris in February, 1987, they agreed to cooperate in order to stabilize it. The key players in this process were Germany, Japan, and the United States **(G-3)**, who agreed to set broad target zones of plus or minus 12 percent for the mark/dollar and yen/dollar exchange rates. This management system has since been called the **Plaza-Louvre Accords** or regime. The EMS thus operated smoothly as long as the G-7 managed the larger dollar problem. This was done largely through rare but concentrated interventions in the currency markets by the central banks of the G-3 countries (who bought up the dollar, for example, when it became too weak). Despite the flimsiness of the target zones, under the Plaza-Louvre regime they kept the dollar's exchange rates within narrower ranges from 1987 through 1992 than for the fourteen years from 1973–1987.[18]

However, the European Monetary System does not stay stable based upon "external" dollar management alone. The internal economic policies of the European Union countries determine the domestic inflation rates, interest rates, and ability of member nations to attract foreign investment. During 1992 the domestic economy of Great Britain slipped into such deep recession that on September 16 of that year, stock prices plummeted. Repeated efforts by Britain and the central banks of Germany and France failed to stop the free fall of the British pound on the exchange markets. Britain was forced temporarily to pull out of the European Monetary System, resulting in chaos that forced weaker currencies, such as the Spanish peseta and Italian lira, to be devalued. A two-tier European Monetary System emerged: Strong currencies such as the Dutch guilder, remained pegged to the German mark, while weaker currencies floated to their market levels. Through French domestic sacrifices and by heavy German buying of francs, a run on the French franc was slowed down. In 1993 the European exchange rate mechanism (ERM) fell apart: The bands of fluctuation were expanded to 15 percent, making them almost meaningless. However, to the surprise of many outsiders, this crisis became an opportunity for the Europeans to move forward on schedule toward creating a single currency. The **Maastricht Treaty** of 1991 provided for a three stage progression to a European currency, "The Euro." In phase one, the nine European Community countries already in the European exchange rate mechanism (ERM) provided for by the European Monetary System harmonized to prepare for phase two, beginning in 1994 when capital markets were further liberalized. The Council of Central Bank Governors was replaced by a new institution, the forerunner of the European Central Bank: The European Monetary Institute in Frankfurt. The final phase was the launching of the "Euro" itself as the official unit of account in 1999, with the European Central Bank coordinating the issuing of the common European currency in 2002.

To be able to join the first wave of those giving up their own national currency for the Euro, the candidate EU countries were required officially to reduce their budget deficits to 3 percent or less of GDP, to reduce their outstanding government debt to 60 percent or less of GDP, to hold their inflation rate equal to or less than 1.5 percent over the rate of the lowest three members, to keep the interest rate on long-term government bonds to no more than 2 percent above the three members with the lowest inflation rates, and to have been within the ERM for at least two years. However, these criteria of convergence pushed by the German Central Bank were relaxed somewhat when the final decision for membership came in 1998: The European Commission ruled that eleven nations were eligible to join the single currency, even though eight were above the Maastricht limit on public debt of 60 percent of GDP and several made it under the 3 percent budget-deficit limit only due to "creative accounting." The eleven and their 1997 percent of deficit and debt in terms of GDP respectively were Austria (2.5, 66.1), Belgium (2.1, 122.2), Finland (0.9, 55.8), France (3.0, 58.0), Germany (2.7, 61.3), Ireland (–0.9, 66.3), Italy (2.7, 121.6), Luxembourg (–1.7, 6.7), Netherlands (1.4, 72.1), Portugal (2.5, 62.0), and Spain (2.6, 68.8). Whether the compromises made to let these eleven all start in the single currency will lead to a Euro as strong as the German Mark, which was the initial intention of the elites planning the European Central Bank (particularly the Germans) is questionable—particularly given pressures by the French and German governments for lower interest rates in order to stimulate more employment. If not, and if the Euro weakens after an initial testing period, the forecast of Euroskeptics such as economist Wilhelm Hankel may be fulfilled, that a weak Euro could spill back and undermine the economic successes that the European Union has enjoyed to date.[19]

INTERPRETATIONS

Adjustments in exchange rates due to balance-of-payments deficits are tips of old icebergs. They are but superficial indicators on the surface of the world monetary system representing the political and money constitutions of the nation-states underlying them. These adjustments can be interpreted differently, depending on whether the observer is from a rich country or a poor one, or is a classical economic liberal, a monetarist, a structuralist, a neorealist, or merely someone who seeks to maintain the status quo. By looking at the alternatives a nation has for solving a balance-of-payments problem from these different perspectives, one can get a sense of the kaleidoscope called the world monetary system.

BALANCE-OF-PAYMENTS ADJUSTMENTS

When the sum of all economic transactions between a state's residents and foreigners is greater than all receipts coming into the state and its residents during a year, that country is running a **balance-of-payments deficit**. Should the amount coming in exceed that going out, that country enjoys a **balance-of-payments surplus**. The objective of conventional monetary theory calls for equilibrium rather than for a surplus or deficit. International management efforts in the world monetary system can often be most easily explained by a maintenance model, which aims toward stability over all else. While stability undoubtedly benefits both rich and poor nations, the adjustment required to recover or to maintain balance-of-payments equilibrium often falls most heavily upon those who are least well off. This explains why conflicting perspectives emerge over the relative value of exchange-rate stability.

Three traditional methods exist for a country to cope with a balance-of-payments deficit:

1. *Internal economic policies*: typically deflationary policies to reduce the deficit such as a tighter budget or higher interest rates.

2. *External measures* to shift expenditures away from imports, securities, and other transactions that lead to payments to foreigners: typically involving import quotas, tariffs, or limiting the outflow of capital.
3. *Financing or raising liquidity:* typically cashing in gold or foreign-exchange reserves or borrowing through private markets or commercial banks.

CLASSICAL ECONOMIC LIBERALISM

Any actual national policy involves some mix of internal, external, and financing measures in adjusting a country's balance of payments. But classical economic liberals stress avoiding policy trade-offs that utilize external measures, arguing that the free flow of capital, goods, and services between nations is essential to increase both economic growth at home and global economic prosperity. Secretary of State Cordell Hull under President Franklin Roosevelt epitomized the classical liberal position. He argued that free markets and free trade would lead to global economic prosperity, that the rising waters would lift all ships (or nations), and that global prosperity would assure world peace.[20] Harry Dexter White represented a more developed extension of this perspective: Balance-of-payments adjustments must focus on internal measures, getting one's own house in order, so as to qualify for financing provided by the IMF or commercial banks.

The Bretton Woods system was inspired from the American side by classical economic liberalism, which sought to deter obstructions to free trade and to head off competitive exchange-rate devaluations or external capital controls by providing a limited but reliable short-term source of liquidity to member states in need. However, the actual institutions of Bretton Woods represented a compromise that political scientist John Ruggie called "embedded liberalism." *Embedded liberalism* is the residue of power and social purpose still remaining in the institutions created by Bretton Woods despite the decline in hegemony or domination of the creator, the United States, in the 1970s and 1980s.[21] At Bretton Woods, the Americans pushed for institutions that would encourage state self-sufficiency, economic growth, and free markets. The means were short-term loans to credible borrowers to supplement adjustments toward free markets made by such states. The Americans wanted a conservative, objective measure of "conditionality." They wanted a "thin" international monetary standard, based on momentary, short-term creditworthiness, to match their "thin" ethical notions of the self as a short-term interest maximizer. While the ideology of the IMF officially matched this American version of liberalism, institutionally the IMF evolved differently than the ideology.

Adam Smith, it will be recalled, thought that an "invisible hand" would steer private self-interest to the public good. The IMF did not become a surrogate "invisible hand," which would, indeed, have constituted a "thin" international monetary standard. Rather, the IMF developed into a collective, norm-governed balancing act between opening markets, on the one hand, and protecting the domestic stability of key states from having to bear undue costs of adjustment to world economic change, on the other. Under Prime Minister Thatcher and President Reagan, Anglo-American efforts to make liberalism (or the praise for free markets and privatization) more pronounced—or to go back to a "thin" monetary system—may have destabilized the Bretton Woods system more than any overload of the regime due to domestic social objectives or protectionism in money and trade.[22]

STRUCTURALISM

From the perspective of the economic school called **structuralism**, Adam Smith's "invisible hand" is too invisible: Nations must use external measures in making balance-of-payments adjustments in a world where the flow of finance, liquidity, and trade is *structured* against them. It is the rich states, after all, who could afford to purchase the most shares in the IMF and who have the largest quotas when it comes time to borrow (the United States, for example, is one of the top borrowers from the IMF).

Structuralists argue that the world capitalist system must be tilted toward the interests of the least-advantaged nations. Nobel economist Gunnar Myrdal suggested that the U.S. redistribution to Europe in the form of the Marshall Plan went to the wrong countries. The "old rich" Europeans were capable of recovering on their own and the historical moment of American goodwill should have been targeted at the poorest countries in Asia or Africa without the training or tradition of economic recovery and development.[23]

Latin American economist Raul Prebisch argued that capital flows from poor countries to rich ones because the terms of trade are structured against the poor, who must live off the low price of commodities, while the rich countries benefit from the higher (and rising) prices of both manufactured goods and high-tech products and services.[24] The rich nations should therefore provide liberal liquidity for the poor countries and accept the external measures the developing countries require to protect their limited markets and resources. Keynesian liquidity creation and long-term soft loans would suit the structuralist perspective of reducing the inequities between the rich nations and the poor ones—not the liberal classical priority of putting one's own house in order first to qualify for short-term, conditional credit.

MARXISM

From the Marxist perspective, the IMF provides a "debt trap" for the developing countries: It renders them forever dependent on external financing by the rich industrialized nations.[25] The world capitalist system is eventually set to self-destruct, breaking down in the contradictions of social and international class conflicts, according to neo-Marxists. Meanwhile, several intermediate Marxist strategies are available for countries with balance-of-payments deficits to follow. One—the former Albanian and North Korean approach—is for such countries to isolate themselves, creating import substitutes, attempting to become as self-sufficient as possible before opening the door to the outside world economy and to vulnerability. This is an extreme policy, one that emphasizes external measures over everything else.

Another strategy is that of the **Cambridge school**. Many of the elites in the developing countries sent their children to study at Cambridge University in England. Partly due to this increasing influx of students from the developing world, a neo-Marxist economic wing developed at Cambridge, which Mexico called upon for advice in the late 1970s when Mexico was haunted by staggering balance-of-payments problems. Advisors influenced by Cambridge neo-Marxist thought persuaded Mexico to borrow as much as the Western commercial banks were willing to lend even though both sides knew the chances of paying back the principal on the loans were not good.* The Cambridge strategy was that even if the loans could never be paid back, Mexico would have the banks by their loans, a sort of reverse debt trap.

The banks, in turn, would have to continue to provide enough liquidity to Mexico to service the interest on the loans or risk a Western financial crisis by officially writing off the loans in reports to stockholders. And the banks ultimately had their governments by the debt. If one of the nine largest banks in the United States threatened to go bankrupt and trigger a financial crisis, the U.S. government would have to step in to bail them out. Mexico, with proximity to the U.S. border and the ability to allow unemployed Mexicans to drift across, thus was able to "restructure" global financial arrangements to create a permanent source of American liquidity. That David Rockefeller, chief executive officer of Chase Manhattan Bank, was one of the American elites strongly promoting this restructuring to make the Cambridge strategy successful is an historical paradox that Marxist theory alone might have a hard time explaining (not to mention the theory of classical economic liberalism).

MONETARISM

Monetarists, such as Nobel economist Milton Friedman, argue that the money supply is the most important factor in a nation's economic policy and that only monetary policy can influence the course of the gross national product.[26] Monetarists usually assume that people tend to keep a fixed amount of money liquid, which they save (for example, the nonconsumed part of income held for convenience). Beyond this, if the nation's money supply provides citizens with easier access to money or credit, they will spend more. If, on the other hand, the nation's money supply is tightened the populace will consume and spend less. Moreover,

---

*Not all of these advisers were neo-Marxists. Carlos Tello, for example, a key Mexican figure behind the borrowing (under President Luis Echeverria) and behind the bank nationalization (under President Lopez Portillo) was educated at Cambridge and influenced by neo-Marxist thinking but often supported neo-Keynesian economic policies for Mexico. Still, the influence of the eclectic neo-Marxist Cambridge school of thought should not be underestimated. See Chapter 5 for details of the Mexican case.

if governments spend more, people or households will spend less since public spending presumably crowds out private and household spending. A nation with a balance-of-payments deficit, according to the monetarists, is probably living beyond its means and must focus upon internal (usually deflationary) measures to tighten up the money supply.

Monetarism is ultimately a free-market ideology advocating an anti-inflation policy above all else, and mostly benefiting those who have something of value to lose from inflation—namely the wealthy. To the extent the IMF demands that countries reduce the money supply and adopt government austerity measures as prerequisites to IMF loans, it is adopting a monetarist policy.

Federal Reserve Chairman Alan Greenspan used the theory of monetarism to decide when to preemptively fight inflationary expectations by raising interests to reduce liquidity, or to head off recession or undue deflation by lowering interest rates to increase the money supply (as in the fall of 1998 in the wake of the Asian financial crisis).

NEOREALISM

Neorealism has its roots in the power precepts of Machiavelli and the nationalistic economic policies of mercantilism. The preoccupation with power—defined as control for the sake of the security, glory, and wealth of the imperial state—traces back to Thucydides in his *Peloponnesian War*. The modern tradition of realism is epitomized by the nine "elements of power" of Hans Morgenthau: geography, natural resources, industrial capacity, military preparedness, population, national character, national morale, quality of diplomacy, and quality of government.[27] The neorealists of the 1980s picked up Morgenthau's concern with calculations of power and national interest in the United States as a reaction against the demise of the nation-state forecast by the global idealists of the 1970s. The inability of nation-states to control or to manage change in the 1970s was not due to the demise of the nation-state, according to the neorealists, but to the power vacuum resulting from the decline of American hegemony following America's defeat in Vietnam.[28]

The neorealist interpretation of optimum balance-of-payments adjustments stresses maximizing the power and internal controls of the state. For nations enjoying a surplus, this means maintaining the surplus as a national security buffer or strong bargaining position, making only superficial compromises to the international community, striving not to weaken the maintenance base of power and wealth. Deficit nations must use their weakness strategically to seduce stronger nations, banks, and international organizations into granting them financing on soft terms. The power base at home is the priority, beginning, of course, with the power of the elites. The maximization of national interest precedes international stability from the perspective of the neorealist: International agreements are nothing more than tough bargains struck between conflicting parties in which the strongest gets its way. Not to strive for hegemony is to lose the game. The rational choice interpretation refines the neorealist position, examining the rational maximization of each actor's choice given full information, but highlighting paradoxes in which short-term interest group choices undermine longer-term national interests. The fiscal interests of the burgeoning class of pensioners in Japan not sufficiently funded for retirement in the 1990s, for example, led the Japanese government to decide rationally to increase savings rates through austerity measures until the outside intervention of the United States and other foreign government pressure groups in 1998 caused the Japanese to reverse priorities in order to stimulate economic growth, to counter recession and the Asian currency meltdown.

IMPLICATIONS

Each of these interpretations or schools of thought has its own insights into how the world money system works. Each has its blind spots. In the rapid transitions of the **post-cold-war world economy**, it may be important to utilize more than one perspective in order to understand what is happening.

The world economy shifted in the late 1980s and 1990s away from centralized "command" economies typical of cold-war socialism toward decentralized market economies and privatization. From the perspective of classical economic liberalism, this shift was seen as a positive move toward tapping free-market potential for economic growth. But the liberal view, in its enthusiasm for chaotic growth, is usually blind to class-structured restrictions of opportunities for equal treatment: While many developed and newly industrializing countries benefited from free-market trends, the poorest developing countries went deeper into global recession and massive unemployment. Both structuralism and Marxism spotlight unequal distributions of the past that discriminate against poor nations in the present—resulting, for instance, in a net capital flow from the poor countries to the rich that still continues. However, these perspectives usually ignore emerging technological innovations that radically recast how money works and how it will be invested in the future. By focusing heavily on the redistribution of the existing economic pie (or wealth), they fail to pay enough attention to how to make the economy grow in the future (or how to create new jobs through entrepreneurship).

Monetarists highlight money flows from the top of each national system downward and keep a close watch on existing liquidity or cash instruments (money, checks, credit). But they risk neglecting existing fiscal and class structures that funnel cash in certain directions rather than others. However, an initial conservative monetarist who developed larger global and social perspectives, such as Federal Reserve Chairman Alan Greenspan (who sometimes seemed to run the U.S. central bank *as if* it were a world central bank), can prove to be amazingly effective as long as the world financial markets and other G-7 members pay attention to his signals. (But if the United States is a hegemon as rare in history as Moby Dick, Greenspan is probably a "monetarist" as rare as Captain Ahab!)

For the neorealists, the more things change the more they stay the same. Politicians who specialize in negative campaigning and champion their realism usually lack a positive vision for the future and underestimate those who act for altruistic motives. They are seduced by power and are often more interested in bringing opponents down than in building the country up. They are what sociologist C. Mills called "crackpot realists." They see the costs of programs and know where power lies. But rarely are they problem-solvers or visionaries. Like neoconservative novelist Ayn Rand, they are apt to be self-righteous defenders of "the virtue of selfishness."

The neorealists flourished during the cold-war era when power was more or less divided into East and West blocs and national security issues were primary. When the cold war was over, there was a shift from "high foreign policy issues" (national security and survival) to "low foreign policy issues" (foreign trade, investment, monetary, and financial issues).[29] The neorealists became mercantilists and shifted their "war-room games" to trade and money issues, with very mixed success. Global money and trade games involve interdependence and cooperation for stability and growth. A collective learning approach that integrates both conflict and cooperation within a global framework is more appropriate than the one-sided, short-term, conflict-oriented perspective of neorealism. The United States, for example, can sell its domination more easily if it is perceived as a moral force for the sake of human rights and global stability, rather than as merely a selfish, short-term maximizer of its own interest.

In an international exchange-rate system of N nations, there are only N-1 exchange rates, rendering one currency redundant.[30] If all N countries attempt actively to manipulate their exchange rates, the system is technically "overdetermined" and to that extent destabilized. Since, in practice, the redundant currency tends to be the key international reserve currency—today's dollar—the clear implication is that key-currency country policymakers should maintain a more or less passive policy except when it is necessary to intervene to keep their currency stable on world markets. To do otherwise not only "overdetermines" the system theoretically but also politicizes the existing international exchange-rate regime unnecessarily, undermining its legitimacy.

The authority of the key-currency country is undermined when others accuse it of mercantilistic currency manipulations for the sake of national interests. Thus American allies protested in the 1970s and late 1980s when the dollar was undervalued, stimulating American exports at their expense, and they complained in the early 1980s when the dollar was overvalued, sucking their capital into the United States as it chased the higher interest rates. In the late 1980s, American policy was to devalue the dollar and to persuade West Germany and Japan to stimulate demand (for imports) domestically in order to help balance the U.S. trade deficit. But by 1990, this short-term policy led to a jump in global interest rates as Japan and West Germany raised their interest rates to dampen the inflation caused by their stimulation of domestic demand. The higher global interest rates hit the United States exactly when it needed lower rates to encourage economic growth and head off a recession. Interest rate roulette played with the world's key currency is a precarious game. As hegemon and superpower, the United States has the greatest stake in the stability of the existing dollar-dominated world monetary system and its more or less "apolitical" acceptance as the legitimate regime by other countries.

But the Americans mismanaged their position of privilege, overexposing their short-term national benefits and putting the very legitimacy of the monetary system in question. Erratic changes in economic policy under President Jimmy Carter undermined the system's stability and U.S. authority as the dollar fell 16 percent in 1977–1978. This mobilized the Europeans to create the European Monetary System—a joint float of European currencies to serve as a buffer to the dollar's instability.

In 1978 Carter appointed Paul Volcker as Chairman of the Board of Governors of the Federal Reserve System. Volcker applied the monetary brakes to bring down the U.S. inflation rate, which was about 13 percent. In so doing he "overdetermined" the international monetary system by refocusing Federal Reserve policy on restricting the base of the entire U.S. money supply and not just on interest rates. The Volcker policy of tightening the money and credit supply drove up U.S. interest rates to historically high levels, causing the dollar to be overvalued.

The high U.S. interest rates attracted capital into American money funds and portfolio investment, draining the world market of liquidity where it was badly needed. American interest rates also helped to lock the United States into a structural trade deficit as the strong dollar made American exports less competitive on world markets. Since the Europeans and Japanese had planned on a strong American recovery to help their own domestic economies, not to mention that of the lesser developed countries, the tight money policy of the Volcker regime had the effect of derailing yet another locomotive theory of economic growth. Late in the recession of 1981–1982, Chairman Volcker shifted to another extreme, loosening the money supply, ignoring M-1 (cash and checking account) fluctuations above his targets.

One reason for Volcker's "overmanagement" of the U.S. money supply was the creation of the *xeno* (foreign or "stateless") money and credit markets—usually known as the Eurodollar markets—in the 1970s. The Eurodollar markets helped recycle back into circulation the money flowing to OPEC for its oil. By the early 1980s the Eurodollar markets had expanded to *trillions* of U.S. dollars, none of which could be governed or controlled by the central banks of the key industrial countries. With their international control through currency monopoly and reserve requirements diluted, to have the slightest impact upon international money markets the central banks such as the Federal Reserve were tempted to overreact or to oversteer—extreme tightening or extreme loosening of the domestic money supply. While this form of defensive management made short-term policy sense domestically, it undermined the legitimacy of the monetary system dominated by the dollar in the long-run when the United States oversteered or overly politicized the exchange-rate regime. American policymakers were exploiting their "privileged position" in the world monetary system either to manipulate exchange rates so as to attract capital to cover U.S. balance-of-payments and federal deficits, or to make U.S. exports more competitive to ease the U.S. trade deficit.

MANAGING THE CRASH OF 1987

The dollar fell with the looser money supply and with efforts of U.S. policymakers to turn their trade deficit around through competitive devaluation in the mid-1980s. Capital flowed out of lower, fixed-interest commitments into a speculative stock market that reached record level highs. Computer-programmed, futures-hedging systems—or "portfolio insurance"—ratcheted up (and later down) these massive speculative investments worldwide. This was done faster than those who would control the world monetary system could keep up with. The American policy of letting the dollar drop to help make U.S. exports more competitive failed to have any appreciable impact upon the U.S. trade deficit in 1987. As a result, the newly appointed head of the Federal Reserve System, Alan Greenspan, let interest rates rise to head off inflationary anticipations stemming from the lower dollar. Despite the February 1987 Louvre agreement among the key Western industrial countries (the Group of Seven), U.S. policymakers again politicized the monetary management system by publicly accusing the West Germans and the Japanese of not stimulating their domestic economies enough to help reverse U.S. trade deficits and to act as locomotives of world economic growth.* Disenchantment with U.S. economic policy became widespread. Congress was taking few significant steps to reduce the huge federal deficit and not enough internal restructuring measures were being taken in the U.S. economy to reverse the large American trade deficit. Then, West Germany raised interest rates rather than lowering them in accord with American wishes that the Germans stimulate demand. U.S. Treasury Secretary James A. Baker openly criticized the Germans on October 16, 1987, stimulating a drop in the prices of U.S. stocks, to be followed on October 19 by Black Monday, when the New York Stock Exchange saw its Dow-Jones average plummet 22 percent in a single day. The world's stock markets fell in tandem with the U.S. market, particularly given international, computerized portfolio systems. Baker's clumsy criticism appeared to undermine the Louvre agreement of industrialized countries to maintain exchange-rate stability, while an anonymous, highly placed American official implied that if the West Germans did not lower their interest rates the Americans would push the dollar down further as an intentional policy (undermining German exports). The threat was another symbol of U.S. politicization of the monetary system for mercantilistic objectives. It epitomized massive disenchantment abroad with a U.S. economic policy that drained the capital of other countries in order to plug up American federal and trade deficits that the Americans appeared unwilling or unable to do much about.

---

*Both the Germans and the Japanese were more concerned with keeping inflation low and their savings rate and export surplus high in the post-World War II period than were the Americans.

The residue of the Bretton Woods system—symbolized by the IMF-G-7 (or "Plaza-Louvre") regime—ensured that October 19, 1987, would not be a repeat of October 28, 1929 (**Black Friday**), even though in percentage terms the stock market actually dropped more on Black Monday than on Black Friday. Late in the day on October 19, the U.S. treasury secretary, the West German finance minister, and the head of the German Bundesbank (central bank) issued a joint statement from Europe assuring the financial markets that the G-7 Louvre agreement was still operative and that they were doing everything to cooperate. On October 20, Alan Greenspan, head of the U.S. Federal Reserve System, publicly announced that the central bank would provide all the liquidity necessary for the American banking system to stem the crisis. This loosening of U.S. monetary policy was the opposite of that of the Federal Reserve after the stock market crash of 1929, when a tightening up of U.S. money policy led to an expansion of the stock market's fall and to a run on the banks, thus helping to bring on the Great Depression. The fact that each individual bank account was insured for up to $100,000 (Federal Deposit Insurance) reassured the American public sufficiently in 1987 that they ran to U.S. banks to put money in this safe haven rather than taking all their savings out.

Once the stock slide started, computer-programmed trading increased the speed and volume of the fall to such an extent that the institutions of the stock exchange—much less federal government institutions—could not cope with what was happening. The managers of stock funds had protected themselves with dollar averaging—that is, as a stock declines, they sell in limited amounts at a time, and when it rises they buy in limited amounts. But this process was stimulated greatly by the difference in the margin requirements in the New York and Chicago exchanges, thus increasing the *arbitrage*, or speculation on the differences between the exchanges. The Chicago Mercantile Exchange, which possessed the largest stock index futures market, had only a 7 percent margin requirement, meaning a buyer had only to put up 7 percent of his or her own money. But the New York Stock Exchange had a 50 percent margin requirement, which stimulated margin buying (a parallel between the 1929 and 1987 crashes).

The process was stimulated because many big traders took out "portfolio insurance," automatically buying futures contracts in Chicago to hedge against a decline in the New York market. Thus the computer trading programs pushed the market in a single direction, faster than money or institutional managers could cope with the change.

All managers could do to recover equilibrium was to try to slow things down— what one could call a policy or *strategy of retardation*. John Phelan, chairman of the New York Stock Exchange, executed this strategy following Black Monday. He prohibited the use of the Big Board's order-distribution system on the New York Exchange for program trading, thus breaking the "financial meltdown" and stabilizing the market. He suspended trading on the ninety-one most volatile stocks, while approximately 1,500 kept trading. Yet his strategy showed moderation. He did not ban margin program trading entirely, but he took it off the computer system and told traders that they would have to do it by hand. Nor did Phelan close down the New York State Exchange (NYSE) for the day, only a couple of hours early on days of the heaviest trading. Hong Kong's more extreme policy of closing its exchange entirely stimulated the 33⅓ percent drop in its stocks the day it reopened. John Phelan also asked major member-dealer firms and the Federal Reserve Bank to provide the NYSE with liquidity in case of need.

When it was all over, Phelan saw the need for institutionalizing what we have called a strategy of retardation. Phelan noted three major lessons learned were (1) to give everyone a little time so that people with knowledge can assess what can be done; (2) to pump liquidity in it "so everything just doesn't dry up;" and (3) to figure out a better way to plug the lender of last resort into the system.[31] The NYSE changed its procedures to be able to cope more efficiently with the next such crisis. It came with the sharp drop in the American stock market on October 13, 1989 ("Friday the 13th"). But this time it was less the new management procedures of the NYSE exchange that slowed the effects of the fall than the cushioning by the globalization of stock markets. The self-confidence of the Japanese buffered the fall of the U.S. market as Japanese investors held onto their stocks. The more risk-shy Germans, in contrast, sold off their stocks and the German market fell 13 percent. Clearly, the power of any government to manage such a financial crisis alone is extremely limited given the globalization of financial markets, not to mention the inability to control the trillions of "stateless" Eurodollars offshore.

Retardation (or slowing things down) alone is ultimately a self-defeating form of crisis management. In addition, there must be international cooperation among the industrialized countries to reform the unstable, private dollar-based world monetary system. The Asian financial crisis a decade later made the need for reform even more obvious.

THE ASIAN CRISIS OF 1997

The "Asian economic miracles" of the 1970s, 1980s and 1990s (see Chapter 9) attracted so much investment capital from the developed countries that these emerging market economies could not handle it, particularly given obscure banking and corporate accounting systems steered more by influential personal ties with the government than by transparent regulations (*crony capitalism*). The result was a contagious Asian crisis in 1997 that was to spread to Japan, and to emerging markets in Latin America and Eastern Europe, ultimately helping to precipitate the breakdown of the Russian economy in 1998 and interrupting the record seven-year economic boom in the United States. The world economy was threatened with serious deflation.

The timeline of the Asian crisis, as developed by Fred Fraenkel of Ing Barings Furmari Selz, is illustrated in Figure 2-1 (on page 66).[32] The first hint came in January 1997 with the bankruptcy of Hanbo Steel, a leading South Korean Conglomerate, under $6 billion in debts. In February Thailand's biggest finance company, Finance One, was unable to make its bond repayments. A month later the Thai

Figure 2-1 Timeline of Asian Crisis

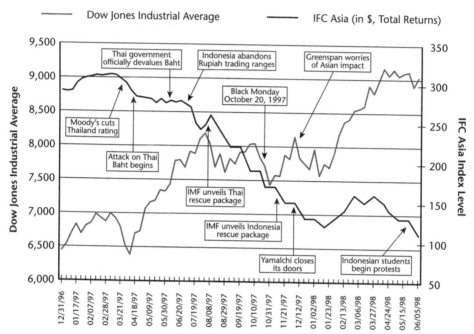

——— Dow Jones Industrial Average   ——— IFC Asia (in $, Total Returns)

government did not keep its promise to cover $3.9 billion in bad property debt from financial institutions. The head of the IMF, Michaell Camdessus announced "I don't see any reason for this crisis to develop further." By April the Moody's credit rating agency downgraded Thailand's sovereign debt rating. Soon thereafter investors began to doubt the stability of the Phillipines banking system. Suggesting they might have to raise interest rates (which they did not) in May, Japanese officials inadvertently set off a sell-off of Southeast Asian currencies and stocks by global investors. Speculators focused on the Thai currency, the baht, given political and economic instability in Thailand. The governments of Thailand and Singapore lost billions trying to defend the baht. After blaming hedge-fund speculator George Soros for the crisis, the prime minister said "We will never devalue the baht." Two weeks later the government effectively did so (through a "managed float" of the currency), calling on the IMF for "technical assistance." This 15–20 percent devaluation triggered the East Asian crisis, as one after another of the region's currencies fell—in the Philippines, Indonesia, Malaysia, and Singapore.

Prime Minister Mahathir Mohamed of Malaysia led the criticism of Western speculators and of George Soros in particular. In a speech July 24 he said: "Presently we see a well-planned effort to undermine the economies of all the Association of South East Asian nations by destabilizing their currencies. Our economic fundamentals are good yet anyone with a few billion dollars can destroy all the progress that we have made. We are told we must open up, that trade and commerce must be totally free. Free for whom? For rogue speculators. For anarchists wanting to destroy weak countries in their crusade for open societies, to force us to submit to the dictatorship of international manipulators. "

After Thailand announced an austerity plan that would restructure the financial sector in August, the IMF unveiled a $16 billion rescue package from both the IMF and Asian countries.

October 20, "Black Monday," ushered in a four-day stock market meltdown as the Hong Kong market fell the most it had ever fallen, the U.S. Dow Jones industrial average declined the most points ever (7 percent), and stock markets throughout Latin America lost value with prices in Brazil, Argentina, and Mexico recording their greatest single-day losses. At the end of the month the IMF granted Indonesia a $23 billion rescue package. In November South Korea asked for an IMF bailout as its currency plummeted, and the crisis hit Japan as the large Hokkaido Takushoku Bank, the regional Tokuyu City Bank, and the fourth largest brokerage, Yamaichi Securities, failed. On December 2, Federal Reserve Chairman Alan Greenspan stated that the Asian impact would be felt but would be temporary, leaving the nations with stronger economies: "There is no reason that above-average growth in countries that are still in a position to gain from catching up with the prevailing technology cannot persist for a very long time, provided their markets are opened to the full force of competition."[33] His remarks, and those by the IMF, were biased toward stability in order to head off a larger panic.

In December, Korea and Malaysia revealed economic plans designed to meet IMF demands. In South Korea the turmoil led to the election of dissident Kim Dae-jung as president, and major foreign banks offered to roll over huge short-term debts. By the end of 1997, the stock markets were down in Thailand 55 percent, Malaysia 52 percent, Philippines 41 percent, Indonesia 37 percent, and Singapore 31 percent, while the currencies were down 55 percent in Indonesia, 45 percent in Thailand, 35 percent in Malaysia and the Philippines, and 16 percent in Singapore.

The year 1998 began with the bankruptcy of Peregrine Investments, the premier local investment bank in Hong Kong. Suharto, leader of Indonesia, gave in to IMF demands but the stock market fell at the news.

Suddenly, investors seemed to think the bottom had been reached and started to reinvest in Asia. Then in mid-February, the Indonesian and South Korean markets fell as investors anticipated social resistance to stiff economic reforms. The first suggestion that the Asian crisis might affect the United States came as the U.S. trade deficit figures were released for December, rising 24 percent to $10.8 billion.

Indonesian officials were attracted to a currency board proposal of American economist Steven Hanke that would have pegged the rupiah to the U.S. dollar but dropped the plan after being pressured to do so by the United States, other members of the Group of 7, and the IMF—which threatened the withdrawal of a $43 billion assistance package. The rupiah suddenly shifted into hyperinflation. Suharto appointed his daughter, golfing partner, and officials associated with family business interests to a new cabinet in defiance of calls for reform from the IMF and world leaders. In May student protests spread, despite orders from the Indonesian military. Six students were killed. Financial and commodity markets and banks were closed as rioting spread. Suharto reversed the turmoil by announcing his resignation after thirty-two years in power.

Japanese stocks dropped as investors showed disappointment that an announced economic reform did not include tax cuts to stimulate growth. Moody's Investors Service lowered Japan's sovereign debt rating. Russian financial markets were hit by investors fleeing another emerging market concerned about Indonesia: The central bank tripled interest rates, and President Boris Yeltsin's government called on the IMF. In May, Pakistan mimicked India and had nuclear tests: The next week the Karachi Stock Exchange plunged, losing $850 million of market capitalization in the first two hours. "That's a very expensive bomb," concluded Munir Ladha of M. L. Securities.

By August 1998, Japan sank into the worst recession since World War II in a stalemated political situation (see Chapter 9). Yeltsin suddenly fired his cabinet, sending Russia into financial collapse (see Chapter 10) and world stock markets into a tailspin. In the week ending August 28 alone there were stock market declines of 22.7 percent in Russia, 19.4 percent in Turkey, 19 percent in South Africa, 12 percent in Brazil, 10.9 percent in Argentina, 10.5 percent in Mexico, 8.5 percent in Canada, 8.4 percent in Israel, 7.7 percent in Spain, 6 percent in the United States, 5.9 percent in Japan, 5.5 percent in Italy, and 4.3 percent in Germany.[34] By the end of August, the U.S. stock market had lost all it had gained for the year; the Asian crisis hit home in the superpower state. One out of two American families with direct or indirect stakes in the stock market felt the fall until Alan Greenspan helped to turn the market around through three cuts in U.S. interest rates.

Globalization served to spill the Asian crisis over into an emerging markets crisis that then impacted the developed countries through their export markets and investor confidence. While appearing to be "chaos," the financial breakdown was actually a constellation of identifiable factors ranging from bank and corporate corruption, government policy incompetence, the greed and fear of investors and speculators, overpriced stock markets and a belated IMF strategy of becoming lender of "first resort" instead of "last resort" to head off panic and a global meltdown (see Chapter 11). Collective learning became a form of herd *contagion* as even experts failed to understand "the global roulette," and uncertainty stimulated disinvestment throughout the world.[35] The apparent initial absence of strong global leadership reinforced this uncertainty as a morally undermined President Clinton (who admitted lying about an affair) met a politically wounded President Yeltsin. But this very distraction reinforced Clinton's delegation of authority for economic policy to his Treasury Secretary Robert Rubin. Rubin ran his department's brain trust like an investment bank, coordinating closely with a "sovereign" Alan Greenspan at the Federal Reserve to help turn the world economy around as they used the rising dollar, the U.S. stock market, and American hegemony as spring boards to cut interest rates and target liquidity. Perhaps it would be wise to consider what makes one of

the technical factors in the financial system work in this volatile world economy—the exchange rate regime.

SINGLE-KEY-CURRENCY ANCHORS VERSUS G-3 COLLECTIVE LEARNING

Much of the successful management of the world monetary system in the last
half of the twentieth century was accidental and a result of the good luck of being
able to anchor the exchange rate system to a key currency. Such a key anchor currency conveniently solved the problem of redundancy (that is, serving as the "redundant" currency or "standard" in a system with N-1 exchange rates).

First, the Marshall Plan of 1948 was meant to use American financial assistance to restore intra-European trade and financial stability. But it had the unin-
tended effect of enthroning the dollar as the unit of account and as the basic
means of settlement in the European exchange rate system (via the European
Payments Union). The IMF faded quickly into the background in the 1950s as the
U.S. Treasury became the world's surrogate central bank. The consumption-ori-
ented U.S. economy served to provide the liquidity and import purchases that
enabled all other countries to run export-oriented growth strategies. But eventually these neomercantilist strategies created a worldwide overcapacity in a deflationary environment.[36] A competitive struggle of downward adjustment ensued
to match the low-cost competition. But this, too, reached a point of diminishing
returns. Nevertheless, hard currency countries such as West Germany and Japan
often used currency reevaluations (or upward floating—hardening their currency) to keep inflation out of their domestic economies, to keep costs down, and to
keep their exports competitive. This amounted to an anti-inflationary policy in deflationary times, reinforced, in the German case, by the costs of reunification.

The Plaza-Louvre regime, or G-3 system, that emerged in the 1980s held more
hope than any single anchor system since it was based on three anchor currencies
rather than just one. The rules of this German-Japanese-U.S. system have been
summed up by economist Ronald McKinnon as follows: (1) Establish broad target
zones of 12 percent of variation in both directions for mark/dollar and yen/dollar exchange rates, but keep agreed-on central rates secret; (2) change implicit central
rates if fundamental disparities among the G-3 currencies emerge; (3) intervene
rarely, but together, if needed, to reverse short-run trends in the dollar that threat-
en to transgress the boundaries of the target zone, and signal G-3 intentions to intervene openly; (4) each of the G-3 should hold foreign exchange reserves
symmetrically in each others' currencies; (5) "sterilize the immediate monetary impact of interventions by not adjusting short-term interest rates"; (6) aim to anchor
each country's monetary policy to the national price level in tradable goods, indirectly stabilizing the world price level and keeping zones viable; and, (7) industrial
countries other than the G-3 should support or at least not oppose G-3 interventions, buying dollars with their national currencies when the dollar is too weak and
vice versa.[37] The G-3 system (underlying the annual G-7 economic summit meetings)
worked surprisingly well. But it, too, may be transitional as the introduction of the

Euro displaces one of the G-3. The European Central Bank may try to "collectively learn" from the remarkable model of Alan Greenspan in terms of the management of monetary policy. The question is to what extent Greenspan's effectiveness depended upon his solo stature, his coordination with a Treasury Department run, for perhaps a unique moment, like an investment bank under Robert Rubin and Lawrence Summers, and relative (hegemonic) autonomy compared with monetary leaders everywhere else in the world at the end of the twentieth century, and whether such hegemony can be transcended in a new financial architecture, perhaps in the form of a world central bank.[38]

QUESTIONS FOR THOUGHT

1. What is the Bretton Woods system "a la White"? In contrast, what have been the propositions of the British economists J. M. Keynes? By enumerating important IMF principles, explain why "the IMF is uniquely positioned to influence national policies of countries threatened with balance-of-payment deficits."

2. Evaluate the assertion that "the constant outflow of dollars from the United States undermined the very monetary system that it serviced." How is the decline of Bretton Woods related to the subsequent rise of oil prices in the 1970s and the debt crisis of the beginning 1980s? Which "three redistributions" of world wealth are identified and why?

3. Describe the "parity grid" and the "basket" systems and how they combined into the "rattlesnake" of the European Monetary Union.

4. Compare and contrast the main ideas of liberalism, structuralism, Marxism, monetarism, and neorealism in regard to the international monetary system.

5. Give examples of how the international monetary management system was politicized in the late 1970s and during the 1980s. Why are "xeno dollars" or offshore currency mentioned when dealing with the "overmanagement" of the U.S. money supply? What were the "rules" of the G-3 system? Speculate on what effects the introduction of the Euro are most likely to have on these "rules." To what extent was the management of Alan Greenspan at the Federal Reserve and Robert Rubin and Lawrence Summers at the U.S. Treasury unique and to what extent was their influence merely an outgrowth of U.S. hegemony and "the U.S. limelight effect?"

6. Compare and contrast the stock market crash of 1987 with the Asian crisis of 1997. How did increasing globalization turn collective learning into contagion? How did increasing liquidity and using strategies of "retardation" help to "manage" these crises?

NOTES

1. John Maynard Keynes noted: "Lenin is said to have declared that the best way to destroy the capitalistic system was to debauch the currency." Keynes, *The Economic Consequences of the Peace* (New York: Harcourt, Brace and Howe, 1920), p. 235.

2. Melville J. and Frances S. Herskovits, *Dahomean Narratives* (Evanston, IL: Northwestern University Press, 1958). Also see Paul Einzig, *Primitive Money* (Oxford: Pergamon Press, 1966).
3. See Wilhelm Hankel, "The Causes, History, and Illusions of Inflation," Part 2 of *Modern Inflation: Its Economics and Its Politics*, W. Hankel and R. Isaak (Lanham, MD: University Press of America, 1983), pp. 25–90. Or, in the German edition: *Die moderne Inflation* (Köln: Bund-Verlag, 1981), pp. 31–114.
4. The best history of the founding of the Bretton Woods System from the conflicting perspectives of Harry Dexter White and John Maynard Keynes is Richard N. Gardner, *Sterling-Dollar Diplomacy in Current Perspective: The Origins and Prospects of Our International Economic Order* (New York: Columbia University Press, 1980).
5. See John Williamson, "Keynes and the International Economic Order," in *Political Economy and International Money: Selected Essays of John Williamson*, ed. Chris Milner (Brighton, Sussex: Wheatsheaf Books, 1987), pp. 37–59.
6. Joan Robinson, *Economic Philosophy* (New York: Penguin, 1981, orig. published 1962), p. 16.
7. John Maynard Keynes, May 23, 1944, address to the House of Lords, in Gerald M. Meier, *Problems of a World Monetary Order* (New York: Oxford University Press, 1974), p. 34.
8. The history of the IMF is reviewed in J. Keith Horsefield, ed., *The International Monetary Fund, 1945–1965: Twenty Years of International Monetary Cooperation* (Washington, D.C.: IMF, 1969). For earlier monetary systems, see Robert Triffin, *The Evolution of the International Monetary System: Historical Reappraisal and Future Perspectives* (Princeton, NJ: International Finance Section, Department of Economics, Princeton University, 1964).
9. See David P. Calleo and Benjamin M. Rowland, *America and the World Political Economy* (Bloomington, IN: Indiana University Press, 1973), Chapter 5, pp. 87–117.
10. See Stanley Hoffmann, "Choices," *Foreign Policy* 12 (fall 1973): 3–42.
11. See, for example, Eugène L. Versluysen, *The Political Economy of International Finance* (New York: St. Martin's Press, 1981).
12. See Karl P. Sauvant and Hajo Hasenflüg, eds., *The New International Economic Order: Confrontation or Cooperation between North and South?* (Boulder, CO: Westview Press, 1977).
13. "Wrangling over IMF Bill at Fever Pitch," *New York Times*, October 8, 1998.
14. David Sanger, "Wealthy Nations Back Plan to Speed Help to the Weak," *New York Times*, October 31, 1998. For a developing country perspective on losers and winners from the process of globalization, see Paul Bernd Spahn, "Globalization, Governance and the Third World," in *Währungsunion und Weltwirtschaft*, ed. W. Nölling, K. Schachtschneider, and J. Starbatty (Stuttgart: Lucius and Lucius, 1999), pp. 411–426.
15. David Sanger, "U.S. Plans to Send Billions to Shield Brazil's Economy," *New York Times*, October 25, 1998.
16. See Peter Ludlow, *The Making of the European Monetary System* (London: Butterworth, 1982).
17. See Luigi Spaventa, "Italy Joins the EMS—A Political History," *Occasional Paper No. 22*, Research Institute, The Bologna Center, June 1980.
18. Ronald I. McKinnon, "The Rules of the Game: International Money in Historical Perspective," *Journal of Economic Literature* 31 (March 1993): 34.
19. See, for example, Wilhelm Hankel, "Das bisher Aufgebaute wird zerschlagen," *Badische Zeitung*, Dec. 2, 1995; and, from a different perspective, Jürgen Siebke, *Zum Geldpolitischen Instrumentarium der Europäischen Zentralbank* (forthcoming). Also see P. B. Kenen, *Economic and Monetary Union in Europe* (Cambridge: Cambridge University Press, 1995).
20. See Cordell Hull, *Memoirs*, Volumes I and II (New York: Macmillan, 1948).
21. John G. Ruggie, "International Regimes, Transactions, and Change: Embedded Liberalism in the Postwar Economic Order," *International Organization* 36, no. 2 (spring 1982).
22. Ibid, p. 413.

23. See, for example, Gunnar Myrdal, *Ökonomische Theorie und unterentwickelte Regionen: Weltproblem der Armut* (Frankfurt, 1974).

24. Raul Prebisch, *Towards a New Trade Policy for Development*, report by the Secretary General of the United States Conference on Trade and Development, E/CONF 4613 (New York: United Nations, 1964).

25. See Cheryl Payer, "The Perpetuation of Dependence: The IMF and the Third World," *Monthly Review* 23, no. 4 (September 1971).

26. See, for example, Milton Friedman, *Tax Limitation, Inflation and the Role of Government* (Dallas, TX: Fisher Institute, 1978). Also, Milton Friedman, ed., *Studies in the Quantity Theory of Money* (Chicago, IL: University of Chicago Press, 1956).

27. See Hans Morgenthau, *Politics Among Nation*, 3rd ed. (New York: Knopf, 1960).

28. J. Martin Rochester, "The Rise and Fall of International Organization as a Field of Study," *International Organization* 40, no. 4 (autumn 1986): 799. Prominent American "neorealists" include Kenneth N. Waltz (see his *Theory of International Politics* [Reading, MA: Addison-Wesley, 1979]) and Robert G. Gilpin (see his *War and Change in World Politics* [Cambridge, MA: Cambridge University Press, 1981]). Also see Richard R. Ashley, "The Poverty of Neorealism," and Robert G. Gilpin, "The Richness of the Tradition of Political Realism," both in *International Organization* 38 (spring 1984).

29. C. Roe Goddard, "Seizing the Opportunity: International Political Economy and the End of the Cold War," *International Studies Notes* 18, no. 3 (fall 1993): 17. The distinction between "high foreign policy" and "low foreign policy" was made by Richard N. Cooper in his "Trade Policy Is Foreign Policy," *Foreign Policy*, no. 9 (winter 1972–73): 18–36.

30. The first part of this section was initially presented at The Research Institute of International Change at Columbia University, and an early version later appeared as R. Isaak, "The International Monetary Crisis and Economic Growth," *Working Papers in International Banking*, no. 4, Institute of International Banking, Pace University, New York, February 1983. For the basis of the "N-1" proposition see Robert A. Mundell, *Monetary Theory* (Pacific Palisades, CA: Goodyear, 1971).

31. George Melloan, "Stock Slide Makes Phelan a Prophet ..." *Wall Street Journal*, October 28, 1987, Op. Ed Page.

32. This quotation and the timeline data are from Fred S. Fraenkel, "Asian Crisis Timeline," presentation to The Global Forum on Management Education: Global Capital Markets and National Sovereignty, Chicago, Illinois, June 16, 1998.

33. Ibid.

34. Data from Bloomberg Financial Markets as reported in "A Shaky Week for the World's Stock Markets," *New York Times*, August 30, 1998.

35. "Global Roulette: In a Volatile World Economy Can Everyone Lose?" *Harper's* 296, no. 1777 (June 1998): 39–50.

36. See Winston Williams, "Waking Up to the Glut Economy," *New York Times*, December 8, 1985, p. 1 of Business Section.

37. McKinnon, "The Rules of the Game," p. 32.

38. See Philip Arestis and Malcolm Sawyer, *The Political Economy of Central Banking* (London: Edward Elgar Press, 1998); and R. Isaak,"A World Central Bank: To Be or Not to Be?" in *Währungsunion und Weltwirtschaft: Festschrift für Wilhelm Hankel*, ed. Wilhelm Nölling, Karl Albrecht Schaftschneider, and Joachim Starbatty (Stuttgart: Verlag Lucius & Lucius, 1999), pp. 255–264. For the investment bank model of the U.S. Treasury Department, see Joshua Ramo, "The Three Marketeers," *Time*, February 15, 1999, 34–41.

THE WORLD TRADE SYSTEM

Who can be blind today to the threat of a world gradually invaded by an identical culture, Anglo-Saxon culture, under the cover of economic liberalism?
—Jacque Toubon, French Culture Minister (1993)

Current-account surplus can't be achieved by all countries simultaneously. Moreover, no country should seek to run its economy and society in such a way as to entrench a massive and permanent trade balance in its favor.
—British Prime Minister Margaret Thatcher (1985)

Every man who lives by supplying any want dreads anything which tends either to dry up that want or to supply it more easily and abundantly. It is to his interest that scarcity should reign in the very thing which it is his function to make abundant, and that abundance should reign everywhere else.
—Philip H. Wicksteed (1910)

INTERNATIONAL TRADE IS TRADE WITH FOREIGNERS—AN IDEA THAT TAKES GETTING USED TO. For people are brought up in sovereign nation-states where they are socialized to believe in the superiority, if not the self-sufficiency, of their own culture. **Ethnocentrism**—the belief in the primacy of one's own people or way of life—is the ultimate motive behind protectionism. Trade blocs create protective barriers separating "them" from "us" in order to ensure one's own economic interests first. From the national perspective, if trade with foreigners is necessary for national prosperity then why not try to arrange it so that there is more money coming in than is going out? It is natural to try to create a trade surplus to protect one's people in case of a downturn in the turbulent world economy.

There are a number of ways to look at international trade. The British (followed by the Americans) came to look at a trade surplus as less important than a world system of free trade. In such a world, they could use their hegemonic power and advanced economy to expand business worldwide for the sake of prosperity at home. With the key international reserve currency backed by the British navy in the nineteenth century, they could run deficits without a short-run problem—unlike any other country. At its peak of power following World War II, the United States adopted the same classical liberal free-trade policy for many of the same reasons. Therefore, the British and Americans scolded smaller nations (which saw trade surpluses as their only long-term security) for not aiming at an equilibrium in their trade balance. That emerging economic powers did not always agree with this Anglo-American free-trade position should come as no surprise.

Developing countries found that the price of their agricultural commodities, upon which their economies were based, did not keep up with the price of manufactured goods or financial services. This put them increasingly behind the developed countries in their terms of trade. From their perspective, the world trade system was structured against them, increasing the gap between their limited wealth and power and that of the rich nations. A banana republic with only bananas to export in exchange for everything else that it has to import cannot be enthusiastic about a world system of free trade that permits wealthy, well-organized, multiresource nations to take advantage of vulnerable, single-commodity countries.

On the other hand, if borders shut down and each nation is forced to live off what it has at home, the developed nations have most, the developing nations least. As uncertainty increases in the world economy, risk-shy, maintenance-oriented wealthy states are tempted to trade with other stable, well-to-do nations in their own image unless their governments or international organizations provide risk-insurance schemes to entice them to do business with less advantaged peoples. Financial crises, such as the stock crash of 1987 or Asian currency meltdown of 1997, merely reinforce the natural conservative impulse and security consciousness of rich consumers, investors, and traders. Crises make protectionism and trade war more tempting unless world leaders cooperate politically to create counter-incentives in the world trading system.

Origins

"Buy cheap and sell dear" is the motto of all business, including international business. Mass production is one way to make things cheaper—through "economies of scale." The ancient Greeks were the first to use mass production.

International trade is furthered by stable, routine relations among different peoples who can use a common currency in exchanges. The Romans provided such international laws and stability—laws that gave even non-Roman citizens certain rights. The Roman dinarius was the first international currency. The hegemony of the Roman Empire provided a predictable basis for international commerce. When the empire broke down through the invasion of the German tribes, international trade languished. The Western world entered the Dark Ages.

The next hegemonic order in the West was the Catholic Church. However, the spirit of the Church was not conducive to stimulating commercial activity or the accumulation of material wealth. Much of international trade was still done by the barter system or exchanging goods for other goods (a system that had shrunk to about 5 percent of total world trade by 1990). During the feudal period, either the Church or ruling lord granted a charter to merchants in one section of the castle, called the *faubourg*, in which limited commercial activities and international trade could take place.[1] Located in most castles, abbeys, and cathedrals beginning in the late eleventh century, the faubourg merchant settlements led to charters granted by lords to merchants for towns. These charters often gave permission for merchants to form guilds or cooperative associations. The guilds were forerunners of modern trade unions.

Initially towns were often granted the right to a guild, commercial court, and a low form of justice, but rarely the powers of self-government. This power deprivation later led the French and Italians to create communes—sworn alliances of groups of people associated for a stated purpose, often in revolt against the local lord. Commune movements ultimately permitted villages to win special rights of self-governance.

Champagne, France, became the meeting place for traders from both the north and the south. In the twelfth and early thirteenth centuries, the Champagne trade fairs became the most important trade centers in Western Europe. The counts of Champagne provided booths, money-changers, police, and judges for the merchants. Modern trade fairs, which still play an important part in European commerce, thus originated in Champagne—not to mention a celebratory form of effervescent liquidity (Champagne wines—with one of the most fiercely protected brand names in history).

From the guilds thus arose the towns and trade fairs that stimulated the modern system of international trade. The guilds had social and religious functions. They paid for the funerals of their members and took care of widows and children. The weakness of the guild system, like that of the trade union system that grew out of it, was its inability to adjust to technological progress. The faubourg, guild, and contemporary trade union can all be seen as maintenance bases or traditional organizational buffers against the creative destruction of global capitalism. They seek to hold on to the rights of those already employed as members according to traditions of the past rather than to focus upon entrepreneurial adaptation to emerging technological and economic trends.

The great Crusades of the feudal era prepared the way for world economic change. Military forces established major trade routes for the sake of ideological beliefs. Secularization was an inevitable trend as religious movements spent their legitimacy in bloody exhaustion.

The feudal order was displaced by national monarchic states at the close of the Middle Ages, marked by the Treaty of Westphalia of 1648. Mercantilism, or the economic nationalism of states, flourished from the sixteenth through the nineteenth centuries. It was exemplified in the writings and policies of men such as Colbert, Burleigh, Cromwell, and Frederick the Great. Nation-states wanted to increase their power in the world and such national leaders viewed trade as a means to this end. They accumulated gold and silver to hire mercenaries and equip fleets of ships. Each state aimed to maximize its share of the world's limited gold supply. Exports were promoted and production costs were kept down to keep state competitiveness lean and mean in the trade struggle. Agriculture suffered hardships, for food prices were held down and luxury goods were considered taboo (enforced with heavy import duties). Foreigners were happily seen as customers, but not as suppliers.[2] It is little wonder that mercantilism often led to both military and trade conflicts.

If one flashes from mercantilism to the neo-mercantilism of the twentieth century, one notes great similarities in their aims: increase exports, reduce imports, and increase employment at home—regardless of the negative effects these policies may have upon other nations. These principles sound almost as if they could be the platform planks in the electoral campaign in almost any contemporary democratic state. Export-oriented growth strategies are the panacea for the collective insecurity generated by turbulent world markets.

FROM MERCANTILISM TO CLASSICAL LIBERALISM

In the eighteenth century a physician in the court of France's Louis XV, Francois Quesnay, propounded a school of economics called Physiocracy, even developing a *tableau économique*—a chart of economy. Insisting that wealth came not from gold and silver, Quesnay went against the tenets of mercantilism. He argued that wealth passed from person to person throughout the nation, replenishing the body politic like the circulation of blood. Quesnay's theory was not of much use for practical policy, however. For the production of "true wealth" was limited to the agricultural classes: The manufacturing and commercial classes were viewed as merely manipulating wealth in a sterile way.[3]

The French Physiocrats offered a doctrine based on free trade and competition to replace the nationalistic bias of mercantilism. Like certain late twentieth-century ecologists, they believed nature to be the only source of wealth; they (inaccurately) categorized manufacturers, artificers, and merchants as unproductive. Their list of proposals was topped by a call for a single tax on the net product of land—a list advising that industry and commerce be exempted from taxation. The phrase *Laissez faire, laissez passer* is attributed to an associate of Quesnay, Vincent de Gournay. The state was not to interfere with the authentic creators of natural wealth from whom society would ultimately benefit.

The *classical liberal school of economics* was enunciated in Adam Smith's *Wealth of Nations*, published in 1776. Smith basically agreed with Quesnay and the physiocratic school apart from the doctrine that artificers, merchants, and manufacturers are unproductive. Gold and silver were asserted to be no more important than other commodities (in contrast to the mercantilist assumption), having their price like the others. Adam Smith spoke of the natural laws of wealth. According to these laws of the market, the drive of individual self-interest in an environment of similarly motivated individuals would result in competition; competition, in turn, would provide society with wanted goods at acceptable prices. The market should be left alone—its productivity would then spill over to the advantage of the public good as if by "an invisible hand." As long as a man does not violate "the laws of justice," he should be left perfectly free to pursue his own interest in his own way, bringing both his industry and capital into competition with those of any other men.

Smith's view was an optimistic, realistic, economic philosophy: Increased competition would lead to increased productivity and increased wealth, making social progress through economic growth inevitable. It was a doctrine devised in a nation of small shopkeepers with limited factories in mind—not a world of giant multinational corporations, which Smith would probably have found abhorrent to the extent that they stifled competition. Nor did Smith foresee that his so-called "invisible hand" might indeed be totally invisible, leading to societies characterized by private wealth and public poverty (John Kenneth Galbraith's description of the United States in *The Affluent Society*).

THE POLITICS OF COMPARATIVE ADVANTAGE, OR ANGLO-SAXON IDEOLOGY APPLIED

By the 1830s the Industrial Revolution had started to disrupt the comfortable mercantilism of the landed gentry in Great Britain, who found themselves at odds with the emerging industrialists. Economist David Ricardo, representing an industrial constituency in Parliament, proposed the theory of comparative advantage as a rationale for opposing the "Corn Law." The Corn Law was designed to protect British grain from cheaper continental competitors—particularly imports from France. The industrialists wanted to keep food prices down so that they could keep wages low in England. Ricardo argued that differences between production costs on soil of maximum fertility and those on less fertile soil give rise to a differential income in favor of the owners of the more fertile soil.

According to Ricardo's theory of **comparative advantage**, even if one of two countries has an absolute advantage in producing two goods, it still pays for both to trade, with each specializing in that which each produces most efficiently. For sexample, assume that England had an absolute advantage in producing both woolen textiles and wine compared to Portugal. Let us say that the English needed only half the number of labor hours to produce the same amount of woolen products (two hours vs. four), but two-thirds the number of labor hours to produce wine compared to the Portuguese (two hours vs. three). In this case both countries would benefit more from trading if England specialized in producing textiles, at which the English were particularly efficient, and if the Portuguese specialized in producing wine, at which the Portuguese were comparatively more efficient than in making woolen products. The key is that the less efficient country, Portugal, was not equally less efficient in producing both wine and woolen products. The cost ratio (or opportunity cost) of producing the two products within the same country compared to the cost ratio in the second country is the decisive factor in determining whether or not a comparative advantage exists (i.e., England needing less labor time proportionately to produce textiles vs. wine in contrast with Portugal). The phrase **terms of trade**, in turn, refers to the exact exchange rate at a particular historical moment of one good or service in terms of another—such as of British woolen products in terms of Portugese wine.

For Ricardo, as pointed out in his *Principles of Political Economy* (1817), the value of a commodity depends on the relative quantity of labor necessary for its production. This is called the labor theory of value, which most modern economists, including many Marxists who favored it, have deserted as inadequate.[4] The terms-of-trade concept growing out of the theory of comparative advantage is critical for explaining the widening gap between the rich industrial nations and the poor agricultural countries in the nineteenth and twentieth centuries.

Perhaps the most persuasive explanation for the Industrial Revolution occurring in Great Britain as opposed to any other country is that Great Britain was the country with the highest agricultural productivity at the end of the eighteenth century. As Nobel economist W. Arthur Lewis has shown, the Industrial Revolution did not create an industrial sector where none had been before. Rather, the Industrial Revolution transformed an existing industrial sector by introducing new ways to make the same old things. According to Lewis, the principal cause of poverty in the developing countries and of their poor factoral terms of trade is that about half of their labor force produces food at very low productivity levels, limiting the domestic market for manufactures and services. This keeps the propensity to import too high, reducing taxable capacity and savings, and brings forth goods and services for export on unfavorable terms.[5] By the middle of the nineteenth century, Britain was the only country in the world where the agricultural population had fallen below 50 percent of the labor force. This signified a very slow industrial learning process even among developed countries. Landed classes well understood the benefits of cheap imports, whereas the advantages of displacing their own power with that of emerging new industrial classes were more mysterious. Resistance to industrial change was for the landed classes a rational form of behavior.

In addition to resistance to industrialization from the top, another reason for the slow impact of the Industrial Revolution on the volume of world trade was that the leading industrial countries—Britain, the United States, France, and Germany—were almost self-sufficient. Except for wool, these core countries had the raw materials they required for their industrialization—coal, iron ore, cotton, and wheat (for food). (So much for the theory that the Industrial Revolution depended upon raw materials from the Third World.) The mercantilist era provided these core developed countries with the maintenance base (typified by agricultural efficiency and relative self-sufficiency) that served as the take-off platform for their industrial development. National trade patterns are shaped by relative self-sufficiency, the stage of agricultural development, and industrial capacity. These factors determine the **absorptive capacity** of the nation—the extent to which a nation can absorb the products of another nation (either because of its own satiation in such products at home or because of a backward stage of development that limits the domestic market for industrial or technological products).

The spread of the Industrial Revolution and resultant increase in the volume of world trade also depended on the financing and developing of railroads and lines of communication. As these increased so did the volume of trade in the nineteenth century. London served as the chief source of financing for these "trade tracks" in North America as well as in Europe—part of the package of "invisible services" that made up for the British balance-of-payments deficit and kept British hegemony afloat.

THE HECKSCHER-OHLIN-SAMUELSON (HOS) THEOREM

The industrialization and trade patterns of the nineteenth century divided the world into the developing agricultural states and the industrializing developed nations. Economists in the twentieth century refined Ricardo's theory of comparative advantage to explain emerging trade patterns within the context of classical economic liberalism. In 1919 Swedish economist Eli F. Heckscher argued that international trade altered factor prices (that is, the prices for land, labor, and capital) and therefore redistributed income within a country. Heckscher's student, Bertil Ohlin, went further in his 1924 thesis, *Interregional and International Trade* arguing that certain countries were disproportionately favored with certain factors that led them to produce those commodities that were most to their advantage. Countries with lots of land produce lots of wheat, for example, or those with a great supply of labor might produce a great number of machines. Capital-abundant nations hold the comparative advantage when producing capital-intensive products for international trade, whereas labor-abundant countries hold export competitiveness in labor-intensive products. Countries, in short, should capitalize on those factors in which they had a particular abundance in order to produce specialized products with a comparative advantage in world trade. American economist Paul Samuelson later extended the work of Heckscher and Ohlin to describe the conditions necessary for equalization of factor prices in international trade. Such equalization would presumably eliminate the need for migration from overpopulated to underpopulated countries.[6]

In sum, the classical theory of free trade assumes that national living standards are raised through the international specialization of production and international trade—even in a country rich in natural resources like the United States. **Absolute advantage** refers to a situation in which one country can produce an item better and more cheaply than another: coal production in the United States or sugar production in Puerto Rico, for example. Comparative advantage is the principle that answers the following question: Supposing that a nation could produce everything more cheaply than any other nation, why should it buy anything from abroad? The answer is that the nation stands to benefit by specializing in those products in which its advantage is the greatest. David Ricardo illustrated the principle of comparative advantage with a classical example:

> Two men can both make shoes and hats, and one is superior to the other in both employments; but in making hats he can only exceed his competitor by one-fifth, or 20 percent, and in making shoes he can excel him by one-third or

33⅓ percent. Will it not be for the interest of both that the superior man should employ himself exclusively in making shoes, and the inferior man in making hats?[7]

To use another example, Babe Ruth began his career in baseball as a pitcher and was an excellent one. But he was an even greater hitter. Knowing that pitchers cannot play in every game, he gave up pitching to specialize in his greater comparative advantage in batting. Thus, it is the ratio between domestic advantages that counts.

If economic growth is the main value priority of a society, comparative advantage is a fairly persuasive theory. But how, exactly, did this "Anglo-Saxon ideology" come to be institutionalized in the world political economy?

FROM GATT TO THE WTO

The General Agreement on Tariffs and Trade (GATT) embodied the theory of comparative advantage with a tilt toward adjustment for domestic stability. Multilateral GATT negotiations modified classical liberalism to take into account the need for political stability and domestic economic adjustments to tariff cuts. These economic adjustments came into play particularly in the case of mature, basic industries such as steel, textiles, shoes, and cars.

GATT was a voluntary commercial treaty representing the third pillar of U.S.-British hegemony after World War II, the other two being the international Monetary Fund and the World Bank (or IBRD). This multinational organization monitored 90 percent of world merchandise trade and stimulated industrial countries to reduce their tariffs more than 40 percent to an average of less than 5 from the time of its founding until it was replaced by the World Trade Organization in 1995.[8]

The origins of GATT can be traced back to the Stock Exchange crash of 1929 and the ensuing Great Depression. While nearly 45 percent of the world's production of manufactures was concentrated in the United States in 1929, and U.S. exports made up 20 percent of world exports, exports represented only 6 percent of the U.S. gross national product. The relative self-sufficiency of the American economy (backed by its unique natural resource base) encouraged Congress to enact the Smoot-Hawley Tariff Act of 1930, expanding the protection of the domestic market to cover an additional 900 items. This legislation set off a chain reaction of import restrictions in other countries, leading to a 40 percent decline in the volume of world trade in manufactures by 1933.[9]

Convinced that world peace depended on the reduction of trade restrictions rather than on their increase, U.S. Secretary of State Cordell Hull lobbied Congress to amend the Smoot-Hawley Act of 1930. This resulted in the Reciprocal Trade Agreements Act of 1934: The president was empowered for three years to initiate trade agreements based on the reciprocal reductions of tariffs. This principle became known as "most favored nation" (MFN) treatment and led to reciprocal agreements with twenty-nine countries before World War II. These agreements had little overall impact on tariffs but served as precedents for GATT rules.

The trade surplus of the United States with the rest of the world at the end of World War II made reciprocity a convenient policy for U.S. hegemony. John Maynard Keynes argued before Bretton Woods for an International Clearing Union in which countries in surplus would disproportionately increase imports to ease the burden of those in deficit. But the American position, which became the trade plank of *pax Americana*, was that strict reciprocity should be the basis for the GATT treaty with an American benefit in exports to other countries for each concession on reducing U.S. import restrictions, regardless of the significant advantages of the United States at the starting line. This principle contrasted with unilateral trade reductions made by the British under the *pax Britannica*.[10]

The development of trade agreements is subject to domestic political pressures in the United States, for the president needs congressional approval for any trade accord. International monetary and financial issues tend to be left in the hands of the elite (that is, central bankers and finance ministers). But trade issues are more broadly politicized and democratic, involving the livelihoods and pressure groups of the butcher, the baker, and the computer-maker. The world trading system that emerged after World War II was largely a product of the constitutional balance of power between the executive and legislative branches of the U.S. government. Congress, not the president, is granted the constitutional power to levy tariffs and regulate foreign commerce.

The executive branch at the end of World War II was dominated by Cordell Hull's liberal vision. This was reinforced by the willingness of American elites to use the economic surplus and security monopoly of the United States to establish a postwar commercial order based on free trade. The liberal vision was articulated in the Havana Charter, the set of provisions to create an International Trade Organization (ITO), which was to be the trade equivalent of the IMF in the field of international monetary management.

The ITO was based on an Anglo-American consensus as World War II drew to a close: Tariff reductions and the free flow of trade were essential to maintain high levels of domestic employment and income. Quantitative restrictions on trade had to be eliminated, and an automatic tariff reducing formula found to assure "substantial" tariff reductions and the "elimination" of discriminatory treatment.[11] Based on these principles, in 1945 the United States proposed a plan for a multilateral commercial convention, providing for the ITO to oversee the trade system. However, the United States and Great Britain were not able to dominate in the international trade negotiations as easily as they had been able to in setting up the monetary system. European countries demanded safeguards for balance-of-payments problems. Even Britain insisted on maintaining its Imperial Preference System. The developing countries pressed for attention to economic development. Although the executive branch under both the Roosevelt and Truman administrations provided strong U.S. leadership for the ITO proposal, congressional opposition proved to be stronger. Protectionists opposed the arrangement for being too liberal, and liberals were against it for remaining too protectionist. In 1950 the Truman administration was forced to withdraw the proposal before it faced certain defeat in Congress. Without U.S. support the ITO was dead.

When the ITO failed to come into being, GATT took over its international trade function by default until the WTO took its place, even though GATT was designed as a commercial treaty between contracting parties rather than as an international organization that states join (such as the IMF). Negotiated by twenty-three countries in 1947, the General Agreement on Tariffs and Trade came into force in 1948 with a minimum of institutional arrangements. About once a year the Session of Contracting Parties was held, where decisions were generally taken by consensus rather than by vote. When voting did take place, each contracting party (or member country) had one vote—in contrast with the weighted voting system of the IMF. For most decisions a simple majority vote sufficed. But for "waivers" or authorization to depart from specific contractual obligations, a two-thirds vote of more than half the member countries was required (i.e., to approve an import surcharge). Amendments to key principles of GATT could only be made with unanimous agreement.

The first principle of GATT was that of **most favored nation (MFN) treatment**—committing all parties to conduct trade on the basis of nondiscrimination. Accordingly, all parties were bound to grant treatment to each other as favorable as the treatment they give to any other country in the application and administration of import and export duties. For example, if the United States reduced a tariff on machine tools from West Germany by 10 percent, it was then obligated to reduce the tariff on machine tools from all other GATT countries by the same amount. The MFN principle created a spill-over effect, helping to make free trade contagious.

The second principle of GATT was **reciprocity**. Because GATT was a commercial treaty, nothing required countries to reduce or abolish tariffs automatically. Tariffs were negotiable: Countries reduce tariffs in exchange for reciprocal reductions from other countries or trading partners. Without such an agreement, a contracting party was not obligated to make a reduction. Without reciprocity, examples of unrequested, unilateral tariff reductions in twentieth-century commercial history were few.[12]

The third GATT principle was **nondiscrimination**. Once foreign goods cross the border into another GATT country, they were to be treated as domestic goods in terms of equal rights of competition. It is the principle of nondiscrimination that was violated most often in the past several decades through "Voluntary Export Restrictions" (VERS), "Orderly Marketing Agreements" (OMAs), and other forms of discriminatory nontariff barriers (such as state subsidies and inspection regulations). State subsidies and obscure nontariff barriers are often difficult to detect, thus violating GATT's **principle of transparency**—namely, that all producers and their governments should be aware of existing trade barriers.

The developing countries failed to achieve the inclusion of a separate chapter in the GATT treaty specifically devoted to problems of economic development. However, they did succeed in Article XVIII in addressing development needs in the context of post-World War II reconstruction. This article recognized that special government aid may be needed to promote the establishment, development, or reconstruction of particular industries or branches of agriculture and that in "appropriate circumstances" granting such assistance through protective measures is justified. Later, developing countries assumed that Article XVIII "reflected the predominance of the import substitution approach to economic development." **Import substitution** is the policy of systematically encouraging the domestic production of goods that used to be imported. The aim is economic self-sufficiency.[13]

The major developed countries gradually restored the convertibility of their currencies after World War II. In step with this process, they used the principles of GATT to reduce restrictions on their trade. This was accomplished in the first eight rounds of multilateral trade negotiations in GATT: Geneva, 1947; Annecy, 1949; Torquay, 1950–1951; Geneva, 1956; Dillon Round in Geneva, 1960–1962; Kennedy Round, 1964; the Tokyo Round, 1973–1974; and the Uruguay Round, 1986–1993. The first five rounds represented renewals of the Reciprocal Trade Agreements Act of 1934. The Kennedy Round was the international counterpart of the Trade Expansion Act of 1962, while the Tokyo Round was made possible by the 1974 Trade Act. The passage of the North American Free Trade Agreement (NAFTA) paved the way for the conclusion of the Uruguay Round by a December 1993 deadline set by the U.S. Congress. American hegemony was still alive in GATT, which initially seemed to be the international extension of U.S. tariff policy.[14]

The first seven rounds of trade negotiations cut import tariffs for ninety-five countries from an average of over 40 percent to 4 percent, and served as a line of defense for governments against demands for protection from domestic interest groups.[15] As a result of the Tokyo Round alone, the weighted average (the average tariff measured against actual trade flows) on manufactured products in the world's nine major industrial markets declined from 7.0 to 4.7 percent—a 34 percent reduction in customs collection.

THE URUGUAY ROUND AND U.S. ASSERTIVENESS

The eighth round of GATT trade negotiations, or Uruguay Round, was launched in 1986 and took seven years to conclude. The difficulty was partly the result of the U.S. attempt to use these talks to do what GATT had not done before—to extend trade reductions to agricultural subsidies and to financial services, as well as to protect intellectual property rights. These talks sought to shore up the shift from bilateral alliances to multilateral systems, which GATT represented. This is particularly true for **nontariff trade barriers**; that is, quotas, customs, export subsidies, "voluntary" restraints, and domestic standards and rules. In the twenty-first century some predict that tariffs will no longer be a serious obstacle to trade and that nontariff barriers will be the primary means of trade restriction.[16]

U.S. assertiveness began with the free-market rhetoric of President Ronald Reagan. Then came targeted hard bargaining with European and Japanese allies by President George Bush. This raised little controversy since Bush was perceived as a strong supporter of GATT. But post-cold-war shifts culminated with President Bill Clinton, who linked trade policy with a new, aggressive U.S. **industrial policy** (state coordination with national business networks). In 1993, President Clinton publicly blamed the loss of jobs at Boeing, the U.S. aerospace giant, upon sales lost to Airbus Industrie, a European consortium, because of state subsidies going to Airbus. Then Clinton came up with government subsidies for an energy-saving, new "supercar" to be produced jointly by the big three American auto manufacturers. Clinton based his policy on job creation data: Between 1986 and 1990 the number of Americans who produced goods for exports increased from 5 to 7.2 million, and export-related jobs paid about $3,500 per year more than the average American job.[17] Trade issues rose to the top of the foreign-policy agenda in 1997, as Clinton tried to get Congress to approve a "fast-track" policy of automatically supporting free trade agreements with other countries proposed by the executive branch without any amendments by Congress.

As a member of the Clinton administration, Jeffery Garten, observed before going to Washington: "In abandoning the rhetoric of Adam Smith, President Clinton only recognized the reality that totally free markets are a myth. But without the kind of clear ideological direction that free-market theory provides, actions will often seem inconsistent and subject to the political winds of the moment."[18]

Clinton advocated a get-tough "pragmatism" that initially focused attention on trade disputes and later on trade blocs. But "pragmatism" at home may be perceived to be selfish nationalism or mercantilism abroad undermining the WTO regime, which is an integral part of American hegemony.[19]

The French reacted strongly against the American position, led by French farmers who saw reduced subsidies as a threat to their way of life. French stubbornness paid off—the cuts in agricultural subsidies were reduced. Arguing for a "cultural exemption," the French also maintained their quota rule on films—60 percent of their television programming must be produced within the European Community. The French Culture Minister Jacque Toubon argued that the world is threatened by the gradual invasion of a dominant Anglo-Saxon culture under the cover of economic liberalism. Since movies are cultural products, nations should be permitted to create barriers to their entry for the sake of preserving their own cultural integrity.[20] The French won in this cultural resistance movement even given protests by the American film industry, which gave major support to Clinton in the 1992 election.

The Uruguay round agreement cut tariffs on manufactured products in most countries by one-third and eased barriers against grain imports. It gradually eliminated tariffs on textiles and clothing and made it harder for countries to impose new quantitative restrictions. Financial services were dropped from the negotiations in order to gain agreement among the 117 countries.

In the Uruguay round process, the developing countries mimicked the trade liberalization of the twenty-some developed countries of the **Organization for Economic Cooperation and Development (OECD)**, which demonstrated such rapid economic growth in the 1950s and 1960s. It represents a proliberal, collective learning process of increasing market access and growth in exports, keeping in-flation rates down, generating foreign exchange, acquiring technology, buying capital goods and supplies: learning by exporting. This, in turn, results in global product specialization and divisions of labor following the principles of compar-ative and competitive advantage. As economist Sherman Robinson put it: "It's Adam Smith with a vengeance."[21]

THE BIRTH OF THE WTO

In April 1994 in Marrakesh, Morocco, 123 GATT members signed the final agree-ment of the Uruguay Round, which not only included the implementation of trade agreements but contained the founding documents of the **World Trade Or-ganization (WTO)**, which went into effect in 1995. As was originally intended in the attempt to create the ITO, the WTO not only replaces and embraces the rules of the GATT but also takes over permanent organizational and monitoring func-tions through its own councils and secretaries housed in the headquarters in Geneva, Switzerland.

The WTO is governed by a Ministerial Conference that meets every two years; a General Council that implements the Conference's policy decisions and is re-sponsible for day-to-day administration; and a director-general, who is appoint-ed by the Ministerial Conference. GATT's legal framework has been expanded into services and intellectual property rights by the GATS—General Agreement on Trade in Services, and the TRIPS—Trade Related Aspects of Intellectual Property Rights. The WTO functions as an arbitrator of trade disputes, particularly among industrialized countries, based upon GATT principles and hence upon free, nondis-criminatory market ideology. Should the United States win more of these dis-putes than it loses, the WTO will be perceived to be just another extension of the Anglo-American hegemony with the comparative advantage of the world's one superpower. But, paradoxically, in areas involving American efforts to enforce en-vironmental regulations abroad—in terms of Mexican fishing techniques that in-advertently kill dolphins and Asian plundering of endangered species such as the giant sea turtle, the United States lost disputes at the WTO: The ruling was that these nations had a right to their own domestic ways of fishing even if such meth-ods resulted in the extinction of species. On the other hand, in 1999 the WTO backed U.S. claims that the European Union's banana-import policies violate in-ternational rules, legitimating the imposition of harsh U.S. retaliatory tariffs on a variety of EU goods.

INTERPRETATIONS

International trade is assumed to be important for economic development by most schools of economic thought. The decisive difference between perspectives is the degree to which trade should be "free" or be regulated by the state. A related issue is the extent to which the domestic economy should aim for self-sufficiency or autonomy. If autonomy becomes the top policy priority, this implies protection-ism and can lead to temporary isolation from parts of the global trading system.

Trade issues are politicized worldwide—first, by their dependence upon the whims of the U.S. Congress, European Union regulations, and Japanese bureau-crats; and second, by the close tie of trade to jobs, to economic growth, and to the very survival of certain sectors and ways of life. Let us consider some differ-ent schools of thought concerning trade.

NEOCLASSICAL THEORY

The neoclassical vision is liberalism modernized—from Adam Smith to David Ri-cardo to Heckscher, Ohlin, and Samuelson. Anglo-American hegemony after World War II focused ideas with the notion that each country should specialize in and export what it could produce more cheaply in exchange for goods and services pro-duced comparatively more cheaply in other countries. International trade thus makes possible the division of labor and specialization upon which the produc-tivity of global capitalism is based. Trade is the engine of economic growth as much as are investment and technological progress. Collective learning takes place as nations, locales, or producers discover which of the various advanta-geous products or services can be produced and exported with most advantage compared to others. Comparatively, this is where the optimum return lies, or the least "opportunity cost." **Opportunity cost** is the cost incurred by a company or nation as the result of foreclosing other sources of profit. **Neoclassical theory** sug-gests that, globally, costs will be cut and economic growth increased in a free-trade system without tariffs blocking the normal shift of production factors in the world market. According to Cordell Hull, economic growth, in turn, fosters global pros-perity and increases the chances of world peace. Despite compromises to permit domestic economic adaptation for the sake of political stability among member states, GATT's liberalism was deeply embedded, tilting the organization toward the ideology of free trade and comparative advantage. The WTO has inherited this bias, having adopted GATT's principles. Even the cases the United States loses in WTO disputes while trying to protect its national economic interests can be seen to constitute a ratification of the ideology of economic liberalism—making the integrity of the trade organization appear to be above the interests of even the most powerful member, and, thereby providing stability for a global economic order which the United States dominates.

In the language of game theory, the neoclassical perspective interprets world trade as a **positive-sum, cooperative game**.* More precisely, it is a version in

---

*The "variable-sum or positive-sum game" in economics is a situation in which two or more players have the option of cooperating for a greater mutual payoff (or the creation of additional "economic pie") than either would gain alone. This contrasts with the "zero-sum game," in which cooperation is not rational since each choice with a positive payoff for one player has a negative payoff for the other player: The focus is upon the distribution of the existing pie (protectionism?) rather than upon the creation of new pie (free-trade capitalism?). (See John von Neumann and Oscar Morgenstern, *Theory of Games and Economic Behavior*, 2nd ed. (Princeton, NJ: Princeton University Press, 1947).

which everyone will be better off if all countries decide to maximize their long-term mutual interests by reducing tariffs and conforming to the rules of reciprocity and nondiscrimination initially set forth by GATT.

Policymakers are constantly tempted to adopt programs of short-term expediency for the sake of national interest, setting the GATT rules now embodied in the WTO aside. But this ensures a better outcome only on the condition that everyone else (or at least almost everyone) continues to observe the rules. Otherwise, to use a metaphor, one person's advantage in standing on tiptoes in a crowd to better see the parade is canceled out as the whole crowd follows suit and stands on its tiptoes too. Infractions of the rules, in short, set precedents. Precedents become models of collective learning for others, who are also then tempted to take shortcuts and break the rules, undermining the entire trading order of intricately specialized but coordinated activity. The thrust of the neoclassical vision of world trade is that if tariffs are dropped and the exchange of goods and services kept free among national borders, a more productive use of given resources (or "factor endowments") will result, with gains in consumption, production, economies of scale, price stability, competitiveness, economic growth, and employment.[22] The GATT rules served as a code of behavior adding predictability and cooperative incentives for the long term to the anarchy of international markets, incorporating efficiency gains through learning effects and the economies of scale of mass production. (Significantly, the neoclassical vision does not dwell upon questions of distribution—i.e., gains in consumption and production for whom?)

Nor is the neoclassical position unaware of the need for protection—temporarily—in certain circumstances, such as sheltering infant industries until they are strong enough to compete internationally. The infant-industry argument goes back to John Stuart Mill (in his *Principles of Political Economy*, [1848]) in which he maintains that the only case where protecting duties can be defensible is when they are imposed temporarily (particularly in a young and rising nation) in hope of "naturalizing a foreign industry" found to be suitable to the circumstances of the country. For, Mill continues, the superiority of one country over another in a sector of production often arises only from having begun it sooner, and it cannot be expected that individuals, risking almost certain loss, will introduce a new manufacturing product, bearing the burden until producers have refined their processes up to par with the competition.

The neoclassical school allows for temporary protection for certain infant industries for the sake of innovation, experimentation, or "vital economic interests" (such as protecting the nation's ability to become agriculturally self-sufficient). But there is an underlying assumption that all nations are potentially equals and can be brought quickly up to the standard of competitiveness in the world economy set by the leaders.

On the one hand, the neoclassical school advocates a form of economic **Social Darwinism** for the sake of economic efficiency and technological progress (only the strong should survive in each economic sector, forcing the weak out of business until they find a niche in which they were meant to succeed given their natural, factor endowments). On the other hand, this perspective assumes that, globally, everyone will be better off if free markets and free trade prevail everywhere. Policymakers in a country like Honduras, which has sustained itself on two basic industries (bananas and rents received from U.S. military bases), must wonder how the global prosperity promised by neoclassical economic theory is supposed to trickle down to them.

STRUCTURALISM

The collective learning through tariff reductions for the sake of free markets and world economic growth advocated by the neoclassical school was perceived to be blocked by many developing nations because of how they were structurally positioned in the global economy. In the 1950s two development economists proposed interpretations of world trade that became the basis of the "structuralist school" and reforms in the GATT—Raúl Prebisch, executive secretary for the Economic Commission for Latin America (ECILA), and Hans Singer.

Prebisch and Singer argued that the world economy was structured or tilted against those countries that depended upon the production of primary commodities for their economic survival (that is, structured against the interests of most developing countries). Rather than an equitable system of comparative advantage in which all countries benefited by maximizing production in those products most appropriate to their factor endowment, the structuralists found an unequal system of trade. The demand for manufactured and industrial goods produced by the *center*, or developed countries, was much greater than the demand for the agricultural and basic mineral commodities in which the *periphery*, or developing countries, specialized. Therefore, the terms of trade were systematically structured against the position of the developing countries and in favor of the position of the developed industrialized countries.[23] This unequal structural position between the center and dependent periphery countries resulted in a *trade gap* between them (that is, a persistent disequilibrium in the trade balance of countries relying primarily upon prime commodities). The trade imbalance, in turn, meant that the periphery countries could not earn enough through exports to cover the cost of the imports they so badly needed for their development.[24]

Initially, the structuralists believed that industrialization was the key to development for the periphery. When it became clear that the center or developed countries would continue to trade predominantly among themselves and, therefore, limit the export earnings that the developing countries could expect from the developed world, Prebisch advocated that periphery countries create their own trading system or bloc until a certain "takeoff" point of modernization was reached. Eventually this could result in a regional or subregional common market made up of preferential agreements for dependent countries.[25]

To achieve this takeoff position, the structuralists usually advocated a strategy of import substitution in order to reduce developing countries' dependence upon exports from the industrialized countries: Brazil's policy of producing automobile fuel from sugar cane to cut down on oil imports is an example. Both the neoclassical and structuralism schools assumed that international trade was an engine of growth. But whereas the neoclassical school stressed leaving things up to the markets alone, the structuralists advocated Keynesian controls, so convinced were they that unregulated markets would not change inequities among countries any more than this economic philosophy solved inequities within them.[26]

The structuralist position was persuasive to the managers of developing economies since export earnings accounted for about three-fourths of their foreign-exchange resources. And primary products, in turn, accounted for about three-fourths of the exports from developing countries. The value of the primary products declined relative to the value of the manufactured products that dominated the trade of the developed countries. Productivity increases in advanced industrial states put a continual upward pressure on wages and other input costs, keeping prices constant or pushing them up. **Productivity** is the measure of how many inputs are required to produce how many outputs—for example, how many hours of work are needed to produce a car. To increase productivity means either to reduce the number of inputs (that is, to pay cheaper wages or to lower the number of working hours) or to increase outputs (produce more products while maintaining the same number of inputs).

However, Prebisch noted that in developing countries productivity increases do not translate into wage increases or constant prices, given weak labor organizations and disguised unemployment. Rather, increases in productivity in the poor countries lead to the decline of prices—a savings passed on largely to consumers in the rich nations. Other factors put a downward pressure on the prices or demand for primary commodities as well. As income increases, the percentage spent on food declines, not to mention the percentage of primary products of the total factor inputs necessary to produce industrial goods. Furthermore, technological innovation provides synthetic substitutes at lower prices for many primary products.[27]

While conventional wisdom often assumes that manufacturing is declining in relative importance, the WTO reports that the shares of manufactures went from 55–60 percent between 1973 and 1985 and then increased sharply, reaching 75 percent by 1995. Indeed the comparison between the rise in dollar value of manufactures compared to the flat export value of mining and agricultural products between 1973 and 1995 lends credence to the structuralist perspective (see Figure 3-1 on page 90).

The original rules of GATT were tilted to the advantage of the multiresource, rich developed countries and to the disadvantage of the dependent developing countries: It was, in short, a "rich man's club"! The most favored nation principle (MFN) prevented rich nations from giving poor nations preferential treatment in importing their manufactured goods for the sake of fostering their development. Reciprocity sounds good in principle as long as there is a wide enough diversity of products to have something to exchange for concessions. But if bananas are all you have, you have nothing to negotiate with: You have to protect your bananas

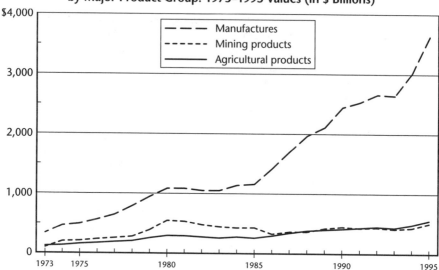

Figure 3-1   World Merchandise Exports
by Major Product Group: 1973–1995 Values (in $ Billions)

with all your might. The American principle of strict reciprocity meant that poor countries would have to make a concession to the United States for each tariff the United States agreed to lower: Clearly the rich countries had much more room for bargaining than did the poor countries when it came to making quid pro quo ("this-for-that") concessions. Thus, the initial GATT regime was a subtle maintenance system of preserving the asymmetrical structures of the status quo, giving most of the payoffs to the rich industrialized countries most able to take advantage of the GATT rules. (All boats might rise with the world economic growth stimulated by global trade but the big boats would stay big and the advantages of those most highly developed at the start of the voyage would be consolidated, their relative position confirmed.)[28]

The **principal supplier rule** of GATT negotiations was also seen by the structuralists to discriminate against developing countries. According to this rule, negotiations begin bilaterally with requests (not offers) for tariff reductions on a particular product made only by the exporter of the largest volume of that product to the market of a second country. Most developing countries were not in this position and were, therefore, not able to request reductions. Their best hope was the "splashing effect" from the MFN clause allowing them to benefit from tariff reductions between developed countries that dealt with products of concern to them. But this "splashing effect" cut two ways: It also precluded developing countries from negotiating concessions just among themselves. The multilateralization process of GATT negotiations was dominated by the strongest trading countries, taking into account the competitiveness and capacity of these countries to overflow their home markets.[29] As the Indian representative noted in regard to the original GATT rules in 1955: "Equality of treatment is equitable only among equals."[30]

A key complaint by developing countries concerning GATT, until it was ad-dressed in the Uruguay round, was that agriculture, one of the largest sectors of commodities, was excluded from the GATT and was, therefore, protected. The United States had received an exceptionally broad waiver for strategic, political, and social reasons.[31] And when the Treaty of Rome creating the European Com-mon Market came into force, the Common Agricultural Policy of the Europeans was similarly protectionist. Later these exclusions from the GATT were expand-ed to include textiles and footwear-products of particular importance to the de-veloping countries, adding salt to the wound.

The acceptance of the Anglo-American hegemony of neoclassical assump-tions behind the GATT was increasingly undermined when large numbers of colonies became politically independent in the 1950s and 1960s and sought eco-nomic independence as well. Provided that the colonizing power that had super-vised them was a member of GATT, these nations were treated as de facto members and permitted to vote, even though all the GATT regulations did not apply to them. In 1958 the Haberler Report by economists Gottfried Haberler, James Meade, Jan Tinbergen, and Roberto Campos provided a fulcrum for building pressures among the developing countries: It concluded that the dilemma of the developing coun-tries was in large part due to the trade policies of the developed countries. Com-mittee III of the GATT was set up as a result of this report to examine the obstacles faced by developing countries in getting their exports into developed countries. But nothing concrete came of the committee's recommendations.

Still the formation of a collective strategy for the developing countries was stimulated. A year after the Haberler Report, fifteen developing countries got to-gether to issue a *Note on the Expansion of International Trade within* GATT. They point-ed out that developing countries were limited in their capacity to initiate negotiations and asked for negotiations on nontariff trade measures that dis-criminated against exports from developing countries.* In the early 1960s, some of the same fifteen nations combined with others to form a group of twenty-one, which proposed a *Programme of Action* calling for the unilateral reduction of tariffs and nontariff barriers affecting the exports from developing countries.** The stage was set for a major collective effort of developing countries to pressure GATT for reform of existing rules and for enforcement of rules on the books of particular in-terest to the poorer nations.

UNCTAD

The structuralist perspective of Raúl Prebisch provided the ideological consensus behind the collective movement of developing countries to establish the **United Nations Conference on Trade and Development (UNCTAD)** as an organ of the

---

*These countries included Brazil, Burma, Cambodia, Chile, Cuba, Federation of Malaya, Federation of Rhodesia and Nyasaland, Ghana, Greece, India, Indonesia, Pakistan, Peru, and Uruguay.

**The twenty-one countries included Argentina, Brazil, Burma, Cambodia, Ceylon, Cuba, Chile, Nige-ria, Federation of Malaya, Ghana, Haiti, India, Indonesia, Israel, Pakistan, Peru, United Arab Repub-lic, Tanganyika, Tunisia, Uruguay, and Yugoslavia.

United Nations General Assembly in 1964. If GATT was "the rich man's club," UNC-TAD was "the poor nations' pressure group," designed to change the GATT rules concerning trade and development for the sake of the developing countries and for a new international economic order.[32] A pressure group is just that, having no institutional power of its own. Indeed, some quipped that UNCTAD actually stood for "Under No Condition Take Any Decisions." But this understates the influence of an organization from which the well-known *Group of 77* (developing countries in the United Nations) emerged, not to mention GATT reforms such as the Generalized System of Preferences (GSP).

UNCTAD, in effect, is a series of conferences sponsored by the United Nations that can make proposals or suggestions but that cannot force compliance. Prebisch, a dynamic Argentinian, was appointed the first secretary-general of UNC-TAD, which he wanted to use to summon developed nations unilaterally to extend preferential treatment to less developed nations for their exports of manufactures. However, the motivating force behind the initial creation of UNCTAD was not so much Prebisch as it was Wadek Malinowski, previously associated with the United Nations. Malinowski believed that the only hope for bettering the position of the developing countries in the world trading system was if they could unify under the prestigious umbrella of the United Nations. The enthusiasm of Malinowski, the intellectual leadership of Prebisch, and the proliferation of developing countries because of decolonialization resulted in UNCTAD.

World trade doubled from 1950 to 1960. But the leaders of developing countries noted that their share of world trade dropped from 41 percent in 1950 to 30 percent in 1960.[33] Diplomats from the East European countries and less developed nations joined forces at UNCTAD I in Geneva, which established UNCTAD as a permanent organ of the United Nations, and pressed for preferential trade agreements and special financial resources for developing countries from the advanced industrialized nations of GATT.

The founding of UNCTAD aimed to improve institutional arrangements and the machinery of the world economic order; to reduce or eliminate all barriers restricting exports from developing countries; to expand export markets for these countries; to create financial circumstances to more easily enable developing countries to increase imports, and to seek better coordination in world trade policies. From the UNCTAD perspective, the GATT market system was structured against the developing nations from the outset. It was buoyed by tariff barriers, protectionist policies, and discrimination on the part of the developed countries that worked to the detriment of their poor neighbors. The northern industrial countries were not only "the center" but were self-centered. And GATT was their greenhouse.

The UNCTAD conferences meet every two to four years at cities in various developing countries (New Delhi, Santiago, Nairobi, Cartagefia de Indias, etc.), focusing on different but related issues: shipping, food problems, difficulties of landlocked countries, disarmament, duty-free entry, domestic production, technological capacity and technology transfer, the brain-drain from developing to developed countries, commodity stabilization, export earnings, and environmental problems.

In the early 1970s, the developing countries succeeded in getting industrialized nations to adopt a **Generalized System of Preferences (GSP)** that eliminated tariffs on manufactured and semimanufactured goods exported by developing countries. No tariff concessions were asked for in return, significantly modifying the reciprocity principle of GATT. The aim of the GSP was to promote industrialization in developing nations by stimulating their exports.

In 1974 the developing countries used the impetus of UNCTAD to push for the *Integrated Program for Commodities* (IPC). The IPC sought to control price fluctuations and average prices of commodities negotiated on a case-by-case basis by exporters and importers. Its aim was to better the terms of trade structured against national economies dependent upon the export of primary commodities for the lion's share of export earnings in a world of falling commodity prices. Targeting ten of the eighteen agricultural and mineral commodities that made up three-fourths of the primary commodity exports of developing countries, the IPC called for stockpiling them to create a buffer zone against price instability. A $6 billion Common Fund was requested that would be made up of contributions from exporters and importers to finance the scheme. However, Western countries, particularly the United States, were wary of any automatic, universal system of price control, such as that implied by the IPC. From their classical, liberal economic perspective, they feared losing flexibility and control and were concerned that such a system would result in continual inflation. The Americans preferred case-by-case, market-oriented arrangements. Structuralism and neoclassical economic theory were at loggerheads blocking the IPC proposal.

Part of this diffusion of energies in the results of UNCTAD conferences is attributable to the group system according to which UNCTAD was organized. For purposes of elections and voting, UNCTAD member states were classified into four groups—Group A: Afro-Asian states and former Yugoslavia; Group B: developed market economies, or the West; Group C: Latin American states; and Group D: states with a centrally planned economy, of the East European bloc. Cross-group alliances were rare except for the steady coalition of the countries of Groups A and C—the well-known Group of 77.

Conventional wisdom holds that the UNCTAD conferences, which meet about every three years, have had but a minor impact on restructuring the world trade system to the advantage of the developing countries. But this misses the point: UNCTAD is but part of a long-term process of delegitimization of Anglo-American (and particularly American) hegemony (or dominant values) in the world economy.

THE EARTH SUMMIT, KYOTO, AND SUSTAINABLE DEVELOPMENT

Such a sea change in values appeared to gather momentum at the Earth Summit —the **United Nations Conference on Environment and Development (UNCED)** in Rio de Janeiro, Brazil, in June 1992. UNCTAD helped to plan for this conference on linking issues such as hunger, poverty, illiteracy, and ill health with the ecological and economic consequences of ozone depletion, climate change, soil degradation, deforestation, declining biodiversity, and the increasing pollution of air, water, and land. New values of equity and environment were defined for the North-South agenda. A number of multilateral agreements resulted: 154 countries signed the climate protection convention, 156 signed the biodiversity protection convention, and 178 agreed to Agenda 21—a 900-page voluntary action plan.

Agenda 21 details strategies and integrated program measures to reverse the effects of environmental degradation and to promote environmentally sound and **sustainable development** in all nations. Chapter 38 of Agenda 21 recommends that the U.N. General Assembly establish a permanent, high-level U.N. *Commission on Sustainable Development* (CSD) to implement Agenda 21 at the national, regional, and international levels. The question for the future is whether or not the CSD will become another "talk shop" with little impact, split by the conflict between the majority of developing countries holding the votes and the rich, developed nations with the cash, and stymied by the limits of national sovereignty that govern international law.[34]

Five years after the Earth Summit there was a follow-up, the Kyoto Summit of 1997. While the U.S. hegemony led the discussion, the United States did not initiate the progress toward **sustainability** at the summit. According to the Kyoto Protocol, most industrialized countries are required to reduce their "greenhouse" gas emissions from 1990 levels between 2008 and 2012: the European Union by 8 percent, the United States by 7 percent and Japan by 6 percent. The industrialized group would cut back such emissions by a little more than 5 percent. The gases included are carbon dioxide, methane, nitrous oxide, and three synthetic gases—fully fluorinated compounds. However, industrialized countries that do not meet their targets can buy the excess "quota" from others who do better than required. Such market incentives were suggested by the U.S. government to head off opposition by large American firms. Individual nations are expected to assign pollution limits for companies, which will also then be able to trade emission credits. A "Clean Air Mechanism" was established by which firms in industrial countries are encouraged to pair up with developing country industries in order to carry out antipollution projects. By so doing, firms from developed countries receive emission trading credits in order to help them meet their emission caps at home. The Kyoto treaty also set up procedures to measure how much CO2 growing and mature forests absorb; it also provided emissions credits for industrial nations that protect or plant woodlands at home or abroad. However, enforcement of the Kyoto agreements was left to future meetings that are supposed to develop means to verify compliance and to establish rules for emissions trading.

The Bush administration had already symbolized the resistance to be expected from those adhering to the doctrine of Anglo-American liberalism: The American government dragged its feet to the point of being isolated at the Earth Summit, fearful that stringent environmental protection measures would force the United States to come up with a unified national energy policy that would cost Americans jobs. From this liberal view, environmental regulation and economic development are perceived to be in inevitable conflict and the threat of global warming is greatly overstated. In contrast, the Europeans and Japanese noted the long-term economic benefits that could be derived from environmental protection, the impact of climate change, and the importance of strengthening ties with the developing countries. The proenvironmental tilt of the Clinton-Gore administration strengthened U.S. commitment to the Agenda 21 program for sustainable development, although financial resources were severely limited given the administration's ambitious domestic agenda and efforts to reduce the American budget deficit. The U.S. support for the Kyoto Treaty was weak since there was not a majority in the Senate willing to approve the protocol. A key obstacle from the position of the world's hegemon was the unwillingness of developing countries to agree to limit their own emissions before the next global environmental summit—a position that those without an industrialized economy were unlikely to adopt. More significantly, American labor unions attacked the treaty out of fear of losing jobs, and corporations forecast resulting economic disaster (based on the dubious assumption that such environmental regulation is incompatible with economic growth).

TRADE BLOCS: THE EU, OPEC, NAFTA, AND APEC

The model of collective behavior of which UNCTAD is such a diffuse and imperfect example is the **trade bloc**—an organized group of nations of limited membership that attempts to create a buffer zone of import, export, and protectionist strategies to maximize the collective economic benefits of its members at the expense of those outside the bloc. Given the increasing tempo of technological innovation, communication, and transnational exchanges in the "creative destruction" of the global capitalist system, it is a natural, human, and conservative impulse to band together with nearby friends to try to structure scarcity to mutual advantage and to protect one's own group from the competitive abundance of the production of others outside the group. Regionalism often serves as the basis for such coalitions given the immense geographical and cultural diversity of the world economy.

Examples of the trade-bloc model of collective learning and positioning, which nations have tried to mimic in various forms in the post-World War II world trade system, are the European Economic Community (EEC), or European Common Market, and the Organization of Petroleum Exporting Countries (OPEC). By limiting the size of their membership to much less than the size of GATT or UNCTAD these organizations have reaped greater proportional rewards for their members and have at times demonstrated a bargaining cohesiveness that has surprised the rest of the international community. New trade blocs formed to counter these successes: the North American Free Trade Association (NAFTA) and the Asian Pacific Economic Association (APEC). There has even been talk of creating a TAFTA (Transatlantic Free Trade Association) between NAFTA and the EU.

The European Union (EU)   The **European Union** (**EU**; formerly the "European Community") emerged from efforts of European businessmen and politicians to put the disintegration of World War II behind them, to cooperate in key economic sectors for mutual advantage, and to protect themselves from future American and foreign competition. Specifically, a continuing Franco-German "axis" is the engine of the European integration movement in terms of trade and industrial cooperation.[35] Konrad Adenauer, the first chancellor of the German Federal Republic, viewed political and economic integration with the French as a strategy for reducing occupation restrictions upon Germany after its loss of the war and for creating a stable basis for future economic and strategic development. In 1950 French Foreign Minister Robert Schuman proposed the "Schuman Plan" for pooling German and French coal and steel production. Steel and coal are vital strategic industries. Schuman saw the advantages of controlling the rich resources of the Ruhr in northern Germany (which had serviced the German war machine in the past). And Adenauer perceived the Schuman Plan as a vehicle whereby the Germans might ease the French occupiers out of the Ruhr through future economic cooperation. The result was the founding of the *European Coal and Steel Community* (ECSC) in 1952, made up of six member states: West Germany, France, Italy, the Netherlands, Belgium, and Luxembourg.

The ECSC abolished customs duties, restrictions, duel pricing systems, and transport rates for coal, coke, iron ore, steel, and scrap for all community members and set production target and investment programs. To head off the dismantling and nationalization of German industries tainted by Nazi leadership, Adenauer promised the unions major participation in the running of private companies. As a result the workers in the ECSC coal and steel industries were allowed to elect 50 percent of the supervisory boards (the policy of **codetermination**) as compared to 33 percent in the rest of German industry. Moreover, the four institutions of the ECSC became precursors of similar European Common Market (EEC) institutions: the High Authority (the EEC's Commission), the Council of Ministers (EEC's Council of Ministers), the Common Assembly (the EEC's European Parliament), and a Court of Justice (the EEC's Court of Justice).

The European Common Market, or European Economic Community (EEC)   The six original members of the ECSC founded the European Common Market, or European Economic Community (EEC), in the *Treaty of Rome* in 1957, led by the Franco-German dynamism and institutional framework of the ECSC. The Common Market, or EEC, succeeded in its basic objective of initially reducing all trade barriers among its members and then essentially eliminating them within twelve to fifteen years. Armed with a common customs tariff—the corollary of an internal customs union—the EEC greatly increased its external trade policy clout with its solidarity. Faced with this economic competition, in 1959 British paymaster-general Reginald Maulding led the way to create a second European bloc, the **European Free Trade Association (EFTA)**, made up of "the Seven":

Britain, Austria, Denmark, Norway, Portugal, Sweden, and Switzerland. This was the first clear example of collective learning from the EEC model for the sake of bettering the collective economic position of a group of allied countries. However, unlike the EEC, the EFTA did not aim to establish a common policy toward the outside world but merely to reduce and eventually abolish tariffs and other trade restrictions among EFTA members. Plagued by Britain's Commonwealth ties with former British colonies, EFTA was not nearly as successful as the EEC, and Britain soon applied for EEC membership.

The small Benelux countries—Belgium, the Netherlands, and Luxembourg—supported British membership in the EEC, calculating that Britain might offset the power of the Franco-German axis. The Germans also favored British entry, hoping it would end the division of Europe into competing trade blocs and knowing that Germany would stand to gain a great deal from trade with Britain and the Commonwealth. Indeed, West German trade with EFTA amounted to three times the sum of French trade with these countries. France, under the leadership of Charles de Gaulle, initially opposed British entry, which could dilute French power in the EEC and make decision making more difficult given Franco-British cultural differences (especially since England carried the baggage of the Commonwealth). De Gaulle also resented "special" British ties with the United States (that is, Anglo-American hegemony). By holding out the longest against British membership, the French managed to tilt the European integration process toward the French position.

Nevertheless, in 1973 the United Kingdom, Ireland, and Denmark entered the European Common Market, following difficult negotiations. In the 1980s Greece, Spain, and Portugal followed suit, and "the Nine" became "the Twelve." By 1984, imports and exports of the Twelve (excluding trade among themselves) represented an average of 12.5 percent of their gross domestic product. This can be compared to 7.5 percent for the United States and 13.5 percent for Japan in 1984. According to GATT figures for that year, the EEC's share of world trade was 18 percent in contrast to 17 percent for the United States and 9 percent for Japan. By 1985 the developing countries absorbed 34 percent of EEC exports.[36] Some 130 countries established diplomatic relations with the EEC, and the EEC received observer status in the United Nations and in some of its specialized agencies. Between 1957 and 1986, trade among EEC countries increased sevenfold while EEC trade with the rest of the world tripled.

By 1985 the EEC was the largest trading bloc in the world in terms of exports and was barely surpassed by the United States in terms of imports. As a percentage of gross domestic product (GDP), the average external trade of the EEC in terms of both imports and exports was greater than that of either the United States or Japan.

In 1985, the European Council (made up of the heads of the twelve member states) agreed to constitute a single market by 1992. This initiative aimed to break down national regulations within the bloc on things such as transportation, banking, copyrights, borders, industrial subsidies, professional certification, and health requirements. In 1986, European Community (EC)* members signed the Single European Act amending the Treaty of Rome by permitting decisions in most areas to be made by a qualified majority instead of unanimously (although still leaving the European Council with the most authority). In principle, the unification of the market has been based upon (1) granting of "mutual recognition" of each other's regulations and standards by members, and (2) home-country control, or the right of a company to operate throughout the community if licensed in one member country.

Such pragmatic principles eliminated the need for the commission to lose energy in "harmonizing" or adopting a single European standard or in pushing for "European companies." As political scientist Stanley Hoffmann noted: "There will be instead a kind of free market of competing national standards."[37]

Nor do the member nation-states seem to "lose" what the European Community "gains" in power since governments and bureaucracies remain the chief players. The European Union (EU) is best understood as a pooling of sovereignties. Still, like de Gaulle before her, British Prime Minister Margaret Thatcher remained convinced that her nation's sovereignty was at stake and resisted any nibbling away of her authority, particularly when it came to issues such as the creation of a common central bank or one European currency. But the persuasive power of Commission President Jacques Delors pushed through a new "European architecture" that became the basis of the Maastricht Treaty. This treaty, which proposed a single European currency, a single European central bank, and unified social and defense policies, was presented at the summit in Maastricht, Netherlands, in December 1991.

Delors's vision of European architecture, which became the official view of the European Commission, was one of three concentric circles: The core circle represented the members of the European Union (EU) made up of the single market, the European Monetary Union (EMU), and the European political union (of foreign, defense, and immigrant policies, etc.); the second circle contained the *European Economic Area* (EEA) confirmed in a treaty of May, 1992, including EFTA members presumably on the waiting list to join the EMU (Iceland, Norway, Switzerland, and Liechtenstein); and the third circle represented the members of the *European Association Accords* (EAA), including the former East bloc countries of Central Europe wanting to join the EMU as well (Poland, Hungary, The Czech Republic, Slovakia, Romania, Bulgaria, Bosnia, Slovenia, etc.) The European architecture of Delors finessed the post-cold-war dispute as to whether the European Union should deepen (integrate internally) before it widens (expands horizontally to take in new members to stabilize their fragile democracies and economies).[38] A more realistic assessment might be that this architecture legitimized the exclusion of the EEA and EAA countries from membership in

---

*EC refers to "European Community"—all political, legal, and economic institutions of the European Common Market (an updating of the more economically focused "EEC"). In 1993 the "EC" was renamed the "EU" for "European Union."

"the club," the European Union, until these would-be members become rich and stable enough to add more benefits than costs.

The deep recession in Europe in the early 1990s slowed down the ratification of the Maastricht Treaty until it finally was confirmed in diluted form in November 1993. The Danes initially rejected it until they received special conditions, Britain delayed deciding, and the French barely approved it. The EU bureaucracy at the headquarters in Brussels moved faster than the general populations of Europe. The elite were slow to come down off their pinnacle to sell their vision to everyday citizens, who mistrusted the centralized "Eurocracy" and were concerned with preserving their sovereignty and cultural identities from further European integration and regulation. The global impact of the European Monetary Union became transparent as the European Monetary Institute in Frankfurt, Germany, established by the Maastricht Treaty, became the European Central Bank that initiated the EURO common accounting unit in 1999 with fixed, unchangeable exchange rates, triggering the transition to the EURO coins and bills three years later in 2002. By 1996 the per capita GDP of the 369 million people in the EU was $20,048 (compared with $4,655 in the world). The three pillars of the EU as provided by the Maastricht Treaty are illustrated in Figure 3-2: (1) European integration (EC Treaty); (2) political integration in external affairs (common security and foreign policy); and (3) political integration in internal affairs (judicial and domestic policy harmonization).

The recession of the early 1990s served to distract attention from the importance of the process of European integration and the long-term political significance of

Figure 3-2   The Three Pillars of European Integration

European Union
15 Members: Germany, France, Britain, Italy,
Belgium, Netherlands, Luxembourg, Greece, Spain,
Portugal, Denmark, Ireland, Finland, Sweden, Austria

FIRST PILLAR	SECOND PILLAR	THIRD PILLAR
EUROPEAN INTEGRATION European Community Treaty EC EMU EAEC EEC ECSC EEA EAA BALTICS Free Trade Agreement	Political Integration: EXTERNAL POLICIES Voluntary Foreign and Security Policy Cooperation	Political Integration: INTERNAL POLICIES Judicial and Domestic Policy Cooperation

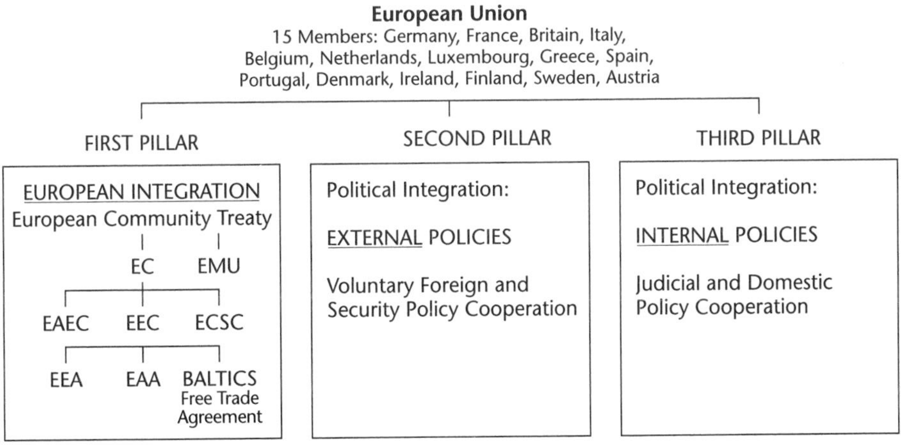

EC = European Community
EMU = Economic & Monetary Union
EAEC = European Atomic Energy Community
EEC = European Economic Community

ECSC = European Coal & Steel Community
EEA = European Economic Area
EAA = European Association Accords

Source: Graph prepared by Victoria Hottenrott.

Maastricht. Economist Lester Thurow even declared the GATT-Bretton Woods system dead and claimed that the world's largest market, the European Union, had already informally written the new rules for the world's trading system.[39] Indeed, by the end of the 1980s the European Union was worth more than $4 trillion in purchasing power and investments from all over the world flowed in, as they did again as Europe began to recover from recession in 1994. The German unification process stimulated the French to push European integration faster, hoping to anchor Germany before her energies were distracted to the East, explaining the aggressive European architecture of Delors and the push for the Maastricht treaty. The percentage of total trade accounted for by intra-European Union trade rose from 35 percent in 1958 to 60 percent in 1990.[40] By 1996, 63 percent of the EU trade was in intra EU trade and EU trade accounted for 40 percent of world merchandise trade. By 1996, exports within the EU totaled $1,249 million and imports $1,182 million, compared to EU exports to the world of $2,041 million and imports from the world of $1,953 million. The 1996 per capita GDP was $20,048 of the fifteen member nations of the EU (covering 3,191,120 square kilometers.) This compared with a world per capita GDP of $4,655. A key trade rule the European Union has introduced is that in areas like banking and public procurement, foreign firms have full access to the EU market if and only if EU companies have similar open access to their home markets—reciprocity with a steel edge.

The success of the EU as a regional trade bloc can be contrasted with other regional integration efforts—such as LAFTA—the Latin American Free Trade Association founded in 1960. The long history of European roots and regional trade traditions gives the EU a tremendous "learning by doing" advantage, based on the experience of centuries. (The first ideological proposal for a federated Europe was advanced by Pierre Dubois in 1306.) Moreover, when the highly developed Western European infrastructure was destroyed by World War II, the necessity for immediate reconstruction and modernization was clear. The cold war heightened the perception of the Soviet threat as seen from the American position, thus stimulating Marshall Plan aid for the sake of Western economic and military hegemony.

In contrast, the impulse for Latin American integration in LAFTA was strongest in times of world economic crisis when the Latin Americans adopted inward-looking policies. And while LAFTA countries also benefited from "learning by doing" in diversifying their export products first in a regional context, as soon as world economic growth was resurrected national interests in global markets displaced regional bloc preoccupations, weakening LAFTA's potential bargaining position immensely.[41]

NAFTA, MERCOSUR, APEC: THE NEW BLOCS ON THE BLOCK

While the Clinton administration pushed for a new GATT agreement globally, it simultaneously helped to support the **North Atlantic Free Trade Association (NAFTA)** and **Asian Pacific Economic Cooperation (APEC)** organization trade blocs to counter the European Union and to benefit from bloc privileges within the GATT. This two-tier strategy was the trade equivalent of the Clinton strategy of attempting to reduce nuclear arms proliferation globally, while supporting other kinds of weapons sales to the Third World (the U.S. share of arms sales in the Third World increased from less than 13 percent in 1987 to 57 percent in 1992; in 1997 the United States was still the biggest arms exporter with a global market share of 36 percent and with 38 percent of all weapon sales in developing countries). The aim in both cases was to boost American economic growth and employment short-term in the post-cold-war era regardless of long-term negative consequences for the world community (i.e., potential trade bloc wars and conventional regional wars in other countries).

Some sort of North American trade agreement became inevitable with the 1982 crash of oil prices. The Mexican and Canadian strategy of 1973–1982 seeking to convert windfall profits from oil price rises into economic development to make them more independent of the U.S.-NAFTA negotiations began under the Bush administration in 1991, building on the 1989 Canada-U.S. Free Trade Agreement. The aim was to counter the clout of the European Union by creating a free trading bloc of 364 million consumers in the United States, Canada, and Mexico with a total output of $6 trillion (25 percent more than the EU). Since Canada's trade with Mexico was but 1 percent of its trade with the United States, the controversy surrounding the final passage of NAFTA in the U.S. Congress in November 1993 centered on trade-offs between the United States and Mexico. In 1992 the United States had a $5 billion trade surplus with Mexico, in contrast, for example, to a $75 billion trade deficit with East Asia. About 70 percent of Mexico's imports came from the United States.[42] President George Bush saw NAFTA as a way to support the open economic reforms and trade liberalization of Mexican President Carlos Salinas that were initiated in 1987. Moreover, without the international investor confidence generated by NAFTA, it is hard to imagine how Mexico would have covered its heavy external savings deficit (5–6 percent of its gross domestic product in 1993).[43] Proponents of NAFTA viewed the agreement as an institutional frame for the natural evolution of an emerging architecture of North America that was happening anyway, and as the first step toward a larger North American-South American bloc.[44]

Opponents to NAFTA argued that after the initial upsurge in exports of the three countries with tariffs removed, factories would be tempted to move from the United States (and eventually Canada) to Mexico, which would result in lower wages and looser environmental regulations. Although the Clinton administration included side agreements to help equalize environmental standards and enforce existing labor laws, skeptics noted that the money allocated for these activities was minimal—particularly in the case of labor law enforcement. Low-skill jobs were expected to shift to Mexico, hitting hardest those in the United States who needed the work most. Americans tended to underestimate the existing training and skills of Mexicans who fill higher-level jobs as well. It is undoubtedly cheaper to train or retrain workers in Mexico than in the United States.

Another problem is that many Mexican corn farmers were put out of work as the lowered tariffs let through a wave of highly competitive agricultural goods from the United States and Canada.[45]

Larger companies, particularly financial services, benefit from NAFTA. And NAFTA may help to stem the tide of Mexicans seeking to emigrate to the United States. The ultimate question is who will benefit the most from the redistribution of benefits, both short-term and long-term? Or will it be a positive-sum game of greater benefit to all? By 1997 public opinion polls in Mexico and Canada indicated much more support for NAFTA than polls in the United States. NAFTA became an institutional means for governments to play catch-up in bringing political and regulatory agreements into line with economic and business changes that had already been completed. For example, corporate consolidation to reduce excess capacity contributed to a situation in which 50 percent of trade was intracompany—that is, within firms. With the peso crisis of 1994, Mexico necessarily became an export platform to try to catch up with its more economically developed partners. There is something of a Lilliputian strategy at work in NAFTA (enough little guys to hold down the big guy); for instance, Canada supported Mexican entry into NAFTA to try to balance U.S. influence.[46] Another strategy with a similar aim is that of MERCOSUR (MERCOSUL in Portuguese), the subregional free trade bloc (or customs union) organized in the 1990s by a handful of nations—Brazil, Argentina, Paraguay, and Uruguay (later joined in 1996 by Chile)—in the southern cone of Latin America: One way to keep the United States out is to start small from the outset. The MERCOSUR thus resists principles in any Free Trade Association for all the Americas that might dilute or undermine its intended primary autonomy—such as those behind the free trade zone that thirty-four democratically elected leaders of the hemisphere agreed to in 1994 at the Summit of the Americas, aiming to establish such a free trade area including the United States by 2005. Subregional trade blocs constitute a trend of "new regionalism" aiming to create buffer zones of local economic interest.

As soon as NAFTA was passed in November 1993, President Clinton went to a meeting of the Asian Pacific Economic Cooperation (APEC) group in Seattle to counter the overselling of NAFTA as an exclusive North American trade bloc and to keep the United States from being excluded from an emerging Asian trade bloc. APEC was founded in 1989 as a consultative forum made up of Australia, Canada, Japan, the Republic of Korea, New Zealand, and the United States, plus the ASEAN nations; Brunei, Indonesia, Malaysia, the Philippines, Singapore, and Thailand. Soon the People's Republic of China, Hong Kong, and Taiwan joined the organization. It has an annual budget of $2 million and a small secretariat based in Singapore. High level ministerial meetings are held once a year according to the APEC charter, aimed at trade liberalization and cooperating on issues such as investment regulations, technology transfer, telecommunications, and energy.

Prime Minister Mahathir Mohamad of Malaysia boycotted the APEC meeting in Seattle, advocating an exclusive all-Asian grouping called the East Asian

Economic Caucus he devised in 1990. He envisioned the caucus, which has failed to develop support, as a counter-weight to the EU and NAFTA blocs.[47]

More recently, Mahathir successfully organized a group of fifteen developing nations to block a U.S.-European move to link preferential access to their markets to workers' rights. In 1998 he closed Malaysia's borders to outside foreign investment in a radical strategy to counter the Asian financial crisis (see Chapters 2 and 11). He said: "Capitalism is not a religion, but some people treat it as if it were." APEC's November 1994 meeting in Jakarta consolidated an investment code drafted by APEC subcommittees—common rules for investing in eighteen nations around the Pacific Rim. As a South Korean diplomat put it, abolishing protective laws is "a necessary evil" in order to expand the trade of East Asian countries. Although APEC is thin, young, and fragile, it may assume growing importance as a trading group, particularly since more than 40 percent of U.S. trade is with the Pacific region. Given the commonality of the Chinese written language (upon which Japanese is based) in many of the APEC countries, it could easily be that a core Chinese language-based trading bloc will emerge. This bloc would functionally exclude those countries incapable of adapting. In this regard, it is well to keep in mind that the major source of direct foreign investment in China is offshore Chinese in other countries....[48]

IMPLICATIONS

Trade blocs may perhaps be best understood as buffer zones in the turbulent process of creative destruction that characterizes global capitalism. Such buffer zones, recently referred to as "the new regionalism," provide time for politico-economic adjustment for member nations inside the zone and time to coordinate policies in order to maximize the advantage of members in the economic competition with nations outside the bloc. The extraordinary success of the European Union (EU) was preconditioned by an unusual set of fortunate historical circumstances. A deep educational, cultural, and technological infrastructure was not difficult to resurrect after World War II, particularly given Marshall Plan aid aimed at shoring up Western Europe against the cold war threat from the Soviet Union. The Americans and British overlearned a lesson from the settlement of World War I—not to break the back of Germany economically, but to help the country reconstruct and be accepted in the family of nations. By giving grants in many cases rather than loans, the United States created the basis for a competitive economic bloc from which it could not ask for loan repayment when its own household went into deficit.

By exaggerating their domination of the world economy, the Americans created the opportunity for the formation of the European Union trade bloc. Some have argued that the formation of such blocs actually helps the United States in the difficult task of steering the multilateral management of the world trade system. But the relative autonomy of decision-making by the EU suggests the decline of American domination more than its extension. And if one considers all the dollars the United States had to print to bankroll European recovery and the resulting U.S. deficit, the case becomes clear.

Thus the American efforts to create trade blocs through NAFTA and APEC can be seen as belated attempts to restore American domination. But the European Union was so far advanced structurally, institutionally, and strategically that its regulations may become the unofficial real rules that govern the WTO. The political and cultural differences between Mexico and the United States and Canada make NAFTA little more than a free-trade zone with limited potential compared to the EU. Mexico, after all, only recently transcended its characterization as a one-party authoritarian state compared to the long-standing, sophisticated American and Canadian governmental systems.[49] APEC represents a fragile trading conference more than an institutionalized decision-making body. Even if it starts to take on more institutional status, the probability is that the Asians will operate as an informal pro-Asian trading bloc behind the scenes, perhaps based on the written Chinese language. Similarly, MERCOSUR operates as a cultural clique and pressure group within NAFTA. As Joanne Gowa has demonstrated, trade with allies produces increased domestic efficiencies that are reinforced because of national security concerns that make power politics among states in a region as compelling as the presumed predominance of stability imposed by one global hegemon.[50] The hegemon, for its part, seems likely to take trade issues ever more seriously in the second century it is likely to dominate. Already by 1999 the United States was looking back at trade deficits in the previous year of $168 billion. The EU and the flood of Asian goods due to the financial crisis pushed imports to record levels as Federal Reserve Chairman Alan Greenspan did whatever he could to keep the Americans consuming in order to maintain investor confidence and to stimulate world economic growth.

In sum, there was a post-cold-war trade revolution to officially extend the free-trade regime of the GATT with the evolution of the WTO, while informally using this framework as an umbrella to legitimate the creation of a world of competing trade blocs. Anglo-American liberalism has been ideologically extended to cover the reality of the rapid development of postliberal coalitions of regional trading regimes. The freeing up of trade globally will help to stimulate economic growth in both the developed and developing countries. Meanwhile, the postliberal trading blocs will determine who benefits most from this growth and who gets which jobs. Some of the rules of competitiveness that determine who gets what, when, and how are illustrated in Chapter 4.

QUESTIONS FOR THOUGHT

1. What is meant by the statement that "export-oriented growth strategies are the panacea for the collective insecurity generated by turbulent world markets"? Why is such a strategy desirable?

2. To what degree should trade be "'free" or "regulated" by the nation-state, and to what degree should a nation-state aim for self-sufficiency?

3. List and describe four important GATT principles. In what respect is the Smoot-Hawley Tariff Act responsible for an advantageous position of the United States at the "starting line" of trade talks?

4. Describe the structuralist perspective of world trade and its critical evaluation of the neoclassical assumptions and principles of the GATT. Is the WTO an improvement from this perspective?

5. Trading blocs seem to be the wave of the future. Is it just a matter of time before trading blocs become political and economic unions (i.e., the direction of the EU)? Or will they disband after their purpose has been served? What are the dynamic forces pushing for change within a trading bloc?

6. Which economic organizations most represent the developed countries and which the developing countries? Where does the U.N. Commission on Sustainable Development (CSD) fit in? To what extent do you think the "commitment" to sustainability mentioned as an abstract goal in the preamble of the WTO is just window dressing? What problems is the WTO apt to have in enforcing its resolutions?

NOTES

1. Sidney Painter, *Medieval Society* (Ithaca, NY: Cornell University Press, 1951), pp. 72–73.
2. See, for example, Jan Penn, *A Primer on International Trade* (New York: Vintage Books, 1967), Chapter 1.
3. See Robert L. Heilbronner, *The Worldly Philosophers* (New York: Simon & Schuster, 1986), p. 49.
4. David Ricardo, *Principles of Political Economy* (London: Everyman's Library, 1911), Chapter 1.
5. W. Arthur Lewis, *The Evolution of the International Economic Order* (Princeton, NJ: Princeton University Press, 1978).
6. See Charles P. Kindleberger, "The 1977 Nobel Prize in Economics," *Science* 198 (November 25, 1977): 813–814, 860.
7. Ricardo, *Political Economy*, p. 83.
8. Arthur Dunkel, Director General of the GATT, "GATT at 40: It's More Needed Than Ever," *International Herald Tribune*, October 30, 1987, Op-Ed page.
9. W. A. Lewis, *Economic Survey 1919–1939* (London: Allen & Unwin, 1949), p. 50.
10. See F. V. Meyer, *International Trade Policy* (London: Croom Helm, 1978).
11. See Richard N. Gardner, *Sterling-Dollar Diplomacy*, 2nd ed. (New York: McGraw Hill, 1969), pp. 101–109.
12. See Diana Tussie, *The Less Developed Countries and the World Trading System: A Challenge to the GATT* (London: Francis Pinter, 1987), p. 19, fn. 4.
13. Kenneth Dam, *The GATT—Law and International Organization* (Chicago, IL: University of Chicago Press, 1970), p. 227.
14. See Meyer, *International Trade Policy*, p. 126.
15. Arthur Dunkel, "To Put the Theory to Work: From Bilateral Alliances to Multilateral Systems," *Innovation* 11/12 (1987): 32.
16. See OECD, *Obstacles to Trade and Competition* (report by Janusz Ordover and Linda Goldberg) Paris: OECD, 1993.
17. Dan Goodgame, "Trade Warrior," *Time*, March 15, 1993, 51.

18. Jeffrey E. Garten, "Clinton's Emerging Trade Policy," *Foreign Affairs* 72, no. 3 (summer 1993): 185. See also Frances Williams, "WTO Enters Uncharted Territory," *Financial Times*, November 18, 1998.

19. For a sampling of the growing literature on neomercantilist trade policies, see Tim Jackson, *The Next Battleground: Japan, America and the New European Market* (New York: Houghton Mifflin, 1993); Laura D'Andrea Tyson, *Who's Bashing Whom? Trade Conflict in High Technology Industries* (Washington, D.C.: Institute of International Economics, 1992); Daniel Burstein, *Turning the Tables: A Machiavellian Strategy for Dealing with Japan* (New York: Simon & Schuster, 1993); Charles Ferguson and Charles Morris, *Computer Wars: How the West Can Win in a Post-IBM World* (New York: Times Books, 1993); and Wayne Sandholtz et al., *The Highest Stakes: The Economic Foundations of the Next Security System* (New York: Oxford University Press, 1992).

20. See "The Culture War," *Wall Street Journal*, October 15, 1993. Also see John Rockwell, "The New Colossus: American Culture as Power Export," *New York Times*, January 30, 1994.

21. Sylvia Nasar, "GATT's Big Payoff for the U.S.," *New York Times*, December 19, 1993.

22. See Richard Blackhurst, Nicolas Marian, and Jan Tumlir, *Trade Liberalization, Protectionism and Interdependence: GATT Studies in International Trade* no. 5 (Geneva: General Agreement on Tariffs and Trade, 1977).

23. The first structuralist works of Raúl Prebisch: United Nations, *The Economic Development of Latin America*, E/CN. 12/89/Rev. 1, New York: U.N., 1950 (Spanish edition, 1949) and United Nations, *Economic Survey of Latin America, 1949*, E/CN.12/164/Rev. 1, New York: U.N. 1951. The seminal article of Hans W. Singer: "The Distribution of Gains between Investing and Borrowing Countries," *American Economic Review*, Papers and Proceedings 11, no. 2 (1950).

24. See Tussie, *Less Developed Countries*, pp. 22–37.

25. Raúl Prebisch, "Five Stages in My Thinking on Development" (Washington, D.C.: World Bank, 1982) (mimeographed), p. 8.

26. Tussie, *Less Developed Countries*, p. 22.

27. Prebisch's viewpoint is summarized in Albert O. Hirschman, "Ideologies of Economic Development in Latin America," *Latin American Issues* (New York: Twentieth Century Fund, 1961), pp. 14–15.

28. See John W. Evans, "The General Agreement on Tariffs and Trade," in *The Global Partnership*, ed. R. Gardner and M. Millikan (New York: Praeger, 1968), pp. 92–93.

29. See S. B. Linder, "The Significance of GATT for Underdeveloped Countries," in *Proceedings of the U.N. Conference on Trade and Development* (New York: UNCTAD, 1964), p. 527.

30. As cited in Tussie, *Less Developed Countries*, p. 25.

31. See Dam, *The GATT*, p. 260.

32. See Joseph S. Nye, "UNCTAD: Poor Nations' Pressure Group," in *The Anatomy of Influence: Decision Making in International Organization*, ed. Robert Cox and Harold Jacobsen (New Haven, CT: Yale University Press, 1973), pp. 334–370. See also Nicholas Bayne, "What Governments Want from International Economic Institutions and How They Get It," *Government and Opposition* 31, no. 3 (1997): 361–379.

33. Michael Zammit Cutajar, *UNCTAD and the North-South Dialogue: The First Twenty Years* (Oxford: Pergamon Press, 1985), p. 13. UNCTAD projects that Latin America and Eastern/central Europe will catch most of the growth in foreign direct investment at the turn of the century. *World Investment Report 1998* (New York: United Nations Publications, 1998).

34. See Kathym G. Sessions, *Institutionalizing the Earth Summit: The United Nations Commission on Sustainable Development* (New York: The United Nations Association, 1992) and *The Global Partnership for Environment and Development: A Guide to Agenda 21* (Geneva: UNCED, 1992). Also see Valerie de Campos Mello, "Economic Globalization and the Contradictions of 'Environmental Management': The Case of the Brazilian Amazon,

Newsletter of the Working Group on Environmental Studies at the European University Institute, no. 16 (fall 1996) (Network of the Working Group on Environmental Studies, Florence, Italy).

35. This Franco-German axis thesis as the basis of Common Market integration is demonstrated in "The Common Market: Organizing for Collective Bargaining Power," Chapter 6 of R. Isaak, European Politics: Political Economy and Policy Making in Western Democracies (New York: St. Martin's Press, 1980), pp. 151–185.

36. These statistics are from "The European Community in the World," *European File* 16/86 (October 1986), Brussels: Commission of the European Communities, pp. 3–4. Compare to European Commission, *European Economy* (Luxembourg) Supplement A, nos. 3/4 (March/April 1998).

37. Stanley Hoffmann, "The European Community and 1992," *Foreign Affairs* 68, no. 4 (fall 1989): 35.

38. Based on discussions with officials in the European Commission in Brussels in May 1992. For background leading up to Maastricht treaty, see *The Single Market in Action* (Brussels: Commission of the European Communities, 1992); and Robert O. Keohane and Stanley Hoffmann, eds., *The New European Community: Decisionmaking and Institutional Change* (Boulder, CO: Westview Press, 1991).

39. Lester Thurow, *Head to Head: The Coming Economic Battle Among Japan, Europe, and America* (New York: William Morrow and Co., 1992), p. 65. However, Thurow's "Europhoria" seems to overestimate the ability of the European Union to master its numerous socioeconomic problems and to underestimate NAFTA's potential. GATT, reborn as the WTO, seems to be outliving Thurow's death sentence.

40. *The Single Market in Action*, p. 10.

41. See Tussie, *Less Developed Countries*, Chapter 5: "The Oscillations of Regional Economic Integration in Latin America: LAFTA-LAIA," pp. 104–135.

42. David Hale, "The Trade Revolution," *Wall Street Journal*, November 3, 1993.

43. Ibid.

44. See, for example, Stephen Blank, "The Emerging Architecture of North America," The North-South Agenda, Paper One, March 1993 (Coral Gables, FL: North-South Center, University of Miami). For a Mexican pro-NAFTA position, see "NAFTA Works for Mexico-U.S. Trade," Summer, 1998 (Washington, D.C.: Embassy of Mexico, SECOFI-NAFTA Office) or http://www.naftaworks.org.

45. See Timothy Koechlin and Mehrene Larudee, "The High Cost of NAFTA," *Challenge* (September–October 1992): 19–26. Also see Sheldon Friedman, "NAFTA as Social Dumping," in the same issue, 27–32.

46. This image from Jonathan Swift is one used by my colleague Stephen Blank.

47. Philip Shenon, "Boycott in Order, Malaysian Says," *New York Times*, November, 21, 1993. And see "Malaysia's Mahathir: Leading A Crusade Against the West," *Business Week*, April 25, 1994.

48. Rong-pin Kang, "Technology Import Policy of China in 1990s," paper presented at International Symposium on Networking of Human Relations and Technology, at Tokyo Keizai University, Tokyo, October 25, 1993. Also see David M. Lampton, "China: Think Again," *Foreign Policy*, no. 110 (spring 1998):11–27. And Ezra Vogel, ed., *Living With China* (New York: W. W. Norton, 1997).

49. See, for example, Anthony DePalma, "Reform in Mexico: Now You See It, ..." *New York Times*, September 12, 1993.

50. Joanne Gowa, *Allies, Adversaries, and International Trade* (Princeton, NJ: Princeton University Press, 1994).

MULTINATIONAL CORPORATIONS

An alliance is a device to reduce costs by creating the opportunity to access or develop different cognitive frames, work arrangements and cultures so that the firm is able to look at both itself and the environment ... in a fundamentally different way, smashing old frames and overcoming organizational inertia.

—Claudio Ciborra, "Alliances as Learning Experiments" (1991)

Giant organizations are nothing new in international trade. They were a characteristic form of the mercantilist period when large joint-stock companies ... organized long-distance trade with America, Africa and Asia. But neither these firms nor the large mining and plantation enterprises in the production sector were the forerunners of the multinational corporation. They were like dinosaurs, large in bulk, but small in brain, feeding on the lush vegetation of the new worlds (the planters and miners in America were literally Tyrannosaurus rex).

—Stephen Hymer, *The Multinational Corporation and the Law of Uneven Development* (1972)

The recent quantum leap in the ability of transnational corporations to relocate their facilities around the world in effect makes all workers, communities and countries competitors for these corporations' favor. The consequence is a "race to the bottom" in which wages and social conditions tend to fall to the level of the most desperate.

—Jeremy Brecher, "Global Village or Global Pillage" *The Nation* (12/6/93)

THE NATION-STATE OFTEN APPEARS TO BE AN ANTIQUE, IF NOT OBSOLETE, STRUCTURE FROM THE perspective of global economic change: To shore up its overloaded maintenance base, national leaders seek to use multinational corporations as the vanguards of economic growth, development, and employment. The locus of economic dynamism has shifted from the state to the global company, which offers more flexibility and higher salaries to its managers than does any government. Given normal geographical fixity, the world of nation-states often seems like an ice-cube tray with global liquidity flowing over it or not, depending upon the capriciousness of external trends.

While multinational companies can invest or disinvest, merge with others or go it alone, rise from nothing or disappear in bankruptcy, the state seems stodgy and stuck in comparison. The state is glued more or less to one piece of territory, fighting off entropy and budget crises, the national community usually assessing the latest foreign attacks upon a condition of declining competitiveness and the vulnerability in its domestic markets. Thus, it is beneficial to examine the sources of dynamism behind the learning strategies of multinational companies. For no small part of the inequality between rich and poor nations is due to the collective learning capacity of multinational companies based in different countries, in terms of responding effectively to shifting business cycles. While national resources, state structures, and access to foreign capital are significant constraints, the collective learning ability of the private sector in cooperation with public sector support may well be the decisive factor in transforming a political economy from deficit-ridden dependence into self-sufficiency, surpluses, and efficient maintenance strategies. The factors contributing to the bargaining power of the multinational corporation (versus that of both the home and host governments) are essential elements of competitiveness. Also vital is the extent to which the economic fruits of this competitiveness are reinvested in long-term infrastructure for the sake of employment and social prosperity, or are diffused in short-term accumulation strategies of private investors (see Chapter 11).

ORIGINS

Generally a multinational corporation in a strict sense refers to a company owned by stockholders in several countries that is also based in two countries—Royal-Dutch Shell and Unilever (in Britain and the Netherlands), for example. But these are the exceptions, not the rule. Usually **multinational corporations (MNCs)** are based and owned in one country with manufacturing facilities in two or more other countries in which profits are not reinvested. Such firms based in one country are sometimes called **transnational corporations** to distinguish them from the purer, two-country-based companies. But everyday usage suggests that it is wiser to retain the term "multinational corporation," although few firms qualify in the purest sense.

In terms of size, multinational corporations are traced back to the East India Company, chartered in London in 1600, which established "outposts of progress" overseas. Ultimately, the British East India Company had its own private army to protect its stakes and employees in unpredictable environments abroad. From the nation of small shopkeepers (and local pin factory) of Adam Smith, to the national corporation, to international representation for trade abroad, to direct investment in manufacturing and the emergence of multinational corporations with global interests, the development of multinational strategies has been evolutionary, often catching government policymakers by surprise. Business managers are compulsively future-directed (although not necessarily long-term oriented); technology is inherently unpredictable (although not necessarily absorbable); and foreign competitors are enigmatic (but not undecipherable). Thus, to get at some of the universals in multinational development despite historical or cultural differences is not easy. A brief comparison of business systems emerging from significantly different cultural traditions illustrates the possibility and complexity of pinning down such principles.

THE EMERGENCE OF U.S. VERSUS JAPANESE MULTINATIONAL CORPORATIONS

From the English, French, and Dutch mercantile families of the seventeenth century, Americans learned that to succeed at international trade it was necessary to have representatives overseas. Typically, Americans would either send independent agents or family members abroad to represent their businesses as foreign commerce grew in the colonial era. Up until the time of the American Revolution, American business development was conditioned by the control of British mercantile policy: This policy aimed to keep a favorable balance of payments for the mother country, to discourage manufacturing within the colonies, and to constrain the colonists to trade within the British Empire.[1] True to their independent nature, the Americans openly disregarded such restrictions.

INDIVIDUALS GO ABROAD: ENTREPRENEURSHIP MULTINATIONALIZED

At the turn of the nineteenth century, cotton became the greatest American export and the basis for establishing an important American textile industry, relying upon inexpensive slave labor. First, canals were built to link the interior of the country with the coast. The mood became one of "Manifest Destiny." However, perhaps due to the tradition of rugged, laissez-faire individualism, many of the businesses started abroad by Americans in the middle of the nineteenth century lasted only for their lifetime or that of their sons. They found themselves under heavy pressure by host governments in the developing countries, and their concessions were often cancelled. This contrasted with more benign treatment in countries like Canada. The Panama Railroad and Nicaraguan carriage-steamboat line were the most important American direct foreign investments preceding the Civil War.

American experience in Nicaragua and elsewhere taught U.S. business people that they had to vary their plans for different cultures. In the second half of the nineteenth century, American business abroad came into increasing competition with the British, particularly in third-country regions such as Mexico and Central America. Transportation and communication developments within the United States made it increasingly possible for companies to become national enterprises—the first step toward becoming multinational concerns. When a U.S. company decided to go abroad, true to the laissez-faire tradition of American liberalism, the government usually had little involvement, leaving the company on its own. In the late nineteenth century, surplus output and the desire to benefit from economies of scale led many U.S. companies to seek export markets. However, again true to the American belief in free trade, there is little evidence of "dumping" by American businesses. Rather, there was a rough adherence to the principle of comparable prices. Communication innovations led to automatic international extensions, as the Western Union Telegraph Company was founded in 1856. The International Ocean Telegraph Company installed the first cable to Latin America between Florida and Havana in 1866. By the 1880s, Tropical American Company had acquired the telephone rights in South America and was selling parts to Latin American telephone companies. At the same time, the Edison Electric Light Company exported to Brazil, Chile, and Argentina and started installing lighting systems in Latin America. But after reaping few profits, Edison withdrew from foreign markets in disappointment.

By the last decade of the nineteenth century, American inventors, manufacturers, and marketers were involved in international business, led by men such as Isaac Singer, Alexander Graham Bell, Thomas Edison, George Westinghouse, George Eastman, John D. Rockefeller, and J. P. Morgan. What Mira Wilkins has termed the "American Invasion" era was in full swing.[2]

The thrust of American international business activity was directed toward forward integration into sales or into horizontal integration—generally in the industrial or industrializing countries. The American government was pulled into becoming more involved. It passed the Sherman Antitrust Act of 1890 (forbidding agreements that restrained trade) and conquered the Philippines (which government policymakers thought would become a base for U.S. trade in the Orient). In the chaotic Third-World markets, the U.S. government was particularly likely to provide American businesses with information and assistance. Rather than directly competing with the Americans, the Europeans preferred a *policy of negotiated environments*. For example, American and European gunpowder industries negotiated market boundaries, some exclusive, some shared, and some free. In coming to terms with European traditions, many American businesses found they had to cooperate with European companies rather than act independently as they were naturally inclined to. Thus, multinational corporate alliances emerged.

German hostility to foreign enterprise at the time, not to mention high tariffs and restrictive patent laws, led American firms to set up manufacturing facilities there (much as the Japanese were motivated out of similar concerns to make direct investments in the United States a century later). High tariffs also induced American companies to start local manufacturing in France. In Russia the American multinational ran into stiff nationalism: Businesses operated under close government scrutiny with the finance minister monitoring almost every deal and with the Russian government serving as virtually the exclusive customer for some companies (such as Westinghouse Air Brake Company). To cope with nationalism abroad, American multinational strategies focused on incorporating in a joint venture with host companies, shifting from sales operations to manufacturing and refining so as to bypass tariffs, hiring local people, buying locally, taking on "national" titles and, if necessary, making security deposits.

In the United States, multinational corporations emerged primarily from an entrepreneurial strategy—businesses and families sending their agents abroad to make foreign trade possible. Innovations in transportation and communication facilitated the emergence of national companies that sought export markets on their own for surplus production and economies of scale. And protectionist international relations led to high risk direct investments to avoid tariffs and cultural obstacles. The government followed with supportive policies long after entrepreneurs had led the way. Many businesses went bankrupt abroad within one or two generations for lack of assistance and continuity. Contrast this with the way Japanese multinational companies evolved.

ZAIBATSU AND SOGOSHOSHA:
HOW JAPANESE MAINTENPRENEURIAL MULTINATIONALS EMERGED

The rise of Japanese corporate groups, the **zaibatsu** (literally "financial clique"), stemmed from the *Meiji Restoration of* 1868. Prior to this radical change in government form toward centralization (setting up the "tight-ship-in-a-storm efficacy" of "Japan Inc." in the world economy) Tokugawa Japan possessed a government (the bakufu) of decentralized personal bonds that linked the *shogun*, the *daimyo*, and the *samurai*, bonds that were more important than institutions. The impetus for changing the governmental structure came from abroad. In 1853 and 1854, U.S. Commodore Matthew Perry forced open Japanese ports to the West. Foreign trade interests began to invade the country, imposing a 5 percent limit on the tariffs the Japanese could put upon imports. The foreigners went so far as to demand the right to **extraterritoriality** so that their citizens could be governed by their own laws rather than those of the Japanese while they resided in Japan. The resentment of the Japanese helped to bring down the *shogun* who ran the country, theoretically returning power to the Emperor Meiji, whose name is used to identify the 1868–1912 consolidation of the Japanese political system.[3]

In *Imitation and Innovation* (1987), sociologist Eleanor Westney details how Western organizational forms were emulated in Meiji Japan—"collective learning" at work. As in Great Britain and the United States, mergers were a favored form of business restructuring in the second half of the nineteenth century. Many of the largest businesses in the early to mid-Meiji era were single industry businesses. By 1896, of the fifty largest manufacturing and mining companies, twenty-eight were cotton textile companies—firms that were to become even more dominant because of the merger movement. In the early twentieth century, the number of cotton-spinning companies fell from seventy-eight to forty-six.[4]

Such Japanese industrial companies were less integrated than American firms and were more comparable to British companies. The insular state depends on companies abroad for sources of raw materials and markets for finished goods, resulting in a relative lack of vertical integration. Japan had a reasonably well-developed marketing system dating back to the early nineteenth century. Manufacturers did not have to set up their own marketing networks. Foreigners (to this day) have found it difficult to penetrate this marketing arrangement.

Thus, huge diversified companies—*zaibatsu*—soon assumed a hegemonic position over the industrial and other business sectors in Japan. More diversified than American or British multinational companies, the *zaibatsu* typically included manufacturing, a bank to finance manufacturing, and a trading company to market the products abroad (the *sogoshosha*). By 1914, Japan was dominated by eight major *zaibatsu*. Three of these (Mitsubishi, Mitsui, and Sumitomo) are still among the largest of the nine main *sogoshosha* (trading companies) that helped to steer Japanese business in the late twentieth century. By the early 1920s, a great deal of the mining, shipbuilding, banking, foreign trade, and industry of Japan was controlled by the *zaibatsu*.

Almost all Japanese firms specialize in a single sector—a specialization nurtured in part by **MITI**—Japan's governmental ministry of industry and trade, which seeks to create appropriate conditions for the competitiveness of the country's major companies over the long run (see Chapter 9). This specialization contrasts with the loose American conglomerate, made up of businesses from different sectors that may be added or dropped depending on short-term market fluctuations. Either companies from a single industrial sector organize for collective learning and clout, or one strong firm from each sector is incorporated into a *zaibatsu*, which is centered around large banks and linked to non-*zaibatsu* groups. The twentieth-century tradition of the *zaibatsu* was to have a holding company at the top, directly controlling the specialized firms in the *zaibatsu* group. Although these holding companies were forbidden and dispersed during the occupation following World War II, the **sogoshosha** or trading companies remaining still operate along the lines of the *zaibatsu*, much as the large companies supposedly broken up in Germany after the war have been recast and still predominate in the German economy.[5] The five largest of the nine major *sogoshosha* are not just trading companies but utilize a strategy to secure sources of basic raw materials and maintain world market share. For example, the largest of the five (Mitsubishi, Mitsui, C. Itoh, Marubeni, and Sumitomo) alone account for about one-third of the energy (gas and oil) imported by Japan.[6] The *sogoshosha* serve not only the big organizations but also the small. They eliminate difficult barriers to entry into new foreign markets for small manufacturing firms that would not normally have the financial or managerial resources to support international ventures. Brazil, Korea, and the Southeast Asian political economies have developed their own forms of *sogoshosha* based on the Japanese model, so convinced are they that these organizations are engines of export-led economic growth.

Overcoming the static concepts of comparative-advantage theories of international trade, the *sogoshosha*'s key strength is to gather foreign marketing intelligence from all over the world, to sift through the information, and to target it for the right company at the right place at the right time.

As information increasingly becomes the basis for power and competitiveness, the Japanese trading company intelligence networks are strategically placed and traditionally cultivated to be highly efficient information processors for both Japanese multinational companies and the Japanese nation. Using something of a "tribal clan mode of organization," the *sogoshosha* serve as large and loyal clearing houses for companies offering diverse goods and services, hooking ultimately into the *senmonshosha*—thousands of specialized, wholesale distributors trading in specific sectors. The *sogoshosha* are flexible organizations, highly leveraged (in terms of debt-equity ratio), and thrive on both dynamic and static economies of scale given a national and worldwide network of market contracts. They are able to barter goods and services among themselves for significant savings and can move in and out of specific markets quickly with the effective collective learning capacity made possible by territorial knowledge bases cultivated over decades[7] (see also Chapter 9).

Perhaps the most significant contrast between the American and Japanese multinational management cultures is the American laissez-faire antagonism between the (government) maintenance base and the entrepreneurial company versus the cooperation between big government and big business in Japan. Early in the twentieth century, American antitrust legislation broke up Standard Oil of California into eleven parts. Each part ultimately became larger than the initial company. In comparison, MITI and the *Keidanren*, the government trade and industry bureaucracies, cultivate mergers between weaker companies to consolidate firms into large, competitive units. The *Keidanren*, the peak industrial association made up of the 700 or so largest companies, works closely with MITI, not only interchanging personnel but calling departments by the same names in both organizations.

The laissez-faire system encourages individualism and entrepreneurial innovation, whereas the *maintenpreneurial* approach stresses long-term targeting and collective adaptation with an institutional structure that assures follow-through on national strategies.

FROM SOFT POWER TO TYPES OF COLLECTIVE LEARNING

As the key basis for hegemony at the end of the twentieth century shifted to the "soft power" of technological and economic competitiveness, at least four universal types of collective learning emerged:

Learning 1: Reduction of error within a rigid frame;
Learning 2: Open, synergistic networking based on trust;
Learning 3: Radical quantum leaps for technological breakthroughs;
Learning 4: Striving for absolute excellence beyond all existing benchmarks.

Reduction-of-error learning (Learning 1) is what American management expert W. E. Deming meant when he said that to increase quality is to reduce variation.[8] For example, a great Swedish tennis player won three of the grand-slam titles in a row by playing 90 percent of his shots to the opponent's weakest side (until the opponent became so bored he would take a risk and often lose the point due to the "variation") and got over 90 percent of his first serves in during the French Open. Deming's corporate examples included reducing the number of suppliers to assure quality and ordering inventory "just in time" as needed to cut down errors and costs. Walmart, a "virtual corporation," anticipates as precisely as possible what customers will want on Monday morning by monitoring purchase receipts for the previous week late on Friday.

Open synergistic network learning (Learning 2) is based on leaps of faith within and between organizations to brainstorm and create new products and processes spontaneously to fit that moment in the business or political cycle. Interactive telecommunication mergers that anticipate shares of markets that do not yet exist and create customized content for short-term demand illustrate this type of collective learning.

Radical quantum-leap learning (Learning 3) challenges old paradigms or technologies and strives for breakthroughs and unpredictable creativity. The discovery of the structure of DNA and the creation of the first IBM PC are examples of this kind of learning that lets no bureaucratic routine or potentially repressive supervisor stand in its way. Maintaining research and development laboratories where this kind of learning can happen by bringing the best minds in the world together is a key to **soft power**, which is "cultural and economic power" that "rests on pull, not on push, on acceptance, not on conquest."[9] Radical, quantum-leap learning is fostered by a learning context that shines and attracts the best and the brightest in the world: Soft power is its inadvertent result.

Striving for absolute excellence (Learning 4) rather than relative quality or meeting existing benchmarks is the ultimate key to competitiveness in the global economy of the twenty-first century. The idea is to build the best mousetrap, not just a better mousetrap. Reject lowest common denominator solutions and seek to meet the highest standards. As management specialist Rosabeth Moss Kanter notes: "CEOs (chief executive officers) build company capabilities by reaching for absolute excellence instead of merely trying to beat today's competition or meet today's regulatory standards. One Japanese quality secret is to seek perfection, not to do one notch better than competitors.[10] This learning paradigm clearly costs more in the early phases but usually proves to be more sustainable in the long run.

ADAPTIVE VERSUS LEARNING ORGANIZATIONS

There is a clear competitive difference between organizations that merely adapted to change in a maintenance mode and those that restructured to become dynamic, risk-taking learning organizations. **Adaptive organizations** react to daily changes as they come up, using maintenance strategies to keep stability, rather than anticipating the future in order to keep up with the cutting edge of innovation. In contrast, as Richard Hodgetts and Fred Luthans have put it, **learning organizations** are able to transform themselves by anticipating change, discovering new ways of creating products and services: They have learned how to learn.

Adaptive organizations see their core competence as improving the same kind of thing. They are preoccupied with the first type of collective learning ("Learning 1")—reduction of error within a rigid frame. They aim for stability, focusing upon market share, compartmentalization, bureaucratic structures, formal rules, hierarchy, disconnected networks, short-term financial rewards, distribution of scarcity, mobility within division or function, a market culture, controlling managerial perspectives aimed at a narrow problem-solving orientation, and a conforming style of response. When interviewing a number of German adaptive companies that sought to qualify for the European Environmental Auditing certificate (of the European Union), the aim was typically to adapt existing processes to continual environmental improvements in order to avoid risk and to cut costs, anticipating threats in order to meet them head on without having to turn the organization totally on its head.[11]

Learning organizations focus less on change than on systemic transformation: They aim to achieve meaningful difference at a core competency, seeking to create markets, facilitating networking structures with lateral rather than hierarchic flows of communication, relying on teams with knowledge-based power, focusing rewards on long-term financial and human resource development (with mobility patterns across divisions or functions), nurturing a clan rather than market culture and a managerial perspective of openness and systemic thinking that asks for creative responses. Learning organizations emerge from the second kind of collective learning ("Learning 2")—open, synergistic networking based on trust. An example of a learning organization is Kodak, which is involved in large-scale experimentation in electronic photography and digital technology to keep up with scientific trends and anticipated future demands.

The most important obstacles in the transition from an adaptive organization to a learning organization are cultural. To change the way people think and to restore collective vitality, every employee in the organization must be engaged in the organization's principal challenges. In the 1990s, denial of the need to change in Sears due to the deep, inbred culture, for example, led the company to include Wal-Mart among its competitor benchmarks only after Wal-Mart had become 60 percent larger than Sears.

FROM VIRTUAL TO WORLD-CLASS ORGANIZATIONS

Ultimately, organizations that have mastered Learning 1 (reduction of error within a tight frame) and Learning 2 (open synergistic networking) may transform themselves to the point where they become **virtual organizations**, which are collective learning networks that can almost instantaneously produce and deliver products or services at any time, in any place, and in any variety, providing instant customer satisfaction. Virtual organizations anticipate reality that is almost there and make it concrete. They operate like the Polaroid camera that produces finished photographs within sixty seconds. Through mastering speed, virtual organizations cultivate collective learning processes that are so economic, target specific, and user-friendly that they are irresistible. Fast, targeted, knockout quality is the objective. The future is now: You can see it, taste it, feel it, touch it, and buy it. But it is not just any future. It is your future, the one you think you want, made to order.

The virtual organization creates a virtual product for a specific customer.

Wal-Mart followed the virtual organization model when each regional store was ordered to analyze purchase receipts each week and reorder customized inventory accordingly for the following week—offering a variety of some 110,000 choices of goods in different styles, colors, and types at the typical outlet. Wal-Mart soon out performed Sears using economies of scale and customized targeting in its reengineering of the inventory process.

The virtual university, for example, might process each student's desired menu of courses instantly at the beginning of each term based on an "individual contract" or curriculum, providing exactly what they want, when and where they want it, whether on site or by distance learning. The virtual democratic government might take an on-line vote by computer on major issues each Sunday evening so that when official business opens every week what was once "polling" becomes a weekly referendum, updating the bureaucracy instantly and holding political feet to the fire. The virtual organization can be considered to be the *reducto ad absurdum* of laissez-faire democratic, economic liberalism, aiming to gratify each individual's customized needs and desires instantly on the basis of immediate market transparency and responsiveness. The best of virtual organizations tap into "Learning 3"—radical quantum-leap learning that goes for broke in risk-taking research to find new technologies and creative designs that constitute the markets of tomorrow. But most virtual organizations are limited by their mere market orientations, which have both the virtues and drawbacks of short-term thinking. There is something more absolute and long-term that some organizations aim for.

World-class organizations create global standards, position themselves socially to dominate soft power, and command the greatest resources across borders. They are guided by cosmopolitan managers with the latest concepts or knowledge, the greatest competence and up-to-date technological sophistication, and they have the best connections with other influential technological and economic elites throughout the world. To maintain their status, world-class organizations take the nurturing of "Learning 3"—radical quantum leaps—for granted and are obsessed with "Learning 4"—the daily struggle for absolute excellence. Like William Gates, founder of Microsoft, and Andrew Grove, CEO of Intel, world-class managers have already developed "the best mousetraps," have monopolized the world market for their products, and relentlessly motivate their organizations to position themselves to create the next best thing that will continue to monopolize and expand their markets. Microsoft monopolizes computer operating systems globally, while Intel dominates the microprocessor market. These organizations invest in inventing processes of continuous perfectionism, ways to raise quality, cut costs, and solve problems more efficiently: They are always driven by the absolute need to find "the best solution" regardless of the efforts or short-term costs this strategy might entail. Indeed, their rationale is often that these very opportunity costs constitute barriers to entry for would-be competitors without the resources, positioning, intelligence, and drive to match them. To maintain their position and to give them space to develop the next best product, world-class firms (particularly American-based companies) engage in constant lawsuits against competitors for any patent infringement that is suspected. Such lawsuits slow the competition down and drain their financial resources.[12] Thus the term "absolute" excellence can have ominous political consequences since it implies achieving the goal by any means necessary. The U.S. government antitrust suits against Microsoft and Intel in the late 1990s, arguing that they unfairly stifle competition, hardly slowed the firms down: The state is almost defenseless in one-to-one battles against such world-class organizations.

JOINT VENTURES OR STRATEGIC ALLIANCES

World-class multinational companies view joint ventures as strategic alliances and collective learning frameworks for consolidating and increasing their share of the world market. As the U.S. boom of the late 1990s peaked, mergers and acquisitions also peaked as U.S. multinationals pushed their efforts to maximize markets to the global limits. The quantity of such mergers declined as the boom softened, although the amount of money spent on the mergers that did take place increased (see Figure 4-1). In the peak year of 1997, for example, the sectors in which the highest prices were offered for mergers and acquisitions were in the "soft power" services: banking and finance, brokerage, investment and management consulting, communications, utilities services, leisure and entertainment, and insurance (see Figure 4-2). In contrast, mergers and acquisitions in the "hard" manufacturing, equipment, and commodities sectors received much lower prices.[13]

The trend toward mergers and joint ventures complemented a corporate shift from focusing on *total quality control* (derived from the W. Edwards Deming's concept of quality as the reduction of variation) to *reengineering*, which calls for a radical restructuring of work processes to create a virtual organization in order to meet the needs of next week's demands by particular buyers. The focus was not merely upon incremental improvement for the sake of reducing errors. Rather, the virtual organization model served as a hidden blueprint behind reengineering and massive merger activity to totally transform the infrastructure and to dominate distribution channels in order to coopt consumer desires, no matter what those desires turn out to be. Bank mergers and telecommunications/media mergers are primary examples. The $10 billion merger in 1995 between Chemical Bank and Chase Manhattan, for example, created the largest U.S. bank, with 25 million customers, ranking first in mortgage servicing and fourth in credit cards and bank mutual-fund assets. In the same year in the media sector, Disney acquired Capital Cities/ABC for $19 billion in order to incorporate ABC's broadcast and cable networks, coopting distribution market share in advance in order to have a monopoly of sorts, no matter what types of programming the customer of the future should happen to desire.

Such aggressive strategies of entrepreneurial risk combine with cost reducing maintenance strategies to keep the stability of one's market position in order to launch the next generation of products and have the infrastructure in place for

Figure 4-1   M & A Activity from 1970 to 1998

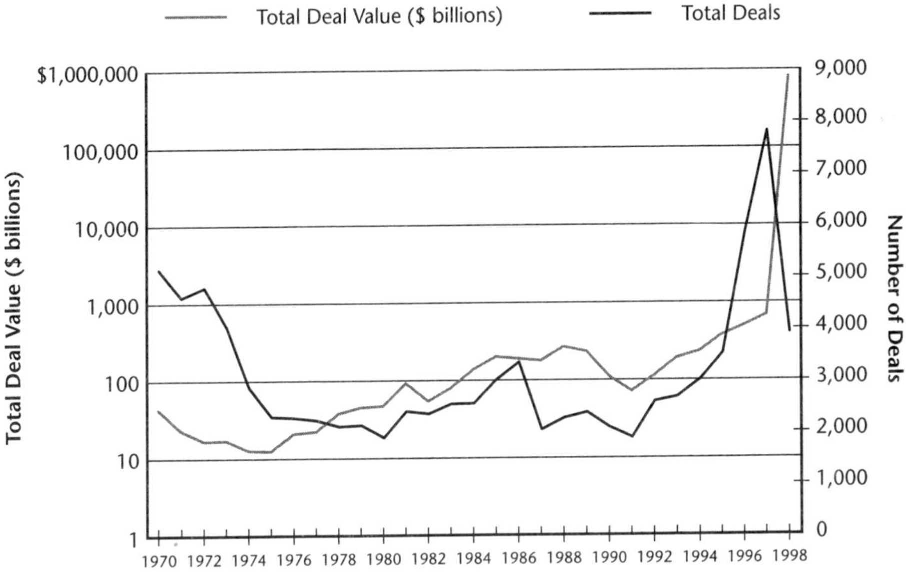

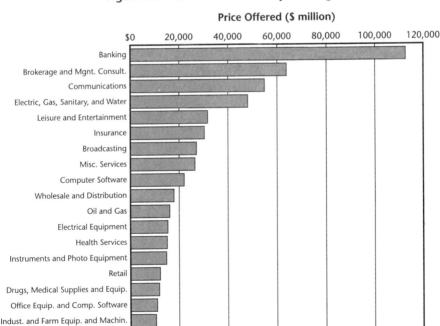

Source: Houlihan Lokey's Mergerstat www.mergerstat.com

Figure 4-2   1997 M & A Industry Ranking

Source: Houlihan Lokey's Mergerstat www.mergerstat.com

future demand. However, the massive downsizing and outsourcing involved in such reengineering and merger activity threatened to create permanent forms of structural unemployment. One-upmanship in downsizing became commonplace: "Look, he needed 450 people to do that job; I can do it with a mere 200 with the help of my new information system!" Moreover, statistically most joint ventures and efforts at reengineering fail, leading those still left in the organization to wonder whether the sacrifices were really worth it. The uncertainty caused by inevitable downsizing led to a sense of meaninglessness on the job: Less-skilled workers are neither loyal nor encouraged to be so since they are often hired as temporaries without benefits.[14]

INTERPRETATIONS

Regardless of which culture one observes, the trend in multinational organization or global direct investment in the twentieth century was one of organizational mergers and foreign direct investment led by oligopolistic industries. Not only did the influence of the state on national political economies grow greatly, but the impact of multinational corporations also expanded to the point of displacing government power on many issues: The turnover of the largest multinational companies is greater than the GNP of some eighty countries. This national and international growth of corporations is made possible by imperfect competition. In a world of perfect competition—the utopia of Adam Smith—there would be many small competitors in each nation supplying all the goods and services demanded with no impetus for direct foreign investment. But in the real world economy, the imperfection of competition provides irresistible payoffs for companies with special access to scarce resources or specialized knowledge or technology for which there is great demand. The increased importance of "soft power" stimulated progressive collective theories of learning, permitting organizations to develop strategies of competitiveness to adapt to globalization. The chaos of imperfect markets, reasserted incessantly by the creative destruction of capitalist innovation, creates the motivation for oligopolistic organizations to maximize their global market share. They merge with their counterparts, making entry into their markets difficult through economies of scale and cooperative pricing. In the process, the world economy becomes increasingly structured into developed and unevenly developing regions—metropoles and peripheries epitomizing the inequality between rich and poor nations.

QUESTIONS FOR THOUGHT

1. Compare and contrast how American and Japanese multinational companies emerged.
2. Compare and contrast the four kinds of collective learning used by companies. Where does "soft power" fit? Give examples.

3. Compare the adaptive organization with the learning organization. Give examples. What is a virtual organization? A world-class organization?

4. Why does merger and acquisition activity speed up near the end of economic booms? Why do you think it declines sharply thereafter, while the amounts involved in mergers increase?

5. There are problems associated with extremes of any organizational type. Consider the thesis that, whether it be state or corporation, one can have it all, although humankind has not yet quite figured out how! Preparation for group project in class: Begin formulating a theory for the corporation (a mature one that tends toward maintenance) that you think would allow the corporation to "have it all"—it would motivate the people and provide for them! (Optimally, the theory could be used for a nation as well.) What do you think is the maximum size group in which entrepreneurship is apt to function effectively and why?

6. What are the probable social and environmental consequences of a world economy dominated by virtual corporations?

Notes

1. Mira Wilkins, *American Business Abroad from the Colonial Era to* 1914 (Cambridge, MA: Harvard University Press, 1970), p. 6. Wilkins serves as the basic source for this section on the American evolution. Ibid., p. 70.

2. Ibid, p. 70.

3. Mansel G. Blackford, *The Rise of Modern Business in Great Britain, the* U.S. *and Japan* (Chapel Hill, NC: University of North Carolina Press, 1988), p. 35. Ibid., p. 80.

4. Ibid, p. 80.

5. See Georg H. Köster, "Germany," in *Big Business and the State:Changing Relations in Western Europe,* ed. Raymond Vernon (Cambridge, MA: Harvard University Press, 1974), p. 138.

6. Anonymous personal interview with manager in Mitsubishi, November 26, 1988.

7. Yoshi Tsurumi, *Multinational Management: Business Strategy and Government Policy,* 2nd ed. (Cambridge, MA: Ballinger, 1984), pp. 107–120.

8. See W. Edwards Deming, *Quality, Productivity and Competitive Position* (Cambridge, MA: MIT Center for Advanced Engineering Study, 1982).

9. Josef Joffe, "How America Does It," *Foreign Affairs* 76, no. 5 (September/October 1997): 24. "Soft" power was first introduced by Harvard political scientist Joseph S. Nye.

10. Rosabeth Moss Kanter, *On the Frontiers of Management* (Boston, MA: Harvard Business School Press, 1997), p. 57.

11. See Robert Isaak, *Green Logic: Ecopreneurship, Theory and Ethics* (West Hartford, CT: Kumarian Press, 1999; originally published: Sheffield, England: Greenleaf Publishers, 1998), Chapter 3. Also see R. Isaak and A. Keck, "Die Grenzen von EMAS," *UmweltWirtschaftsForum* 5 (September 1997): 76–85.

12. See Tim Jackson, *Inside Intel* (New York: Dutton, 1997).

13. Merger data is from 1998 *Mergerstat Review,* December 31, 1997.

14. R. Isaak, "Virtual Organization," *Working Paper* (spring 1996); New York: Pace University, Center for Applied Research. See also W. H. Davidow and M. S. Malone, *The Virtual Corporation* (New York: Harper-Collins, 1992). For negative social consequences of the virtual corporation and what might be done, see David Korten, *When Corporations Rule the World* (West Hartford, CT: Kumarian Press, 1996).

THE NORTH-SOUTH SYSTEM

The wealthiest fifth of the world's population consumes 86 percent of all goods and services while the poorest fifth consumes 1.3 percent. The richest fifth consumes 45 percent of all meat and fish, 58 percent of all energy used, 84 percent of all paper, and owns 74 percent of all telephone lines and 87 percent of all vehicles.

—United Nations Human Development Report, 1998

The fastest-growing source of funds flowing to the developing world is private investment capital, which seeks out the turnaround economies and avoids the back-sliders.... Poorer countries ignored by the multinationals and investors are left to rely on the aid mills in the industrial nations, which face new demands around the world and budget constraints at home....

—Tim Carrington, Wall Street Journal (9/27/93)

With respect to development, we should note that economic growth is not the only factor. There are countries, such as Venezuela and Brazil, which, in spite of strong economies, suffer from great instability because their economic growth does not translate into more options, better opportunities or higher living standards for the people. Economic growth that does not produce food, drinking water, housing and health and education represents a great security risk.

—Oscar Arias Sanchez (1993)

THE MOST HUMAN FOCUS OF INTERNATIONAL POLITICAL ECONOMY IS THE "NORTH-SOUTH structure"—the asymmetrical or unequal relationship between the developed and developing countries in the world economy. The shift toward a high technology/high information global economy accelerates the widening of the gap in levels of development between rich and poor as money, technology, and skilled personnel flow to the secured, developed nations of the world. The poorest countries find themselves without the resources to begin to catch up. The increasing speed of technological change works to the disproportionate benefit of the advantaged over the disadvantaged. Hence, movements by lesser developed countries to slow the pace of technological transformations on their home ground should not be surprising: Their traditional way of life, the very cultural essence of their collective existence, becomes increasingly vulnerable to disruption if not eradication. From this perspective, resistance to technological change may be more rational than irrational as people desperately try to preserve the integrity of their own culture.

From the perspective of the rich nations of the "North"* the initial temptation is to maximize the self-interest of one's own people regardless of the consequences for the poorer developing nations of the "South." But this short-term viewpoint has become problematic in an interdependent world economy in which exports from the North can only be purchased by customers in the South if the North helps to provide the South with money or credit to make such purchases. Moreover, many regions of the so-called rich countries of the North are as poor in some ways as the poor developing countries of the South, which, in turn, are often studded with their own rich elites or minor metropoles. Hence some analysts argue the North-South split is a myth.

For instance, who is more "developed"—the man who dies at forty-five from a heart attack in a high-pressure, future-oriented, workaholic metropolitan center of the North or the man who dies at a similar age of a snake bite on a present-oriented, developing Pacific island of the South? The Northerner lives to work and sacrifices his present for a future that never materializes. The Southerner lives each day to the hilt and dies as naturally as he lives—often with neither the promise nor the hazards of modern technology or drugs. Technology and drugs are making their way to the peripheries of the South, but will this really improve the quality of life and constitute a more meaningful level of human development?

Regardless of the meaning attributed to the process of Western modernization, one can identify dominant structures and strategies in North-South relations since World War II, highlighting northern institutional efforts to "manage the economic problems of the South" and attempts by the developing countries to change the game rules in their favor. One paradox is that Western industrial nations often assume that the leaders of developing countries are primarily after wealth, whereas they may be aiming first for control and less vulnerability. Conversely, the southern developing countries often assume the industrial North is seeking imperialistic control as a primary motive whereas the rich countries may be in pursuit of more wealth.

From the perspective of collective learning, the management of North-South relations is a chaotic, politically charged adventure in which ideological blinders often obstruct long-term blueprints, tempting both sides to give up on each other or to insulate themselves from the other's problems. Meanwhile, the interdependent world economy demands constant communication, negotiation, and adjustment on all sides to keep the global economy healthy. This is particularly true when the richest 20 percent of the world's people increased their share of global income from 70 percent in 1960 to 83 percent in 1989 (The ratio between the richest fifth and the poorest fifth thus grew from 30 to 1 to 59 to 1). According to the UN *Human Development Report*, by 1998 the 225 richest individuals in the world, of

---

*"North" usually refers to developed, industrialized nations of the Northern Hemisphere, while "South" designates developing countries of the Southern Hemisphere, but many countries and regions have a North-South economic split within them (e.g., the U.S. rural south, the EU's southern members).

whom 60 were American with assets of $311 billion, had a combined wealth of more than $1 trillion—equal to the annual income of the poorest 47 percent of the entire world's population. In fact, in 1998 the three richest people in the world held assets exceeding the combined gross domestic product of the 48 least developed countries. Just compare real GDP value in the developed regions of North America and Western Europe with real GDP in South Asia, the Middle East, and Sub-Saharan Africa (see Figure 5-1).

ORIGINS

The nation-states, which were first established in Europe (e.g., England and France), had the advantages that all first arrivals enjoy. They had their choice of colonies, whereas nation-states united later (e.g., Italy and Germany) were forced to choose from leftovers. These late colonial efforts were perceived as illegitimate, given the tides of late liberalism and parliamentary democracy that swept over Europe in the course of the nineteenth and early twentieth

Figure 5-1   Real GDP (in Billions of 1996 U.S. $)*

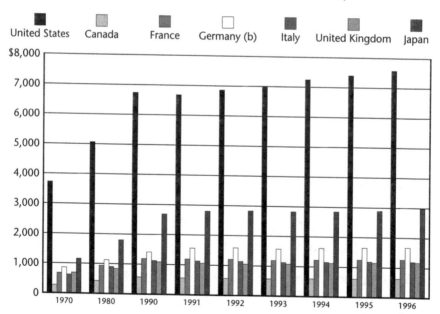

*GDP estimates have been revised from figures published in previous issues of the Handbook of International Economic Statistics and the CIA World Fact Book. Those publications used purchasing power and the CIA World Fact book. Those publications used purchasing power parity conversion rates based on Summers and Heston (PENN World Tables). The present estimates are based on purchasing power parity conversion rates published in the World Bank's World Development Report (1996).

Source: Central Intelligence Agency, Handbook of International Economic Statistics, 1997; Aggregate Trends http://www.odci.gov/cia/publications/hies97

centuries. Even when France and England were eventually forced to give up their colonies in the course of the twentieth century, they left deeply rutted cultural and administrative traditions behind that would work in the favor of British and French trade: The former colonies usually preferred to do business with "the bastards they knew the best."

By the end of the nineteenth century, most prime global real estate was tied up one way or another by established interests, dominated by European nations. They had the advantages of relatively unregulated flows of trade, capital, and labor, thus allowing them to profit as efficiently as the state of technology would allow from their colonial investments. With minor exceptions, this colonial business could be consolidated without any interruption from war. The colonial powers learned from each other how to set up colonies for power and business so that benefits soon flowed to the home country.

Advocates of the developing country position argue that global economic opportunities have changed drastically since the nineteenth century. Goods and labor cannot move as freely over borders as they did for Europeans and Americans a century ago. Protective tariff barriers and strict immigration quotas block Third-World goods and labor from moving freely to the developed industrialized world, thus hindering modernization processes of the poorer countries. Dr. Mahbub ul Haq, former director of Policy Planning and Program Review at the World Bank, maintained that the poor countries are not asking for a massive redistribution of wealth, even though at least three-fourths of the world's income, investment, and services and most of the world's research facilities are in the hands of one-fourth of its population. Rather, the developing nations want greater equality of opportunity, which is made impossible by existing economic imbalances and international structures skewed toward the rich nations.[1]

Whether speaking for the rich nations or the poor, no one denies the imbalance between the economic structures of the developed and developing nations. The conflict of perspectives focuses on whose fault it is and which means are most appropriate for improving the situation. The international institution dealing most with the practical long-term consequences of this North-South gap is the World Bank.

THE WORLD BANK

The perspective of the developed countries toward the South or developing countries was initially set forth by the American dominated Bretton Woods philosophy after World War II. As noted in Chapter 2, this philosophy initially represented a partial resurrection of classical economic liberalism according to which international credit should be given only to countries and projects that were "economically sound" (that is, "hard banker terms," not "soft loans"). The exception that proved the rule was the Marshall Plan program of outright grants for European reconstruction. But the ruling constitution for managing the economic problems of the developing countries in the postwar era was the "embedded liberalism" of the Bretton Woods regime, spearheaded by the International Monetary Fund (IMF) and the World Bank, or its formal name—the International Bank for Reconstruction and Development (IBRD).

While the IMF was founded to provide international liquidity and short-term credit to alleviate balance-of-payments problems of its member nations, the World Bank's major function has been to stimulate the flow of capital into long-term investment across national boundaries (although not always from the rich countries to the poor). When founded on December 27, 1945, the International Bank for Reconstruction and Development was overshadowed by the IMF and focused on making loans to war-damaged countries in Western Europe, not to the underdeveloped countries where the credit risks were higher. As with the IMF, the site chosen for the headquarters of the World Bank was Washington, D.C. This upset John Maynard Keynes, who preferred London or even New York, but not a location "under the thumb of the U.S. government." Actually the IMF and World Bank headquarters are housed in the same building in Washington, "Siamese twins," with representatives going to each other's meetings despite their different functions. Membership in the World Bank has always been contingent upon membership in the IMF, and any nation expelled or withdrawing from the IMF automatically ceases to be a member of the World Bank.

With the adoption of the Marshall Plan or European Recovery Program (proposed in 1947 by U.S. General George Marshall), the World Bank was able to shift its priorities from reconstruction to development. However, the World Bank's role is not restricted to raising money in developed countries so it can lend to developing nations: The bank borrows from and makes loans to both groups. Loans are targeted for specific, viable economic projects—typically to build up the infrastructure of developing countries as a prerequisite to industrialization: highways, railroads, power and port facilities, irrigation and flood control (as contrasted with public health projects, schools, seeds, or houses). Normally, loans by the World Bank cover only hard-currency import needs and have to be repaid in hard currency at long-term rates. Initially, the daily operations of the IBRD were steered by a group of executive directors, five appointed by the five member governments with the largest subscriptions to the bank, the rest elected biennially by the remaining members. A president was hired (and could be fired) by the executive directors, who, with their approval, could select a staff made up of as diverse a geographical representation as possible. Traditionally, the president of the World Bank has been American, and the president of the IMF a European. But this convention may change when a Japanese president is selected for one of these international bodies in an effort to draw Japan into more obligations in the management of a global economy from which the Japanese have benefited handsomely. Such an institutional development would be a natural outgrowth of the trilateralism that has emerged de facto in the management of the global economy.

In 1960 the **International Development Association (IDA)** was created as part of the World Bank Group in order to provide loans to developing countries on a more liberal basis than was permitted within normal IBRD guidelines—typically fifty-year, interest-free loans. Moreover, there is normally a ten-year grace period before loans must start to be repaid, and the repayment can be in local currency, provided that it is convertible. With resources of its own, the IDA loan projects go through the same World Bank evaluation process as do regular credit applications. The purpose is to provide liquidity on a more liberal, long-term basis to the poorest countries. But the amount of funds is never enough to keep up with the requests that qualify for support.

The post-cold-war world economy has put increased pressure on the **concessional financial assistance** (that is, either outright grants or soft loans) of the IDA. Because of the consequences of the war between Iran and Iraq, 1990 grants doubled to $29 billion, and rose again to $32 billion in 1991.[2]

The former Soviet Union and eastern European governments were clearly not able to maintain the aid programs to which they contributed before 1989. Since 1991 at least eight new low-income member countries have been admitted to IDA membership. The "Tenth Replenishment" of funds for the IDA, which did not keep up with growing demand, extended from 1993–1996.

Another key organization within the World Bank Group is the **International Finance Corporation (IFC)**, formed in 1956 to provide risk capital for productive private enterprises, to encourage the development of local capital markets, and to stimulate the international flow of capital. Loans by the IFC to private companies in developing countries are normally for seven- to twelve-year periods. Such loans can also be made for joint ventures between investors in developed and developing countries and cover projects in such fields as mining, manufacturing, steel, textile production, food processing, machinery production, local development finance companies, and tourism. The aim is to foster entrepreneurship and job creation.

In 1988 the *Multilateral Investment Guarantee Agency* (MIGA) was established to issue loan guarantees and protect investors against noncommercial risks such as currency transfer, war, civil disturbances, and expropriation. This agency provided stimulus for direct investment and new concessional aid to the IDA but was tilted in its priorities toward areas favored for strategic support by the United States. Guarantees are granted depending on the assessment of the economic soundness of development projects by the agency as well as upon approval by the host government.

ORGANIZATIONAL "MODELING": REGIONAL DEVELOPMENT BANKS

Collective learning is illustrated when one international organization is seen to have economic success and other countries view it as a model to shape their own economic organizations. With the World Bank model in mind, regional development banks were created: the *Inter-American Development Bank* (IDB) in 1959 to provide World Bank-type services to countries in the Western Hemisphere (particularly the United States and Latin America); the *African Development Bank* (ADB), organized by a group of newly independent African countries in 1963 under United Nations auspices; and the *Asian Development Bank*, which set up headquarters in Manila in 1966. In addition, the World Bank has been instrumental in helping to found more than fifty development banks (mainly national banks) in member countries.

An illustration of how the regional development banks work is the African Development Bank, Africa's premier source of credit. With fifty African members and an additional twenty-five from the industrialized world, the ADB is structured like a mini-World Bank, financing projects in most African countries and granting soft, long-term loans to the poorest. By 1987 the ADB had approved about $10 billion in loans, including $4 billion interest-free, through the African Development Fund (ADF)—the soft-loan window of the ADB modeled after the International Development Association. The money for ADF comes from the rich developed members of ADB, while the operating funds for the ADB come from all its members in addition to the loans raised on international markets, where the ADB has the same blue-chip rating as does the World Bank. With more than $19 billion in capital, the ADB worked toward doubling its rate of lending to more than $10 billion from 1987 through 1991.[3] But what about the World Bank itself?

MCNAMARA'S BASIC-HUMAN-NEEDS ORIENTATION

When Robert McNamara became president of the World Bank in 1968, he shifted the bank's priorities away from focusing on the modern sector of developing countries (usually cities) toward alleviating absolute poverty through direct action at the rural level. He defined **absolute poverty** as "conditions of deprivation that fall below any rational definition of human decency" in his speech at the Annual Meeting of the World Bank at Nairobi in 1973. In his first five-year term McNamara not only doubled the amount of lending by the World Bank (without losing its AAA-credit rating for never having anyone default on a loan). But he also changed bank policy, aiming to break the main constraints on development (such as population increase, malnutrition, and illiteracy) rather than limiting credit to conventional infrastructure projects. Thus, much more money went for agriculture, education, and the control of population growth (McNamara's original, controversial contribution) and to the poorest developing countries, particularly Africa. The basic human-needs orientation (not original with McNamara) focuses on alleviating the needs of the poorest individuals in the world as the appropriate orientation to the North-South dilemma.

McNamara himself was a somewhat Faustian figure as head of the World Bank. He had learned the cold, efficient techniques of managerial decision-making theory at Harvard, applying his cognitive skills later at Harvard as an accounting professor, at Ford Motor Company as chief executive officer, and then at the Pentagon as secretary of defense during the Vietnam War, where efficiently maximizing "body counts" was the indicator of success rather than the reduction of absolute poverty. The legendary Faust, it will be recalled, sold his soul to the devil in exchange for knowledge, which he knew to be worldly power. By 1966 McNamara realized the Vietnam War was morally wrong. He stated in a speech in

Montreal that peace and stability in the world depended less on building up armaments than on raising the living standards of the poorer two-thirds of mankind.

McNamara, who left the Pentagon for the World Bank, had discovered he was using technological means to the wrong ends. In his new job he set about to improve health care for the world's poor rather than to wage war against the Vietcong. There may be a moral in this tale that can be applied to the asymmetrical balance in world markets in terms of payoffs for arms and war versus support for health care and the alleviation of world poverty. The North knows its Faust well....

While aware that four-fifths of the resources must come from the developing country itself, McNamara sought to use the other one-fifth to create a critical mass of financial and technical power through the World Bank so as to accelerate the process of development to a high but sustainable level. His purpose, using decision-theory methodology, was to maximize whatever small impact the World Bank funds had. He expanded the research arm of the bank to make it one of the world's most authoritative centers for studies of key development problems. Under McNamara's leadership, the IDA portion of IBRD loans became even greater, given the targeting of the poorest of the poor countries. While Nobel economist Arthur Lewis suggested separating the two organizations so that the IDA could focus solely upon development without the drag of banking orthodoxy, McNamara rejected this advice. Forced to choose between the two, he said he would select development over banking orthodoxy, but that this was a false choice: By submitting all projects to the same procedures, development could be made more effective and the financial credibility of the World Bank preserved. McNamara pushed the IFC to select developmental projects benefiting the poor masses rather than more short-term profitable undertakings and to support local, home-grown enterprises instead of large multinational companies. The developed nations were split on their support of McNamara's policies. Several OECD nations observed that the IBRD poverty program was less than helpful in their export of capital goods.[4]

But the Scandinavian countries and the Dutch stood strongly behind the new stress on poverty-oriented projects: It is no accident that these are nations known for contributing more than the average share of GNP in foreign aid.

WOLFENSOHN'S WORLD BANK STRATEGY

In 1995, fourteen years after McNamara stepped down in 1981, James D. Wolfensohn became president of the World Bank and refurbished McNamara's passion for the poorest of the poor countries. But Wolfensohn brought a new perspective to bear: As a former Australian investment banker who had a record of philanthropy and was famous for helping to engineer the U.S. government bailout of Chrysler, he had switched to U.S. citizenship to qualify as a candidate for the World Bank post, since Americans traditionally receive the job. He set about restructuring the World Bank to speed up the bureaucracy and to encourage "field" experience by employees who previously were tempted to sit comfortably in Washington. He sought to relieve the debts of forty-one of the poorest countries. In a world in which private capital accounts for some 75 percent of net capital flows to developing countries, Wolfensohn wanted to make sure that these funds not only reached the "emerging" developing countries (which attract three-quarters of that private capital, one quarter alone going to China) but that nations left out of the economic boom receive at least a greater share of official aid, which he used to leverage and attract private capital inflows.

Wolfensohn argued that self-sustained development in poor countries is only possible with large initial investments in the infrastructure not only of roads and dams, but of micro-bank credits, marketing advice, health, and education. The focus was on the decentralization of competencies and responsibilities and upon environmentally benign development. Decentralization at the World Bank led to efforts to reach out to cooperate with hundreds of environmental, human rights, and poverty-fighting *nongovernmental organizations* (NGOs) in joint strategies—organizations that had previously been among the bank's sharpest critics. He asked local government and organizational leaders of poor nations to propose plans in order to increase their stakeholder motivation rather than merely imposing World Bank blueprints. Even before the 1997 Asian crisis, Wolfensohn noted that at least one in five developing countries had a banking crisis, and he made strengthening banking systems a priority, complementing the objectives of Michael Camdessus, head of the IMF.

On the political right, the World Bank was criticized for becoming an obstacle in the necessary adaptation of developing countries to a free market economy. Simultaneously, from the left Wolfensohn was criticized for still embodying the idea that globalization will bring prosperity to poor workers and farmers around the world rather than exploiting them and leading to a downward spiral in their living standards and working conditions.[5]

The World Bank set up an office for special financial operations with a staff of twenty-four and a $60 million budget to help modernize the financial and legal institutions of Thailand, Indonesia, and South Korea after they received IMF bailouts in 1997. This longer-term, "collective learning" perspective was aimed at coordinating technical assistance, from drafting new commercial laws to devising training programs for bank supervisors. The "model" was first tested on Thailand, involving 150 consultants from McKinsey and Co., restructuring experts, and central bankers from Japan, Germany, and Britain. As a result, 68 failed financial institutions were shut down and their $23 billion of loans were sold at deep discounts to foreign investors.[6] Of course, a Marxist perspective might claim that the IMF bailouts were really a setup by the United States and other rich nations to put the austerity squeeze on potentially profitable developing countries so that their multinational companies and investors could go in after the inevitable disarray to pick up the assets of these desperate countries on the cheap.

FROM OPEC TO THE NEW INTERNATIONAL ECONOMIC ORDER

As modeling goes, the most influential pro-Southern example in the world economy was OPEC, the organization of oil-producing countries that other less successful would-be commodity cartels tried to mimic. As documented in Chapter 8,

OPEC's successes stemmed to a large extent from its oligopolistic roots in the oil industry, which has a history and structure different from other commodity businesses.[7]

Of course the effectiveness of managerial structure cannot be separated from cyclic trends in the sectoral market: Since 1890, roughly every decade the dollar price of oil in real terms appears to go from trough to peak and then from peak to trough in the following decade. With a peak in oil prices in real terms reached in 1981 (a 225 percent increase over the previous decade), a long price decline was anticipated to bottom out in the 1990s if the pattern was extended.[8] And it did in 1999.

After each trough in this twenty-year boom-and-bust pattern, the oil industry reorganizes. Collective learning and cooperation at this critical juncture set the stage for the relative efficacy of the cartel as demand again begins to outstrip supply. Thus the efficiency of the maintenance learning base is prerequisite to the effectiveness of the collective, entrepreneurial bloc demand for certain prices and production quotas. As the coordination or efficiency breaks down, OPEC's power is undermined—to the point that at the end of the twentieth century, with oil prices in a deep trough along with prices of other commodities, some experts even (prematurely) wrote the organization's obituary (see Chapter 8).

The success of OPEC at pushing up oil prices in the 1970s had great impact upon Third World countries. Some attempted to form other commodity cartels—in copper and bananas, for example—without much success.[9] The OPEC situation was unique. Even given the development of other energy sources and oil discoveries in the world, by 1980 OPEC still accounted for two-thirds of the world's petroleum reserves and for over 40 percent of the world's petroleum production. OPEC's success was contingent on high demand, inelastic oil prices, tight supplies, a small number of producing countries, common political interests, a tradition of "collective learning," and a sufficient supply of financial reserves. The falling prices of other commodities and the great number of alternative suppliers did not make them likely candidates for successful commodity cartels.

Nevertheless, the OPEC model inspired developing countries to band together to demand the establishment of a **New International Economic Order (NIEO)** at the United Nations' Sixth Special Session in 1974. Observing that between 1952 and 1972 per capita real income in developed market economies went up from about $2,000 to $4,000 (1973 prices) while in developing countries per capita income rose from $175 to $300, the developing countries concluded that the international economic system was skewed against them. Rather than catering only to improvement of standards of living in the developed countries, the objective of the NIEO was to make the basic needs of developing countries a priority as well, by restructuring the world economy to allow greater Third World participation and effectiveness.[10]

The New International Economic Order movement pressured for a change in financial flows, beginning with a target of 0.7 percent of industrialized countries' GNP for aid to developing countries. While the North resisted NIEO pressures, they served to change global consciousness on economic matters. U.S. Secretary of State Henry Kissinger reversed his policy of benign neglect in 1975 and the European Economic Community (EEC) signed the first **Lomé Convention** with forty-six developing countries from Africa, the Caribbean, and the Pacific to stabilize their export earnings and to make EEC capital and technical assistance available to them through a Center for Industrial Development. This was a major breakthrough in the Northern establishment for the sake of Southern interests.

THE LOMÉ STRATEGY: A MODEL FOR NORTH-SOUTH ECONOMIC TIES?

The world's largest regional agreement, linking over 500 million people in industrialized European and developing countries, was signed on February 28, 1975, as the result of hard bargaining inspired by the NIEO movement. The **African, Caribbean, and Pacific states (the ACP nations)** began from a maximal position in negotiations, demanding that export and import prices should be indexed in a stabilization system to guarantee the purchasing power of the developing countries based upon their major export products. The European Community (EC) opposed this indexation of export and import prices on two grounds: (1) Such indexation could hurt some of the ACP states, since trade took place not only between industrialized and developing states but also between developing states themselves; and (2) interference with the market mechanism could have negative, bottleneck effects, such as the EC experienced in the expensive subsidies for the EC's Common Agricultural Policy.[11]

A European Commission study of major ACP exports discovered that variations in quantities of key exports as well as price changes were responsible for the instability of ACP export earnings.[12] The EC agreed to stabilize export earnings instead of focusing on prices and proposed a list of key exports from the ACP countries: groundnuts, cocoa, coffee, cotton, coconut products, and bananas. The ACP states responded with tough bargaining that resulted in a list of twelve major products plus seventeen more derived from them. The twelve were groundnut products, cocoa products, coffee products, cotton products, coconut products, palm nut and kernel products, rawhides, wood products, fresh bananas, tea, raw sisal, and iron ore. With sugar, the stabilization guarantees go even further than with this dozen. Southern bloc unity at a propitious historical moment, with a negotiating partner with long-term economic interests in the bloc, were the main ingredients of the Lomé success. The European Community, for its part, assured itself privileged access to the resources and markets of an important bloc of developing countries, which could become invaluable in the event of any future protectionist trade war in the global economy. Indeed, the potential power of the agreement could serve as a deterrent to exactly such a trade conflict.

By the mid-1980s, sixty-six ACP states had signed the Lomé Convention, which was renewed in 1979 and again in 1984. These include all the former French colonies, illustrating the shrewdness of French diplomacy within the European Community. The Lomé Convention frees ACP members from all customs duties on 99.5 percent of their exports to the EC with no reciprocal concessions required. Also, the EC grants the ACP countries technical and financial aid. When the export earnings of the major ACP products listed above fall below the average of preceding years, the EC compensates them in repayable advances for the more prosperous ACP nations and in nonrepayable grants for the rest. An agreement was reached in 1979 to cover support for a certain level of production or export potential for key ACP minerals as well (called *Sysmin*). A 1985 agreement expanded cooperation in areas of rural development, energy, industry, fisheries, and social and cultural problems.[13]

Programmed aid under the Third Lomé Convention (1980) slowed down the allocation of aid due to the administration of the large-scale rural development programs involved. The import program financing was dispersed more efficiently, however. And extra money was targeted for **structural adjustment** (basic institutional economic adaptation to world economic change) for the Fourth Lomé Convention (Lomé IV), covering 1991–1995, given the overload put on the Lomé's STABEX system.[14]

STABEX is limited to stabilizing the export earning from products that affect employment and cause a deterioration in the overall terms of trade in ACP countries. By the 1990s, aid requests far exceeded available financial resources, particularly given the heavy indebtedness of many ACP nations. These nations also worried about the erosion of their preferential access to the European markets because of the Single Market evolution of the European Union and the GATT Uruguay Round.

But the positive model of the Lomé Convention broke beyond defensive, riskshy maintenance strategies and stimulated collective learning adaptation to world economic change, targeting economic growth while supporting social equity and cultural integrity. In June 1992, non-European industrialized nations, including the United States, agreed to the Lomé Convention in principle by supporting Chapter 33 of Agenda 21 at the Earth Summit (United Nations Conference on Environment and Development) at Rio de Janeiro[15] (see Chapter 3).

Chapter 33 of Agenda 21, "Financial Resources and Mechanisms," proposed that since the 5–6 percent of Gross National Product (GNP) industrialized countries spend on defense was declining and 1–3 percent went to environmental cleanup, it would be possible to shift levels of official development assistance from 0.35 percent to 1.0 percent of GNP, and call this the **Earth Increment**. In theory, the Earth Increment could add $150 billion to fund projects aimed at protecting the ozone layer, biodiversity, and international waters. These funds could also be used to limit emissions of greenhouse gases, perhaps halving the debt of developing countries through such plans for sustainable development. In practice, only Norway, Denmark, and Sweden are close to 0.8 percent of GDP as official development assistance, making the prospects for the adoption of the Earth Increment dim. The future green house gas emissions limits of the Kyoto protocol, described in Chapter 3, are about the best that can be hoped for; and, *if* enforced, these apply at present to the industrialized rather than to the developing countries.

UNCTAD AND UNIDO: TRADE AND INDUSTRIAL PRESSURE GROUPS

The demand for a New International Economic Order in the 1970s motivated new efforts by existing international economic pressure groups for the developing countries, sponsored by the United Nations. As described in Chapter 3, UNCTAD, or the United Nations Conference on Trade and Development, had been organized to promote the interests of the countries disadvantaged by the unequal world trading system. Recall the structuralist Raul Prebisch of Argentina, first head of UNCTAD, who argued that the Northern center of world trade was so structured as to keep the South on the periphery and to increase the North-South gap. Southern countries typically produce commodities and basic resources with prices that tend to fall, whereas developed countries specialize in finished manufactured goods with rising prices. Only by providing import substitutes for Northern goods could the South catch up. Prebisch concluded that the North was preoccupied with a maintenance strategy concerned with furthering the well-being of industrialized countries in the status quo. The concerns of the South were not even on the agenda of the North. GATT had become a de facto rich man's club—a commercial treaty organization that best served those who could afford its terms. UNCTAD, then, was the economic pressure group for the poor countries.[16]

The NIEO helped to promote the implementation of UNCTAD's Integrated Program for commodities and the establishment of its Common Fund.[17]

On the industrial side, the **United Nations Industrial Development Organization (UNIDO)** was established in 1966 to help the developing countries in the private industrial sector. Headquartered in Vienna, UNIDO set a target of at least 5 percent economic growth in gross domestic product for the developing countries, advocating that by 2000, 25 percent of all industrial output should be by the developing countries. Nations must come to UNIDO, which uses its Industrial and Technology Bank (established in 1976) to help them with marketing and capital financing strategies. In addition, there is a Special Industrial Services program (SIS) to provide specific project help in industrial development through, for example, a fellowship program for technological and managerial training for key personnel.

The Industrial Development Board, which governs UNIDO, was set up with forty-five seats elected from the General Assembly of the United Nations: fifteen seats for developed countries, eighteen seats for Africa, Asia, and Yugoslavia, seven seats for Latin America and the Caribbean, and five seats for socialist countries. Industrialization is not seen as an end in itself by UNIDO, but as a means to economic growth in developing nations. Projects are analyzed for visibility, cost-benefit ratios, and the promotion of financing. UNIDO encourages nations to focus first upon agricultural projects before moving to other projects.

At its 34th Conference in New Delhi in 1980, UNIDO proposed a $300 billion fund by 2000 for industrial financing, long term rather than short term. However, countries prefer short-term financing. Conventional state development programs fail to reach the people who have the greatest need for financial services in the developing countries. This is particularly true for women. Large-scale, regulated, subsidized programs fail to reach the poor. Successful alternative financial services rely instead on reducing barriers to access to money, such as high transaction costs for lenders and borrowers, high collateral requirements, and low levels of literacy and numeracy.[18]

A new *microcredit strategy* has, therefore, come into being that creates incentives and technical and financial assistance to those who will provide employment and growth in the micro and small business sector. The focus is not on grants but on more or less cost-recovering loans in order to achieve the long-term objective of less and less reliance on subsidized funds. Quasi-market structure and repayment discipline are the key notions. A prominent example, a "collective learning model" for government programs in at least forty other countries, is the Grameen Bank in Bangladesh, which has repayment rates of over 90 percent. Reaching out to the rural poor, by 1995 the Bank had two million members, 94 percent of whom were women, spread over 35,000 villages. Group pressure and peer pressure mechanisms have helped to successfully maintain a consistent repayment rate and correct imperfect enforcement in order to counter adverse selection of borrowers and the dilemma of moral hazard (or expectations of subsidized risks that will be covered if repayment is not possible). The Grameen Bank's track record suggests that it is possible to develop a profitable financial institution that works exclusively with the poor.[19]

Still, such frail international economic organizations were no match for the debt crises of the 1980s and 1990s—crises "resolved" by commercial banks and private investors as substitutes for governments and international organizations—a role for which they were not designed.

THE DEBT CRISIS

The seeds of the debt crisis were planted with the quadrupling of oil prices in 1973. Transfer of wealth to the oil-producing Third World countries amounted to a "tax" equivalent to 2–3 percent of the GNP (on average) of the industrialized countries. And this economic cost of some $30 billion was soon recycled from the North to the non-oil-producing South—those poorer countries that produced no oil and were least able to cope with the price increases.

Meanwhile, the OPEC nations, most of which were sparsely populated, found themselves with more wealth on their hands than they could absorb domestically. So they deposited their funds in "safe," short-term accounts in banks of the North—in Europe, the United States, and Japan. This game of "hot capital" (same rules as hot potato) was then continued by the commercial banks of the North who wanted desperately to get rid of this abundance of cash and hired hundreds of young graduates to fly around the world to sell loans to developing countries. Given that the economic growth rates in the oil-importing developing countries between 1973 and 1980 averaged 4.6 percent annually, compared to a mere 2.5 percent in the industrialized countries, one can understand why the bankers were attracted.[20]

Citibank, the Bank of America, Chase Manhattan, the First National Bank of Chicago, the Bank of Tokyo, and other world-class banks acted as turntables. They recycled the petrodollars deposited by OPEC to provide liquidity in the non-oil-developing countries who needed cash to pay for higher oil bills. Because some of these banks actually calculated that they probably would not get the principal back on the loans, planning to live a long time on high rates of interest, this massive commercial loan program has been referred to as "the third redistribution" (the first two redistributions from wealthy to disadvantaged nations being the Marshall Plan and OPEC's success in raising oil prices). Since both industrialized governments and the international organizations they supported were under great financial pressures in the 1970s, they applauded the action of commercial banks without attempting to discern the long-term consequences. The outstanding debt of developing countries shot up from $161 billion in 1974 to $599 billion in 1982, and by 1982 debt service payments claimed 24 percent of the export earnings of developing countries compared with 14 percent in the mid-1970s.[21]

Nevertheless, in the late 1970s the Marxist-oriented Cambridge School of economics in England sent advisors to Mexico who recommended that the Mexicans borrow all they could as long as North Americans were willing to lend. The loans would indirectly be insured by the U.S. government and even if the loans went bad, Mexico would have the Americans by their debt.

By 1982 some forty developing countries found themselves in a cash squeeze. Interest rates on their variable-rate loans were skyrocketing in tandem with the Paul Volcker tight-money, anti-inflation policy of the United States at the same time that their export earnings were falling because of a recession in the industrial world and because of plunging commodity prices. As economist John Maynard Keynes observed, if you owe your bank a hundred pounds, you have a problem; but if you owe your bank a million pounds the bank has a problem. And in a global economy, if a number of countries owe banks billions of pounds, everybody has a problem.

Poland, with $27 billion in debts, was the first casualty. Because of the imposition of martial law in Poland, the United States pushed for calling the loans in default, but was dissuaded from doing so by West European allies whose banks had large stakes in Poland.

In Latin America the debt stakes were even higher—$90 billion in Brazil, close to the same amount in Mexico, and $38 billion in Argentina. But it was not Poland but the Mexican debt crisis that shocked the financial markets severely in August 1982. The advice of the Cambridge School came home to roost.

THE MEXICAN CASE, THE DEBT TRAP, AND THE COVER OF PRIVATIZATION

Commercial banks had been particularly anxious to lend money to developing countries where new oil had been discovered, as in Mexico, assuming that oil prices would continue to rise and back up the loans. And since the Mexican economy grew an average of 8 percent annually between 1978 and 1981, all looked well on the surface. But a structural crisis resulted when the oil price forecasts by the banks proved to be wrong. The demand and price for oil began to go down, not up.

Underlying this structural crisis, we discover the hegemony of Anglo-American economic theory at work (see the Introduction). Most policymakers from the developed world accept the assumptions of Keynesian economics that savings always equals investment, that whatever is not consumption is defined as savings, and that whatever is not consumption is defined as investment. While these assumptions might work in the economy of a closed domestic system (which does not exist in a global world economy), in an open economy imports and exports have to be worked into the definition of savings equaling investment. In the daily practice of balance-of-payments statistics, a **current account deficit** (or the total export of goods and services that is less than the total import of goods and services) goes down as a deficiency of domestic savings vis-à-vis investment. Since foreign savings (that is, foreign debt) can be tapped to supplement a shortfall in the domestic savings rate, according to this economic philosophy, the growth process for developing countries cannot help but be associated with foreign indebtedness. Current account deficits are perceived to be the normal way of life in this formulation.

No great collective learning motivation exists for developing economies to concentrate on suitable production for exports to balance foreign exchange requirements. Mexican President Luis Echeverria used foreign commercial bank loans in the early 1970s to back up state enterprises and public credit agencies for loans to small and medium-sized businesses. But the Mexican economy became overheated in the late 1970s and too dependent on foreign sources of financing to repay both its old debt and to keep the hyped-up economic growth going.[22]

From the late 1970s onwards, Mexico's President José López Portillo pretended all was well until the election was won in July 1982. But in one week in August 1982, the peso lost half its value and the Mexican government declared it could not pay the $20 billion in principal repayments due on government debt through 1984. Mexico was broke and $10 billion was owed to the banks within a few months. The money borrowed by Portillo was to be used ostensibly for an ambitious industrial development program based on greatly expanded petroleum production. However, a large amount of the money lent—perhaps as much as half of it—was never invested in Mexico. The cash wound up in the Swiss bank accounts of corrupt government functionaries or was used by businessmen for secure investments and real estate purchases in the United States and Europe. Portillo's own assets and summer villas flourished. By August 1982, Mexico had only $200 million remaining in its central bank; it suspended commercial debt principal payments and requested a three-month moratorium on its debt. Mexico's decision to suspend payments on its foreign debts and to request $10 billion from the United States to bail itself out shocked the world and functioned as a model: Other Latin American countries followed suit, acknowledging their unserviceable debts publicly, igniting the world debt crisis.

Following exhaustive negotiations, the United States agreed to purchase $1 billion of Mexican oil at $25 to $30 a barrel to go to the Strategic Petroleum Reserve and the Pentagon. The U.S. Federal Reserve was willing to put up $750 million for Mexico through the Bank for International Settlements if the Swiss, German, and British central banks would together put up the same amount. Nearly $4 billion was provided in emergency credit, almost $3 billion by the United States, and the rest by other central banks of the North. Another credit of about $4 billion was granted by the IMF after negotiations with Mexico; the credit was contingent on stringent austerity measures that Mexico would enact.

A major Mexican problem was capital flight—Mexico was the largest of any debtor nation. Some $60 billion left the country between 1977 and 1984, and about $5 billion flowed out in the first half of 1985.[23] Capital flight depleted foreign-exchange reserves, reduced the tax base, and eliminated investment resources, thus undermining economic growth. Traditionally the Mexicans tried to keep foreigners from acquiring a majority share of stock in a Mexican company. This deterred high-tech companies from investing a great deal or transferring technology to a situation that the companies could not control. The class structure of traditional wealthy Mexican families, who are jealous of foreign competition, reinforced this trend of cultural resistance.[24] This class structure appears to be compatible with the corruption of the Institutional Revolutionary Party, which ruled Mexico for more than half a century.

However, the Mexican government made an exception to the rule for the **maquiladora** industrial plants just below the U.S. border that assembled parts from abroad and exported the finished products. Between 1978 and 1988 the maquiladoras grew 14 percent annually, employing over 350,000 workers in some 1,500 plants. The government used these plants to rent cheap workers to American firms to do piece work. But the new economic policies of President Carlos Salinas de Gortari, which tilted toward economic liberalism, converted the function of the maquiladoras to upgrade the skills of the workers in order to achieve prize-winning quality production in the auto industry. By 1992, although the pay of the average Mexican worker was but one-sixth of that of his or her American counterpart, the level of Mexican productivity growth was double that of the United States.[25]

The image of privatization projected by policies of Salinas served to cover up the existing heavy levels of Mexican debt in order to pull in foreign investment and bring about NAFTA approval. Behind the scenes Salinas fixed salaries through *el pacto*, a business-labor agreement that keeps inflation and wages down while increasing productivity, employment, and worker training. But the poor Mayan Indians of Chiapas, who saw their minimum wage drop 24 percent (adjusted for inflation) since 1988, revolted after NAFTA was approved in 1993, focusing the 1994 elections on the issue of social justice.[26]

Mexican debt, which faded from view, upstaged by all the liberal economic rhetoric and surface action of Mexican and American administrations, refused to go away. Already, by 1986, Mexico's total debt was $99 billion, with most of the $25 billion U.S. share held by the ten largest U.S. financial institutions.[27]

In 1992, Mexico's ratio of total external debt to its Gross National Product (GNP) or total annual economic output was still over 40 percent (outdoing Brazil's ratio, which was less than 25 percent, but better than Nigeria's disastrous 118 percent, not to mention the Ivory Coast, with an almost inconceivable 204 percent).[28]

External debt is defined by the World Bank as the sum of portfolio investments and long-term capital inflows by nonresidents. It does not include foreign direct investment by nonresidents (the key category that causes the United States to be called the "world's largest debtor nation").

Brazil and Argentina mimicked Mexico's behavior in seeking aid from the IMF and a rescheduling of their debts. By 1982 the Third World and Eastern European countries combined had foreign debts totaling $626 billion—three times as much as in 1976.[29]

Key international economic organizations that the North used to attempt to manage or analyze the world economy—the OECD and World Bank—both initially underplayed the debt crisis. These organizations focused on the largest debtor country problems, hoping to prevent a general loss of confidence in the Western financial markets. For if the commercial loans could not be rescheduled and were officially declared in default and written off as losses, the stocks of the large banks involved could plummet, risking a run on the banks or, at the least, a great crisis in confidence in the stability of world finance. A comment made in 1982 attributed to Arthur Burns, former chairman of the Federal Reserve Board, summed up the situation: "The international banks have made many foolish loans and now we can only pray they will make some more of them."

However, to receive IMF-sponsored loans, which permit developing countries to reschedule their debts with lower interest rates spread out over a longer period, the debtor governments usually were forced to agree to austerity conditions that initially cut economic growth and caused unemployment, lower living standards, and domestic political unrest. Mexico, for example, had to agree to cut government subsidies and employment, curb imports and inflation, and permit the peso to float against the dollar. Between 1982 and 1987, real income in Mexico fell 40 percent and annual inflation reached 160 percent. Thousands of workers lost their jobs.

The following year, preceding the national election of Salinas, the government's six-year-old austerity plan finally slowed the inflation rate and foreign trade surpluses doubled to $8.4 billion. Mexico also followed the advice of Ronald Reagan's treasury secretary, James Baker, to start selling state enterprises, reduce tariffs, ease restrictions on foreign investment, and encourage nonoil exports. To make the economy look good before the election, the government negotiated the wage-and-price pact with workers and manufacturers and increased the availability of consumer goods. But the successful political strategy, which barely gave the incoming president over 50 percent of the vote in a contested election, caused chaos in Mexico's balance of payments, already suffering from a drop in oil prices. Capital fled to safer havens abroad.

Mexico illustrates the "debt trap" situation of debtor developing countries caused by economic policies of the Reagan administration: A nation can either aim for an external balance-of-payments policy or it can try to meet the population's demand for a higher quality life—but not both. Most of the resources needed to service Mexico's external debts come out of domestic investment. Between 1982 and 1988 the investment rate within Mexico fell 6 percent and Mexico's GNP shrank, even though the population grew by 13 percent.[30] About 4 percent of Mexican GNP went to foreigners for debt servicing. So the $3.5 billion loan given to Mexico by the United States in 1988 paradoxically sank Mexico deeper into the debt trap.[31] Nor did the landmark deal completed in 1990 with American bankers under the Brady plan, under which most banks reduced the value of Mexico's debt by 35 percent (by lowering the principal on existing loans or accepting lower interest payments) change this structure of dependence. With the subsequent peso devaluation crisis of 1994 and the Mexican financial instability from contagion stemming from the Asian crisis of 1997, the benefits of the North American Free Trade Agreement of 1993 have so far been insufficient to significantly reduce Mexican dependency.

INTERPRETATIONS

The tempo of global economic change and technological innovation has speeded up, putting increased psychosocial and financial pressures upon rich and poor alike. The rich have the resources to create more buffer zones between themselves and socioeconomic change. Nevertheless, Swedish economist Staffan Linder has argued in *The Harried Leisure Class* that the higher one is on the class scale, the more harried one's "leisure" time becomes as the goods and opportunities to be consumed grow geometrically while the time one has in the day is still finite— 24 hours for the rich as well as for the poor. Or, as poet Antonio Machado put it: "Speed kills the soul."

Whether this increase in speed has increased the gap between the rich and poor nations is less often asked than this question: How great has the gap become and how fast is it increasing? Still, among economists based in the classical liberal school, such as W. W. Rostow, it appears that the poor have gotten richer while the rich have slowed down.[32] Growth rates among the developing countries, particularly those in the **Newly Industrialized Countries (NICs)**, have often exceeded those of the developed countries (see Chapter 9). On the other hand, developing countries start with much less so there is more room for growth (or the numbers are easier to double). From the reformist liberal perspective, world capitalism can be made to work for the poor if it is better targeted for economic growth in the less developed regions—as in the case of Michael J. Camdessus's growth-before-austerity policy at the IMF.[33]

The basic human needs perspective represented by the philosophy of Robert McNamara at the World Bank (resurrected in the decentralized policies of James Wolfensohn) focuses on helping the poorest of the poor individually.[34] The microcredit strategy of the Grameen Bank illustrates how poor women can become increasingly self-sustaining. But such an individual-focused target seems unrealistic to the realist school: The power, security, control, and vulnerability of the nation-state make up the dominant reality for these analysts.[35] The **interdependence** school stresses the increasing global dependency of rich and poor nations upon each other.[36] Finally, the neo-Marxists perceive global capitalism as a system headed for self-destruction.[37]

A brief look at how such perspectives conflict in their interpretation of foreign aid as a means to lessen the gap between rich and poor nations may serve as a useful illustration.

FOREIGN AID: PARTIAL SOLUTION, DRUG, OR PANACEA?

The success of OPEC and demands for the New International Economic Order set the stage for an expansion of multinational financial aid for developing countries in the 1970s. Bilateral foreign aid—which is defined as official financial assistance, excluding military aid, private philanthropy, and private investment—dominated the discussion concerning economic relations between developed and developing countries in the 1950s and 1960s, but came to be viewed with skepticism not only by the poor nations but also by the mass publics of the industrialized world. *The Ugly American*, a best-seller, told the tale of the United States donating thousands of sacks of wheat to malnourished countries only to have Soviet agents stamp the sacks upon arrival as gifts from the USSR. The American share of total Western financial aid fell from 59 percent in 1961 to 27 percent in 1980, when the United States ranked only thirteenth among the top seventeen Western aid donors in terms of percentage of aid relative to GNP.[38]

In terms of absolute quantity, Japan in 1989 surpassed the United States as the number-one giver of foreign aid. Given the pressures in the 1990s for budget reductions in U.S. domestic programs, foreign aid bills have had a difficult time getting through Congress. The "postliberal" nations of Scandinavia and the Netherlands, on the other hand, have continued to strongly support foreign aid, leading the world in 1992 in terms of aid as a percent of GDP. So have Japan and West Germany, after their postwar reconstruction was assured. In 1989 Japan targeted $65 billion for recycling to indebted countries from 1990–1993. China more or less stopped its foreign-aid program in the late 1970s, while aid from Russia and Eastern bloc countries declined to insignificance in the post-cold-war economy.

Although foreign aid typically makes up only 10 percent of the cash received by developing countries (compared with some 70 percent for export receipts), this amount can be more easily targeted by governments for specific projects than can commercial money, giving foreign aid more influence on national economic development than its percentage weight might suggest. Clearly, foreign aid cannot be more than a partial solution to the North-South economic imbalance, but as Robert McNamara and James Wolfensohn were well aware, aid can be targeted as a strategic tool to influence national policies.

While McNamara used foreign aid via the World Bank to target the poorest individuals in the poorest countries, others have found this nonstructural approach too diffuse to have anything but a short-term effect. McNamara's focus on individuals is a typical example of the humanism of Western culture. Taking the viewpoint of the power realists, the Soviet Union and Eastern European countries targeted long-term strategic states for aid—Cuba, North Korea, and Vietnam—as did OPEC in targeting Islamic states Syria, Jordan, and Egypt—and the United States in shoring up Middle Eastern allies, Israel and Egypt. According to the realist perspective, foreign economic assistance becomes a form of political war fought by means other than force. For the realist the national security of the nation and its allies becomes the criterion for granting aid—a criterion that may better serve the interests of one-party, authoritarian economies than of multiparty, factional democracies.[39]

The cold war motivation of Marshall Plan reconstruction of Western Europe, for example, served as a defense against Soviet influence only in the short-term, while at the same time building up the economies of future competitors in the world economy. Opposing the dispensing of foreign aid as a gift (except when the beneficiary is a developing country with deep structural problems) as unwise, structuralist economist Gunnar Myrdal noted in 1970: "The whole international exchange situation would have been more wholesome now and in the past decade if the United States could have called for repayments of loans from West European governments—gradually and with due considerations."[40]

Myrdal noted that aid policies cannot be morally neutral: From a realist's state-centered focus, the Swedish government's criterion for aid is to promote political democracy and social equality, not to preserve antiprogressive social structures (too often the case in the use of shortsighted cold war realism as an aid criterion).

As a structuralist (see Chapter 3), Myrdal agreed with the reformist school of liberalism to the extent that he suggested the capitalist world economy can be fixed to be more human and just. Myrdal has much in common with what has been called the "interdependence school": the stress upon the mutual dependency of developed and developing countries. This school of thought grew out of the momentum of the NIEO movement and the growing consensus that international organizations gave more bargaining leverage to developing countries in **multilateral aid negotiations**, where norms and rules are more clear than they would be in **bilateral aid negotiations** (between two states) preferred by the realists, where asymmetry of inequality is likely to be the dominant perception.[41]

The interdependence school rejects the realist's state-centered focus, arguing that this form of analysis cannot capture the reality of many transnational flows that have little to do with the nation-state transactions of multinational companies, for instance. State sovereignty has become as leaky as a sieve. The global political economy is a network of domestic, business, cultural, political, and economic linkages that perforate the pretentious control of the nation-state. Technology and financial flows are cited as evidence of the need for an interdependence perspective.

Perhaps the ultimate example of the interdependence perspective is the initial report of the Independent Commission for International Economic Cooperation chaired by Willy Brandt of West Germany—the well-known Brandt Report of 1980[42]. Using a vision of global Keynesianism, the Brandt Commission argued that the Third World must carry the main share of its own burden but cannot be left alone to the world markets or to the haphazard nature of the liberal or basic-human-needs perspectives. Rather, aid must be shifted from bilateral to multilateral forms and focus for the sake of the South, based on an automatic international tax on armaments, the trade of luxury goods, and the use of the global commons (that is, the international seabed). Without general increases in aid levels based on these and other policies, economic forces left to themselves produce growing inequalities.

From the radical or neo-Marxist perspective, foreign aid is a tool for imperialism and social control, aiming to undermine the independence of developing countries.[43] In *The Debt Trap*, Cheryl Payer, for example, implies that the solution to this dilemma of becoming dependent upon the debt trap cultivated by foreign aid donors from the industrialized world and the growth-dampening austerity measures of the IMF is to go it alone as much as possible. The North Korean constitution is cited as a model.[44] In the postwar period Albania tried this strategy only to face ever-greater poverty until reluctantly the Albanians rejoined the world economy, only to be pushed into further dependence by the 1999 war in Kosovo.

On the other hand, the People's Republic of China successfully modernized its agricultural base largely in isolation, joining the world economy officially as it was becoming a net exporter of food, thus giving the country a less dependent bargaining position. From the contemporary radical perspective, models of the ideal socialist society must be established to be ready to take over when global capitalism breaks apart from its own contradictions.

MARXISM AND DEPENDENCY THEORY

Marx himself, however, believed that the role of capitalist or bourgeois imperialism was revolutionary and would transform all traditional societies until they used the same mode of commodity production. In his *Communist Manifesto of* 1848, Marx wrote: "It compels all nations, on pain of extinction, to adopt the bourgeois mode of production ... compels them to introduce what it calls civilization into their midst.... creates a world after its own image." But in going beyond the continent, Marx discovered that his European theory of development did not seem to apply. In Asia and the Middle East, precapitalist stages did not appear to exist. These societies were stuck in what Marx termed the "Asiatic mode of production," based on the unity and autarchy of agriculture and manufacturing at the village level and an autonomous, parasitic state split from the rest of society at the top. Since nothing existed internally to change such a conservative social structure, Marx thought the external force of Western imperialism would be the agent of change.[45]

Thus, nineteenth-century-England's role in India was both the destruction of the old Asian society and the laying of the groundwork for the material basis of

Western society in Asia. Lenin extended this thinking to conclude that the inherent contradiction of capitalism was that it developed, not underdeveloped, the world, spreading its technology and industry to lesser-developed nations, thus undermining its position, preparing the competitive basis for its own destruction.[46]

Picking up Marx's theory of capitalist imperialism and Marx's concern for the domestic distribution of wealth, **dependency theory** arose in the mid-1960s, adding a strong dose of economic nationalism. Disenchanted with the inadequacy of the structuralists' strategy of import substitution as a means to wealth for the developing countries, dependency theorists were convinced that the failure lay in the inability of this strategy to change the traditional social and economic conditions of peripheral states. Whereas the Marxist-Leninist thesis of capitalist imperialism suggests the necessity of foreign aid as part of the process of inevitable capitalist development, dependency theory argues that dependency causes underdevelopment and is apt to be critical of aid. According to Brazilian scholar Theotonio Dos Santos, **dependence** is "a situation in which the economy of certain countries is conditioned by the development and expansion of another economy to which the former is subjected."[47]

Whereas liberals perceive underdevelopment as a condition of countries that have not kept up with the leaders in the world economy, dependency theorists view it as a process inherent in an asymmetrical system that continually restructures developing countries into underdeveloped positions compared to developed countries.[48]

Rather than the liberal vision of developing countries as split between modern sectors well integrated into the national and international economies and backward sectors that have not yet adapted, the dependency school sees the developing countries locked into a backward position on the periphery of an integrated global economy. This position of "negative self-fulfilling prophecy" is characterized typically by an overdependence on raw materials with unsteady prices; inequitably distributed national income catering to the tastes of the elite and not targeted toward the needs of the masses; distorting investments by multinational companies that stymie local entrepreneurship and technological innovation as profits are recycled abroad; an undermining of the local labor market as foreign firms pay higher salaries, creating structural unemployment; and dependence on foreign capital that fosters authoritarian governments, which provide multinational companies with the stability they require.[49]

The underdevelopment of dependent countries is caused, according to dependency theorists, by transnational class linkages between the metropolitan international centers of world capitalism and the parasitic, feudal clientele class dominating the political system of the country at the periphery. True nationalists must rise up against this international class hegemony and pursue the welfare of the entire society, not just of the class in which they find themselves. The aim is to create an autonomous, industrialized state characterized by equality, not parasitic dependence. As this goal is achieved, foreign aid presumably becomes less and less necessary. While dependency theory describes certain cases of poor, exploited, commodity-producing states—such as the Philippines of Ferdinand Marcos—it cannot account for the higher growth rate characterizing lesser developed countries as a group over that of the developed countries in the recent past.[50]

Rather than systematically underdeveloping the developing countries, the global economy appears inadvertently to have helped many of them, although in a sporadic way that has worked to help the least advantaged nations the least (such as those of sub-Saharan Africa). Thus, the 40 percent of the developing countries that are the richest get about twice as much aid per head as the poorest 40 percent. Other theories, such as the world-system perspective, fault dependency theory for neglecting the implication of the global division of labor.

THE WORLD-SYSTEM PERSPECTIVE

From the viewpoint of sociologist Immanuel Wallerstein's world-system perspective, foreign aid is no more than a transitory epiphenomenon, distracting one from the essential structural transformations, macro-cycles, and trends of global capitalism. In his book *The Modern World System II* (1980), Wallerstein argues that the modern world system emerged from the transformation of European feudalism and mercantilism into a capitalist world economy colored by Europe's particular redistributive or tributary mode of production. This transformation originated in the economic expansion of the sixteenth century (phase A) and subsequent contraction, depression, or "crisis" in the seventeenth century (phase B). Since then, the capitalist world economy has expanded to cover the entire globe, manifesting a cyclical pattern of economic expansion and contraction (phases A and B) with shifting geographic locations of economic roles (the rise and fall of hegemonies and hierarchical displacements of particular core, peripheral, and semi-peripheral zones). It has continued to undergo a process of secular transformation (that is, of technological advance, industrialization, proletarianization, and of the emergence of structural resistance to the system itself).

According to Wallerstein, the French Revolution and its Napoleonic continuation catalyzed the ideological transformation of the capitalist world economy as a world system, creating three new sets of cultural institutions central to this system: the ideologies (conservatism, liberalism, and Marxism), the social sciences, and the social movements. The antisystemic national and social movements are created by growing economic constraints at those cyclical moments when world economic production is in excess of world demand, precipitating stagnation (or phase B-contraction). Labor unions, socialist parties, and other kinds of workers' organizations are examples of social movements, emphasizing the growing polarity between successful bourgeois groups and the proletariat caught in the economic squeeze. Paradoxically, according to Wallerstein, these worker movements turn to the state to maximize their collective interests, further strengthening the governmental structural supports of the bourgeois classes against whom they feel the sting of increasing inequality.

While in the nineteenth century the process of the social movement spread from core to periphery in the world economy, the national movement went from periphery to core. But in the late twentieth century, Wallerstein argued, they are no longer ideological rivals: "Today there is scarcely a social movement which is not nationalist, and there are few national movements which are not socialist."[51]

This questionable supposition (given national conservative movements in the United States and Great Britain, as well as in France, West Germany and Eastern Europe) permits Wallerstein to project that we are living in a global transition from capitalism to socialism that may take more than a century to complete, given capitalism's tendency to reemerge in cyclic ways. Such a transformation would presumably bring more equity to a world system now flawed by the absence of an overarching international political authority to match the global scope of the world economy.

There appears to be a meeting of the minds in the rejection of foreign aid on the part of the extreme, socialist perspective to the left and the extreme capitalist viewpoint on the orthodox, liberal right. Orthodox liberal economists Peter T. Bauer and Basil S. Yamey argue that foreign aid serves to magnify and politicize the state in a developing country, giving power to corrupt leaders who have their own personal and political interests in mind rather than the interests of the poorest people in their nation. Thus, Dr. Julius K. Nyerere of Tanzania used aid to force millions of people to move from their homes into socialist villages, devastating food production. And President Mobutu of Zaire, who received a great deal of aid, expelled traders, bringing the society back to subsistence production and widespread deprivation. Aid, according to this perspective, lowers international competitiveness of a developing country by permitting governments to disguise the worst aspects of their economic policies—such as creating or maintaining overvalued exchange rates or increasing the domestic money supply, leading to inflation, a lack of confidence, and a flight of capital.[52] Indeed, economists Bauer and Yamey observe: "The concept of the Third World and the policy of official aid are inseparable. Without foreign aid there is no Third World."[53]

Economic growth has been negligible in many of the countries that receive the most aid and have the highest levels of capital investment. For example, while aid made up more than 5 percent of the GNP of some 47 countries in 1988 (particularly in sub-Saharan Africa), GDP per head was flat for twenty-five years.[54] Foreign aid is similar to a drug that corrupts the economic competitiveness of a country, rendering it dependent upon the aid-giving North as long as the drug is consumed.

THE RATIONAL CHOICE PERSPECTIVE

The rational choice perspective points to a similar conclusion: As long as individuals and nations are given incentives to become free-riders or to take moral hazard for granted, they would be "irrational" not to increase their debt and their risk, given that some lender of last resort has always been willing to pick up the tab. The "free rider" notion is therefore rational and the U.S. effort to redistribute "the burden sharing" of maintaining the international system onto other allies can be interpreted as a rational counter strategy on the part of the world's frustrated hegemon in an effort to cut the costs of being the lender of last resort. Since the United States has the most to lose if the economic stability and security of the global "public commons" should be undermined, it is rational for other nations in the international system to stand back and wait for the United States to spend resources first to shore up any weakness in the global system.

THE ENVIRONMENTAL PERSPECTIVE

If aid is a drug, there is always the chance of taking it to the point that a nation goes crazy in stimulating short-term economic growth no matter what the consequences are for the environment in the long-term. Thus the primary rain forest of Sierra Leone, which covered about 60 percent of the country when it achieved independence in 1961, had shrunk to 6 percent by 1994 due to harvesting for economic survival. The rain forest in the Ivory Coast has been reduced from 38 percent to 8 percent. While the coastal areas of China have boomed economically, the quality of the vast expanses of land in the interior have declined rapidly, due to deforestation, loss of topsoil, and salinization. Water supplies have been lost or contaminated, population growth climbs (projected to be 1.54 billion by 2025), and crime and corruption are rampant.[55] Since 1970, the world's forests have declined from 4.4 square miles to 2.8 square miles per 1,000 people and a quarter of the world's fish stocks have been depleted or are in danger of being depleted. In terms of rain forest, we lose 2.4 acres *per second* and 78 million acres per year (the size of Poland)! And 137 species of plants and animals become extinct *each day* and 50,000 species every year.

Environmental theorist Thomas Fraser Homer-Dixon projects that future civil violence, war, and floods of refugees will often be caused by scarcities in resources such as water, cropland, forests, and fish. The countries most threatened by such resource scarcities will be most likely to turn to "hard regimes" of concentrated authoritarian military power.[56] Such developments are stimulated by existing foreign aid priorities: Big military spenders get about twice as much aid per head as do the less belligerent.

Environmental journalist Robert D. Kaplan projects that West Africa symbolizes the future for much of the developing world: deforested, hungry, waterless areas with massive population riddled with disease, crime, and anarchy. He notes: "Part of the globe is inhabited by Hegel's and Fukuyama's Last Man, healthy, well fed, and pampered by technology. The other, large, part is inhabited by Hobbes's First Man, condemned to a life that is "poor, nasty, brutish, and short." Although both parts will be threatened by environmental stress, the Last Man will be able to master it; the First Man will not."[57]

Another school of environmental thought accepts this analysis and argues that the management of global environmental change must be linked to definable processes of social and collective learning if improvement is to be expected.[58] Aid policies must be targeted to convert nations suffering from policies of negative transparency, in which they are overwhelmed with news of pollution, sickness, crime, inflation, and underdevelopment, to policies of positive transparency, which place hard facts in a context of hope with a concrete plan for sustained local economic development. Collective learning, in short, must be made a tool of concrete, targeted recipes for "green-growth consciousness" and self-help to create increasingly self-sufficient communities of environmentally sustainable access to work, food, water, and community self-confidence. The principle is to go from powerlessness to a sense of agency or positive self-determination by keeping money and jobs at home, adding value to existing resources and products, doing surveys to determine local and regional needs, upgrading the community aesthetically, refurbishing local cultural traditions, and involving everyone with enthusiasm in the project.[59] (See Chapter 10.)

IMPLICATIONS

From a collective learning perspective, foreign aid must be targeted for the economic interests of the countries involved, according to a model that links short-term help to long-term rewards and mutual benefits. Leaving the world markets alone to run their own course—an orthodox liberal policy—amounts to a de facto maintenance strategy that leaves existing inequalities between the North and South in place. This causes the gap between rich and poor to widen as the high technology and information revolutions speed up economic transactions, putting the underequipped or less informed farther and farther behind.

The North-South gap widened the decade after the debt crisis, which discouraged commercial banks from lending any new money to debtor nations (reinforced by new banking regulations). Money was granted for interest repayments on outstanding loans. But this caused increasing political unrest in Latin American democracies, which saw such a large share of scarce export earnings going to pay interest on debt rather than reinvested in their own economies.

By 1989, Latin American governments had paid $160 billion in interest on their $420 billion foreign debt, and to avoid default many of them cut back essential imports, reduced government spending, and watched economic growth and political support evaporate.[60]

The largest Latin American debtors saw themselves caught in a vicious circle or debt trap in which the banks granted them just enough money to tide them over until the next payment was due to avoid having to formally write off the loans and cause a crisis in world financial markets: This sense of running in place and never catching up with their collective economic problems led to a widespread political and economic malaise throughout Latin America.[61] Thus, in terms of change in per capita gross domestic product from 1981 to 1989: Mexico −9.2, Venezuela 24.9, Colombia 13.9, Brazil −0.4, Ecuador −1.1, Peru −24.7, Bolivia −26.6, Chile 9.6; and Argentina −23.5.

In the 1990s Chile and Bolivia benefited from tough austerity and free market measures (although at significant social cost—particularly for the poor). The younger generation of the established elite classes made a killing on privatization. Most people were not so fortunate, however, and poverty deepened.[62]

The 1985 plan of U.S. Treasury Secretary James Baker—to encourage more World Bank and commercial lending to debtor countries in return for privatization and opening up of their economies to foreigners—did not work. Nevertheless, as Baker was appointed secretary of state under President George Bush, the ideology behind the Baker Plan continued: Broken down on a case-by-case basis, a reformist liberal tried to head off political and economic crises in key countries (starting with Mexico) in terms of U.S. national interests on a cost-effective basis. Since the United States had itself run up debts amounting to nearly four times that of the greatest Latin American debtor (Brazil) by the end of the 1980s, there were financial constraints on how far the United States could go on its own to alleviate Third World debt. Europe and Japan became increasingly involved, whether they liked it or not. Indeed, the Lomé Convention provided one model that worked quite well in targeting aid to a large number of developing countries—sector-specific support benefiting donors and recipients alike in the long run. Rather than its typical short-term, put-out-the-fire crisis management, the U.S. government might do well to create its own form of Lomé Convention, building on the NAFTA agreement. The Japanese could do the same for their region. Both could do this by following through with their voluntary agreement to Agenda 21 of the Earth-Summit, targeting 1 percent of GNP for the "Earth Increment" in their own regional areas.

In the decade of the 1980s official development assistance from all sources ran about $55 billion annually, 90 percent of this coming from the industrialized countries of the OECD.[63]

In the 1985–1996 period, U.S. defense spending declined by 54 percent and was the lowest share of the GDP since 1940 (3.8 percent of GDP in 1996)[64] But this savings was not passed on in significantly increased development aid.

Until the Kosovo war in 1999, Clinton's defense spending reflected post-cold-war philosophy: No money for new fighter planes or tanks, but more money for environmental clean-up and U.N. peacekeeping operations. Clinton's budget had to fight the big deficits inherited from the Reagan and Bush administrations and follow strict spending caps legislated by Congress, leaving him little room for increasing items without much domestic support, such as foreign aid. As a result, the odds of the United States putting the "Earth Increment" on the agenda seem slim indeed. To move beyond what sociologist C. Wright Mills called "crack-pot realism," industrialized nations need to look beyond short-term economic and power interests to long-term regional and global strategies that integrate idealism and realism in mutual benefit packages. From Myrdal and the Swedes one learns not only that foreign aid is not morally neutral but that it can also further national ideological objectives to the extent these are long term and exportable. The prerequisite here for successful long-term support and success is not to mix kinds of aid just to get one bill through a parliament but to clearly distinguish humanitarian aid, development or modernization aid, and military assistance for national security from each other; and, as one moves from the humanitarian to the military, also shift from multilateral to bilateral organizations for financing.[65]

It is unrealistic to expect governments of developed countries to give foreign aid without targeting it to be consistent with their national interest. But those nation-states with long-term visions of global strategy and a positive, community-oriented rationale for foreign aid will reap the benefits of solidarity with allies, while those with short-term, defensive, national security band-aid policies will find themselves lining the pockets of corrupt authoritarian leaders, who in turn, generate more animosity than good-will toward the donor.[66]

Models of equality of economic opportunity should be cultivated as the rule in targeting aid, not the exception. Apart from aid, developing countries look to Newly Industrialized Countries (NICs) for models of successful internal development—longing for more independence (see Chapter 9).

In the post-cold-war economy, the International Labor Organization (ILO) reported in 1994 that some 30 percent of the world's labor force was unemployed or underemployed—more than ever before. By the end of that year, unemployment would reach over 8 percent in the industrialized nations alone. By 1998 global unemployment reached the highest level of joblessness since the Depression of the 1930s.[67]

QUESTIONS FOR THOUGHT

1. What characterizes the relationship between the South and the North in terms of attitudes toward one another, trade, and ways of living?

2. Briefly summarize the borrowing policies of the World Bank. What changes were introduced by McNamara taking over the presidency? By Wolfensohn?

3. What are the key achievements of the Lomé Convention and why can OPEC be said to have inspired the push for a New International Economic Order (NIEO)?

4. Outline the mechanisms that led from the quadrupling of oil prices to the debt crisis. Illustrate a "debt trap" situation by briefly discussing the case of Mexico. Why weren't the loans officially declared in default and written off as losses?

5. Evaluate the concept of foreign aid for the developing countries after considering the different schools of thought and facts mentioned in the text. Consider the dependency thesis, the Brandt Report, and the environmental perspective. Without foreign aid, is there really no Third World? (Bauer/Yamey)

6. How might one account for the highest world unemployment since the Great Depression emerging simultaneously with the record 1990s economic boom in the United States?

NOTES

1. Mahbub ul Haq, "The New International Economic Order," paper presented at the Faculty Seminar on International Economy at Columbia University, December 17, 1975. See Haq's *The Poverty Curtain: Choices for the Third World* (New York: Columbia University Press, 1976).

2. *World Economic Survey* 1992 (New York: United Nations, 1992), p. 74.
3. Fiametta Rocco, "ADB Becomes Premier Source of Credit," *International Herald Tribune*, September 28, 1987, p. 10.
4. William Clark, "Robert McNamara at the World Bank," *Foreign Affairs* (fall 1981): 171–174.
5. See Richard W. Stevenson, "The Chief Banker for the Nations at the Bottom of the Heap," *New York Times*, September 14, 1997. Also see Bruce Stokes, "Wolfensohn's World," *National Journal*, 29, no. 38 (September 20, 1997): 1846.
6. "Cleaning Up Thailand's Mess: The Long Struggle Ahead," *Business Week*, October 12, 1998, 120–122.
7. See Stephen D. Krasner, "Oil Is the Exception," *Foreign Policy* 14 (spring 1974): 68–84.
8. Edward L. Morse, "After the Fall: The Politics of Oil," *Foreign Affairs* 64, no. 4 (spring 1986): 793.
9. On prerequisites for successful producer cartels, see C. Fred Bergsten, "The Threat from the Third World," *Foreign Policy* (summer 1973): 102–124; and Benson Varon and Kenji Takenchi, "Developing Countries and Non-Fuel Minerals," *Foreign Affairs* 52 (1974): 497–510.
10. See Karl P. Sauvant and Hajo Hasenpflug, eds., *The New International Economic Order. Confrontation or Cooperation between North and South?* (Boulder, CO: Westview Press, 1977).
11. Ibid, pp. 165–166.
12. Commission of the European Communities, "The Lomé Convention: The Stabilization of Export Earnings," *Information Development and Cooperation*, no. 94 (1975): 2–3.
13. "The European Community in the World," European File, Commission of the European Communities (Brussels, Belgium, October 1986), pp. 9–10.
14. Adrianus Koetsenruijter, "A Review of Financial Cooperation under the Lomé Convention," *The ACP-EEC Courier* (Brussels: Commission of the European Communities), no. 132 (March–April 1992): 4–9.
15. See *The Global Partnership for Environment and Development: A Guide to Agenda* 21 (Geneva: UNCED, 1992).
16. Michael Zammit Cutjar, *UNCTAD and the North-South Dialogue. The First Twenty Years* (Oxford: Pergamon Press, 1985).
17. See Donald J. Puchala, ed., *Issues Before the 35th General Assembly of the United Nations 1980–1981* (New York: United Nations Association of the United States, 1980), pp. 73–104.
18. Sharon L. Holt and Helena Ribe, "Developing Financial Institutions for the Poor and Reducing Barriers to Access for Women" (Washington, D.C.: The World Bank, 1991).
19. See S. R. Khandker, Z. Khan, and B. Khalily, "Grameen Bank: Performance and Sustainability," *World Bank Discussion Paper* 306, 1995; and "Sustainability of a Government Targeted Credit Program: Evidence from Bangladesh," *World Bank Discussion Paper* 316, 1995 by the same authors.
20. Christopher A. Kojm, ed., *The Problem of International Debt* (New York: H. W. Wilson Co., 1984), p. 14. See also Philip A. Wellons, *Passing the Buck: Governments and the Third World Debt* (Cambridge, MA: Harvard Business School Press, 1987); Miles Kahler, "Politics and International Debt: Explaining the Crisis," *International Organization* 39, no. 3 (summer 1985): 357–382; and Michael Palmer and Kenneth R. Gordon, "External Indebtedness and Debt Servicing Problems of Developing Countries," *Columbia Journal of World Business* (spring 1985): 37–43.
21. C. Bogdanowicz-Bindert, "Financial Crisis of 1982: A Debtor's Perspective," in *International Banking and Global Financing*, ed. S. K. Kaushik (New York: Pace University, 1983), pp. 203–204.
22. Luis Catan, "The Future of Debtor Countries in Latin America," in *The Debt Crisis and Financial Stability*, ed. S. K. Kaushik (New York: Pace University, 1985), pp. 17–31. Also see Jorge I. Dominguez, *Mexico's Political Economy* (London: Sage Publications, 1982); and C. W. Reynolds and C. Tello, *U.S.-Mexico Relations* (Stanford, CA: Stanford University Press,

1983). On money going into Swiss accounts, see Curtis Skinner, "The Next Earth-quake," *Commonweal* (July 11, 1986): 397.

23. Ibid., p. 398.

24. Brian O'Reilly, "Doing Business on Mexico's Volcano," *Fortune*, August 29, 1988, 74.

25. "The Mexican Worker," *Business Week*, April 19, 1993, 85–92.

26. Paul B. Carroll and Craig Torres, "As Elections Approach, the Uprising in Mexico Is Shaking Up Politics," *Wall Street Journal*, February 7, 1994.

27. House of Representatives, Committee on Foreign Affairs, "Global Debt Crisis: Mexican Debt Situation" (Washington, D.C.: U.S. Congress, July 30, 1986), p. 58. See also "U.S. Senate Committee on Finance, Subcommittee on International Debt, Hearings on Third World Debt," April 6, 1987, 100th Congress, 1st session, U.S. Superintendent of Public Documents, 1987.

28. *World Debt Tables 1991–92* (Washington, D.C.: The World Bank, 1992), p. 25.

29. Kojm, *Problem of International Debt*, p. 38.

30. Karin Lissakers, "More Funds for Mexico, More Debt Trap," *New York Times*, November 8, 1988. For alternative views, see Benjamin J. Cohen, "International Debt and U.S. Policy," *International Organization* 39, no. 4 (autumn 1985): 699–727; and Henry S. Bienen and Mark Gersovitz, "Economic Stabilization, Conditionality, and Political Stability," pp. 729–754 in the same issue.

31. For a neo-Marxist interpretation of the debt trap, see Cheryl Payer, *The Debt Trap: The IMF and the Third World* (New York: Monthly Review Press, 1974).

32. W. W. Rostow, *Why the Poor Get Richer and the Rich Slow Down* (Austin, TX: The University of Texas Press, 1980).

33. For an example of the reformist liberal perspective, see Albert Fishlow, "A New International Economic Order: What Kind?" in A. Fishlow et al., *Rich and Poor Nations in the World Economy* (New York: McGraw-Hill, 1978). Also see Robert E. Wood, *From Marshall Plan to Debt Crisis: Foreign Aid and Development Choices in the World Economy* (Berkeley, CA: University of California Press, 1986).

34. See Robert S. McNamara, Address to the Board of Governors, International Bank for Reconstruction and Development, October 2, 1979 (Washington, D.C.: IBRD); and R. McNamara, "The Population Problem," *Foreign Affairs* 62 (summer 1984).

35. See Hedley Bull, *The Anarchical Society* (New York: Columbia University Press, 1977); Robert W. Tucker, *The Inequality of Nations* (New York: Basic Books, 1977); and Stephen D. Krasner, *Structural Conflict: The Third World Against Global Liberalism* (Berkeley, CA: University of California Press, 1985).

36. Robert Keohane and Joseph Nye, *Power and Interdependence* (Boston, MA: Little, Brown, 1977). See also *World Economic and Social Survey 1998: Trends and Policies in the World Economy* (New York: United Nations, 1998).

37. See, for example, André Gunder Frank, *Latin America: Underdevelopment or Revolution* (New York: Monthly Review Press, 1969); Arghiri Emmanuel, *Unequal Exchange: A Study of the Imperialism of Trade* (New York: Monthly Review Press, 1972); and Samire Amin, *Accumulation on a World Scale: A Critique of the Theory of Development*, 2 vols. (New York: Monthly Review Press, 1974).

38. Organization for Economic Cooperation and Development, *Development Cooperation 1980 Review* (Paris: OECD, 1980), p. 99.

39. See Robert S. Walters, *American and Soviet Aid: A Comparative Analysis* (Pittsburgh, PA: University of Pittsburgh Press, 1970), p. 240.

40. Gunnar Myrdal, *The Challenge of World Poverty: A World Anti-Poverty Program in Outline* (New York: Random House, 1970), p. 338.

41. See Leon Gordenker, *International Aid and National Decisions* (Princeton, NJ: Princeton University Press, 1976), pp. 57–58, 67.

42. Willy Brandt and Anthony Sampson, eds., *North-South: A Program for Survival* (Cambridge, MA: MIT Press, 1980).

43. See, for example, Steven Weisman, ed., *The Trojan Horse: A Radical Look at Foreign Aid* (San Francisco, CA: Ramparts Press, 1974); and Teresa Hayter, *Aid as Imperialism* (Middlesex, England: Penguin, 1971).

44. Payer, *The Debt Trap*.

45. See Shlomo Avineri, ed., *Karl Marx on Colonialism and Modernization* (Garden City, NY: Anchor Books, 1969).

46. V. I. Lenin, *Imperialism: The Highest Stage of Capitalism* (New York: International Publishers, 1917, 1939), p. 65

47. Theotonio Dos Santos, "The Structure of Dependence," *American Economic Preview* 60 (May 1970): 231.

48. Robert Gilpin, "The Issue of Dependency and Economic Development," Chapter 7 in *The Political Economy of International Relations* (Princeton, NJ: Princeton University Press, 1987), p. 282.

49. Ibid, pp. 285–286. See, for example, Peter Evans, *Dependent Development: The Alliance of Multinational, State and Local Capital in Brazil* (Princeton, NJ: Princeton University Press, 1979).

50. Krasner, *Structural Conflict*, pp. 97–101.

51. Immanuel Wallerstein, "The Future of the World Economy," in *The Global Agenda*, ed. Charles Kegley and Eugene Wittkopf (New York: Random House, 1984), p. 279. For a critical view of Wallerstein, see Theda Skocpol, "Wallerstein's World Capitalist System: A Theoretical and Historical Critique," *American Journal of Sociology* 82 (March 1977): 1075–1090.

52. See Hans O. Schmitt, "Development Assistance: A View from Bretton Woods," *Public Policy* (fall 1973).

53. Peter T. Bauer and Basil S. Yamey, "Foreign Aid: What Is at Stake?" in *The Third World: Premises of U.S. Policy*, ed. W. Scott Thompson (San Francisco, CA: Institute of Contemporary Studies, 1983), p. 117. See also Bryan Johnson et al., *1998 Index of Economic Freedom* (Washington, D.C.: The Heritage Foundation, 1998).

54. "Foreign Aid: The Kindness of Strangers," *The Economist*, May 7, 1994, 20.

55. The statistics above are from Robert D. Kaplan, "The Coming Anarchy," *Atlantic Monthly* 273, no. 2 (February 1994): 48, 60. Also see Paul Kennedy, *Preparing for the Twenty-First Century* (New York: Random House, 1993).

56. Thomas Fraser Homer-Dixon, "On the Threshold: Environmental Changes as Causes of Acute Conflict," *International Security* (fall 1991); and T. Homer-Dixon, *Environment, Scarcity and Violence* (Princeton, NJ: Princeton University Press, 1999).

57. Kaplan, "The Coming Anarchy," p. 60.

58. See, for example, E. Parson and W. Clark, "Learning to Manage Global Environmental Change: A Review of Relevant Theory," *Discussion Paper 91-13 of The Center for Science and International Affairs* (Boston, MA: John F. Kennedy School of Government, 1991). Also see Hilary French, "Rebuilding the World Bank," in Lester Brown et al., *The State of the World 1994* (New York: W. W. Norton: 1994), pp. 156–176.

59. First presented in R. Isaak, "Developing Country Recipes for Collective Learning, Economic Development and Global Environmental Responsibility," a paper given at the International Environmental Institutions Research Seminar at Harvard's Center for Science and International Affairs, Dec. 11, 1992. Revised version presented at the International Studies Association Convention in Acapulco, Mexico, March 27, 1993. Published as *Working Paper No. 116*, November 1993, The Center for Applied Research, The Lubin School, Pace University, Pace Plaza, NY, NY 10038. See also R. Isaak, *Green Logic: Ecopreneurship, Theory and Ethics* (West Hartford, CT: Kumarian Press, 1999; Sheffield, U.K.: Greenleaf Press, 1998).

60. Alan Riding, "Latins Want Bush to Help on Debts," *New York Times*, November 29, 1988.

61. Sarah Bartlett, "A Vicious Circle Keeps Latin America in Debt," *New York Times*, January 15, 1989.

62. Henry Veltmeyer's analysis of Latin America, which illustrates deepening and broadening poverty as the social cost of privatization: Panel on "Neoliberal Programs of Adjustment," International Studies Association Convention, Acapulco, Mexico, March 26, 1993.

63. See *Development Cooperation*, Paris: Organization of Economic Cooperation and Development, Dec. 1991, p. 172.

64. "The Morning after High Noon," *The Economist* 340 (August 10, 1997): 20.

65. See "Public Opinion, Foreign Policy Making and Foreign Aid," Chapter 6 of R. Isaak, *American Democracy and World Power* (New York: St. Martin's Press, 1977).

66. Or, as economist Barbara Ward put it: "In all this welter of Western insistence upon self-interest and self-defense, one looks in vain for any consistent exposition of a positive policy of foreign aid, some general political philosophy to match the Communist confidence in world brotherhood based on Socialist production, some framework of solidarity between givers and takers of aid, some aspect of human concern beyond the narrow limits of common fear." In B. Ward's "For a New Foreign Aid Concept," in *Readings in American Foreign Policy*, ed. Robert A. Goldwin and Harry M. Clor (New York: Oxford University Press, 1970), p. 582.

67. ILO statistics and projections as cited in "The Labor Letter," *Wall Street Journal*, February 8, 1994. For the knowledge gap between the developed and developing countries see The World Bank, *World Development Report: Knowledge for Development* (New York: Oxford University Press, 1999). See also Nancy Birdsall, "Life Is Unfair: Inequality in the World," *Foreign Policy*, no. 111 (summer 1998): 76–93.

MULTINATIONAL STRATEGY, DIRECT INVESTMENT, AND TECHNOLOGY

Capitalism places every man in competition with his fellows for a share of the available wealth. A few people accumulate big piles, but most do not. The sense of community falls victim to this struggle. The good of the private corporation is seen as prior to the public good. The world market system tightens control in the capitalist countries and terrorizes the Third World. All things are manipulated to these ends.

—Donald Barthelme, "The Rise of Capitalism" (1972)

Although the purpose and tone of a Greenpeace executive meeting in Tokyo will differ from a meeting of IBM executives in New York, both sets of executives will use the language of scientific rationalism. Like the automatic weapon, the U.S. dollar, the business suit, and the English language, scientific rationalism is now a global tool.

—Ralph Pettman, "Limits to Rationalist Understanding" (1997)

THE LINK BETWEEN THE MULTINATIONAL CORPORATION AND DEVELOPING COUNTRIES IS INITIALLY a rational, strategic one from the perspective of multinational managers. Since they hold the upper hand, it is useful to take this rational, strategic perspective for a moment and to view individual, corporate, and state economic behavior in this all-too-clear light. The factors that make up the bargaining power of the multinational company in the host developing country can be more easily understood in terms of the structural limits such strategic behavior encounters. And technology, that ultimate extension of applied scientific rationalism, plays its role as well in this struggle of the elite to get the most of what they can get in negotiating with those more dependent who will grant what they must.

ORIGINS

STRATEGIC BEHAVIOR

An examination of individual, corporate, and state economic behavior in the late twentieth century in terms of the maintenance model (see Chapter 1 and Figure 1-1) revealed at least four types of strategic behavior (expressed here as

Weberian ideal types—or characteristic typifications of particular categories of behavior):[1]

1. *Defeatist*: takes as few risks as possible, cutting costs rather than risking assets; past-oriented, passive, defensive, plagued by a fear of loss and a neurotic conservative impulse; thrifty in consumption with a security-oriented portfolio mix.
2. *Free-Rider*: takes high risks at no cost or low cost, specializing in living at someone else's expense; present-oriented with active-passive motivation or *maximin*—*max*imizing individual gains and *min*imizing personal costs; high individual consumption when others pay, low otherwise; portfolio mix centered on cheap money or upon debt at low interest rates.
3. *Maintenance*: takes limited risks at moderate cost to keep up with business cycle and inflation; present-oriented, short-term realism guided by passive-active motivation, seeking to co-opt change in order to assure stability; consumes high quality now before costs go higher; portfolio mix stresses stable returns, liquidity, diversity and flexibility.
4. *Entrepreneurial*: takes high risks even at high costs; aims to come out ahead of inflation and present stage of business cycle; aggressive motivation stemming from tension between perception of handicap and potential advantage; seeks to thrust all energy and resources into direction of highest probable payoff, future-oriented; all-or-nothing consumption: "prince or pauper"; portfolio mix focused upon highest return through astute gambles on the business cycle.

These four types of strategic behavior were derived from analyzing individual, corporate, and state reactions to inflation. But they have wider applicability. For our purposes, they can be consolidated into two basic types, which can then be described in terms of how they are mixed: the maintenance versus the entrepreneurial. (The "defeatist" type can be dropped as descriptive of "sick" or pathological strategic behavior that does not get us further in terms of knowing what types of positive behavior to adopt.)

The "free-rider" behavior pattern, however, is more interesting. The work of Professor Howard Stevenson at Harvard University implies that the entrepreneur or "promoter" may actually be one particularly creative variety of "free-rider." Stevenson argues that *entrepreneurship is a behavior or process by which individuals pursue opportunities without regard to the resources they currently control.*[2] The wise entrepreneur, in fact, may specialize in taking risks with *other* people's resources. For Stevenson, the contrast with the entrepreneur is the administrative "trustee"— what we call the maintenance man or mode of behavior. The **maintenance manager** or **trustee** is driven by resources currently controlled, tends toward formalized, promotion-oriented hierarchy in organization, and is security-driven. The **entrepreneur** or **promoter**, in contrast, is driven by the perception of opportunity or is value-driven, is often team-oriented, and relies on performance-based, flat, informal modes of organization.[3]

These two basic types of strategy can be mixed to give a recipe for managing economic change. Economist Paul Samuelson maintained that to cure the economic dilemmas of the United States required more savings in order to prepare the way for more investment.[4] Or, translated into our strategy types, by making the maintenance base more efficient through cost-cutting and saving on the part of government and corporate trustees or maintenance managers, more capital can be targeted for investment by entrepreneurs or promoters in order to create new businesses, economic growth, and jobs. Paradoxically, the American boom that continued through 1999 was based on a reverse variation of this strategy: Maximize individual consumption through almost unlimited credit as the economic engine, while reducing government deficits (the government's maintenance base) to keep taxes down and to stimulate entrepreneurship (job creation) and consumer spending (see Chapter 9).

A **strategy** is a blueprint or intentional plan for the future, a cognitive design that can be both personal and organizational. **Strategic behavior**, on the other hand, refers to patterns of individual or collective behavior after it has occurred. Strategy stems from the "in-order-to motive" whereas strategic behavior is analyzed from the "because-of motive." Changes in the environment lead to adaptations of strategic behavior as collective learning takes place through the adoption of a series of strategies.

In many cases people do not *choose* a specific type of strategy as much as they *fall into it* as a result of the socioeconomic and information sources available to them at that moment. For example, in coping with inflation, rich individuals, corporations, and states have overwhelmingly illustrated the *maintenance* strategy. This strategic behavior is probably not due to rational choice (since maintenance is often not the best strategy), but more apt to be due to the future-shock effect of being overwhelmed with more change than can be digested.[5]

Strategies, in short, are symptoms of structural positions in the world economy as much as they are constellations of choice. This is what Kierkegaard meant when he said, "I feel like the piece in the chess game that is not allowed to be moved." Decision-makers in Ethiopia and Bangladesh with little structural flexibility can identify with Kierkegaard's remark. Given that almost all human institutions and organizations are being "outpositioned" by the pace of technological and socioeconomic change, there are times when almost anyone can sense that the strategy they have chosen is the inevitable outgrowth of the structural position in which they find themselves as much as it is due to any freedom of will.

This does not mean that global structures *always* penetrate to individual cognition or that theorists always reflect the structural interests of countries from which they emerge. Free will exists, but not in a cultural or structural vacuum. The individual's *strategy* today—that is, his or her future-oriented intentional plan—must be distinguished from individual or group *strategic behavior* tomorrow—the actual behavior performed in cultural, structural, and historical context. Effective collective learning can be measured by the extent to which groups of individuals overcome traditional patterns of behavior or habits that have become maladaptive and replace them with effective strategies that result in more opportunities for the exercise of free will or autonomy by the company or state in the world economy.

Major American automobile companies, for example, found themselves outpositioned by foreign competition in the late 1970s—thrust into the defeatist category by the latest wave of creative destruction in the global economy. Rather than adopting entrepreneurial strategies to escape from their position of structural stalemate and noncompetitiveness, these U.S. companies fell back on defensive maintenance strategies, which blocked their potential adaptiveness. Chrysler even found itself in a free-rider position, accepting subsidies from the U.S. government, which also introduced "voluntary export restraints" (tariffs by another name) to keep out the Japanese competition until the American companies had time to adapt. The automakers responded with more sophisticated maintenance strategies, forming joint ventures with Japanese car companies so as to be competitively positioned when the export restraints were removed: "If you can't beat them, join them."

The wave of mergers and joint ventures among multinational companies in the 1980s and peaking in the late 1990s (see Figure 4-1 and Figure 4-2, page 119, and Figure 11-1, page 291) represented maintenance strategies of coping with the creative destruction of global competition. Smaller car companies (American Motors) were taken over by bigger ones. Chrysler joined Daimler-Benz.

A similar shakedown occurred in the airline industry. Three major airline manufacturers emerged from the competitive trauma: Boeing, McDonnell Douglas, and Airbus. Airbus Industrie illustrates an astute blend between maintenance and entrepreneurial strategies. Founded in 1970 as a consortium of Western Europe's leading aircraft manufacturers (the maintenance base, supported by billions of dollars of state subsidies), the Airbus 320 became the fastest selling plane in aviation history during the 1980s, given its technological edge with a fully computerized flight-control system (the entrepreneurial innovation of the strategic mix).

Nor had the American competitors much grounds for complaint: U.S. government military contracts in the era of American hegemony after World War II enabled Boeing, Lockheed, and McDonnell and Douglas (which had not yet merged) to account for about 90 percent of all airline sales outside the Communist bloc by the late 1960s. Building on the mixed experience of the French-British Concorde, Airbus became the European symbol of a joint industrial policy of technological competitiveness to match the *Pentagon Inc.* industrial policy of the United States. As *Pentagon Inc.* was scaled back after the collapse of the U.S.S.R., the Clinton administration began to intervene on the side of the American airlines industry in head-to-head industrial policy exchanges with the Europeans.[6] Such differences in industrial policies in reaction to the cycles of creative destruction that characterize global capitalism can only be explained by defining the structures that make up these different political economies.

STRUCTURES AND DEPENDENCE

At least five primary structures make up the maintenance base of each state (or multinational organization) in the world economy, which together determine its competitive structural position and relative independence or dependence:[7]

1. *The security structure*: the maintenance of order both within the organization or state and outside—within the international system at large.
2. *The money and credit structure*: the stability and relative value of the currency and the sources and flexibility of short- and long-term finance.
3. *The knowledge structure*: literacy rates, technological competitiveness, training systems, and the distribution of critical economic information and skills throughout the population.
4. *The production structure*: the way resources are organized and the knowledge structure is utilized to determine what is produced.
5. *The value structure*: a cluster of psycho-cultural beliefs and ideological preferences that transcend and color "the rational"—what the people predominantly *choose* to learn. In many cases traditional value structures block states from becoming what Karl Deutsch called "adaptive-learning states" (post-1868 Japan, for example), which are able to change political and economic structures to cope with some major problem in the environment.[8]

Thus, **political economy** can be viewed as the collective capacity of a state or multinational organization to structure payoffs for effective learning or adaptation in the global system—or the study of learning by paying if such adaptation is blocked.[9]

The particular combination of these five primary structures determines the potential power of one state or multinational organization compared to others in the world economy. **Power** is the social capacity to satisfy human needs or wants relative to competitors: It is always increasing or diminishing.* Powerful states, for example, can be described in terms of surpluses in their **structural assets**. What sociologist Max Weber might have termed the "ideal type" of Great Power state would be characterized by a surplus of security (nuclear deterrents, armed forces, military preparedness); a surplus of money and credit (a strong international reserve position, a creditor nation); a surplus of production (high gross national product growth, balance of trade surplus, a diverse, competitive industrial capacity); a surplus of knowledge (a deep and wide infrastructure of research and development, high productivity in innovative technologies, a national literacy rate higher than required for most job functions); and a surplus of value consensus (a widespread anti-inflation, prosavings consensus, absence of ideological polarization, a community spirit that comes together to permit adaptation to new global challenges).

---

*This definition stresses the ability of collective consensus to create solutions to adapt to change rather than power as mere materialistic distribution or authoritative allocation of values in the status quo. See R. Hummel and R. Isaak, *Politics for Human Beings*, 2nd ed. (Belmont, CA: Wadsworth, 1980), p. 34.

Thus, the world political economy can be envisioned as a hierarchy of states spread between structural surpluses and structural deficits, between relative independence and dependence.

The aim of the nation-state is to use its potential power and influence to achieve self-sufficiency and independence with enough surpluses to serve as a buffer against global change. But absolute self-sufficiency or independence is no longer possible to achieve. As political scientist Richard Rosecrance put it: "To be fully independent, an aggressor would now need the oil of the Persian Gulf, the iron ore, bauxite, and uranium of Australia, the chromium of Zimbabwe and South Africa, and the granaries of Canada, Australia and the American West."[10]

The typical cycle of creative destruction or of capitalism is oversimplified for the sake of illustration in Figure 6-1. The cycle begins with creation. For example, in political economies still at the traditional premoney barter stage of trading, the creation of money and credit structures makes possible the technological innovation that is the engine of creative destruction. Historically, financial innovation (through the creation of money and credit structures) precedes technological innovation (or productivity increases in the maintenance base through industrial revolutions). In traditional barter societies, the same individuals perform the functions of producing, saving, and investing—"Jacks of all trades." But the creation of money, or credit financing through debt, permits a splitting off (or "specializing") of producers from savers on the one hand, and of savers from investors, on the other. Individuals who have not earned, saved, or inherited capital can borrow it on credit to make dynamic, risky, innovative investments, the "entrepreneurship" leading to **syntropy** or economic integration in the cycle. **Inflation,**

Figure 6-1   Strategies, Structures, and Cycles of World Economy

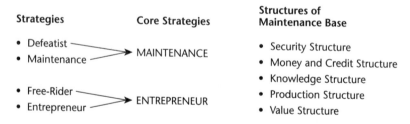

Strategies	Core Strategies	Structures of Maintenance Base
• Defeatist • Maintenance	→ MAINTENANCE	• Security Structure • Money and Credit Structure • Knowledge Structure
• Free-Rider • Entrepreneur	→ ENTREPRENEUR	• Production Structure • Value Structure

Cycle of Creative Destruction (or Capitalism)

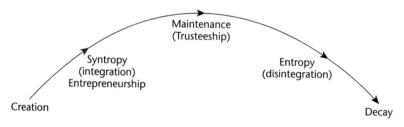

Maintenance
(Trusteeship)

Syntropy
(integration)
Entrepreneurship

Entropy
(disintegration)

Creation

Decay

or more money chasing fewer goods, is the inevitable result. Inflation serves as the lubricator for innovative investment and as the liberator of resources held by conservative property-owning individuals through the mechanism of credit. The creation of money and credit structures thus leads to technological innovation, which leads to entrepreneurship, industrial revolution, and a diffusion of power of the propertied classes. Societies are democratized through inflationary financing (the creation of credit cards, for instance). But as this environment risks becoming overheated with economic growth, the maintenance managers or trustees of organizations and states have to worry about reducing the costs of maintenance of their organizations and about financing entrepreneurial innovation to keep up with the technological state-of-the-art of global competition. To fail at either of these management functions prevents another positive cycle of economic growth from emerging and leads inevitably to **entropy** or disintegration, ultimately resulting in the decay of the economic organization.

Managers of all nation-states and multinational organizations have to cope with domestic and global waves of creative destruction simultaneously. Those able to build up surpluses in security, money and credit, knowledge, production, and value structures position themselves for a moment of global hegemony. Inevitably their maintenance managers or trustees slip and hegemony begins to slide toward entropy and decay, making space for other states to rise economically, using the stability provided by the declining hegemon as a springboard. To revive, a country needs to attract direct investment. But here, as in most places in the world economy, the playing field is uneven and the same places receive the lion's share of the resources as the largest firms tend towards oligopolistic concentration.

DIRECT INVESTMENT: OLIGOPOLY AND THE LAW OF UNEVEN DEVELOPMENT

In tracing the development of companies from workshop to factory to national corporation to multidivisional corporation to multinational corporation, economist Stephen Hymer argued that oligopolies were the leaders in direct investment, which is concentrated in the metropolitan centers (or metropoles) of advanced developed countries, leaving everywhere else—the periphery—underdeveloped.[11] It is not just a question of increase in size: Corporate growth is qualitative as well as quantitative, evolving increasingly complex administrative and communication systems, or "brains." The statistics support Hymer's argument: By the early 1980s, of the top fifteen recipients of direct investment only four were generally not classified as developed countries: South Africa, Brazil, Mexico, and Hong Kong. The less developed countries (LDCs) accounted for only about 31 percent of foreign-owned affiliates, 54 percent being in Europe.[12] Hymer forecasts that money and new plant construction from the rich nations will continue to flow disproportionately to the most developed sections of the rich countries, financing technological and economic innovation and development there at the expense of all the peripheral areas of the world where the investment could have gone. Because of the "learning-by-doing" effects of this deepening of capital, two different worlds of education and economic sophistication emerge as the gap between them grows.

Hymer's vision is one of an emerging imperial economic hierarchy headed by oligopolistic multinational corporations that eventually reach an "oligopolistic equilibrium" following an acute competitive phase aimed at increasing global market share. This "Imperial System" will follow the "Law of Uneven Development" as it creates poverty as well as wealth, underdevelopment as well as development. The division of labor between geographic regions corresponds to the vertical division of labor within the company. High-level decision making in the system will be centralized in the metropoles—a few key cities in the advanced countries. The metropoles, in turn, are surrounded by a number of regional subcapitals. The rest of the world (the periphery) is confined to low levels of activity and income—having the status of villages or towns in the Imperial System. The metropoles monopolize income, status, authority, and consumption. They share some with the regional subcapitals but with declining curves of these values as one moves from the (metropole) center to the periphery, perpetuating a pattern of inequality and dependency. New York, London, Tokyo, Berlin, Paris, and Beijing become the major centers of high level strategic planning in the Imperial System, while lesser cities deal with day-to-day operations. And the "best" and highest-paid professionals—administrators, doctors, lawyers, scientists, educators, government officials, actors, and servants—will be concentrated in or near the metropoles. Even *within* the developing world, advantages concentrate in regions with budding metropoles. See, for example, the flows of the direct foreign investment into developing Asia, China, and Latin American in contrast with Africa and the Middle East (see Figure 6-2).

**Figure 6-2   Cumulative FDI Inflows (in $ Billion)
into Selected Developing Regions, 1988–1994**

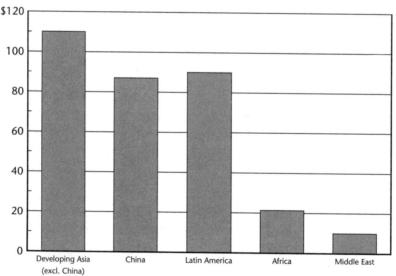

Source: IMF, Balance of Payments Yearbook, 1995.

Hymer's vision is prophetic in terms of the concentration of economic and political power. Statistically, the metropoles and their suburbs are responsible for being the greatest producers of new patents—the indicator of cutting-edge research and development. Corporate, government, and academic institutions in the metropoles often have a leadtime of at least six months in receiving information on new technological and economic innovations, giving them a competitive edge in a fast-moving global economy and perpetuating their dominance over subsidiary and lesser institutions located in the periphery. If information is power in the high-tech/high-information global economy, then sitting at the source of new information is a prerequisite to political and economic competitiveness. And the most sophisticated technologies for sorting out the quick from the dead are often concentrated in the metropoles in such quantity as to make a qualitative difference in the levels of information flows received by inhabitants of these privileged areas. Collective learning happens faster here and in a concentrated manner, thus intensifying the learning and experience curves hypothesized by economist Kenneth Arrow and the Boston Consulting Group.[13] The metropoles are staging grounds for static and dynamic economies of scale that propel institutions there ahead of others.

HOST COUNTRY VERSUS HOME MULTINATIONAL BARGAINING POWER

Having one's headquarters in one of the world's key metropoles can help maximize the bargaining power of a multinational corporation in dealing with host countries in the periphery where it makes direct or portfolio investments. Theodore H. Moran identified three other variables perhaps even more crucial in determining the negotiating balance of power between multinational corporations and host countries: (1) the extent of competition in the industry (or, How unstable are the oligopolies?); (2) the changeableness of the technology (or, How fast is it changing?); and (3) the importance of marketing and product differentiation. Bargaining power for the multinational corporation is high relative to the host country if competition is low, if technology is changeable, and if the importance of marketing is high. On the other hand, host countries can be expected to have high bargaining power if competition is high, if technology is stable, and if marketing is of little importance. Moran projects increasing power for Third-World host countries as bargaining power changes over time, as the host countries move up a learning curve, and as the viability of economic nationalism in Third-World countries increases.[14]

The shift in bargaining power from First-World-based multinationals to Third-World host countries began in the 1970s with the success of OPEC stimulating Third-World economic nationalism and largely frustrated efforts at forming other commodity cartels. Host governments became more sophisticated in their bargaining conditions. However, with the widespread debt crisis in developing countries in the 1980s, bargaining power shifted back the other way. Desperately in need of new capital, developing countries had to make major concessions—particularly on initial corporate tax rates in order to lure First-World multinational companies into uncertain political and economic environments. Standing to gain from better use of production factors and idle resources and from upgrading resources and production with new technology and investment, developing countries bent over backward to attract foreign companies.

The risks involving the exploitation of their prime resources, the replacement of local firms by the multinationals, the potential destruction of local entrepreneurship—not to mention increasing dependence upon foreign influence—were understated for the sake of short-term economic gains that could bolster the power position of elected officials in the Third World.

In the late 1980s and 1990s, a strategy emerged in the Third World to consolidate the gains in bargaining power of the nation-state made in the 1970s with the economies of scale made possible through organizing large multinational enterprises by subsidizing the creation of Third World-based multinationals.[15] The success of efforts to use homegrown multinationals as arms of state economic policy depends not just on obtaining start-up financing but upon the previous success of transfers of technology.

THE PRODUCT CYCLE AND TECHNOLOGY TRANSFER

That which has been called "the product cycle" almost always begins in the developed countries where high-income market economies provide an environment conducive to both technological innovation and the flexibility and maintenance risk insurance facilitating the commercial applications of technological change. The United States is the prime example. Its large domestic market; loose, flexible labor structure; high-income consumption; and collective tendency to try out "the new" make it an optimal testing ground for new products. The entrepreneurial culture spawns new product innovation. It also serves as a basis for the hegemonic role of the United States (as the entrepreneurial culture *par excellence*) in the world economy since World War II, attracting direct foreign investment and portfolio investment with combinations of inventive investment options, political stability, attractive interest rates, receptiveness to innovation, a skilled and mobile labor pool, and multiple sources of capital and technology.

The **product life-cycle theory**—sometimes called the **neotechnologist school**—is divided into four stages: *introduction* or *innovation, growth, maturation,* and *decline.* At the *introductory stage,* a new product is created in a developed market economy where the cost of innovation is not a problem and the innovator does not have to worry about the product having a high initial price. Then, if the product succeeds, the *growth stage* commences and the product becomes widespread in the national market. When the product reaches the *maturity stage,* its production has become standardized and, therefore, cheaper to produce with unskilled labor. At this stage the product is exported, having satiated the domestic market. But given the standardization of production it soon becomes cheaper to produce the product in developing countries where the wages are lower than in the home country. Competition emerges as the technology is copied or adapted or bought. The foreign developing country then starts exporting the same product back into the home, developed country where it was born—the final *phase of decline.*[16]

Product-cycle theory assumes that information does not flow freely across national borders: Key technological processes related to production and marketing are concentrated and protected in certain developed countries—at least initially. Moreover, it assumes that each country has its own peculiar milieu, which is more or less conducive to technological change and which steers the direction of that change. Finally, the theory assumes that international trade is often directed by the particular stages that products happen to be in during their life-cycles, combined with the changing matrix of international marketing opportunities for the product.

The product life-cycle theory applies to many but not all products.[17] For example, the fashion industry moves so quickly, the creative destruction occurs so fast, that the product life-cycle theory hardly applies as the new is constantly replacing the old.[18] But if it can be established that the theory covers most products, a major cause for the inequality between the developed and developing countries will be confirmed. For the rich, developed countries where the innovations initially take place get the most profits out of the products in the early phases of their life cycle. By the time the products are in decline, the multinationals in the metropoles have more innovative replacements ready to launch on the markets in order to maintain market leadership, if not domination.[19] The developing countries are given recycled technologies by the developed countries after quite a bit of the juice has been drained from them.

Benjamin Franklin argued that technological innovations of any kind should be shared freely with mankind. But that was in the eighteenth century. He would never have dreamed that the United States might one day attempt to live more off selling the patents for technological innovations and their servicing than from producing agricultural or manufactured goods. In service-sector-dominated developed economies, the control of technology transfers to potentially competitive economies has become a key to maintaining economic, if not political, hegemony.

To understand the dynamics of the multinational corporation in a global context, it is not sufficient to focus on the product cycle and technology transfer. Longer-term economic and business cycles are significant as well for managers who seek to cope effectively with change by systematically reducing uncertainty into calculable risk (see Chapter 11). A failure to understand these cycles—or the error of mistaking one for another—tempts corporate managers to become preoccupied with mere maintenances strategies rather than those of the dynamic entrepreneur. And the larger the corporation, the more tempting it is to be predominated by maintenance strategies. The U.S. manager, for example, is shackled with the short-term scrutiny of stockholders (unlike longer-term bank-financed Japanese managers). The stockholders block the U.S. manager from "going for broke" with everything in terms of innovation or the direction of the highest long-term payoff. So the American manager "satisfices"—maintaining low risks in some areas while taking high-risk gambles in others.*

CORPORATE STRATEGY

Step, for a moment, into the shoes of the corporate manager who is responsible for strategic plans that assure not merely the corporation's survival but also a significant return on investment for owners and shareholders. It is easy to understand why a conservative maintenance strategy is tempting in an era of erratic change and uncertainty.

The timing of business cycles often appears to be inscrutable. International markets and sources of supply are politicized. Flexible exchange rates and money-market funds revolutionized the international monetary system. Productivity growth is erratic. Technological breakthroughs appear to be in capital-intensive rather than labor-intensive sectors. Future inflation hovers like a black cloud above the aspirations of industrial democracies where most multinational corporate headquarters are based. It seems reasonable under such circumstances to think in terms of Social Darwinism—the strong survive, the weak go under. And it is tempting to adopt a defensive strategy to preserve the value of existing assets and investments, to shore up existing bulkheads in the structure, and to tighten up on efficiency controls within the organization.

An examination of corporate strategies that were employed to fight inflation in the 1970s in terms of four Weberian ideal types—the Defeatist, the Free-rider, the Maintenance Man, and the Entrepreneur—revealed that the maintenance strategy predominated. These four types of strategies were classified according to risk orientation, time horizon, guiding motive, consumption pattern, and characteristic portfolio mix as illustrated in Table 6-1.[20]

Table 6-1 is not meant to be exhaustive either in the number of strategy types or in the range of portfolio mixes. Weberian ideal types are just typical patterns or typifications of striking features in social reality, like the tips of icebergs that serve to indicate the massive structure that lies invisible beneath the surface. Actual corporate behavior patterns usually draw from more than one strategy type, and sometimes from all of them. Nevertheless, particular strategy types appear to be dominant in specific organizations at certain historical moments. Organizational survival in the late twentieth century depended on the company's ability to transcend defeatist and free-rider strategies. But the international climate of uncertainty did not stimulate healthy, risk-taking behavior. Concerns about losing because of change or inflation reinforced a normal conservative bias of organizations that favors maintenance strategies and penalizes the entrepreneur in an environment calling for the opposite.[21]

To understand the rationale for the defensive, risk-avoiding attitude that

---

*Economist Herbert A. Simon coined the term *satisfice*—a combination of *satisfy* and *suffice*—to describe the tendency to choose an alternative that looks like it will "make do" rather than choosing the best alternative.

TABLE 6-1 CORPORATE STRATEGIES

STRATEGY TYPE	RISK ORIENTATION	TIME HORIZON	DOMINANT MOTIVE	CONSUMPTION PATTERN	PORTFOLIO MIX
Defeatist	Low	Past	Passive	Thrifty	*Security-oriented:* divest weak holdings insure areas of vulnerability consider declaring bankruptcy exploit cash cows/mature products
Free-Rider	High	Present	Active/ Passive	High when others pay	*Cheap credit-oriented:* refinance at cheaper interest rate relocate where taxes are lower and public transportation and infrastructure can be exploited relocate abroad for cheap labor speculate in exchange markets
Maintenance	Medium	Present short-term	Passive/ Active	High	*Stable return and diversity-oriented:* maximize short-term profits reorganize business units within firm, targeting specific markets buy back company's own stocks shorten reaction time within business units with limited computer planning develop better inflation indicators diversify in firm to cover risks mergers with large companies in similar fields
Entrepreneur	High	Future long-term	Aggressive	All or nothing	*High return orientation:* acquire smaller companies to reduce resource dependence and increase innovation and technology R&D bring in outside consultants to plan better financing and R&D increase individual payoffs in company for those who create plans for long-term gains foreign expansion to follow or create customers, increase world market share, overcome international currency and tax fluctuations or government regulatory barriers lobby in government for tax subsidies for R&D, capital formation, and less regulation

prevails in many corporations and institutions, it is helpful to recall economist Mancur Olson's thesis in *The Logic of Collective Action*:

> Unless the number of individuals in a group is small, or unless there is coercion or some other incentive to make individuals act in their common interest, rational, self-interested individuals will not act to achieve their common or group interest.[22]

There has to be some principle or policy of motivation and deterrence that cuts through large organizations and corporations to constantly remind individuals to maximize the organization's interest, not just their own. In capitalist free-market systems or mixed economies, this is no easy task and management can never be sure of the effectiveness of efforts to assure company loyalty. Moreover, in the large, anonymous group context of the corporation, the individual is often tempted to become a free rider (or a defeatist). There is a rational temptation to settle for mediocre group compromises in which strategies are targeted not for high gains (entrepreneurial strategies) but are rather spread to reduce risks and to keep things going as they are for the sake of job security or promotion (maintenance strategies). Thus the corporation in turbulent times appears to be caught in a double bind: For organizational survival certain "maintenance" rules and conventional loyalty codes must be established, but healthy organizational growth depends upon entrepreneurial risk-taking, which is obstructed by this very maintenance activity. Security and stable returns predominate in an era of economic uncertainty. Stockholders in American firms reinforce the problem by annually pushing for short-term profits rather than long-term world market share and research and development (R&D).

There is one way out of this corporate dilemma: The corporation must clearly define limited maintenance objectives for the sake of organizational and group stability (centralized within the organization) and simultaneously select a number of entrepreneurial target areas and creative pilot tests aimed at high returns and adaptation to change in the long term (usually decentralized).

In looking at Table 6-1, it is clear that *maintenance thinking* has a low or medium risk orientation, with a focus on cutting costs and maximizing benefits within the firm, whereas *entrepreneurial strategies* focus on long-term planning and investment in new areas of greatest potential growth with a high risk orientation, seeking to maximize benefits or cut costs by investing outside the firm either nationally or internationally. This observation is consistent with Peter Drucker's thesis in his book *Management*: Within the organization the focus is upon efficiency, whereas outside the organization the focus is upon effectiveness, and corporate strategies cannot be effective unless they go from the inside out.[23]

To survive and expand, corporations require a maintenance base from which to take long-term entrepreneurial risks in the search for new technologies, markets, and sources of resource supply. The Japanese, for example, became hypercompetitive on the world market in many sectors, such as automobiles, through a unique blend of maintenance and entrepreneurial strategies (or maintenpreneurial strategies). For example, according to the maintenance principle, about one-quarter of Japanese workers in the late twentieth century were guaranteed that once hired they would not lose their jobs until "retired" in their mid-fifties.* This and other conservative maintenance preconditions built into the Japanese culture gave company managers a freer hand in times of change or crisis, permitting them to introduce radical reorganization and technical innovation—such as the introduction of robots on the assembly line.

In the mid-1970s, when major automakers were threatened with bankruptcy, a communitarian culture integrating companies and banks permitted Toyo Kogya (the producer of Mazda cars) of Hiroshima to radically shift its strategy, restructure, double its productivity, cut its debt, and to fire no one for five years. The "maintenance base" was provided by the traditional loyalty of the Japanese local community, labor force (given job security), and private creditors. The Sumitomo Bank appointed six of its people to major management positions in the auto company, including chairman (a standard practice in Japan where banks usually own companies and supply managers). These personnel shifts together with worker-participation groups offering suggestions gave Mazda both the financial basis and flexibility needed for effective entrepreneurial adaptation to the changed environment. Parts inventories were cut back, even given the risks of stopping assembly lines; new equipment was purchased to improve efficiency (including robots); new hiring was frozen; workers agreed to accept smaller wage rises; and several thousand unneeded workers on the assembly line were rerouted to serve temporarily as Mazda car salespeople at distribution centers and from door-to-door. In the 1992–1993 recession, Mazda successfully repeated this strategy, shifting managers to production lines.[24]

Whereas the development of Western industrial societies involved the evolution of separate institutions with autonomous spheres of influence, and it was assumed that the spiritual and social life of the individual should reside *outside* the workplace, this is not the case in Japan or China.[25] The Japanese company concerns itself with the worker's full range of social and spiritual needs, creating a maintenance base that is tightly knit and integrated with the culture. For example, Toyota Motor Company, Japan's largest automaker, created an entire town ("Toyota City") to satisfy the needs of its workers, ranging from houses, dormitories, baseball fields, gymnasiums, swimming pools, tennis courts, and sumo rings, to a company stadium. This is perhaps the most efficient automobile production center in the world. Toyota managers long resisted the temptation to attempt to apply their manufacturing formula outside Toyota City before reluctantly setting up a plant with General Motors in California in the 1980s.[26] Toyota

---

*At this point, they typically either accepted more difficult (and usually less desirable) assignments abroad or lived off personal savings until their pensions started at 65 (thus stimulating the Japanese savings rate throughout the life-cycle). The earnings of Japanese are more conditioned by the number of dependents, age, and seniority than those of American workers. See Ame Kalleberg and James Lincoln, "The Structure of Earnings Inequality in the United States and Japan," *American Journal of Sociology*, supp., 94 (1988): p. S1 49.

strictly adhered to three manufacturing objectives, assuring the efficiency of the maintenance base: (1) Keep inventories to a bare minimum, (2) ensure that all phases of the manufacturing process are completed correctly the first time even if it slows down the assembly line, and (3) reduce the amount of human labor expended on each automobile. The efficient maintenance base of Japan's effective entrepreneurship is grounded on a "shame culture." Kenichi Ohmae, former managing director of McKinsey & Company in Tokyo, observed: "The Toyota system is based on shame culture—that it is shameful to stop the whole plant. It would be risky in the United States. One guy could sabotage the whole plant. A lot of Toyota's advantage is not directly transferable."[27] The resulting Japanese advantage over American automobile manufacturers during their recovery of the 1980s is sharply revealed in statistics showing much lower inventories and quality defects and higher productivity and teamwork in Japanese, compared to American and European automobile assembly plant performance.[28] The **just-in-time delivery** of parts to the point of assembly by a few, well-trained suppliers reduces the costs of storing inventory in Japan. The high percentage of Japanese workers in teams on the work force increases productivity and reduces defects (through Deming-derived "quality control circles").

The ways in which a society such as Japan was able to create such an efficient maintenance base, which permits such effective entrepreneurial strategies in the world market, remain somewhat mysterious. However, an hypothesis can be suggested. When the samurai of Japan lost status in the disintegration of their feudal society, they turned to business to recover their sense of purpose.[29] A similar pattern of entrepreneurial reaction resulted from the downward mobility suffered by the Balinese aristocracy.[30] The hypothesis is that acute downward mobility or outright disaster in a feudal society brings maintenance and security needs to the surface if the society is to survive, forcing upper-class elites into focused entrepreneurial patterns initially oriented toward reconstructing an efficient maintenance base. This hypothesis (complemented with the investment of U.S. capital and technology) could explain the incredible Japanese and German economic reconstructions after World War II (see Chapter 9 on "Economic Miracles").[31]

However, despite its feudal past, the British case following World War II provides a contrast to the German and Japanese, given that most of the outdated British industrial plant was not destroyed during the war. Hence there was less incentive to reconstruct a modern and efficient maintenance base (meaning the British had to compete with old factories and equipment). Many of the British upper class were led to believe they could preserve their status without having to modernize their industries or to stoop to become merely upwardly mobile entrepreneurs.[32] The limits of Anglo Saxon liberalism in Britain and the United States played a role in fragmenting domestic power and their success in World War II made them complacent.

If a society, because of downward mobility or destructive experience, takes care of creating and sustaining an efficient maintenance base (through, for example, the Japanese culture of shame or the German culture of order), the business sector is free to focus its energy on export-oriented growth and entrepreneurial strategies. This assumes that government policies permit the corporate flexibility they have in Germany and Japan. In short, there are numerous cultural and maintenance-base preconditions to "the German economic miracle" and the efficiency of Japan's global "laser beam" market analysis. Such prerequisites also facilitate corporations from these countries in *hedging and positioning* strategies aimed at ensuring against the risk of downturns in the business cycle on the one hand, and at preparing them to be in the right place at the right time for upturns in the cycle on the other.

Thus, in terms of "hedging," in 1982 Toyota sought a more international stance by going into negotiations with General Motors Corporation concerning the possibility of jointly producing small cars in the United States. Although the negotiations succeeded, this was less important for Toyota than the fact that they were held. Such cooperative gestures ease American protectionist pressures aimed at keeping Japanese cars out of the American market, whether by tariff or "voluntary restraint." However, there may be a limit to which the Americans will be satisfied with symbolic gestures. Between 1970 and 1994, the cumulative U.S. trade deficit with Japan was over a trillion dollars. In 1993, alone, the U.S. trade deficit with Japan reached $59 billion, over one-half of the overall $116 billion U.S. trade deficit for that year. In 1994, the Clinton administration demanded quantitative quotas to prove results in changing this deficit, but the Japanese refused on the grounds of pushing for deregulation at home and advocating voluntary solutions. The probability of a U.S.-Japanese trade war significantly increased. The United States was no longer as concerned with not offending the Japanese for fear they would dump their holdings of U.S. Treasury securities (which help to finance the U.S. deficit) since Japanese banks, strapped by recession, only bought about 10 percent of the securities offered by early 1994 compared to about 25 percent in 1988.[33] By 1998 the United States reached another record trade deficit with Japan and its overall trade deficit reached $168 billion.

IMPLICATIONS

This analysis of corporate strategy suggests many reasons that corporations are tempted to adopt maintenance strategies to assure their survival. If a country does not have a secure and efficient maintenance base—the case of most countries in the world including most developed industrial nations—companies may be more tempted than otherwise to focus on a maintenance strategy rather than a high-risk entrepreneurial approach. Indeed, companies in many countries may have to establish certain infrastructural maintenance prerequisites, which they cannot take for granted that their culture or government will provide. (This may explain why business interests in capitalist cultures ask the government both for subsidies [maintenance prerequisites] and freedom.) One cross-cultural study concluded that Japanese managers place social and security needs higher than self-actualization needs because these needs are less well satisfied than in British and American cultures.[34]

At a certain stage of development, industrial societies with a maintenance or conservative set of value biases may socialize or indoctrinate managers and companies with maintenance strategies to such an extent that entrepreneurial long-term risks cannot break through. Such collective learning patterns and their effect on strategies of social planning have been substantiated cross-culturally by anthropologist Gregory Bateson.[35] But what is the role of big companies as compared to small business in this process of collective adjustment within particular cultures in terms of global economic change?

BIG-BUSINESS BUFFERS AND SMALL-BUSINESS FLEXIBILITY

The trade-offs between big business and small business involve extreme claims of both sides: "Bigger is better" versus "Small is beautiful." Let us assume that the survival of the business enterprise is a common value that all firms share, whether they be large or small. The question then is whether large or small companies best assure survival. And further, which size firm has greater advantages in addition to mere survival?

Big business, ultimately incorporated in the multinational organization, is an organizational form that emerged from the Industrial Revolution, illustrated by enterprises such as the Hudson's Bay Company and British East India Company and later by American companies such as Singer, Standard Oil, and American Bell. The promise of bigness was the promise of combining maintenance and entrepreneurial strategies in an organization large enough to buffer its interest against the storms of creative destruction in the world economy on the one hand, and providing the base for research and development, and investment risk-taking on the other. In a famous chapter on "Monopolistic Practices" economist Joseph Schumpeter argues that the very imperfection of the world market creates conditions appropriate for large corporations since the big company can use its resources strategically, adapting to change through its research and development capacity while buffering against unexpected change with its very size and ability to set or control prices.[36] Economies of scale given corporate size and large world market share allow big companies to deter new competitors from entering the market, thus assuming the stability afforded by a limited number of suppliers of a goods or service. Investors are attracted by the security of bigness, particularly when governments are reluctant to permit large corporations to go bankrupt because of the increase in the unemployment rate that would result or because of the strategic nature of certain industries in terms of the national interest (the steel and semi-conductor industries, for example).

Paradoxically, as the world economy becomes more interdependent, mercantilist state philosophies are stimulated that view major corporations as critical arms of state economic objectives in the competition for world trade, resources, and development. Some have even claimed the corporate era is an improvement over earlier eras since "corporate pluralism" is more viable and progressive than the rugged individualistic pluralism upon which democratic Western state ideologies were founded.[37] Many multinational corporations have the communications, technological, financial, and personnel capacity to have a global view of change and collective interests. Ultimately, many have a corporate foreign policy that transcends that of any particular nation-state, ideology, or region.

However, not everyone is pleased with "the global bargain" struck by the multinational corporations abroad or the monopoly effects of the big corporation at home. The opposing viewpoint was elegantly expressed by economist E. F. Schumacher in his populist classic *Small Is Beautiful*. Schumacher argued that the "bigger is better" thrust of the corporate economies of advanced industrial states contributed to the error of treating capital as income, particularly "natural capital" (such as fossil fuels) as if it were expendable without limits. Developing countries, accordingly, should not aim for this insatiable big business model of capitalist Westernization but wisely accept the limits of nature and the earth's resources and utilize **intermediate technologies** targeted for their own unique capacities and situation. Economic growth per se is not a higher priority for Schumacher than the dignity of man or the respect for the natural environment: "The substance of man cannot be measured by the Gross National Product. Perhaps it cannot be measured at all, except for certain symptoms of loss."[38]

On a philosophical level, who can deny that small is beautiful, that humans should "cultivate their gardens," that human dignity resides in the creation of one's own limited niches, and that in small, limited, but carefully targeted plans lie flexibility as well as independence?[39] The motivational allure of independent small business entrepreneurship is, of course, one of the classical seeds of the capitalist economic model. One "Eureka" or "ah ha!" experience transformed into a marketable product or niche and one has the future key to all individual happiness—is this not the New World dream of going into business for oneself, becoming independent of any boss, becoming free, and one day becoming rich (which is what "making it" means in capitalist society)?

Moreover, small young businesses are where most of the jobs are created in advanced stages of capitalist society, contrary to "bigger is better" mythology. The M.I.T. Program on Neighborhoods and Regional Change discovered where the net new jobs emerged in a sample of 5.6 million businesses in the United States between 1969 and 1976: Two-thirds were created by companies with twenty or fewer employees, and about 80 percent were created by companies with 100 or fewer employees! As David L. Birch observes: "Smaller businesses more than offset their higher failure rates with their capacity to start up and expand dramatically. Larger businesses, in contrast, appear rather stagnant."[40] In addition, the M.I.T. study indicated that 80 percent of replacement jobs are created by firms four years old or younger. So large companies are no longer the major providers of new jobs for Americans. Nor are old companies. And in Italy, where macroeconomists were surprised at the economic recovery and growth rate in the late 1970s, the basis for the growth was found to be in small- and medium-sized firms.

Globally, in the 1990s economist Daniel Hamermesh showed that one-third of jobs created come from new start-up firms.[41] Evidently, at a certain advanced stage of capitalist development, as a national economy shifts increasingly away from the manufacturing and toward the service sector, small young businesses become the engines of economic growth and job creation as large corporations reach a point of stalemate or diminishing returns.

CENTRALIZATION AND DECENTRALIZATION

Of course the *either-or* thinking behind the split between big and small business organizations is a Western habit of collective learning that may be more a part of the economic problem than of the solution. Schumacher notes that while large-scale organization is here to stay, the fundamental task is to achieve smallness within large organization. A large organization normally goes through alternating phases of centralizing and decentralizing, like swings of a pendulum: "Whenever one encounters such opposites, each of them with persuasive arguments in its favour, it is worth looking into the depth of the problem for something more than compromise, more than a half-and-half solution. Maybe what we really need is not *either-or* but, *the-one-and-the-other-at-the-same-time*."[42]

This non-Western approach of simultaneously centralizing and decentralizing within the large organization, or as the Zen sage might put it, seeing the *yin* and *yang*, big and small, black and white, good and evil as interdependent, appears to be one of the reasons for the effectiveness of Japanese management in competing on world markets in spite of the turbulence of global change. Consider one of the world's largest manufacturer of electrical appliances, Matsushita. In the 1930s, Matsushita combined four decentralized functions with four centralized functions within the organization. The four decentralized functions included independent managers and distinct product categories; strong consumer orientation on the part of these self-sufficient managers; the flexibility of small companies; and the cultivation of specialized expertise among these managers to allow them to mature rapidly.

At the same time, Matsushita countered these characteristics with four centralized functions: controllers reporting to a centralized accounting system at headquarters; a company bank that took in divisional profits and gave out funds for capital improvements; centralized personnel recruitment; and centralized training. The managerial genius of Matsushita (the founder) resided in the fact that he refused to choose "once and for all" between decentralization and centralization (the trap of Western either-or rigidity). Rather, he accepted the uncertainty of an unresolvable conflict between these organizational alternatives. This allowed Matsushita to view centralization and decentralization as a kind of alternating spiral, and he could draw on one aspect or the other depending upon what each historical moment called for.

Thus, in the confusion following World War II, Matsushita replaced his decentralized divisional organization with strong centralization under himself. He headed the advertising department personally to stimulate consumer confidence in his products. In the early 1950s, with greater need for flexibility to match increasing competition, he shifted the company back to a phase of decentralization, bringing back independent product groups. In the late 1950s he recentralized to adjust to the turbulence of an historical stage of growth and increasing interdependence in international markets. But when the business cycle in the early 1960s swung into recession and stagnation, he decentralized again to give his people in the field more flexibility and initiative. Following the oil crisis in the early 1970s, centralization was again instituted as a buffer against this disruptive rush of creative destruction.[43]

Thus the astute corporate manager can use centralization as a means to solidify maintenance objectives in times of historical crisis or disruptive change and can shift to decentralization to stimulate entrepreneurship among his people when the business cycle permits. Effective corporate strategies depend upon managers getting the feel for the relativity of unexpected change; upon sensing when to shore up the maintenance base and when to throw all energies toward entrepreneurial risk; upon knowing when to take a business cycle downturn or upturn seriously and how to react without overreacting: *both-and*, not either-or, *big-small*, not big or small, *long-short-term* planning, not long-term or short-term, *centralization and decentralization*, not centralization or decentralization. Governments can promote, or retard, such strategies of corporate adaptation by providing information, subsidies for sunrise industries, and protection for sunset industries.[44] But to be effective, their ability to apply such policies based on scientific rationality in an effective strategic manner is conditioned by the specific culture, class, and educational systems that shape the life chances of the societies they govern—the themes of the next chapter.

QUESTIONS FOR THOUGHT

1. Spontaneously list all the "structures" you can think of that determine the power of a nation to be independent of others. Which are the most important? Now compare your list with the structures at the beginning of the chapter.

2. What is "The Law of Uneven Development" and how does it relate to the bargaining power of multinational companies based in rich as opposed to poor countries? How does the product cycle fit into this?

3. Consider Table 6-1 in the context of government. Is the dilemma that the state has to motivate and provide for its people the same as that of the corporation?

4. There are problems associated with extremes of any organizational type (e.g., centralized versus decentralized decision making in a corporation; free-market versus socialism [welfare state] for a nation), but there are advantages as well. The thesis in the text, whether it be state or corporation, seems to be that one can have it all; humankind has not yet quite figured out how! Preparation for group project in class: Begin formulating a theory for the corporation (a mature one that tends toward maintenance) that you think would allow the corporation to

"have it all"—it would motivate the people and provide for them! (Optimally, the theory could be used for a nation as well.) What do you think is the maximum size group in which entrepreneurship is apt to function effectively, and why?

NOTES

1. Robert Isaak, "Modern Reactions to Inflation: Private and Public Strategies," Part II in Wilhelm Hankel and Robert Isaak, *Modern Inflation: Its Economics and Politics* (Lanham, MD: University Press of America, 1983). German version: *Die moderne Inflation* (Köln: Bund-Verlag, 1981). Also see R. Isaak, "Inflation on Strategies in the 1980s," *The Adherent* 9, no. 1 (March 1982): 32–47.
2. See H. H. Stevenson, M. J. Roberts, and H. J. Grousbeck, *New Business Ventures and the Entrepreneur* (Homewood, IL: Irwin, 1989).
3. See Michael Warshaw, "The Mind-Style of the Entrepreneur: Q&A: Howard H. Stevenson," *Success* (April 1993): 29–33. The term "entrepreneur" was first introduced by Richard Cantillon (1697–1734), who used it to refer to a specialist in taking on risk, "insuring" workers by buying up their products or labor for resale before consumers have shown how much they are willing to pay for them.
4. Steven Greenhouse, "The Man Who Wrote the Book Suggests Econ 101 for Presidents," *New York Times*, October 31, 1993.
5. The conservative psychological impulse that results in the choice of maintenance strategies due to overwhelming loss or change is perceptively documented in Peter Marris, *Loss and Change* (New York: Pantheon, 1974); see also R. Isaak, *European Politics: Political Economy and Policy Making in Western Democracies* (New York: St. Martin's Press, 1980).
6. "Pentagon Inc." is the description of U.S. industrial policy used by Yoshi Tsurumiin, *Multinational Management: Business, Strategy, and Governmental Policy*, 2nd ed. (Cambridge, MA: Ballinger, 1984), p. 8.
7. The primacy of security and then of money and credit among the first four of these structures is propounded by Susan Strange, "Protectionism and World Politics," *International Organization* 39 (spring 1985): 234.
8. See Karl W. Deutsch, "State Functions and the Future of the State," *International Political Science Review* 7 (April 1986): 209–222.
9. Illustrated in *European Politics*.
10. Richard Rosecrance, "International Theory Revisited," *International Organization* 35 (autumn 1981): 709.
11. Hymer made the oligopoly-leading-direct-investment argument in his 1960 doctoral dissertation at the Massachusetts Institute of Technology. For the relation of this argument to the "Law of Uneven Development," see Stephen Hymer, "The Multinational Corporation and the Law of Uneven Development," in *Economics and World Order from the 1970s to the 1990s*, ed. J. Bhagwati (New York: Collier-Macmillan, 1972), pp. 113–40. See also Gary Gereffi and Richard S. Newfarmer, "International Oligopoly and Uneven Development: Some Lessons from Industrial Case Studies," in *Profits, Progress and Poverty: Case Studies of International Industries in Latin America*, ed. Richard S. Newfarmer (Notre Dame, IN: University of Notre Dame Press, 1985), pp. 385–442.
12. United Nations Center on Transnational Corporations, *Transnational Corporations in World Development*, Third Survey (New York: United Nations, 1983), pp. 318–326.
13. See Y. Tsurumi, *Multinational Management*, pp. 193-196.
14. Theodore H. Moran, "A New United States Policy toward Multinational Enterprises,"

a paper presented at the Faculty Seminar on International Political Economy at Columbia University, New York, November 19, 1975.

15. For initial efforts at forming such Third World companies, see David A. Heenan and Warren J. Keegan, "The Rise of Third World Multinationals," *Harvard Business Review* (Jan.–Feb. 1979): 102–103; Also, United Nations Commission on Transnational Corporations, *Transnational Corporations in World Development: Trends and Prospects* (New York: United Nations, 1988).

16. See Raymond Vernon, "International Investment and International Trade in the Product Cycle," *Quarterly Journal of Economics* 80 (May 1966): 190–207.

17. See James M. Lutz and Robert T. Green, "The Product Life-Cycle and the Export Position of the United States," *Journal of International Business Studies* 14, no. 3 (1983): 77–94; and Alicia Mullor-Sebastian, "The Product Life-Cycle Theory: Empirical Evidence," *Journal of International Business Studies* 14, no. 3 (1983): 95–106.

18. See Ian Giddy, "The Demise of the Product Life-Cycle Model in International Business Theory, *Columbia Journal of World Business* (spring 1978): 90–96.

19. See Richard Barnet and John Cavanagh, *Global Dreams: Imperial Corporations and the New World Order* (New York: Simon & Schuster, 1994).

20. R. Isaak, *Modern Inflation*, pp. 32–47.

21. Ibid. For the conservative bias of organizations, see Ruth Mack, *Planning on Uncertainty* (New York: Wiley, 1971); Robert Townsend, *Up the Organization: How to Stop the Corporation from Stifling People and Strangling Profits* (London: Michael Joseph Ltd., 1970); and Peter Drucker, *Managing for Results* (New York: Harper & Row, 1964). On being overenamored with the process of management stressing order, efficiency, and predictability (what I have referred to as the "maintenance syndrome") see Abraham Zaleznik, *The Managerial Mystique* (New York: Harper & Row, 1989).

22. Mancur Olson, *The Logic of Collective Action* (Cambridge, MA: Harvard University Press, 1965), p. 2.

23. Peter F. Drucker, *Management: Tasks, Responsibilities and Practices* (New York: Harper & Row, 1973).

24. Andrew Pollack, "Japan Finds Ways to Save Tradition of Lifetime jobs," *New York Times*, November 28, 1993.

25. Richard Tanner Pascale and Anthony G. Athos, *The Art of Japanese Management* (New York: Simon & Schuster, 1981), Chapter 1, pp. 19–27. For the global implications from a Japanese perspective, see Takashi Inoguchi and Daniel I. Okimoto, *The Political Economy of Japan* (Stanford, CA: Stanford University Press, 1988).

26. For a critical view, see Mike Parker and Jane Slaughter, "Behind the Scenes at Nummi Motors," *New York Times*, December 4, 1988.

27. Steven Lohr, "The Company That Stopped Detroit," *New York Times*, March 21, 1982, Section 3, p. 26.

28. These comparisons are from James P. Womack, Daniel T. Jones, and Daniel Roos, *The Machine That Changed the World* (New York: Macmillan, 1990), pp. 92, 118.

29. See Everett Hagen, *On the Theory of Social Change* (London: Tavistock Publications, 1964), Chapter 14.

30. See Clifford Gertz, *Peddlers and Princes: Social Development and Economics in Two Indonesian Towns* (Chicago, IL: University of Chicago Press, 1963).

31. For the German case interpreted from this perspective, see R. Isaak, *European Politics*, Chapter 2, pp. 27–62.

32. Ibid., Chapter 4: "Great Britain: A Socialized Economy in Crisis," pp. 99–125.

33. Bob Davies and Jacob M. Schlesinger, "Trade War? Unlikely, but Shifting Relations Do Increase the Risk," *Wall Street Journal*, February 18, 1994.

34. Mason Haire, Edwin Ghiselli, and Lyman W. Porter, *Managerial Thinking* (New York: Wiley, 1966). But also see C. J. McMillan, "Social Values and Management Innovation: The Case of Japan," in *Management under Differing Value Systems*, ed. Günter Dlugos and

Klaus Weiermair (Hawthorne, NY: Walter de Gruyter, Inc., 1981); and Fons Trompenaars and Charles Hampden-Turner, *Riding the Waves of Culture*, 2nd ed. (New York: McGraw-Hill, 1998).

35. Gregory Bateson, "Social Planning and the Concept of Deutero-Learning," in *Steps to an Ecology of Mind* (New York: Ballantine Books, 1972), pp. 159–176. It may be time to take one step backward in order to take two steps forward and learn how nonhuman animals learn collectively. For example, big horn sheep transmit home range knowledge from generation to generation *if* individual lambs are not dispersed from their home range (see Valarius Geist, *Mountain Sheep: A Study in Behavior and Evolution* [Chicago, IL: University of Chicago Press, 1971]). And wolf pups raised without the social structure of a wolf pack adapt poorly to life in the wild (see Barry Holstun Lopez, *Of Wolves and Men* [New York: Charles Scribners' Sons, 1978]). Individual freedom (that is, mobility) is not always the recipe for health, survival, or collective adaptation to global change. The cultural constraints upon mobility in West Germany and Japan may help to explain their efficacy at collective learning after World War II.

36. Joseph Schumpeter, *Capitalism, Socialism and Democracy* (New York: Harper & Row, 1950), pp. 87–106.

37. See Neil H. Jacoby, *Corporate Power and Social Responsibility* (New York: Macmillan, 1973).

38. E. F. Schumacher, *Small Is Beautiful: Economics as if People Mattered* (New York: Harper & Row, 1973), p. 20.

39. See, for example, Kempe Ronald Hope, "Self-Reliance and Participation of the Poor in the Development Process in the Third World," *Futures*, 15, no. 6 (December 1983): 455–462. And Charles Hampden-Turner, *From Poverty to Dignity* (Garden City, NY: Anchor-Doubleday, 1974).

40. David L. Birch, "Who Creates Jobs?" *The Public Interest* 65 (fall 1981): 7.

41. Daniel Hamermesh, *Labor Demand* (Princeton, NJ: Princeton University Press, 1993).

42. Schumacher, *Small Is Beautiful*, pp. 242–243. International Management consultant Stanley Davis confirms the need to overcome false either/or, centralization/decentralization dichotomies and to deal with the simultaneity of business opposites. See S. Davis, *Future Perfect* (Reading, MA: Addison-Wesley Publishing, 1987), p. 188. And also S. Davis and C. Meyer, *Blur: The Speed of Change in the Connected Economy* (Reading, MA: Addison-Wesley, 1998), Chapters 1, 5, and 8.

43. Pascale and Athos, *Art of Japanese Management*, Chapter 2, "The Matsushita Example," pp. 28–57.

44. See Daniel Yergin, *The Commanding Heights: The Battle between Government and the Marketplace that Is Remaking the Modern World* (New York: Simon & Schuster, 1998).

Life Chances, Class, Education, and Culture

Americans spend $8 billion a year on cosmetics—$2 billion more than the estimated annual total needed to provide basic education for everyone in the world. Europeans spend $11 billion a year on ice cream—$2 billion more than the estimated annual total needed to provide clean water and safe sewers for the world's population.

—UN Human Development Report 1998, *New York Times* 9/27/98

In general, women in developing countries with seven or more years of education (and presumably from the better-off classes?) marry approximately four years later than those without education, have higher rates of contraceptive use, and enjoy lower maternal and child mortality rates—so both they and their offspring have better chances in life.

—Paul Kennedy, *Preparing for the Twenty-First Century* (1993)

Crisis, the Greek term that has designated "choice" or "turning point" in all modern languages, now means "driver, step on the gas" … understood in this way, crisis is always good for executives and commissars, especially those scavengers who live on the side effects of yesterday's growth: educators who live on society's alienation, doctors who prosper on the work and leisure that have destroyed health, politicians who thrive on the distribution of welfare which in the first instance was financed by those assisted.

—Ivan Illich, "Useful Unemployment and Its Professional Enemies" (1987)

NO HUMAN BEING CAN CHOOSE WHERE OR WHEN TO BE BORN. EACH INDIVIDUAL REPRESENTS a collective throwing of dice at this starting position, a cluster of probabilities thrust into a particular culture, family, and historical set of circumstances. Life chances are first born, then made. Those born rich naturally try to maintain their position: They can never really understand those in poverty without experiencing poverty themselves. Thus, the human condition is inherently tragic: Individuals are arbitrarily thrown into cultures, classes, languages, and historical conditions that are exceedingly difficult to transcend if they are to understand those born otherwise. Collective learning for the sake of a national or global community involves a lifetime of unlearning parochial habits, languages, and ways of seeing with which one is inevitably born.

From 1950 to 1987 the world population had doubled to 5 billion. If all 5 billion stood shoulder to shoulder they could fit into Hong Kong: It is more the relative distribution of people upon the earth's surface that determines their life chances than the absolute quantity of people. Globally, the population is growing too rapidly in the wrong places, creating dense pockets of poverty and deprivation.

By 1994 one out of four human beings was absolutely poor in terms of living in conditions of malnutrition, illiteracy, disease, high infant mortality, and low life expectancy. More than half of these poor were small farmers, while 20–25 percent were landless laborers. Eighty percent of poor workers in these categories live in India, Pakistan, and Bangladesh. In the developing countries, only 20 percent of the 300 million people above age sixty have any form of income security; 17 million people die annually from infectious and parasitic diseases; 800 million people do not get enough food; two-thirds of the illiterates are women; 850 million people live in areas of desertification; tropical forests are being destroyed at the rate of the equivalent of two soccer fields per second; and these nations are home to 80 percent of the 12–13 million people infected with the HIV virus.[1] By 1997, the world population stood at 5.9 billion. Thirty million people were afflicted with HIV, a number that will increase to more than 40 million in 2000, according to the UN. By 2000, 1.5 billion people will live in absolute poverty on less than one dollar a day.[2] The population forecast for 2050 is about 9.4 billion.

However, the problem today is not the absolute number of people, but *where* the population growth takes place. In the richest countries there is a slowdown in which any two people are not producing two more people. In Spain and Italy, for example, fertility is as low as 1.24, compared to a 2.1 level of offspring necessary just to replace the existing population. The rich nations are the producers, consumers, and donors, and falling fertility rates could foreshadow economic trouble with global consequences. For the life expectancy is greatest in the developed regions where the population growth of future workers to support these old people is the smallest.

Some scholars—all living in the rich, developed countries—argue that the world's poor were materially better off in the late twentieth century than they were in earlier times.[3] The majority of the world's population no longer earns its living from agriculture, for example.[4] But what if I, as a human being, believe that I am worse off in a situation where I am no longer able to live off the land as a self-sufficient farmer? The industrial process of modernization works to homogenize life chances worldwide, rendering people impotent to satisfy their own basic needs independently.[5] Global industrialization makes the masses of the world population increasingly dependent upon ever-accelerating *global* market processes.[6]

An overabundant global food supply is mismanaged and maldistributed: As with any domestic economy, the global economy cannot depend alone upon the "invisible hand" of surplus production automatically to spill over and satisfy public needs. Life chances are indeed chancy for most people if left merely to laissez-faire markets. Poor nations provide few opportunities for those with talent to develop. Of course the world economy in no way approaches a total laissez-faire free-market system. Still, the collective management implied by the doctrine of global Keynesianism seems more hopeful to the disadvantaged of the earth than the winner-take-all premise of Adam Smith's laissez-faire capitalism. The creative destruction of global capitalism is a greater threat to those down the class scale without the resources to buffer themselves from the uncertainties of change than it is to the wealthy minority, who may well perceive change to be more an opportunity than a threat. Sociologists have noted that those in the underclass tend to perceive life chances merely as a matter of "luck," whereas those up the class scale have the resources and educational tools to give them the self-confidence that their life chances can, at least in part, be "managed."[7]

ORIGINS

The notion of "life chances" can be traced back to Aristotle's conception of human beings as political animals, inclined to live in cities or states, who often want more than they need but are constrained by existing social and economic conditions and the competition of others. Early in the twentieth century, sociologist Max Weber used the concept of **life chances** to imply a competitive struggle for survival among individuals or types of people.[8] In the late twentieth century, sociologist Ralf Dahrendorf interpreted life chances as the odds of fulfilling the full range of human possibilities, given the individual's social ties and options.[9] Weber's vision has a pessimistic tone of Social Darwinism, stemming in part from the social struggle for the survival of the fittest in the wake of the Industrial Revolution. Dahrendorf's more positive view of life chances, on the other hand, grew out of socioeconomic conditions created by the abnormally high economic growth rates in advanced developed countries in the 1950s and 1960s. Then it was sometimes assumed that affluence could be taken for granted—along with lower-level material needs. By the last decade of the twentieth century this assumption did not seem to hold, except for a wealthy minority of the world's population.

Life chances is the concept that allows one to locate an individual in the class structure or stratification system of his or her society at a particular historical moment. From a materialistic point of view, **class** refers to how much you have got of what your society considers it important to get. **Status** is how much others think you have got or the degree of deference others give to you based on how you got the goods or go about getting them. *Social class constrains or supports an individual's life chances. If you are born rich, you usually sense social support for your efforts to maximize your life chances, whereas if you are born poor, your daily experience is more apt to be one of constant constraints.* Of course if the capitalist society into which you are born has a socialist revolution, you may find the rules of the game reversed, leading to social discrimination against the rich. Since the French Revolution, the importance of equality as a social value in Western democratic countries has become ingrained in public consciousness. Often the rich find it more comfortable to understate their wealth and social standing in order to reduce envy and potential social and political animosity from the majority down the class scale. The French Revolution served to delegitimize the aristocratic upper classes of the *ancien regime* once and for all. We are still experiencing its social effects.

Class position depends on how many people are living together on how much space under which economic conditions. Before the Industrial Revolution, life for the majority of people was more often than not, as philosopher Thomas Hobbes described it, "nasty, brutish and short." The Industrial Revolution of the eighteenth century introduced technologies that were soon to lift the life standards of the masses far beyond the expectations of pessimists such as Karl Marx, who projected (wrongly) that the poor would become increasingly worse off. Indeed, despite the pockets of poverty and deprivation still remaining, by the 1970s much of the population of the United States lived as well as did the wealthy of the colonial era.[10] Such technology did little to sweeten the fate of those born in Bangladesh rather than the United States, however: In Bangladesh some 110 million people survive on one of the smaller gross national products per capita in the world, and two-thirds of the country was flooded in 1988, causing rampant medical and malnutrition problems. Numbers, space, and natural resources (or disasters) are all determinants of class position in the world economy, not to mention the level of technological and educational development.

The impact of numbers on personal welfare is notable in the differences in the sizes of generations within countries as well. The coming of mass production in industrialized countries served to diminish the importance of being born high or low on the class scale. But in the period between the world wars, industrial society brought on a new form of economic uncertainty: Periodic recessions (or depressions) brought mass unemployment that could undermine an individual's life chances overnight. Fortunately, since that time unemployment insurance has been provided in most developed countries (such as the 1946 Employment Act in the United States). Nevertheless, if one is lucky enough to be born in a generation when the birthrates are low, one will find oneself to be relatively much better off than a generation in the same country born when birthrates were high. Thus, between the end of World War II and 1960, individuals born in the low-birth rate 1930s found their services in high demand given labor shortages (aggravated by losses of manpower during the war): They prospered and tended to have large families. They were the baby-boom generation of the 1950s, who, in turn, found the competition keen, their standard of living under financial pressure, and the temptation to limit the size of the family they intended to have an accepted social reality. Baby-bust generations tend to bring baby-boom generations into the world, and vice versa, creating an economic cycle of life chances unforeseen a century ago.[11]

SOCIAL CLASS AND EDUCATIONAL LEVEL

The higher the social class, the higher the educational level for most people. This has important economic and political implications in a high-technology, high-information global economy. *Nam et ipsa scientia potestas est*—"Knowledge is power," wrote Francis Bacon in 1597. These days—in an age of uncertainty when people are distrustful that such a thing as objective knowledge truly exists—"information is power." Hence, Kenneth Boulding's definition of knowledge as the systematic loss of information makes modern sense of Bacon's proposition in a postmodern world. The key question in terms of social class is: Which kind of information is an individual from the lower class most apt to lose—or, more important, to keep and cling to—compared to someone from the upper class? And what is the difference in lower-class and upper-class time horizons?

People from lower classes tend to lose the abstract and to cling to the concrete, focusing upon the present at the expense of thoughts about the past or the future. Low-status or working-class individuals are typically characterized as lacking an adequate frame of reference or general perspective—or of possessing a fixed, rigid one. Such a mind-set opens them to suggestibility in terms of participation in extremist movements.[12] Lack of education of lower class individuals means that they do not have a sophisticated worldview nor the ability to form abstractions from concrete experience. They demonstrate an absence of imaginative flexibility. They lack a prolonged time perspective, without an historical sense of continuing tradition reaching toward the past and without a cultivated ability to make imaginative, strategic plans to shape their own future. Typically, they react immediately to the present, absorbed by its daily routine business.[13] They feel driven to adjust to the outside world rather than to cultivate their own impulses by fantasy and introspection, according to studies of lower-class children.[14] Working-class people are not as apt as middle-class people to see the *structure* of an object, but are characterized in their perception by an action-oriented behavior in reaction to an object's content.[15] American attitude surveys show that elites are interested in abstract values such as freedom and stability in foreign affairs, whereas the masses focus upon simple, concrete values such as improving their own income, housing, and schools.[16]

The correlation between social class and educational level extends from the national to the international level. There is a direct relationship between high national economic growth and levels of primary and secondary school enrollment and national literacy. For example, the ten nations with the highest percentage of children aged six to seventeen enrolled in primary and secondary schools in the mid-1980s—Denmark, France, New Zealand, Finland, the United States, Norway, Canada, Spain, the Netherlands, and Japan—were all among the top fifty countries in the world in terms of GNP. Six of the ten with the highest enrollment percentages were among the top fourteen nations in terms of GNP.[17] A comparison of country literacy rates in Europe in the mid-nineteenth century reveals a strong correlation with rates of economic development in the same countries a century later.[18] Emmanuel Todd's 1970 data on literacy rates in various areas of civilization ranked those areas highest in literacy from which a number of the most dynamic newly industrialized countries emerged in the late twentieth century: (1) *Buddhist and Confucian Asia* (Taiwan, China, Vietnam, and Korea): 83 percent average literacy; (2) *"Indian" America* (Peru, Ecuador, Bolivia, Paraguay,

Mexico, Venezuela, Colombia, El Salvador, Honduras, Guatemala, Nicaragua, and Panama): 70 percent literacy; (3) "*Small Vehicle*" *Buddhist Asia* (Sri Lanka, Thailand, Burma, Laos, and Cambodia): 63 percent literacy; (4) *South India* (States of Kerala, Tamil Nadu, Karnataka, Orissa, Andhra Pradesh, and Maharashtra): 37 percent, (5) *Central and Western Moslem World* (Syria, Tunisia, Egypt, Algeria, Iraq, Morocco, Sudan, Iran, Afghanistan, Pakistan, and Bangladesh): 35 percent; and (6) *Northern India* (Indo-European) (Gujarat, Punjab, Uttar Pradesh, Rajasthan, Bihar, Madhya Pradesh, and West Bengal; Nepal): 26 percent.[19]

In France, for example, only half of the economy's post-World War II growth rate can be accounted for by changes in capital and labor: The other half is ascribed to "residual" factors, the most important of which is education.[20] Powerful group learning potential is enhanced in countries like China, Japan, Korea, and overseas Chinese communities where the common Confucian culture represents a dynamic force in the receptivity to learning and in the collective capacity for cultural and economic development.[21] In Japan, for instance, neo-Confucian respect for knowledge and teachers extends basic learning throughout the life-cycle; information gathering becomes focused and "takes on a special campaign-like intensity when an organization recognizes an issue as preeminently important."[22]

The United States demonstrates a particularly heavy correlation between high levels of education and high lifetime earnings. Education, of course, provides only a potential power basis or springboard for socioeconomic clout. The richest Americans explain their wealth overwhelmingly in terms of entrepreneurship, to a much smaller extent in terms of inheritance, with financial acumen and invention being even less weighty factors.[23]

Paradoxically, although the American economic boom of the 1990s marginally increased the number of 18-to-24-year-olds taking college courses, from 30 percent in 1989 to 35 percent in 1998, and provided more jobs at all levels of education, the quality of American performance in math and science education before the college level did not improve. The "best" American students in physics and advanced mathematics were at the bottom of the list among industrial countries in performance: Not one country involved in a 23-country study—including less well-off-nations such as Greece, Cyprus, and Latvia—scored lower than the United States.[24] Perhaps the paradox is that identified by economist Joseph Schumpeter: Capitalism becomes so successful that it tends to do itself in, with richer, spoiled people seeking leisure and easier paths to the point that it undermines the rational, efficient work ethic necessary to keep successful capitalism going. Quantitative fields like math and science are perceived by many young Americans to be too difficult and frustrating: If jobs appear to be readily available in other areas in which one can earn good money without going to all that trouble, why not take the easier, practical route? Obviously a rigorous math and science education is not the only criterion for economic competitiveness.

National competitiveness—the transformation of an efficient maintenance base into dynamic, export-oriented entrepreneurship—is a function not merely of the level of education and literacy in the country, but of the degree to which this education is entrepreneurial (proeconomic growth and technology) in orientation and group-consensus building in terms of social equity and cultural values. There are conflicting interpretations of this "efficiency-equity trade off" that can lead to such ideological polarization that the political economy can make little headway either toward more economic growth or toward greater social fairness.

INTERPRETATIONS

Societies, and Western societies in particular, develop cultural splits or polarizations that undermine economic effectiveness and are rooted in the educational and class structure. Knowledge itself has no edge to it: It is infinite, overwhelming, diffusing, forgiving, and unforgiving. The individual, guided by class and culture, must give knowledge an arbitrary edge—a slant or niche to render it useful for specific purposes.

THE GENTLEMAN VERSUS THE CRAFTSMAN OR TRADESMAN

Within the industrial society—particularly in its British manifestation, which served as the model for so many countries*—the archetype of educational success is the gentleman. According to economist Thorstein Veblen in his classic *The Theory of the Leisure Class* (1899), this role model of leisure-class life was characterized by a conspicuous exemption from all useful employment. Typically the occupations chosen by "gentlemen" symbolizing this characteristic are government, war, sports, and devout observances.[25] Veblen did not have a high opinion of the ability of these occupations to contribute to a society's economy. The solution, as he saw it, was to resurrect the status of the craftsman and technician (or engineer), demoting "proper" or "useless" occupations to their appropriately low rank of contribution to productive enterprise. In the process, the "invidious distinctions" created by the leisure class to shore up their status—their pecuniary trophies of material success and ownership and conspicuous consumption of unnecessary luxuries—would be shown up for the decadence they symbolized.

The decline of the British economy in the twentieth century is often attributed to the gentleman's narrow, invidious distinctions, which are the soul of elitist British education. British elitist education is marked by the values of exhibition, symbolization, self-expression, sociability, and consumption—as opposed to spectatorship, the management of things, social utility, task, and production. This being-before-doing culture of sociability and polite behavior looks down upon entrepreneurship and mere money-making. The gentleman looks down on the mere tradesman, and in the process the basis of the British economy is slowly undermined as the hard-working producers are discriminated against socially.[26] This

---

*Another example of the worldwide influence of Anglo-American ideology capped with English as the global language of business.

class-based snobbism is epitomized by a story told by British journalist Claude Cockburn following World War II about his father, who had a first-class upbringing. "A friend said there was a position available as chief of an interallied financial mission to oversee the finances of Hungary. My father replied that he knew almost nothing about Hungary and absolutely nothing about finance. Would this not be a disadvantage? The friend said that this missed the point: They had a man doing this job who knew all about Hungary and a lot about finance, but he had been seen picking his teeth with a tram-ticket in the lounge at the Hungaria Hotel and was regarded as socially impossible. My father said that if such were the situation he would be prepared to take over the job."[27]

The British model of elitist education had great influence, as elites in the developing countries sent their children to Oxford and Cambridge to study and "ape the British gentleman" before coming home to manage their own societies. By socially discriminating against pragmatic, mundane, "hands-on" models of the mind, traditional British priorities undermined the will to self-sufficiency so important for the autonomous development of the developing countries. As British writer C. P. Snow noted, literary intellectuals are often "natural Luddites"—a reference to a band of workers in the early nineteenth century who tried to prevent the use of labor-saving machinery by destroying it and burning down factories. Snow observed the following:

> Industrialisation is the only hope of the poor. I use the word "hope" in a crude prosaic sense. I have not much use for the moral sensibility of anyone who is too refined to use it so. It is all very well for us, sitting pretty, to think that material standards of living don't matter all that much. It is all very well for one, as a personal choice, to reject industrialisation—do a modern Walden, if you like, and if you go without much food, see most of your children die in infancy, despise the comforts of literacy, accept twenty years off your own life, then I respect you for the strength of your aesthetic revulsion. But I don't respect you in the slightest if, even passively, you try to impose the same choice on others who are not free to choose.[28]

THE TWO CULTURES AND EDUCATIONAL CONSEQUENCES

The passage above is from C. P. Snow's influential 1959 Rede lectures, published as *The Two Cultures and the Scientific Revolution*. Deploring the fact that academia was divided into two mutually-incomprehensible intellectual camps—the literary intellectuals versus the scientist/technologists—Snow argued that this cultural divide split societies and helped to explain why, at the time, the Soviet Union trained so many more engineers than were trained in the West. The higher status of literary intellectual studies in traditional British centers of elitist institutions of education drew highly qualified minds away from careers in science and engineering, diminishing the technological power base of Great Britain compared to the USSR. Critics accurately noted that Snow's thesis applied particularly to Anglo-Saxon cultures and was not as universal as Snow implied. Yet given the domination of the British Empire followed by American hegemony and the residual status of British and American universities as educational models, the consequences of the cultural split between the humanities and scientific technology should not be underestimated.

During the 1980s and 1990s, the United States continued to graduate many more lawyers and liberal arts graduates than required for existing job positions in the information-processing, technological economy, and too few electrical engineers and computer scientists for existing slots—particularly on university faculties. Already by the late 1970s, Japan was graduating 21,090 electrical engineers annually, compared with 14,085 for the United States, 6,649 for West Germany, and 1,749 for France. Computers and electronics represented 4.3 percent of the gross domestic product in Japan, compared to 2.7 percent of the U.S. GDP, 2.1 percent for West Germany, and 2.3 percent for France.[29] This educational mismatch with the job market suggested a lack of competitiveness at the time in the United States compared to Japan. *The major educational debate for the twenty-first century is to what extent high-technology developments will further aggravate structural unemployment and unemployment and what the training policy implications are for the sake of international competitiveness and social well-being.*

The U.S. economy shifted away from manufacturing (about 25 percent of workers employed) toward the service sector (75 percent of workers). Productivity growth, a key to competitiveness, is harder to achieve in the service sector than in manufacturing. Indeed, in the 1980s, productivity growth annually averaged only 1.1 percent in the United States and only rose marginally in the 1990s—1.3 percent.[30]

Many information-processing jobs in the service sector may not require high tech skills. Yet if American educational institutions aim merely to satisfy the needs of the existing low-skill job market with vocational, pragmatic curricula to boost their enrollments in the short term, the long-term needs in terms of theoretical and experimental research and development will be shortchanged. The United States will pay the price in global competitiveness. What is at stake here is not just a college "major" nor a professional goals portfolio but the education *structure* of the entire society: Short-term entrepreneurship does not always result in long-term economic competitiveness nor necessarily in social respect for the work required for such competitiveness.

To take another example, in the West German educational system, the computer market pressure (and opportunities) grew immensely by the 1990s, and there was a shortage of trained teachers as well as computers in all countries of the world. Student frustration with the existing educational system in West Germany extended to the point that the share of *Abitur* (the high school passport to the almost totally subsidized university system) graduates planning to go to the university dropped from 90 percent in 1972 to 62 percent in 1983, according to the German Federal Bureau of Statistics. Instead, by 1984 nearly a fourth of the *Abitur* graduates opted for job training programs in an apprenticeship system that brings the workers in Germany to the highest technological level in the world. That by the end of the 1990s there were not enough apprenticeship training slots available for the demand, only served to underscore a basic principle: Economic competitiveness depends on how a society treats and trains its non-college bound population.

With one of the highest percentages worldwide of high school graduates going on to study at the university level, the United States inadvertently declasses the value of high school education and those in American society who perform low-skill jobs not requiring academic qualifications. High school is thus seen as a mere transition to a higher-level education and is often not taken seriously. Those individuals (with or without high school degrees) desperately needed to perform blue-collar and low-skill, white-collar jobs do not receive sufficient respect in American society, making their job functions socially unattractive. This class discrimination effect exists also in Germany, but not to the extreme that it does in the United States, largely because of the apprenticeship system that receives high respect from most people in German society. Ranging from glass-blowing to high-tech robotics to training to become a bank teller, the apprenticeship system in Germany permits students of about age 16 to divide their time for two or three years between on-the-job training and theoretical studies (regulated by the state but paid for by firms including training salaries for students).* The *structure* of the German society allows respect for blue-collar and low-skill white-collar workers and for those who have no university education—the majority. The system structures everyone "in" and almost no one "out" in terms of social respect. One senses this in meeting people socially where it may be months or years before one person finds out what another does for a living, whereas in the United States one usually finds out within ten minutes. Social respect, in short, is accorded to the *human being per se* first and to his or her status in a job hierarchy only in retrospect. While the Germans have a well-articulated social class structure, basic social politeness calls for understatement concerning one's job status and for sensitivity in asking what could be embarrassing questions of another in terms of how he or she earns a living. Politeness implies that social solidarity or equal human dignity overshadows social competitiveness or divisive class discrimination—at least formally. And social consensus fosters an efficient national maintenance base that provides a reliable take-off platform for effective global export-oriented entrepreneurship.

EQUALITY AND EFFICIENCY? THE SWEDISH MODEL

The commonplace Western assumption is that an inverse relationship exists between equality or solidarity and efficiency or economic competitiveness. According to this premise, the Western society with the highest taxes and greatest percent

---

*By 1990, these dual German training programs had been "exported" to sixteen other countries, including a two-year applied international banking studies program in New York City sponsored by eight German and Swiss banks for local American B.A. students. For the origins, see Stephen F. Hamilton, "Apprenticeship as a Tradition to Adulthood in West Germany," *American Journal of Education* 95, no. 2 (February 1987).

of government spending compared to gross domestic product (that is, welfare spending for the sake of solidarity) should not be an efficient or economically competitive society. But, in fact, this society—Sweden—has often been remarkably efficient and competitive given its expensive welfare system.

The Swedish model assumes that whether equality is compatible with efficiency or not is a question of organization. If the society is overwhelmingly committed to full employment, equality, and democracy as basic values, work can be used as a proxy for efficiency instead of profit or money. In other words, if efficiency is defined as the optimal use of resources, a maximum amount of work performed in a competitive market economy approximates an efficient situation (that is, a situation when the benefit or value of production cannot increase anymore).[31] Sweden's commitment to full employment resulted in an unemployment rate of less than 2 percent in the late 1980s—a period in which most Western economies had an unemployment rate six to eight times higher. In a country characterized by a strong labor and Social Democratic movement (typical for Scandinavian countries), the apparently dispassionate Swedes seem to have a passion for work, which they believe is vital for individual welfare. *Work brings self-esteem, a sense of a significant social role, a means to create social prosperity and self-respect.* The work ethic in Sweden appears to be almost universal, transcending the motive for profit maximization and permitting the society to limit the income gaps between people (that is, equality for the sake of solidarity). The cultural schema is one of *social* individualism.

In Sweden, the life chances of all citizens are given higher priority than extraordinary salaries for competent superstars. Sweden developed the highest labor force participation rate among Western industrialized countries: 82 percent (compared with 76 percent in the United States, 73 percent in Great Britain, 65 percent in France, and 64 percent in West Germany).[32] This high participation rate may be partly a result of more than 80 percent of Swedish blue-collar workers, and even more telling, 70 percent of white-collar workers, belonging to unions. Swedish unions assume that even a small amount of unemployment signifies great losses in potential production and wealth, thus undermining the welfare state as it is forced to distribute money for unproductive unemployment benefits.

The inequality of family income is lower in Sweden than in other industrialized countries. In order of least inequality in family income are: Sweden, Norway, United Kingdom, Canada, West Germany, and the United States (with the most market-oriented wage structures having the greatest extremes). The Scandinavian welfare system is universal, giving all children (not only the poor) an equal right to good, free education and all people (not only the poor) access to free medical care—the best available. The aim was to restructure society toward becoming a classless society by organizing the public sector for everyone. The most needy stages of the life cycle—those of children, families, and the aged—are supported, while the most prosperous phases—those of the young adult and middle-aged—are tapped for progressively greater contributions.

But what does all of this cost? Lots! In the early 1990s, the Swedes achieved a world record in terms of public expenditure as a percentage of GDP—70 percent under the Social Democratic government, reduced to 58 percent by 1999. And the volume of Sweden's GDP increased 35 percent between 1970 and 1986, compared to an average of 47 percent for European OECD countries and 59 percent for all OECD (developed) countries. During the 1980s, inflation in Sweden was higher than the overall OECD average and higher than in European OECD countries (averaging 9 percent compared to 3.5 percent in West Germany, one of Sweden's most important competitors). And tax rates in Sweden were also among the highest in the world. A typical secretary earned about $22,800 annually in 1998, but took home less than half that after taxes, for example. But given Sweden's generous welfare system, the secretary had more disposable income than this indicates and did not need as much income as would a secretary in a country with a greater market orientation, such as the United States.[33]

What is striking in the Swedish equation is that, until the economic crises of the 1990s, despite the high costs in taxes and government spending, the Swedish economy remained competitive, the unions remained responsible, and the system delivered a GDP per capita that was higher than that of West Germany, Denmark, Finland, France, the Netherlands, Belgium, and the United Kingdom (and is just behind Japan, Norway, and the United States)—all with close to full employment! Even unemployment among Swedish youth was down to 6 percent in the 1980s—substantially below the corresponding figure for the OECD countries as a whole. So while Sweden did not deliver the highest abstract growth rates in the world and spread taxes as thick as peanut butter, hardly anyone was out of a job, education was free, health and pension benefits were among the best in the world, the average wealth level was significant, and the companies maintained high liquidity. During the 1980s, the Swedish stock market outperformed that of almost all other industrial countries. Exporting 40 percent of its manufactured goods, Sweden is the most "international" economy of all except for "island economies" like Hong Kong and Singapore.

This stable, work-oriented welfare state formed the basis of an unusual program for the handicapped as well. In 1980 the Swedish government centralized employment for the handicapped under the Samhall Group—an amalgamation of all sheltered workshops and industrial relief work facilities in the country that were owned by the government. Based on the principle that meaningful work is more important than meaningful products, twenty hours of work were demanded per week in this group of twenty-four companies made up of 350 factories. But no one was fired for absenteeism or low productivity. Of the 34,000 workers in the Samhall Group, 29,000 were handicapped. The centralization provided more equality for the handicapped all over the country, more equal competitiveness, and a more equal cost structure, lowering the support necessary from society. Beginning with a 70 percent level of government support in 1980, by 1988 the Samhall Group lowered the subsidy level to 50 percent, making up more than a half-billion dollars in savings for the government. The Samhall Group became the biggest producer of Swedish furniture and a large producer of textiles, with 20 percent of their products exported. The 1980 centralization resulted in 7,000 more people obtaining jobs by 1988 at less expense per employee (despite a 12 percent rate of employees leaving the group each year). Thus, a universal commitment to full employment and equality of opportunity in Swedish society provided a framework for self-respect and economic competitiveness for even the most disadvantaged groups in the population.[34]

For the 1945–1990 period, Sweden showed that equality and efficiency need not be mutually exclusive in a *growing, supportive, international economy*. But "hedging" all equality risks can lead to bureaucratic stalemate, motivational malaise, and social instability.[35] And this extreme form of social insurance made the Swedish economy less competitive than other "leaner" nations in the global recession of the early 1990s. In 1991, the Swedes voted the Social Democrats out in favor of a center-right coalition government on a platform of drastic cutbacks in the welfare system to restore national competitiveness. In 1992 and 1993 cuts pushed through parliament amounted to more than 6 percent of the gross domestic product (GDP)[36] From the state with the world's heaviest tax burden (over 57 percent of GDP in 1990 compared to 30 percent in the United States or the 38 percent average for industrialized nations), Sweden managed to cut the top tax rate from 50 percent in 1986 to 20 percent in 1993 (compared to U.S. cuts of 50 percent to 31 percent).[37] The **social capital** or widespread consensus that enabled Sweden to establish a generous welfare state permitted the Swedes to cut back sharply when necessary for the sake of solvency, competitiveness, and a more private-oriented vision of their still-sacred collective work ethic. In 1996 public spending constituted 72 percent of GDP and by 1997 the budget was balanced. Yet the Swedes are haunted by the threat of "swedosclerosis": The welfare state could become a problem and drag down productivity growth, reducing Swedish competitiveness. In 1998 Sweden remained the nation with the second highest tax burden in the world (after Denmark). And in 1999 the Social Democratic government was confronted with "a creeping brain drain" as entrepreneurs and multinational companies left the country since the globalized economy permitted them to move work wherever they liked—to less isolated nations *inside* the Euro zone where taxes were lighter.[38]

COLLECTIVE LEARNING AS UNLEARNING IN KENYA

Equality versus efficiency is not the only polarity that must be brought into synthesis in the process of collective learning. "Work smarts" versus "school smarts" is another split to be overcome, particularly in developing countries like Kenya, which is undergoing rapid modernization. In the case of Kokwet, a rural farming community in Kenya, the natives found themselves having to unlearn traditional models of childrearing. They needed to refocus educational development upon training children to work in the home economy at a tender age for the sake of adapting to compulsory schooling introduced with the modernization process.

Whether the loss of traditional cultural values is worth the sacrifice for the sake of western modernization goals is an open question.

Given the differences in physical settings, Kokwet babies sleep less than their American counterparts: Americans have more rooms and Kokwet children sleep with their mothers, not in separate places. By the time the Kokwet child is seven years old, half its time is spent in work activities in the household economy—processing food, cooking, tending the fire, taking care of animals and siblings. In contrast to the emphasis upon play in the development of the middle-class Western child, work is considered the main task of the traditional Kokwet childhood.[39] Language development for the natives of Kokwet is minimal, stressing commands and socialization for obedience and responsibility in contrast to the focus on expressive verbal individuality in the American culture.[40] A traditional concept, *ng'om*, translated as intelligence, implies responsibility to group obligations. But after compulsory schooling was introduced, which meant that work time had to be sacrificed to homework and test preparation, this concept had to be "unlearned" or differentiated into *ng'om en ga* ("intelligent at home") and *nq'om en sukul* ("intelligent at school"). Moreover, these two kinds of "intelligence" are generally agreed to be uncorrelated.[41] Whether such language differentiation, which is absolutely necessary for modernization toward the Western industrial model, makes the individual human being "more whole" than the old traditional model (or a better citizen, for that matter) is a question worth pondering.

IMPLICATIONS

Each society has its relevant fictions or utopias, which guide its educational system, structure its class system, and condition the life chances of its citizens.[42] In Sweden, equality through full employment was the predominant vision. In the United States, individual freedom through various checks and balances of prevailing governmental powers is the ideology. The market dominates the United States, and extreme disparities of income mark its socioeconomic structure. The state is the largest actor in the Swedish system, and organizations within it usually tend to work to lower disparities of income as much as they can for the sake of equality, while still striving for competitiveness. Swedish individualism is social individualism.

Game theorist Anatole Rapoport did a comparative study of values in the United States and in Denmark (which is similar to Sweden in its tilt toward equality) using the famous "Prisoners' Dilemma" as a tool. The Prisoners' Dilemma gives two people, who cannot communicate, the option of maximizing their own interest at the heavy expense of the other person or the choice of settling for a more moderate payoff, which would be better for both people and maintain the basis for long-term cooperation. Two-thirds of the American students in Rapoport's experiment opted for maximizing their own interests (the tilt toward freedom whatever the social costs), whereas the Danes overwhelmingly selected the more moderate reward for the sake of cooperation (respecting equality despite the individual cost to themselves). Value frameworks or structures are passed on as if by osmosis in each society, predisposing individuals to behave in one way rather than another and to strive for socially acceptable goals. In Kokwet, Kenya, as we have seen, "work intelligence" shifted to "school intelligence." Collective learning begins with individual adaptation to specific social norms, whether or not these norms are the best for the society as a whole or are helpful in national adaptation for the sake of competitiveness in the world economy. These norms become schemata or prototypes for learning.

As a society is industrialized, knowledge is organized for the sake of certain human interests over others.[43] In Great Britain, the values of the gentleman have traditionally been ranked above those of the craftsman or merchant, and the most prestigious universities have cultivated a certain disdain for the mere man of affairs. This ideology was a contributing factor in the decline of the British economy in the late twentieth century.

In contrast, the strong work ethic in Sweden helped to keep that country competitive economically despite its heavy government spending and tax burdens. The freedom *not* to work was favored in old England; the equal opportunity *to* work was the guiding motivation of the Swedish economy. And a shift away from work responsibility in the household characterized modernization in rural Kenya.

THE COLLECTIVE WORK ETHIC AND A SENSE OF CALLING

The collective work ethic waned in Great Britain and waxed in Sweden, resulting in Sweden's greater relative success in the 1980s in producing sufficient economic development to service its welfare state while maintaining its competitiveness in the world economy. This interpretation is based on German sociologist Max Weber's *The Protestant Ethic and the Spirit of Capitalism*. In this classic work, Weber argues that the Industrial Revolution occurred first in Western Europe (and then America) not because of accident but because the asceticism of the spirit of Protestantism had prepared European society psychologically for this form of economic development. Weber derived the spirit of capitalism from the development of rationalism as a whole: Capitalism is a special form of rationalism in which the individual is dominated with acquisition and action in rational pursuit of more acquisition as the ultimate purpose in life. Idle pleasure and spontaneous enjoyment are not "rationally" part of this Protestant asceticism in which both uncontrolled consumption and spending are regarded as sinful; acquisition and profit-making become a calling or vocation, causing the capitalist to be a constant innovator in order to be better positioned for new acquisition and material achievement.

According to Weber, "The most important opponent with which the spirit of capitalism ... has had to struggle was that type of attitude and reaction to new situations which we may designate as traditionalism."[44] Innovative action in pursuit of profits and acquisition regardless of the impact upon the status quo is the calling of the capitalist. The future-oriented, business entrepreneur is set into conflict with historical traditions. If a whole society is socialized and taught in this tradition, a collective capitalism can emerge based on an ethos of "workaholics" who define collective economic growth, efficiency, and international competitiveness to be the main sources of their international pride (as in the case of post-World War II Japan). A nation sets people up for certain kinds of collective learning, which may or may not encourage the calling of "ascetic, accumulative entrepreneurship" over the callings of roles that maintain existing traditions of the past. But if certain nations become tightly integrated "hit teams" of efficiency, information-gathering, and competitiveness regardless of the social consequences at home or abroad they can set the tone of international competition in the world economy, setting the standards to which other nations must adapt or else pay the price. The threat perceived of Japanese displacement of American economic power in the 1980s is a case in point (despite decline of influence in the 1990s of the "Japanese model" after the financial bubble burst). The collective model seems to work only if it is consistently supported (as in the case of Denmark at the end of the twentieth century): Otherwise it is likely to produce corruption and to break apart, as the recent unraveling of Asian societies has illustrated.[45]

The significance of Weber's distinction between entrepreneurial capitalism based on the work ethic and the maintenance of traditions of the past in terms of economic development must be separated from Protestantism. Critics have pointed out that the spirit of capitalism was not the creator of capitalism as much as was the emerging class of businessmen, and that people need not be "called" to riches to devote themselves fully to their pursuit without stopping to enjoy them.[46] In fact, the capitalist spirit appears to have existed long before the Reformation. Protestantism was more a product of intellectual, social, and cultural changes toward a more secular, rational world-view than it was a father of this secular shift. Indeed, although the economic development of the Netherlands, England, France, and Germany, as well as other European countries, can be correlated with Protestantism, it could well be that prosperity leads to Protestantism rather than the other way around.[47]

One must avoid throwing the baby out with the bathwater, however. Weber's contribution was to stress the *psycho-cultural* prerequisites involved in dynamic industrial development and to focus on the importance of the cultural milieu in preconditioning individuals' selections of one "calling" and educational path over other possible options.

For Weber, a *social event* was an empirical or existential occurrence plus the significance with which it was imbued. One must go beyond Marx and the proposition that existence precedes and determines consciousness to recognize that certain ideological, religious, and value constructs precondition occupational and economic choices. One is, in other words, not just "called from" but "called to." Cultural schemata legitimate particular career paths. Certain societies are more apt to raise the status of the calling to become an electrical engineer or technician than others and these will reap collective economic benefits in the high-tech global economy of the twenty-first century. The German apprenticeship system is a case in point. Research has demonstrated that crafts or occupations create their own states of consciousness (or what Thorstein Veblen termed "habits of mind") that are independent from other bases of knowledge such as an individual's social origins, the market position of a person's occupation, or even someone's own economic interests.[48] The logics and schemata of an individual's cultural milieu are sharply differentiated in the world economy. Family, class, occupation, craft habits, tax incentives, religious and ideological affiliations all can play independent roles in influencing economic behavior. To maintain national competitiveness, the state must "call" individuals into certain fields over others in order to become collectively more effective in targeted niches of the increasingly differentiated world economy. Otherwise, the mismatch between traditional educational paths and emerging economic and technological opportunities will grow worse.

VALUES AND CULTURE

To know which values to preserve in order to maintain a culture when adapting a society for competitiveness, consider the growing literature on cross-cultural differences. Anthropologist Edward Hall noted in his classic, *The Silent Language*, that it is helpful to think of culture as analogous to music: If another person has not heard a piece of music, it is almost impossible to describe. Fons Trompenaars and Charles Hampden-Turner define culture as "the way in which a group of people solves problems and reconciles dilemmas.[49] Geert Hofstede views culture as "the collective programming of the mind which distinguishes the members of one human group from another."[50]

On the basis of 100,000 IBM questionnaires in the 1970s, Hofstede identified four dimensions of work-related value differences: (1) *power distance* (importance of inequality, pecking-order, hierarchy), (2) *uncertainty avoidance* (lack of tolerance for ambiguity, need for formal rules), (3) *individualism/collectivism* (concern for yourself as an individual versus concern for priorities and rules of the group to which you belong) and (4) *masculinity/femininity* (emphasis on work goals and assertiveness versus personal goals [getting along with others] and nurturance).

Germans, for example, feel more comfortable in formal hierarchies, while the Dutch have a more relaxed approach to authority.[51] Life-time employment is more common in high uncertainty avoidance nations like Japan, Portugal, and Greece, in contrast with job mobility in low uncertainty avoidance countries like Singapore, Hong Kong, Denmark, and the United States.[52]

For only a minority of the world's population do individual interests prevail over group interests (in which people think of themselves as "I" as distinct from other people's "I's"). In one experiment, Chinese participants performed best when operating with a group and anonymously in contrast with American participants who performed best when operating individually with personal work identified (and who performed poorly when operating in a group and anonymously).[53]

In Hofstede's study, the Scandinavian countries are the most feminine, with Swedish women having worked both on Volvo's assembly line and as top executives for decades. In contrast, the "masculine" cultures of Japan and Austria generally expect women to stay at home and care for children without working outside the home, particularly in their middle years.

To reconfirm Hofstede's findings, the Chinese Culture Connection asked about the work culture of the Chinese: Uncertainty avoidance disappeared, the other three cultural dimensions were supported, and a different dimension was uncovered—"Confucian dynamism" or long-term versus short-term (i.e., thrift versus conspicuous expenditure).[54]

From analyzing over 15,000 questionnaires from managers in 28 countries, Fons Trompenaars identified seven dimensions of culture, which complemented the findings of Hofstede: universalism versus particularism, analyzed specifics versus integrated wholes, individualism versus communitarianism, inner-directed versus out-directed, time as sequence versus time as synchronization (time-as-a-race versus time-as-a-dance), achieved status versus ascribed status, equality versus hierarchy. Thus, for example, Americans who have a small private and large public space in social personality (according to Trompenaars) may find the Germans to be reserved, who have a large private core and small public space. The Germans often address people formally with whom they work for years, whereas Americans leap to a first-name basis immediately, which from a German perspective may be perceived to be intrusive.[55]

Individual behavior must be moderated by appropriate collective norms which are culturally specific in order to create an organizational environment of competitiveness and solidarity. On the way it is necessary to explore briefly the typical phases of national economic development in order to identify viable strategies at each stage. This will be the focus of the following chapter.

QUESTIONS FOR THOUGHT

1. How does social class determine or influence life chances within a society? Compare life chances in one developed and one developing country.

2. Account for the relationship between education, social consensus, and effective global entrepreneurship by briefly describing and comparing the relevant particularities of the educational systems of the United States and Germany. How does Sweden overcome the seeming inverse relationship between equality and economic efficiency?

3. Suppose a nation-state wanted to choose between the "culture of the literary intellectuals" and the "culture of the scientists/technologists" as the path for its society. Follow each course to the extreme as a hypothetical exercise and describe the characteristics of a society on its chosen course. (Remember, not both in the same society at the same time.)

4. Compare and contrast two cultures using the cultural dimensions uncovered by either Hofstede or Trompenaars. Which of the two cultures is apt to adapt

most effectively to compete in the global economy emerging in the twenty-first century given existing trends? Which cultural values are apt to be lost if the culture that is less apt to adapt is overwhelmed by forces of globalization?

NOTES

1. United Nations Development Program (UNDP), *Human Development Report* (New York: Oxford University Press, 1993), p. 12.
2. Paul Lewis, "Debt-Relief Plan Is Flawed, 5 Nations Say," *New York Times*, April 24, 1999.
3. See, for example, Raymond Vernon, "Global Interdependence in a Historical Perspective," in *Interdependence and Co-operation in Tomorrow's World* (Paris: OECD, 1987), pp. 22–35. Also, Jonathan Power, "Population: Don't Be Frightened by the Numbers," *International Herald Tribune*, April 27, 1987.
4. Karl Deutsch dwelled on this point in a lecture at the University of Mannheim, Germany, June 7, 1988.
5. See Ivan Illich, *Toward a History of Needs* (New York: Pantheon Books, 1978).
6. See Theodore Levitt, "The Globalization of Markets," *Harvard Business Review* 61, no. 3 (March–June 1983).
7. See, for example, Frank Parkin, *Class Inequality and Political Order. Social Stratification in Capitalist and Communist Societies* (New York: Praeger, 1975), pp. 76–77.
8. See Max Weber, *Wirtschaft und Gesellschaft* (Tübingen, 1956), p. 20.
9. Ralf Dahrendorf, *Lebenschancen* (Frankfurt: Suhrkamp, 1979), pp. 48–50.
10. Lance E. Davis et al., *American Economic Growth: An Economist's History of the United States* (New York: Harper & Row, 1972), p. 84.
11. See Richard A. Easterlin, *Birth and Fortune: The Impact of Numbers on Personal Welfare* (New York: Basic Books, 1980).
12. Hadley Cantril, *The Psychology of Social Movements* (New York: Wiley, 1941), Chapters 8 and 9; and Seymour Martin Lipset, *Political Man: The Social Bases of Politics* (New York: Doubleday-Anchor, 1963), Chapter 4.
13. Richard Hoggart, *The Uses of Literacy* (London: Chatto and Windus, 1957), pp. 158–159. For the American case, see E. D. Hirsch, *Cultural Literacy* (Boston, MA: Houghton Mifflin Co., 1987).
14. B. M. Spinley, *The Deprived and the Privileged* (London: Routledge & Kegan Paul, 1953), pp. 115–116. Also see W. T. Grant, "The Forgotten Half; Non College Youth in America," *Phi Delta Kappan* 69 (February 1988): 408–414.
15. B. Bernstein, "Some Sociological Determinants of Perception," *British Journal of Sociology* 9 (1958): 160. Also see Harry C. Triandis, *Variations in Black and White Perceptions of the Social Environment* (Urbana, IL: University of Illinois Press, 1976); and Christine Oppong, ed., *Female and Male in West Africa* (London: George Allen and Unwin, 1983), esp. pp. 10–15 and 223–235.
16. Philip E. Converse, "The Nature of Belief Systems in Mass Publics," in *Ideology and Discontent*, ed. David E. Apter (New York: Free Press, 1964), pp. 206–261.
17. "School Enrollment Ratio, 1984," in *The World Bank Atlas* 1987 (for 184 countries and territories) (Washington, D.C.: The World Bank, 1987), pp. 24–25.
18. C. M. Cipolla, *Literacy and Development in the West* (London: Penguin, 1969), p. 115.
19. Emmanuel Todd, L'enfance du monde, as cited in Jean Boissonnat, "World Economic Development: Some Observations," in *Interdependence and Co-operation in Tomorrow's World* (Paris: OECD, 1987), p. 38.
20. Boissonnat, "World Economic Development," p. 36.
21. William Theodore de Bary and John W. Chaffee, eds., *Neo-Confucian Education: The Formative Stage* (Berkeley, CA: University of California Press, 1989).

22. Ezra A. Vogel, *Japan as Number One: Lessons for America* (New York: Harper & Row, 1979), p. 31.

23. Michael Cieply, "Mutiny in the Galley," *Forbes*, September 12, 1983, 126–137.

24. Ethan Bronner, "U.S. Trails the World in Math and Science," *New York Times*, February 25, 1998. Data is from the Third International Mathematics and Science Study, which tested samplings of fourth, eighth, and twelfth graders in the spring of 1995.

25. Thorstein Veblen, *The Theory of the Leisure Class* (New York: The New American Library, orig. 1899, 1953 Mentor ed.), p. 44.

26. See Charles Hampden-Turner, *Gentlemen and Tradesmen: The Values of Economic Catastrophe* (London: Routledge & Kegan Paul, 1983, especially Chapter 2).

27. *The Autobiography of Claude Cockburn* (Harmondsworth, Middlesex: Penguin, 1967), pp. 37–38. Also see R. Isaak, "Great Britain: A Socialized Economy in Crisis," Chapter 4 of *European Politics: Political Economy and Policy Making in Western Democracies* (New York: St. Martin's Press, 1980), pp. 99–125.

28. C. P. Snow, *The Two Cultures* (London: Cambridge University Press, 1969), pp. 25–26.

29. James Botkin, Dan Dimancescu, and Ray Strata, *Global Stakes: The Future of High Technology in America* (Cambridge, MA: Ballinger, 1982), p. 13. Also R. Isaak, "Mismatches Between Jobs and Education: Collective Learning Across Cultures," a paper presented at the International Studies Association meeting April 12,1990, in Washington, D.C.

30. Louis Uchitelle, "Muscleman, or 98-Pound Weakling: Taking the Measure of an 8-Year Economic Expansion," *New York Times*, October 18, 1998.

31. Anna Hedborg (Director of Swedish Association of Local Authorities), "The Swedish Model—A Happy Marriage between Efficiency and Equality," paper presented at the "Sweden: Equality and Efficiency?" Conference at Indiana University, Bloomington, September 30–October 1, 1988. This section draws heavily on insights derived from this conference, organized by Professor Tim Tilton of Indiana University.

32. Ibid., p. 4. Statistics from 1987.

33. The above statistics (except for the 70 percent public expenditure as percentage of GDP figure, which is from the OECD) are from "The Swedish Economy: Facts and Figures 1988," published by the Swedish Institute of Stockholm. For Sweden's role as one of the most international economies in the world, see Michael Maccoby, ed., *Sweden at the Edge* (Philadelphia, PA: University of Pennsylvania Press, 1991).

34. Based on a personal interview with president of the Samhall Group, Gerhard Larsson, on October 1, 1988, in Bloomington, Indiana.

35. See Hugh Heclo and Henrik Madsen, *Policy and Politics in Sweden* (Philadelphia, PA: Temple University Press, 1987). But also see "Sweden's Social Individualism: Between Raging Horses," Chapter 10 in Charles Hampden-Turner and Alfons Trompenaars, *The Seven Cultures of Capitalism* (New York: Doubleday, 1993), pp. 233–260.

36. Richard W. Stevenson, "Swedes Facing Rigors of Welfare Cuts," *New York Times*, March 14, 1993.

37. Stevenson, "Swedes ..."; and "Tax Reform," *Wall Street Journal*, February 3, 1993.

38. Tom Buerkle, "Sweden Pays the Price of High Taxes," *International Herald Tribune*, March 16, 1999.

39. Sara Harkness and Charles M. Super, "The Cultural Structuring of Children's Play in a Rural African Community," in *The Many Faces of Play*, ed. R. Blanchard (Champaign, IL: Human Kinetics, 1986), pp. 96–103.

40. Sara Harkness and Charles M. Super, "Why African Children Are So Hard to Test," in *Cross-Cultural Research at Issue*, ed. L. L. Adler (New York: Academic Press, 1982), pp. 145–152.

41. Charles M. Super and Sara Harkness, "The Developmental Niche: A Conceptualization at the Interface of Child and Culture," *International Journal of Behavioral Development* (North Holland: Elsevier Science Pub.) 9, no. 4 (December 1986): 545–69. Also see

R. H. Munroe, R. L. Munroe, and B. B. Whiting, eds., *Handbook of Cross-Cultural Human Development* (New York: Garland, 1981), particularly pp. 181–270.

42. See Karl Mannheim, *Ideology and Utopia: An Introduction to the Sociology of Knowledge* (New York: Harcourt, Brace and World, 1936).

43. For an analysis of the victory of positivism in this process of development, see Jürgen Habermas, *Knowledge and Human Interests* (Boston, MA: Beacon Press, 1972).

44. Max Weber, *The Protestant Ethic and the Spirit of Capitalism*, translated by Talcott Parsons (New York: Scribner's, 1958), pp. 58–59.

45. See, for example, Peter Waldman, "Crisis Management: 'Asian Values' Concept Is Ripe for Revision as Economies Falter," *Wall Street Journal*, November 28, 1997.

46. See H. M. Robertson, *Aspects of the Rise of Economic Individualism: A Criticism of Max Weber and His School* (London: Cambridge University Press, 1933).

47. See Kurt Samuelsson, *Religion and Economic Action*, translated from the Swedish by E. Geoffrey French, ed. by D. C. Coleman (New York: Basic Books, 1961).

48. See Joseph Bensman and Robert Lilienfeld, *Craft and Consciousness: Occupational Technique and the Development of World Images* (New York: Wiley, 1973).

49. Fons Trompenaars and Charles Hampden-Turner, *Riding the Waves of Culture*, 2nd ed. (New York:McGraw Hill, 1998), p. 6.

50. Geert Hofstede, *Cultures and Organizations: Software of the Mind* (London: McGraw-Hill, 1991).

51. Lisa Hoecklin, *Managing Cultural Differences: Strategies for Competitive Advantage* (Reading, MA: Addison-Wesley Publishing, 1994), p. 29.

52. N. J. Adler, *International Dimensions of Organizational Behavior* (Belmont, CA: PWS-Kent Publishing, 1986).

53. C. P. Earley, "Social Loafing and Collectivism: A Comparison of the United States and the People's Republic of China," *Administrative Science Quarterly* 34 (1989): 565–581.

54. Hoeklin, p. 39.

55. Trompenaars and Hampden-Turner, pp. 83–88.

STATE STRATEGIES
AND STAGES OF DEVELOPMENT

But where do the moral values that drive wealth creation come from? They originate in culture—the word actually means "to work upon," as in agriculture, which means "to work upon soil or ground."... In any culture, a deep structure of beliefs is the invisible hand that regulates economic activity.

—Charles Hampden-Turner and Alfons Trompenaars,
The Seven Cultures of Capitalism (1993)

FROM THE GLOBAL PERSPECTIVE, THE STRIKING SUCCESS STORIES IN THE WORLD ECONOMY IN the late twentieth century initially appeared to be Japan and the newly industrializing "dragons" of Asia, namely Taiwan, South Korea, Hong Kong, and Singapore. These were tight ships in a storm of economic turbulence that set the standards for manufacturing competitiveness in many key areas and seemed to be models for others to learn by, until the Asian financial crisis of the 1990s. Other looser, more democratic communities enjoyed more freedom individually at home only to find that their individualism had a high economic opportunity cost in the form of trade conflicts with other nations. Japan was permitted by others to rise quickly economically following World War II, using protectionism to cultivate many "infant industries" until the Japanese could compete as equals on the world market. This opportunity was available partially because it was the only newly industrializing country systematically using these strategies at the time. Had Japan and the four dragons risen simultaneously, they might well have been slowed down, if not stopped, by the key countries in the world economic community. Japan benefited by a strategy out of sync with most other states.

The Japanese example of turning a situation of wartime defeat and dependence into one of economic competitiveness and independence shone through the world economy like a lantern in the dark. The Japanese mastered the principles of the world economy, organized themselves collectively to be effective in it by targeting their efforts, and converted weakness into strength, poverty into wealth. It was not a matter just of strategies but of structures—educational and learning structures; industrial structures of close government-business cooperation; financial structures of long-term local financing for firms; job structures of lifetime employment and commitment for that portion of the working population employed in key sectors of manufacturing competitiveness; and value structures of group solidarity and community loyalty, which encouraged short-term savings and sacrifice for the sake of long-term collective gains and security (see Chapter 9).

Theories of international political economy are abstract; the astonishing Japanese results are concrete—a poor country that rose to major industrial status in the world in a mere 100 years. This chapter relates theoretical abstraction to comparative concreteness in state strategies at various phases of economic development. In the process, polarizations of Western thought—capitalism versus socialism, short-term versus long-term, homogeneity versus duality—seem to collapse.

As striking as the successes of the Japanese and Far Eastern "dragon" economies in the 1970s and 1980s was the unraveling of industrial economies in processes of deindustrialization, deregulation, and cutbacks in welfare-state development. The linear Western assumption of progress was turned on its head with regressive taxes replacing progressive taxes, disintegration replacing integration, illiteracy replacing literacy, and economic dualisms of various sorts replacing any single homogeneous standard of national economic development in so-called developed countries. The "postindustrial" society has proven to be a misnomer: The competitiveness of the "service economy" depends on the efficacy of its manufacturing base much as the competitiveness of industrial development depends on the efficiency of the agricultural sector. The deindustrialization of Great Britain in the second half of the twentieth century demonstrates that imperial economic designs have points of diminishing returns—as the Soviet economy demonstrated in the Eastern bloc with its desperate *perestroika* program. In 1989, *perestroika* released grass-roots democratic revolutions from below throughout Eastern Europe—from Poland and Hungary to East Germany and Rumania—making a shell of the one-party Communist state, which broke up as mass movements demanded political freedom and market-oriented reforms. But efforts of socialist states to move toward market incentives were not always one-way streets: In the late 1980s the People's Republic of China rolled back its free-market strategies after price increases outstripped wage increases and a 50 percent inflation rate, and economic corruption caused disenchantment among the masses of the Chinese population. National student demonstrations for reforms were crushed with the massacre at Tiananmen Square in Beijing, June 3, 1989. And the Chinese government repression of human rights with a later loosening of economic restrictions proved to be more effective for economic development than many Western analysts thought possible. Moreover, liberal economic "shock therapies" were countered with postliberal reactions in Poland and Russia in the 1990s (see Chapter 10).

Despite discontinuities stemming from the linear, progressive sequence of development posited by Western theorists, it is useful to summarize briefly the origins of these assumptions as a point of departure.

Origins

Conventional Western theories of national economic development assume a universal process of modernization, rationalization, secularization, and democratization. This focus is Eurocentric. Most of the social theorists came from the European tradition (and its American extension). The conventional modernization paradigm is the story of how the agrarian, feudal societies of Europe were transformed by the Industrial Revolution and the applied techniques of capitalism into modern, industrial societies of expanding markets, secular values, and institutions of democratic pluralism. The universality of this paradigm was taken for granted by Westerners. It was just a matter of time until other fortunate parts of the world would undergo European modernization, flavored with the egalitarian ideals of the French Revolution and the worldly aims of export-oriented, economic growth, using the manufacturing sector as the engine and trade as the means. That everyone would be better off after this transformation was also taken for granted, as the prosperity of free markets supported the growth of democratic political institutions, thus increasing individual rights and autonomy.

MODERNIZATION AND PURPOSIVE RATIONALITY

Modernization as understood in the Western tradition is a process of disenchantment in which reason, science, and technology systematically undermine traditional belief systems, mythologies, and spontaneous ways of doing things. Knowledge itself involves a process of disenchantment. The knower tests hypotheses against empirical experience, learning what the truth is as false assumptions are displaced in the process. Western modernization, however, turns this scientific testing process into a systematic ideology of applied reason or purposive rationality.

Modernization involves a cooling-off process in collective learning as people learn to detach themselves from their traditional habits and opinions and to test their behaviors for efficacy in the real world. To be modern is to be cool. Science and technology reign; superstition and emotion are edited out. Armed with reason—or technology, which is but reason applied—the individual becomes more autonomous and free of traditional social bonds. The state bureaucracy, in turn, becomes more powerful and centralized in order to keep individuals from spinning out into chaos or violence against the law. But how does this process of modernization get going and take off?

In 1861 Sir Henry Maine suggested that progress entailed a shift from a "status" society to a "contract" society. An individual in a status society is accorded rights and duties on the basis of family and kinship ties, whereas a contract society relies on contractual relationships between individuals, grounded on territorial ties and enforced by the acceptance of a universally defined code of ethics.[1] In 1887 Ferdinand Toennies elaborated upon Maine's distinction, contrasting *Gemeinschaft* (community) with *Gesellschaft* (society). *Gemeinschaft* is characterized by human association based on affective, nonrational, emotional ties of kinship, community, and neighborly spirit. *Gesellschaft*, in contrast, is marked by neutral human relations of rational, calculating individuals whose relationships are distinguished by contractual arrangements aimed at maximizing an individual's strategic goals. Belongingness was displaced by cool, contractual exchange as a society was modernized by the Industrial Revolution.[2]

In his *De la Division du travail social* of 1893, sociologist Emile Durkheim stressed the positive advantages of modern society (which he termed "organic") in terms of its potential for individual development. This contrasts with the repressive and "mechanical" nature of traditional society. Rather than seeing the danger of class conflict in greater role differentiation in a modern society, Durkheim perceived greater individual opportunities and a social solidarity based upon diverse but authentic interests in contrast to the more authoritarian form of solidarity imposed by traditional societies.[3]

At least three distinct phases of modernization can be identified—the traditional, the legal-rational, and the technological. After creation, a society hardens into routines and traditions—the traditional phase. The **traditional society** is based on affective or prerational community relationships (blood ties), diffuse role structures (jack-of-all-trades), and ascriptive notions of social and political authority (that is, deference for being the son of the king or a witch doctor). Eventually, the traditional society becomes so encumbered with routines and rites that people are obstructed from satisfying their needs—the original purpose of the society. At this point, sociologist Max Weber notes that a social crisis usually occurs: Political authority flows away from traditional roles (such as the king) to a charismatic leader who symbolizes the solution to the crisis. For Weber, the key to modernization was the shift in authority patterns from the traditional to the legal-rational, with the charismatic performing the function of transitions.[4]

A **legal-rational society** is one made up of contractual community relations (work prescribed by legal contracts), specific role structures (specialization rather than jack-of-all-trades), and achievement-oriented modes of social and political authority (deference given on the basis of accomplishment rather than blood ties to the king or the witch doctor). Of course legal-rational societies retain some of their traditional aspects, for no pure legal-rational societies exist anywhere in the world. The traditional, legal-rational, and charismatic are what Max Weber called *ideal types* of authority patterns—abstract theoretical constructs that represent or typify certain kinds of social realities.

Traditional societies become modern when their cultural norms of legitimacy are undermined and overwhelmed by the forces of rationalization and bureaucratization. Social thinker Jürgen Habermas defined this Western process of rationalization as the proliferation of *subsystems of purposive-rational action*. And far from being "value-free" or neutral, Habermas stressed the ideological nature of the uses of science and technology in this process of modernization.[5] Such forces of rationalization are marked by new bureaucratic reorganizations in legal-rational societies and by the dominance of applied scientific technology in technological societies.

In **technological societies** technologically exploitable knowledge undermines both traditional cultural norms and the social cooperation made possible by the legal-rational framework. Traditions are overwhelmed by scientific techniques, monarchs are replaced by technological maintenance professionals, roles dominate personalities, conditioning steers socialization. Humans as traditionally cultured beings are overwhelmed and dominated by the so-called apolitics of scientific technique and expertise. When Habermas in the late 1960s first pointed to purposive-rational action as being destructive of existing social bonds and community ties, the counterculture student rebellion (which latched on to his work) prevented him from being taken too seriously. But as foreign-language requirements (the study of at least one other traditional, cultural world) were displaced with computer science "literacy" in American high schools and colleges in the 1970s and 1980s, Habermas' insights became conventional wisdom. Technological societies tend not toward technological limits but toward technological satiation as an ever-greater percentage of the population clamors to get on board.

The ideological nature of purposive-rational action or the transformation into a technological society is manifest in the unwillingness to see social reality in any *other* way without identifying this alternative as "old-fashioned" or "archaic." For example, some of the world's greatest poets (perhaps the least economically motivated of people) insist on writing first in longhand rather than composing on a typewriter. Similarly, they may keep to an old typewriter rather than switch to a computer. Each of these technological innovations speeds up the writing process, but the poet wants to slow down the process for the sake of quality and tone. Modern technological society pays no one to slow down—even when slowing down may be in society's best interest. I recall being annoyed when first arriving in Bologna, Italy, from Manhattan to discover that the mail was not picked up each day (much less several times each day, as I was used to) at the Johns Hopkins University Center where I taught. For six months I lambasted this lack of efficiency, this hopeless lack of modernization, as my letters sat for three days before they were taken out. By the end of my three-year stay I found that I either withdrew or changed one-third of my letters, improving their quality. Back in the United States, I miss the slower pace and opportunity to retrieve my flawed work before it officially becomes "an anonymous product." Similarly, in Spain I was amazed to see a plumber use the palm of his hand in a pumping fashion to unclog a bathtub drain. Without the modern technology of a "plumber's helper" nearby I'd forgotten many of the original uses of the hand. It may be that the failures of the technological society will eventually teach us to slow down and to become more human. Technology is ideology insofar as it becomes a way of life, displacing other ways that may be more humanly satisfying.

In sum, the modernization process from the agricultural, traditional society to the industrial, legal-rational society, and finally to the technological, high-information society presupposes a process of systematic rationalization and a cooling down of values—sometimes in abstract, dehumanized forms. That there is often cultural resistance to this linear assumption of economic development or "progress" is hardly surprising and may, indeed, be wholesome. There is something in humans that demands a balance between the "hot" (emotional belief) and the "cool" (rationalization and industrialization). To neglect this need for balance is to invite another Iranian Revolution—a case in which a Westernized, technocratic Shah attempted to modernize his people too quickly on the Western model and was insensitive to the resistance on the part of the traditional segments of Iranian culture until fundamentalist leaders struck back with a vengeance from which the world still reverberates.

INTERPRETATIONS

Given the immense literature on Western modernization, the best one can do is to highlight a few basic themes as they relate to the fundamental thesis of the book—that there are patterns of collective learning that go a long way toward explaining the economic positioning of both the developed and developing nations in the global economy.

NEOCLASSICAL VERSUS TRANSFORMATIONAL SCHOOLS

Perhaps the main "civil war" between schools of thought on economic development since World War II has been the debate between the neoclassical and transformational schools. Derived from Adam Smith, neoclassical models stress the linearity of economic growth with collective learning most effectively triggered by market mechanisms (as opposed to being imposed by state intervention). In contrast, the transformational school argues that the neoclassical argument is too simplistic and that successful modern capitalist societies involve major restructuring of sectors, social relations of production, investment targets, and institutional frameworks conducive to entrepreneurial risk and innovation. Indeed, Charles Lindblom's *Politics and Markets* could be seen as a response to this debate in which Lindblom suggests that the most useful political economy question is how much state and how much market? This either/or framework, however, leads him to a rather typical American liberal stress on the antagonism between the state and the business sector, with the nontypical surprise ending: Big companies have won the struggle in the American economy by out-positioning every other potentially threatening interest group.[6] However, the oversimplifying abstraction—state versus market—underestimates the subtleties of mixed economies.

Rather than asking "How much state and how much market?" it may be more compelling to ask "How much capitalism is necessary for modernization?" And "How much modernization is possible without undermining cultural integrity?" In the late twentieth century, many developing countries headed by governments publicly "anticapitalist" privately sought financial and technological support from developed capitalist nations. Ideological compromises were made to achieve the "takeoff" from agricultural to industrial stages of economic development—as in the de-Maofication of China and the early 1980s emphasis there upon private economic incentives and "zones."[7] Mao Zedong saw that "purposive rational action" was overwhelming his socialist agenda, thus causing him to try to turn back the clock with his Cultural Revolution (against the intellectuals and technocrats) in the late 1960s. But it was too late. Once the forces of technological society have been released from the bottle, no magician can wish them back into it again merely by waving an ideological wand. Nevertheless, the leaders of the People's Republic of China reversed themselves again in 1988, fearing that entrepreneurial individualism, soaring inflation, and economic corruption were getting out of hand in Chinese society.[8] The question they confronted was: "How much capitalism is really necessary for the modernization of China?" In Eastern Europe the question was reversed after the revolutions of 1989: "How much socialism can we afford to keep if we are to become autonomous and competitive nations in the world economy?" (See Chapter 10.)

CAPITALIST INCENTIVES AND ECONOMIC GROWTH

The historical evidence since World War II suggests that "the inevitability of capitalism" is less a passing phase of modern development than Marx or Lenin supposed. On the one hand, socialist economies were forced to introduce capitalist or private-market incentives to stimulate economic growth and industrial production. On the other hand, the postindustrial phase has proved to be elusive for developed Western economies, which have resorted to fiscal austerity and tax-cutting measures to rekindle falling growth rates in productivity and to raise stalemated national growth rates and national competitiveness in world markets.[9]

Economic growth depends on the effective collective motivation of human activity—ultimately on a large scale. But human motives start small.[10] Economic motives necessarily address the self-interest of the individual. Noneconomic, social, or ideological motives may spark unusual individual initiative at certain critical, charismatic phases of historical development and revolutionary transformation, but as passions abate so does the influence of this "selfless" collective form of motivation in the economy.[11] The stick replaces the ideological carrot and when the stick no longer works, the private market incentives of Adam Smith are (re)introduced through the back door. Consider the private garden plots promoted to reverse agricultural stalemate in the Soviet Union, or the capitalist economic zones set up in the People's Republic of China to attract foreign investment and technology.

Stages of Economic Growth   Perhaps the best-known summary of the vision of inevitable capitalist stages of economic development in the modern state is W. W. Rostow's influential book *The Stages of Economic Growth: A Non-Communist Manifesto*

(1960). According to Rostow, all modern societies since about 1700 can be located within one of five categories in terms of their economic dimensions: the traditional society; the preconditions for takeoff; the takeoff; the drive to maturity; and the age of high mass-consumption.

While not static, the initial traditional phase is limited in attainable output per head by "pre-Newtonian science and technology and pre-Newtonian attitudes toward the physical world." Traditional societies generally devote a high proportion of their resources to agriculture. This, in turn, involves an hierarchical social structure with relatively narrow scope for vertical mobility.

Rostow compares the second stage, "preconditions for takeoff," to the process of building up compound interest in a savings account by leaving in interest to compound with principal. Growth normally proceeds by geometric progression, and this requires a transition involving education, increased receptivity to modern science, and the assumption of the necessity of growth; increased investment in transportation, communications, and raw materials; and the emergence of entrepreneurs in the private sector and in government willing to mobilize savings and to take risks in pursuit of profit or modernization. The scope of commerce expands as modern manufacturing evolves using new methods. Still, the socioeconomic pace remains traditionally slow with low-productivity methods predominating. A decisive feature at this stage is the development of an effective, centralized state, fostering a new nationalism and creating coalitions in opposition to traditional landed regional interests and colonial power.

The third stage of economic growth, the "takeoff phase," is the watershed of modernity. Growth becomes the society's normal condition as old ways and resistances are overcome: "Compound interest becomes built, as it were, into its habits and institutional structure."[12]

In the terms of *this* book, a collective learning or adaptation process has taken place and becomes part of the infrastructure of social institutions and the motivational milieu of the citizenry. Rostow maintains that the main stimulus for takeoff in the Anglo-Saxon countries (Britain, the United States, and Canada) was technological. Not only is there a buildup of social overhead capital and technological development in agriculture and industry, but also a group comes to political power determined to make economic modernization a high priority on the government's agenda. Typically, the rate of effective investment and savings doubles and new industries expand rapidly.

The fourth stage of economic growth, the drive to maturity, involves a 10 percent to 20 percent investment of the national income. This allows output to keep ahead of population increases and stimulates the spread of technology throughout the nation's economy. Fluctuations in progress and ceaseless shifting in economic sectors lead the society to discover its role in the world economy. About sixty years after the beginning of the takeoff phase, maturity is usually attained, involving refined and technologically complex economic processes. At this point the economy demonstrates the capacity to move beyond the key industries that powered its takeoff to apply modern technology and efficiency to managing the resources throughout the nation. The society shows that it has the technology and entrepreneurial skills to produce whatever it decides to produce (although it may lack the resources or preconditions to provide everything).

Finally, the economy moves into the fifth and final stage of economic growth, the age of high mass-consumption, which stresses durable consumer goods and services. Basic needs have been met. In this "postmaturity" phase, the further extension of technology is no longer accepted as an overriding objective. Social welfare and security emerge as primary areas of state spending in the society where consumer sovereignty reigns. Beyond this mass-consumption phase, Rostow envisioned the possibility of a value shift, subsequently termed "postindustrialism," in which basic material satisfactions could be taken for granted and most people would seek higher-level satisfactions.[13]

Rostow called this hypothetical future "the pattern of Buddenbrooks dynamics" after the novel by Thomas Mann that traces several generations of the Buddenbrook family: the first seeking money; the second taking money for granted and desiring social and civic position; and the third, born of both comfort and family prestige, looking toward music for satisfaction. The "Buddenbrooks behavioral dynamics" epitomized the changing aspirations of succeeding generations as they give low value to that which they take for granted while seeking newer sources of satisfaction.

As the late twentieth-century world economy shifted back toward promarket, procapitalist models, Rostow's influential stage-model appears somewhat prophetic, which is why his theory is detailed here. Yet one must be wary of its oversimplification, pretense of universality, and Eurocentric (if not Anglo-American) bias. The experience of Latin American industrialization illustrates that takeoff stages were never really reached. Takeoff was blocked by production bottlenecks, the saturation of domestic markets for consumer nondurables, and the difficulty that countries discovered in graduating to the manufacturing of consumer durables without foreign corporate ownership of such manufacturing enterprises. As a recipe grounded in various interlocking forms of collective learning, Rostow's sequence is more viable as a blueprint than as a forecast.

Social Costs of Capitalist Growth   Every recipe has its opportunity costs: One may not like the taste of the meal that results, no matter how abundant it may be. Capitalist growth has social and environmental costs. Most of the negative social effects of capitalism are well known. Indeed, they are too often taken for granted by those of the "capitalist habit of mind" and too often underestimated by developing societies that hunger for the material luxuries of advanced Western nations. The free pursuit of individual self-interest creates a society of winners and losers. Moreover, capitalism appeals to those with a winner's instinct; socialism to those with a loser's. Assuming he or she will win, the capitalist wants the greatest share of the economic product that he or she had a hand in producing, paying as little as possible to the government umpire in the form of taxes. However, assuming one will sooner or later lose leads one to desire social insurance and security provided by the state even if the cost in taxes of this risk-reducing insurance keeps going up. Thus, the priority of economic growth accentuates the distance between the winning and losing social groups, constantly redirecting resources to the winners in order to make them self-fulfilling prophecies and "locomotives" for the economy. To the extent capitalist incentives are inevitable, so are manifestations of social inequality.[14]

Karl Marx, of course, took this as his point of departure, saying that the winners in capitalism were few and the losers many: Eventually he anticipated a point in economic development and polarization in which quantity would be transformed into quality as the many rejected a system in which they, as the absolute majority, were structured to be the losers. However, rather than the many becoming increasingly impoverished, the poor have become at least marginally better off in capitalist societies, undoing the collective motivation that Marx believed would lead to revolution. And, when interviewed, even those who are not better off in capitalist society are against turning over the system, for they seem to be confident that their children or grandchildren will be better off. They want a better shake and a larger share rather than a revolutionary transformation. Perhaps these attitudes can be explained by the findings in Chapter 7 on education and class, which demonstrated those down the class scale are more likely to focus on concrete values today rather than upon abstract ideological convictions: mass consumerism *ad absurdum*.

Thus the classical liberal ideology of maximizing national economic growth over all other values is inherently unlimited. The increase of anything is equal to the additions minus the subtractions: More additions mean growth. Growth tends to expand until its ecological niche is filled—and the niche is ever-changing. The concept of equilibrium is thus a fiction—it is a mere temporary state when an ecological niche has momentarily been filled. Even the earth is an open system of disequilibrium in that when fossil fuels are exhausted, solar energy from outside the terrestrial sphere provides an alternative. Because everything is either in growth or decline—in a normal state of *dis*equilibrium—the natural, democratic political appeal has to be for more growth (not decline). The crucial question of political economy is: Whose growth is it or who will it belong to? And further, At what social and ecological cost will this growth take place? The natural tendency is for each nation to run an export-oriented growth policy in order to maximize domestic wealth even at every other nation's expense, using the rest of the world in free-rider fashion as a dumping ground for industrial waste, unemployment, inflation, wars, and so on. Because there is no international police force, there is nothing to prevent the most powerful nation from maximizing its own growth at everyone else's expense and distributing the benefits of this growth to a small minority of its people. In a world economy that has become a global village, any one nation's growth has social and ecological implications for every other nation.

However, even the successful state operated like an economic growth machine needs to keep its legitimacy going to maintain itself. The key question for the legitimacy of the state is whether or not the marginal inequality necessary for economic growth incentives is based upon an "open" meritocracy or on a "closed" concentration of resources. The development of democratic institutions fosters openness. Even if one does not go as far as to accept Marxian class analysis, which argues that the appropriation of surplus labor in the form of surplus value by the upper classes will undermine legitimacy, a process of "delegitimization" appears to accompany the progressive "rationalization" of society as scientific and technical development is institutionalized. Sociologist Jürgen Habermas observed that the technical and organizational conditions under which social wealth is produced by industrially advanced capitalism make it increasingly difficult to assign status in an even subjectively convincing manner through the mechanism for evaluating individual achievement.[15] In other words, as the "rational" status-hierarchy of achievement of the industrial stage of development is undermined by technological advances in the "casino capitalism" of the high-tech, high-information economy, profit and social status often seem less associated with greater productivity than with successful speculation. Take corporate takeover efforts or computer stock arbitrage, for example. As the old industrial class system is undermined, individuals shuffle between social categories more loosely in society, particularly in the United States where status, not class, is the measure of social significance, and the cash nexus in the 1980s and 1990s became the driving force behind the achievement of status.[16]

The classical liberal ideology of growth assumes that capitalism will generate enough opportunities so that the disadvantaged can pick themselves up by their own bootstraps, thus eliminating the need for extensive redistributions of wealth by the state. The bootstrap theory of growth as a substitute for redistribution has failed exactly to the extent that most existing capitalist societies shortchange open meritocracy or opportunity for the sake of established concentrations of resources and interest groups.[17] Democratic institutions have become too abstractly representative and technocratic, if not oligarchical.

Greater economic production pulls up the entire society and provides for employment, but usually at the social cost of creating greater gaps between the rich and the poor and of sharpening the competition for access to meaningful jobs.[18] If the gap between the high earners and low earners becomes too great for the legitimacy of the social system to bear, a political shift to the left for the sake of fairer redistribution is a probable result. If, on the other hand, the pendulum swings too far to the other end of the spectrum in providing and redistributing more social services than the economy can bear, a deficit-cutting austerity policy and shift to the political right tends to result.[19]

Such pendular extremes in societies heavily reliant on capitalist incentives have helped to lead some to conclude that capitalism has a tendency to create a social context in which it "self-destructs."[20] According to this interpretation, capitalist growth results in such a level of affluence that an overdose of leisure time and overeducated citizens are spawned—forces that undermine the bureaucratic rationality of industrial efficiency with counterculture lifestyles and socialist attacks by intellectuals. Antigrowth, antibusiness, antitechnology constituencies emerge in this "destructive" Buddenbrooks behavior scenario, undermining the legitimacy of the economic growth as the highest priority in society.

The challenge confronting postmodern managers is to find a way to structure the inevitable capitalist incentives and inequalities necessary for economic growth in a socially acceptable framework of meritocracy and opportunity so that both social equity and prosperity are furthered, thus making legitimacy self-sustaining as well as growth. Full employment is not possible without economic growth, but economic growth is quite feasible without full-employment. And as if it were not difficult enough to find out how to establish social limits for the sake of legitimacy without killing the goose that lays the golden egg, different rates of economic growth in different sectors of the economy complicate the problem.

DUAL ECONOMIES AND ENGINES OF CREATIVE DESTRUCTION

Capitalism is a philosophy of winners who become self-fulfilling prophecies of success. Winners consolidate their positions and attract resources, sometimes to the point of monopoly. Successful centers of development tend to draw off resources from peripheral areas where they are more badly needed. **Dual economies** operate at many levels during all phases of a nation's economic development. Indeed, to the extent that the world economy is driven by capitalist incentives, and technological progress is permitted to drive out the old with the new at an ever-increasing tempo, any existing economic sector in any society could be considered "dual." What exists will soon and inevitably become obsolete and be displaced by a more dynamic and adaptive development. State strategies may be most effective in assuming themselves to be obsolete upon birth. By permitting national institutions to cushion their infancy and to pay back their "opportunity costs," they plough themselves under with their own self-spawned technological replacements. But if effectiveness is the only social criterion, vast regions of the country may be left temporarily unemployed, in the dark, as it were, as the limelight shifts to the newest technological development. Few are in the economic sunshine at any one moment, while the majority exist in some kind of shadow economy.

The reality of **dualism** and discontinuity in even the most developed technological economies shatters the myth that one homogeneous national economy can be managed with supply-and-demand tools from a centralized cockpit and that macroeconomic trends can be projected only "from the top." While some centralization and use of supply-and-demand tools are necessary, they are not sufficient to explain, control, or project national economic trends. "The system" is a composite of systems.

Dualism and discontinuity are most obvious in developing countries predominated by small domestic markets and industries with low output. The emerging modern sector in these countries produces high output over time, composed of enclave economies directed toward large **metropoles** (metropolitan centers of large, developed economies) or toward the world market. And given the larger sizes of these developed or extensive markets, the modern sector tends to consist of large, capital-intensive enterprises. Dualism in both developing and developed economies results from factors relating to the market, the division of labor, and productivity. But the specific causes of dualism are usually different in the two cases. In the case of the lesser-developed country, dualism usually emerges because of industries of different sizes. In the developed country, on the other hand, dualism most often stems from the varying degrees of the stability of markets within the same industries.[21]

In *Modern Capitalism*, John Cornwall demonstrates that the *dual-economy model* can be a powerful mode of explaining growth-rate differences in the more advanced OECD (developed) market economies in the period since World War II. Cornwall stresses the importance of entrepreneurship and investment in manufacturing technologies as catalysts in bringing about qualitative changes or structural transformations.[22] The key is the importance of demand and of the opportunity of absorbing less productive workers in a traditional sector (say agriculture) into a more productive manufacturing sector without unduly raising their wages. The beginning of the development process entails the enlargement of the advanced sector (usually but not necessarily the industrial). At this stage there is no emphasis upon wages, for the backward sector has a backlog of underemployed workers who can be released for the advanced sector—workers who demand only slightly higher salaries due to their marginal productivity. Thus the industrial sector can be widened without the deepening of capital through hefty wage increases and expanding employment. At a certain point the backward sector becomes so small that stable wages cannot be maintained and intense structural change results.

VIRTUOUS VERSUS VICIOUS CIRCLES AND LEARNING BY DOING

Cornwall's explanation takes **Engel's law** into account—that at different levels of income people have an elasticity of demand that differs (for example, in becoming richer, at a certain point you cannot continue to buy more steak instead of chicken for dinner, and shift your money somewhere else). Accordingly, various sectors of the economy grow at a different pace. In the process of structural change, technology gaps emerge in different areas in different countries. But the manufacturing sector is "the engine of growth." And following Verdoorn's law (the "learning-by-doing approach"), there are numerous advantages that are derived from a fast-growing manufacturing sector due to learning-by-doing as workers go through new technological steps.

The learning-by-doing approach depends on a distinction between static and dynamic economies of scale in the manufacturing sector. A **static economy of scale** refers to a reduction of unit costs (and a rise in average productivity) as output over a given production period goes up. Typically, static economies of scale come from increases in plant, firm, or industry size. Longer production runs in the same production time reduce unit costs since production does not have to be stopped and started up again, less inventory has to be kept, and there is less loss of downtime to make adjustments for running through different models. The Deming principle of increasing quality by reducing variation seems to be at work here.* In contrast, **dynamic economies of scale** are "learning economies" since they involve continuous reductions in unit costs and increases in productivity attributable to continuous increases in output of a corporation, industry, or economy over time. The key of **Verdoorn's law** is the stress on the growth of output in determining the rate of growth of productivity rather than the level of output determining the average level of productivity.[23] Productivity growth results from a learning process, particularly in the capital goods industry, a process that can be maintained only by constant new investment.[24] The industrialization of Japan and the de-industrialization of Great Britain since World War II provide two illustrations of learning-by-doing in the context of economic dualism.[25]

Thus, the manufacturing sector acts as an engine of economic growth (or **creative destruction**) in having not only backward but also forward linkages as it propels the dynamic-learning economy in a virtuous economic circle and demonstrates positive learning reactions. The strategic nature of manufacturing output becomes clear in the links between domestic economic conditions and external export and monetary results.

The dual-economy structure sets the state up for either vicious or virtuous circles, which are critical for international competitiveness. In the post-World War II period, Britain, for example, often slipped into a **vicious circle** of sluggish productivity, which led to difficulties in exports, problems in the balance of payments, lower productivity growth, excessive wage increases, and a decline in competitiveness in world markets. Typically, a vicious circle strategy involves devaluing the currency in order to stimulate export sales in the short term by making them cheaper; but this has the effect of increasing inflation at home, thus causing workers to demand higher wages to match rising living costs, driving up the costs of production, and making exports less competitive, until the government intervenes with another devaluation to start the circle anew. An economy in a virtuous circle such as West Germany after World War II, on the other hand, shows a steady or improving level of productivity at home, leading to competitiveness abroad with export growth resulting in opportunities for employment and investment, which, in turn, help to stimulate productivity, revalue the currency upwards to head off inflation, maintain competitiveness, and lead to an avoidance of balance-of-payments problems.

---

*W. Edwards Deming's essential fourteen points for managers aim to create constancy of purpose toward improvement of product and service by ceasing dependence on inspection to achieve quality, eliminating the need for inspection on a mass basis by building quality into the product in the first place, moving to minimize total costs by awarding business on the basis of price tag, and moving toward a single supplier with long-term trust and commitment. See Bruce Serlen, "W. Edwards Deming: The Man Who Made Japan Famous for Quality," *New York University Business* (fall 1987/winter 1988): 18. Or Andrea Gabor, *The Man Who Discovered Quality* (New York: Penguin Books, 1990).

NEOCORPORATISM

Neocorporatism is another interpretation of successful capitalist economies since World War II that stresses not the underlying economic factors of production, labor cost, inflation, investment, and learning-by-doing but the institutional relationships among major business, labor, and governmental interest groups that are conducive to harmonious collective management and equity in representation by various levels of workers in society. The original notion of **corporatism**, or state corporatism, stems from a belief in political representation through functional, occupation-related institutions, not geographically defined electoral units. State corporatism was embodied in the right-wing **Fascist** regimes of Mussolini in Italy and Franco in Spain. The "new" or "neo" or "liberal" corporatism is used to describe post-1945 Western economies that still guarantee certain functional labor, management, and employee interest groups more or less a monopoly right to represent their part of society in government negotiations but without the coercive aspects of state corporatism negatively associated with the Fascist governments.[26] Free elections, democratic rights, and the ability to withdraw from negotiations voluntarily as an interest group are political characteristics of neocorporatism, as contrasted with corporatism. Yet neocorporatism still maintains integrated, functional "peak" organizations as the chief labor-management bargainers in the government-labor organizations for workers, business federations for employers, agricultural organizations for farmers, and so forth. Each worker or employer is automatically a member of the organization relevant to that economic sector in government policy-making. Neocorporatist states can be contrasted with noncorporatist states with fragmented economic interest groups without such widespread membership that are only intermittently consulted by the government and where such interest groups rarely carry out administrative duties on behalf of the state.[27]

Neocorporatist states tend to have large working-class movements, a heavily unionized labor force, and a social democratic tradition. The neocorporatist states of Norway, Sweden, and Austria, for instance, have a unionized labor force making up the overwhelming majority of the work force. The Social Democratic Party has also done well in these countries, particularly in Sweden, where it dominated the government for half a century until the 1990 austerity program—which froze wages, prices, rents, local taxes, and stock dividends, plus banned strikes for two-years—undermined the Social Democratic Party, leading to electoral defeat (see Chapter 7). And in Germany, often identified as having many neocorporatist characteristics, unionized labor plays a strong role in labor-management-major parties. A country with strong corporatist traditions is one in which the trade union leadership and employers' associations are committed to an ideology of social partnership and where the trade unions, employers, and the state cooperate in some economic policy areas. Usually the number of labor strikes is low in such states and "authoritarian" income policies are not imposed by the state. Switzerland is sometimes interpreted as a liberal form of corporatism with comparatively low state involvement.[28] And Japan is sometimes described as "corporatism without labor" or "private corporatism." The Japanese represent a consortium of big business and government with labor largely coopted in unions organized *within* specific firms that at one time promised lifetime employment.

The countries with corporatist modes of policy coordination, whether of the liberal (meaning less state) or more heavily social democratic versions—Austria, Japan, Norway, Sweden, and Switzerland—managed to maintain relatively low levels of unemployment from 1974 into the 1980s compared to the mass unemployment that plagued all other OECD countries during this period.[29] The consensus on social cooperation reinforces the stability of the maintenance base of these welfare states. The key questions raised is: To what extent can these societies afford the trade-off costs in terms of economic growth and entrepreneurial innovation implied by state-centered, as opposed to more pluralistic market-oriented, economies?

Let us consider a contrast to the neocorporatist model in which the state, in cooperation with others, focuses upon a single sector with great success and bargaining power at certain historical moments.

COMMODITY PRODUCER CARTELS: THE CASE OF OPEC

While OPEC is referred to as a commodity producer cartel rather than as a trading bloc, the effect in terms of the world economy is similar: A limited group of member nations strive to cooperate to increase their internal development benefits, shifting the costs to those outside the club wherever possible through joint pricing policies. The rationale for comparing OPEC to a trading bloc is increased when one notes that world economic data in the late twentieth century were usually broken down into "oil-producing" versus "non-oil-producing" developing countries, reflecting the importance of the OPEC bloc from the 1960s into the 1980s. In the late 1980s and early 1990s OPEC appeared to decline into insignificance as alternative energy sources and suppliers grew, energy consumption and environmental emissions controls became popular, oil prices fell, and OPEC members failed to keep up with technological developments on the one hand, or to manage their quotas seriously, on the other. By 1996 the combined estimated population of the OPEC member countries was 463 million.Functionally, OPEC served like the EU as a buffer zone against the creative destruction of turbulent change of global capitalism—an effort at cooperative management by individual states or organizations in order to cope with change to their mutual benefit. Buffer zones such as trade blocs or commodity cartels can be seen as arenas of opportunity for collective learning and structural positioning, which succeed through solidarity and joint traditions of learning by doing, and fail to the extent solidarity and such mutually beneficial learning traditions break down. While other commodity cartels, in commodities such as copper and coffee, failed after consumers soon found substitutes or found that they could do without, the OPEC oil cartel was to prove more successful given the economic and strategic importance of oil.

After World War II the global economy was characterized by excess oil supply over demand, dominated by "the Seven Sisters"—the major multinational oil companies of the West: Exxon, Texaco, Mobil, Standard of California, Gulf, Shell, and British Petroleum. These seven companies controlled both production levels and prices throughout the 1950s and 1960s, more or less dictating management policies to the host developing countries whose oil provided the basic resource for the business. Given the surplus of supply over demand, oil prices were kept low, thus providing a cheap energy basis for the extraordinary economic growth rates of Western nations through the 1960s. In 1959, the Seven Sisters, actually lowered oil prices, triggering the formation of OPEC by developing nations who defensively banded together in an initially impotent gesture in 1960 to try to hold the line on the price of the commodity upon which their economic survival seemed to depend.

OPEC was first made up of Iran, Iraq, Kuwait, Saudi Arabia, and Venezuela. Later, Indonesia, Algeria, Libya, Nigeria, Ecuador, Qatar, Abu Dhabi, Dubai, Sharjah, and Gabon joined them. Thus, one could say that OPEC was symbolically created from the threat imposed by a cartel of multinational corporations who overplayed their dominant hand to the point of making economic injustice patently blatant.

At the end of the 1960s, major shifts were occurring in the global oil industry. Independent oil companies—such as Occidental Petroleum—sprang up alongside the Seven Sisters, establishing their own sources of supply and diffusing the power of the major oil firms. High growth rates in the Western economies increased energy consumption to such an extent that the international oil market became tight as demand came in sight of matching supply. The dollar—the currency in which oil is priced—was devalued, increasing inflationary pressures already hitting the oil-producing developing countries hard. Col. Muammar el-Qaddafi, the unpredictable leader of Libya, correctly perceived an unusual bargaining opportunity in the changed world economy. He demanded a higher price from Occidental Petroleum for Libyan oil than the price asked in the Middle East, arguing that Occidental's transport costs for Libyan oil were cheaper and that the low sulfur content of Libyan crude gave it a special value to ecologically minded Western consumers with their rising environmental standards. Because Occidental Petroleum depended almost solely upon Libya as a source of supply, this independent company was eventually pressured to give into Qaddifi's demands despite counterpressures by other oil companies.

Anticipating that Libya's success would lead to similar demands on oil companies by other Middle Eastern states, which in turn would stimulate Qaddafi to raise Libyan prices even more—resulting in a vicious circle—the major oil companies got the oil-producing nations of the Middle East and North Africa to agree to the Teheran and Tripoli Agreements of 1971. These agreements were designed to manage world oil price increases in a stable structure of multinational cooperation. Alas, the major multinational companies had "learned" too late.

OPEC's breakthrough, largely inspired by Qaddafi, was based on the willingness of major OPEC members to take concrete and concerted actions in the event that negotiations should fail.[30] Libya cut back its oil output to convince oil companies to lower their prices—at a moment when Libyan oil (supplying about a quarter of Western Europe's needs) was in great demand. When Occidental Petroleum agreed to Qaddafi's demands, other companies followed suit and that set the stage for the Teheran negotiations of February 1971, largely tilted in favor of the oil-producing countries.

However, global economic and political events quickly outstripped the Teheran and Tripoli Agreements—the 1971 and 1973 dollar devaluations, the outbreak of war in the Middle East in October 1973, and the resulting oil embargo by the Arab oil-producing states against the United States, the Netherlands, and Portugal for their support of Israel. Afraid that their vital oil-supply lines could be disrupted, Western nations bid up the price of oil. OPEC took advantage of this great uncertainty in the world oil markets to quadruple the price of petroleum. Given domestic political uncertainties in the United States (of which the Arabs were well aware), the Americans were in no position to follow political scientist Robert Tucker's risky advice to invade and occupy the Saudi Arabian oil fields until oil prices came down. OPEC's world energy "revolution" was thus a *fait accompli* (see Figure 8-1).

Figure 8-1 History by the Barrel (Cost per Barrel in Constant Dollars)

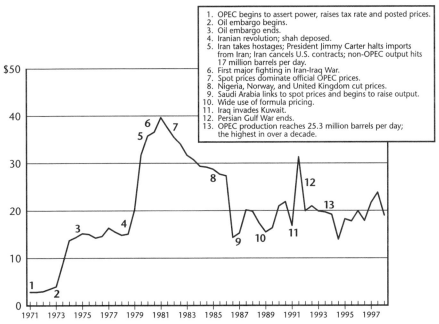

Source: Edited from Energy Information Administration, U.S. Department of Energy.

From the perspective of the developed oil-importing countries, the quadrupling of oil prices in 1973 and the subsequent doubling of oil prices in 1979 following the revolution in Iran were seen as "crises." But from the perspective of the oil-producing states these price rises were perceived as "adjustments of imbalances" long overdue. As Dr. Fadhil Chalabi of Iraq, the second in command at the OPEC Secretariat in Vienna, noted in 1980, given the dollar devaluations and inflation of the 1970s, if the same quantities of oil continued to be pumped at the same low prices, the oil reserves would be depleted much sooner than anticipated. This would not give oil-producing developing countries the time to use their oil revenues to invest in infrastructure development and alternative industries to complement their lopsided oil economies.

Financially, the oil-producing countries would be better off to leave their oil in the ground than to deplete their lifeblood resources at low prices in an inflationary environment when developed Western countries were anxious to stockpile all the oil they could in case their supply should be cut off. Moreover, Chalabi argued that a consistently rising price of this finite fuel was in the interest of Western economies, which desired to become less dependent upon OPEC oil and needed higher oil prices to stimulate the search and development of alternative sources of energy.[31]

OPEC's 1973 and 1979 price rises had a deflationary rather than an inflationary impact on the world economy of the 1980s for a complex set of reasons. Most of the OPEC oil-producing nations had an absolute preference for liquidity in their investment strategies, putting their petrodollars into short-term (usually off-shore) bank accounts where they could not be easily taxed or frozen by governmental authorities. This liquidity preference meant that the OPEC states served as a transformer of real investment capital into short-term liquidity, creating a worldwide liquidity surplus. Meanwhile, in the rich developed countries, inflationary fears led to anti-inflation policies and austerity measures, resulting in tight money policies and high interest rates. Inflation was subdued at significant social costs (for example, the severe U.S. recession of 1981–1982). Conservation measures in the energy field and massive oil stockpiling by governments and companies led to an oil glut in the disinflationary environment of the mid-1980s. Paradoxically, this temporary situation of oil abundance diluted OPEC's power. By 1988 OPEC found it necessary to invite non-OPEC oil producers to their negotiations in order to consolidate the petroleum trading bloc and reduce production enough to keep prices rising (a strategy repeated in 1999). But these efforts were mixed given that OPEC members did not carry out all the promises made at the negotiations (that is, producing more oil than they were supposed to), particularly given the uncertainties of the war winding down between Iran and Iraq. And if OPEC members themselves refuse to abide by their own agreements, compliance by non-OPEC oil producers is also undermined.

However, during the last three years of the 1980s the demand for oil steadily grew, along with the exports of crude oil by OPEC members. Moderates, such as Saudi Arabia's oil minister, Hirsham Nazer, saw to it that oil prices were kept

stable and relatively low in order to take away the incentive for Western countries to develop their own new sources of energy. And to prevent other OPEC
members from attempting to outposition Saudi dominance in the cartel, the
Saudis threatened to pump oil freely if any other member tried to reduce its 25
percent share of total OPEC output. As the country with the largest proven un-
tapped oil reserves, Saudi Arabia would like to extend the dependence of others
upon its oil for as long as possible in order to have time to modernize and create non-oil sources of wealth. The Saudi fear of loss due to the threat of revolutionary change motivated the Saudi government to make its alliance with the
United States explicit during the Gulf War of 1990–1991.

   Although the United States took only 10 percent of its oil from the Persian
Gulf, while Japan and Europe depended on oil from the region for more than half
of their energy needs, the Bush administration saw an opportunity to manage
the crisis caused by Iraq's invasion of Kuwait for both economic and strategic
gains. By organizing the United Nations coalition of developed countries who
could pay for the war, the United States subsidized its military risks and restored
American hegemony. The compliance of the Arab states with the trade embargo
against Iraq confirmed U.S. primacy and set the stage for not only restoring OPEC's
ability to function after the war but for the wider Middle East peace agreements
that emerged between Israel and her Arab neighbors in 1993. U.S. stability depends in part on the moderate management of the OPEC cartel by the Saudis. This
assumption of permanent dependence prevents the American government from
having to bite the bullet of a painful reform of its energy policy. Twenty years after
the 1973 Arab oil embargo, the United States continued to use approximately
the same amount of oil. But in 1993 it imported 44.6 percent of its oil compared
to 37.2 percent in 1973. And 11.6 percent of the oil in 1993 came from Arab members of OPEC as opposed to just 5.3 percent in 1973.[32]

   As oil-producing Arab countries recovered from the Gulf War, the impact was
deflationary, supporting U.S. complacency in terms of its energy policy. For example, by 1993 Kuwait was again producing almost as much oil as it had before
the August 1990 Iraqi invasion—the third largest Arab producer after Saudi Arabia and Iran.[33] OPEC was confronted with how to share world oil markets without
pushing down the prices of petroleum. OPEC attempted to impose quotas on
the producers who recovered from the war. But their motive was to make up for
the revenues lost when they had no oil revenue and quotas were not very effective. The result was continuous cheating within OPEC, increasing production beyond agreed upon targets, keeping oil prices down. This, in turn, helped keep
inflation and gas prices down, encouraging Americans to continue their profligate
uses of energy and their policy of increasing dependence upon foreign sources of
oil. By 1994 crude oil prices hit a 5-year low and OPEC accounted for 37 percent
of world oil production. Whereas in the mid-70s, OPEC oil accounted for 56 percent of global energy requirements, by 1997 it accounted for only about 26 percent. In the same period, the number of major oil producing countries grew from
19 to 33. And rather than being 50 percent of the world's primary energy supply

in 1973 (with nuclear being 1 percent; and gas 18 percent), by 1996 oil provided barely 40 percent of primary global energy, while nuclear energy's share had risen to almost 8 percent and that of natural gas to almost 24 percent. Last but not least, whereas the annual price of oil increased 30 percent per annum in 1973–1981, it increased only 2 percent per annum between 1991 and 1996.

In an "obituary" for OPEC, Fadhil Chalabi wrote in 1998 that to survive, OPEC had to learn to give up old habits and face the new realities of a competitive, transparent, environmentally sensitive high tech economy.[34] A new strategy mix emerged in 1999 when decline in oil revenues by a third in 1998 caused Norway and Mexico to unite with OPEC to cut production by 3 percent with the support of big oil firms.[35]

* * *

Since 1973, the emergence of the floating exchange-rate regime, the volatility of oil prices, and the policy-linked distortions of the value of the dollar warped the context of global economic development and severely limited the strategy options available to all nation-states, rich or poor. Still, the hard-currency countries had much more flexibility than did the majority of the world's soft-currency nations, whether the fashionable policies were inflationary or (more commonly) anti-inflationary. Able to take their maintenance domestic frameworks for granted, these hard-currency countries were able to pursue entrepreneurial strategies using the Eurodollar markets as free-riders to reduce the cost of imported inflation. The successful West German strategy in the "floating game," for example, was to appreciate the value of the mark to push down imported inflation, but not to the level of global inflation, thus preserving West German export markets.[36] Hooking their own currency to the value of the West German mark, the Austrians maintained a hard-currency policy, using foreign-exchange-rate subsidized capital imports to finance domestic restructuring and development.[37] West Germany and Austria used the priority of stable maintenance strategies as a base for secondary entrepreneurial and free-rider strategies in order to protect themselves from inflation and to maintain their international competitiveness.

The Swiss had another effective brand of "maintenpreneurial" strategy.* They used monetary policy to neutralize foreign inflows through a wide range of controls. And they used their effective federal Export Risk Insurance scheme to protect Swiss exporters from all sorts of risks stemming from transfer, bad debts, production, politics, and particularly the threat to their prices and profits resulting from the appreciation of the Swiss franc.[38]

The strategies of weak-currency countries in the agricultural development category, on the other hand, aimed for mere maintenance as a goal. They used depreciation to improve their balance of current accounts and to substitute for imported depression or unemployment. Taking economic advice from the Cambridge School, developing countries in Latin America, such as Mexico, took all

---

*A "maintenpreneurial" strategy is one in which overwhelming concentration on efficiency at the maintenance base provides the opportunities for entrepreneurial effectiveness at home and abroad (e.g., using the maintenance base as a launching pad for entrepreneurial risk).

the credit they could get from private commercial banks (the OPEC-dollar recycling agents of the 1970s)—a consummate free-rider/defeatist strategy blend. But such vicious-circle strategies are expensive in terms of stimulating world inflation and creating burdens for future domestic development when the foreign debt mortgages must be repaid. Carefully timed, one-shot free-rider strategies (suspending payments on international debts) combined with short-term, anti-inflation shock treatment (deep cuts in wages and state spending) may work to break states out of vicious, inflationary cycles if democratic populations are patient enough—as in Bolivia in 1985 and in Poland in 1990[39] (see Chapter 10).

Another weak-currency-country strategy variation is the free-rider indexation scheme used by nations whose credit is good because of their strategic importance, such as Israel and Iceland. **Indexation** refers to automatic, indexed hikes in industrial wages linked to inflation or rises in consumer prices. But the Italians discovered that the benefits of redistribution to those down the class scale resulting from such indexation schemes can reach a point of diminishing returns. Attempting to restore international competitiveness and to break free of vicious circles, the Italians began in the 1980s to dismantle their system of indexation. After all, the free-rider has to know when to get off since the status quo is no streetcar named desire.

The United States used yet another version of a complex free-rider strategy, manipulating dollar exchange rates and U.S. interest rates to keep international money flowing into the United States to offset the crowding out of U.S. private investment by government borrowing that was feared due to the large federal deficit. The shift in the mid-1980s to use a falling dollar to make American exports cheaper and to improve the large U.S. trade deficit appeared to many critics to be another free ride on the world economy—a potentially vicious-circle-strategy of devaluation that permitted the Americans to postpone inevitable internal (budget cuts or tax increases) and external (protectionist tariffs to match competitors subsidy for subsidy) adjustments that are politically unpopular at home.

IMPLICATIONS

In a global capitalist economy, rational choice for the individual citizen is apt to be maximized in a free-wheeling, deregulated domestic market like that of the United States. As a consequence, a small minority of individuals in the national community—the professional speculators—are positioned to make the most rational use of available choices given the information overload of a system in which the set of available choices is the greatest in the world.

A political economy maximizing laissez-faire entrepreneurship pays off in the great range of freedom or the range of choice in professional work, investments, and so forth, as the American boom of the 1990s demonstrated. By the same token, the overwhelming majority of citizens at any one historical moment are structurally in a position where they will probably make less than rationally optimal decisions or even make irrational decisions, thus increasing the gap between their own life chances and those of the rational few. Such nonadaptive, ill-informed decision making, in turn, risks undermining the basis of the large middle class, which Aristotle believed to be the prerequisite to his ideal form of balanced, democratic-aristocratic state, the **politea**.

As a contrast, the trade-off of neocorporatist political economies is to give citizens a more limited range of freedom of choice for the sake of greater social stability and coverage of the risk of social failure (falling to the bottom, "down-and-out"). Governmental bureaucracies tend to make routine decisions concerning health, old-age pension, unemployment insurance benefits, and educational structures, leaving citizens with less routine decisions (and less decision stress), thus freeing time for the kinds of decision making they most enjoy.

In *The Overworked American* (1992) economist Juliet Schor demonstrated that although the level of productivity of the U.S. worker more than doubled between 1948 and 1990, none of this increase went into more leisure time. American workers could have used this productivity increase to take every other year off *with pay*. On the contrary, the average American owns and consumes more than twice what he or she did in 1948 but has less free time. Americans are trapped in an insidious cycle of work-and-spend.[40]

Sociologist Philip Slater, in *The Pursuit of Loneliness*, argued that Americans have to make more decisions than do people in any other culture in the world.[41] The opportunity cost of this freedom is to be overwhelmed as an individual, having to make more decisions than one wants to in any one day, eating up time with "busyness," and leaving the individual autonomous but lonely as he or she sorts out everything individually. The neoconservative solution of Alan Bloom in *The Closing of the American Mind* is to reduce this "openness" for the sake of cultural calculability.[42] Or, in W. Edwards Deming's terms, by reducing the amount of variation, the quality of any process can be increased. The problem, of course, is whether in an antistate liberal society, such as that of the United States, the majority of citizens would tolerate the arbitrary closing down of options or openness by the state for the sake of increased predictability collectively desired. Evolving U.S. health care and social security reforms may suggest the answer.

Americans, for example, typically want improvements in public services, but no increases in taxes to pay for such improvements—a free-rider strategy of improving the maintenance base grounded on borrowing from others, a policy that may not be able to last indefinitely. Indeed, by 1990, national opinion polls suggested a shift toward tolerating a marginal tax increase if the money were spent to fight drugs and to improve the environment. The problem lies not just in getting the majority of people in a nation to choose differently at any one moment, but in restructuring the society so that all individual choices are perceived as social choices, and so that the individual and community learn to work in harmony for the sake of long-term social adaptation and economic competitiveness. Structure, in short, seems to precede strategy rather than the other way around. In the United States, individual freedom has been structured as primary in the social system no matter what the cost in social or economic distance between individuals or groups.[43] In the neocorporatist economies, autonomy for the "peak" interest groups of labor, management, and government bureaucracies is structured to predominate over individual choice, limiting individual freedom somewhat but increasing social harmony and decreasing social distance between individuals and groups.

Still, at certain transitional phases of economic development, nations collectively appear to have strategic choices between strategy mixes that can restructure their economies toward more industrial competitiveness or not. One concrete measure of the existing political economy strategy mix in a society is the amount of the nation's economic product devoted to government spending.

STATE SPENDING AS A MEASURE OF POLITICAL ECONOMY CONSTITUTIONS

To compare how different national political economies are structured, the nature and amount of government spending is the best point of departure. The OECD publishes these data annually under the title "Total Outlays of General Government." Government outlays include goods, services, public investments, interest payments on debts, and the cost of social (welfare) transfer payments. These comparative data show how limited the room for political flexibility since 1960 became. The states most heavily burdened with government spending (note the correlation with *social democratic neocorporatism*) have been Sweden, the Netherlands, Denmark, Belgium, and Luxembourg. Between 1960 and 1985, government outlays as a percentage of the annual total GNP rose for Sweden from 31 percent to 65 percent (the government outlay as a percentage of the GNP is called the **state quota**). Similarly, the state quota for the Netherlands and Denmark rose to 60 percent in the same period. West Germany's state quota—somewhat representative of the average for Europe—rose from 32 percent in 1960 to 48 percent in 1985. In contrast, *liberal neocorporatist* states such as Japan and Switzerland had much lower state quotas—about 30 percent in 1985. And the state quota of the most liberal of nations, the United States, rose only from 27 percent to 36 percent between 1960 and 1985. By 1993, the state quota of Sweden fell to 54 percent, that of the Netherlands to 54 percent, and that of Denmark to 45 percent in reaction to global competitive pressures. During 1991 the state quota of the United States was 24 percent, that of Germany 34 percent, and that of Japan 16 percent.[44]

The key questions in terms of strategic choices available for restructuring of a political economy are (1) Why are the differences between the state quotas so different—from 30 percent to 60 percent, and (2) What are the consequences of a large or small state quota for international competitiveness and social welfare? One way of explaining these differences is the "openness-of-the-economy hypothesis." Political scientist David Cameron demonstrated that political economies that were more strongly integrated in the world economy in terms of international trade have higher state quotas, whereas nations with a small portion of their GNP made up of foreign trade have much smaller state quotas.[45]

Thus, European countries that are heavily integrated into the world economy have high state quotas, whereas the United States and Japan, which are heavily oriented domestically in terms of their political economies (foreign trade making up some 15 percent of the U.S. economy and 20 percent of the Japanese), have low state quotas.

The second well-grounded hypothesis explaining the differences in state quotas is the "power-and-party-division hypothesis." Political scientist Manfred Schmidt demonstrated that, since 1960, the countries with the smallest state quotas—the United States, Japan, and Switzerland—have been dominated by bourgeois right-wing parties, whereas Denmark and Sweden, with high state quotas, have been dominated by Social Democratic parties. This Social Democratic tradition has seeped into the cultures of Denmark and Sweden to the point that politicians take social democracy for granted, while in the United States and Switzerland the state plays a more restrained role. In strategic terms, one could say that political economies with high state quotas are more maintenance-bound, whereas those with the more liberal, less Social Democratic tradition are more entrepreneurial in orientation (self-help versus state-security).

As to the second question—the consequences of high state quotas for international competitiveness—the empirical findings are less conclusive and dependent on changing global economic conditions. In his book *Sozialdemokratische Krisenpolitik*, political economist Fritz Scharpf showed that Sweden, Austria, West Germany, and Great Britain developed successful Keynesian recipes for coping with the world economy dilemmas of the late 1970s: There was a consensus among their unions not to push for wage hikes to match the rising inflation rates. This enabled their governments to carry on state-deficit economic politics with low interest rates. Austria had full employment with a low inflation rate. Sweden maintained full employment as unemployment declined. West Germany held the world record for fighting inflation, but lost jobs in the process. And for two years Great Britain slowed down unemployment and inflation only to have the government lose control over the unions, which raised their demands.

However, in the 1980s these successful Keynesian recipes no longer worked. The high real dollar interest rates transformed the international capital market, which had become globally integrated. Money flowed toward the highest real return wherever that happened to be in the world. Consequently the incomes of taxpayers stagnated while the profits of investors soared. Given the high interest rates and loss of domestic capital, governments had to pay more money to cover their budget debts and thereby nearly lost the flexibility to use the Keynesian instrument of intervention in the domestic economy.[46] Thus the high-real-interest-rate strategy of the United States to attract the money needed to service its deficits skewed the world economy toward the American position—a policy perceived by Europeans as a free-rider tactic on the part of the United States. This delayed the inevitable long-term economic adjustment domestically in America at the cost of making mere maintenance in European economies more expensive.

By 1994 the long-delayed American economic adjustment began to kick in, pushed by Treasury Secretary Robert Rubin. Clinton's proposed $1.5 trillion budget preserved the strict spending limits imposed in the 1993 deficit-reduction law and reduced the deficit for the third consecutive year. Clinton's defense budget actually went up $3.2 billion from 1993–1994.[47] By the end of the 1990s, the Americans were able to eliminate the federal budget deficit. Clinton led the way to transform the United States into what Philip Cerny has called a "competition state"—an engine of globalization that leaves its former social buffer role in the dust for the sake of "the economy, stupid!" The state is no longer able to act as a decommodifying hierarchy (i.e., taking economic activities out of the market). It must act more and more as a collective commodifying agent (i.e., putting itself *into* the market) and even as *a market actor itself.*[48] In the future, American commitment to human service programs will have to expand, particularly given inevitable health and welfare reforms, crime prevention, educational crises, and job retraining programs. Largely stagnant American incomes among the bottom 80 percent (until 1996—despite the boom of the 1990s) mean that taxes will be difficult to raise. And Americans do not see themselves as getting the services for their taxes that Europeans do, thereby magnifying the problem. Given the excesses of the conservative liberalism of Reagan and Bush, postliberal consciousness has been raised in the United States, particularly in terms of defense spending (stimulated by the war in Kosovo). But the follow-through to restructure America's maintenance base to make it more efficient and communitarian is unlikely to come soon, given the conservatism of the American liberal tradition and voter resistance to state intervention and taxes. And the foreign debt, already in the trillion dollar range, hangs like a permanent storm cloud in the background, unmentioned by politicians in both mainstream parties and claiming ever more of the annual budget in interest payments. It may take a decline of the dollar's value when the babyboomers (born in the decade after World War II) retire to make it an issue on the political agenda. Until then, the hegemon is apt to continue to live it up.

QUESTIONS FOR THOUGHT

1. Describe briefly the three different phases of modernization. What is the usefulness of the term "purposive rationality" within this context?

2. Characterize as precisely as possible Rostow's five stages of economic growth in key terms. Give examples of countries in the different stages. Could it be that a stage is missing or that Rostow got the number five wrong? (Never assume a theory is the *same* as the reality!)

3. Why does capitalist growth seem inevitably to be related to social inequality? Consider as well the cases of export-oriented growth, "casino capitalism," and oligarchism. If efficacy is the only social criterion, why is there a high probability of a "dual economy"?

4. A dynamic, i.e., "learning," dual economy easily sets the state up for either

a virtuous or a vicious economic circle. Describe both in the form of a circular graph. Then use the graph to explain the examples of Germany and Great Britain. Instead of stressing economic factors, what do neocorporatist states like Sweden and Austria focus on?

5. Which factors determine whether or not a commodity cartel such as OPEC will be successful?

6. Discuss the trade-off between individual freedom and social stability. Compare relevant situations in the United States and in Sweden. What is your personal preference? Is it fair to impose U.S. preferences on all other countries through "globalization"?

NOTES

1. Henry Maine, *Ancient Law: Its Connection with the Early History of Society and Its Relation to Modern Ideas* (London: Lardon J. Murray, 1861).

2. Ferdinand Toennies, *Gemeinschaft und Gesellschaft* (1887), translated by Charles P. Loomis, *Fundamental Concepts of Sociology* (New York: American Book Co., 1940).

3. Emile Durkheim, *De la Division du Travail Social* (1893), translated by George Simpson, *The Division of Labor in Society* (Glencoe, IL: The Free Press, 1947).

4. See Max Weber, *The Theory of Social and Economic Organization*, translated by A. M. Henderson and Talcott Parsons (Glencoe, IL: The Free Press, 1947).

5. Jürgen Habermas, *Toward a Rational Society* (Boston, MA: Beacon Press, 1970).

6. Charles Lindblom, *Politics and Markets: The World's Political-Economic Systems* (New York: Basic Books, 1977).

7. See, for example, Christopher S. Wren, "China's Courtship of Capitalism," in *New York Times*, December 25, 1983; and C. Wren, "China Turning Back to Its Educated for Help," *New York Times*, March 4, 1984.

8. See, for example, Edward A. Gargan, "China Explains Policy Shift Retightening Economic Grip," *New York Times*, October 28, 1988.

9. See Sylvia Ostry, "The World Economy in 1983: Marking Time," *Foreign Affairs*, "America and the World," vol. 62, no. 3, 553–560.

10. According to an MIT survey of 5.6 million firms between 1968 and 1976, 80 percent of the jobs in the United States were created by companies that were four years old or less and employed 100 or fewer workers. See David L. Birch, "Who Creates Jobs?" *The Public Interest* 65 (fall 1981). On the theory of motivation in the welfare state, see Kenneth E. Boulding, *The Economy of Love and Fear* (Belmont, CA: Wadsworth Publishing Co., 1973); and Thomas C. Schelling, *Micromotives and Macrobehavior* (New York: W. W. Norton, 1978).

11. Economist Albert Hirschman has identified alternating cycles of public involvement and return to private interest maximization: See A. O. Hirschman, *Shifting Involvements: Private Interests and Public Action* (Princeton, NJ: Princeton University Press, 1982).

12. W. W. Rostow, *The Stages of Economic Growth: A Non-Communist Manifesto* (London: Cambridge University Press, 1960), p. 7.

13. For other interpretations of "postindustrial" values, see Ronald Inglehart, "The Silent Revolution in Europe: Intergenerational Change in Postindustrial Societies," *American Political Science Review* 65 (December 1971); Fred Hirsch, *The Social Limits to Growth* (London: Routledge & Kegan Paul, 1978); Daniel Bell, *The Coming of Post-Industrial Society* (New York: Basic Books, 1973); and Daniel Bell, *The Cultural Contradictions of Capitalism* (New York: Basic Books, 1976).

14. See, for example, Frank Parkin, *Class Inequality and Political Order: Social Stratification in*

Capitalist and Communist Societies (New York: Praeger, 1975); and "Social Liberalism: A New Political Economy," Chapter 11 in R. Isaak, *American Democracy and World Power* (New York: St. Martin's Press, 1977), pp. 172–186.

15. Habermas, *Rational Society*, p. 122. For a Marxian class analysis, see Stephen Resnik, John Sinisi, and Richard Wolff, "Class Analysis of International Relations," in *An International Political Economy*, International Political Economy Yearbook, Vol. 1, ed. W. Ladd Hollis and F. LaMond Tullis (Boulder, CO: Westview Press, 1985), pp. 87–123.

16. See Part 3: "The Loose Individual" in Robert Nisbet, *The Present Age: Progress and Anarchy in Modern America* (New York: Harper & Row, 1988), especially pp. 122–125.

17. See Charles S. Maier, "The Politics of Inflation in the Twentieth Century," in *The Political Economy of Inflation*, ed. Fred Hirsch and John H. Goldthorpe (Cambridge, MA: Harvard University Press, 1978).

18. See Hirsch, *The Social Limits of Growth*; and Staffan B. Linder, *The Harried Leisure Class* (New York: Columbia University Press, 1970).

19. See R. Isaak, *European Politics: Political Economy and Policy Making in Western Democracies* (New York: St. Martin's Press, 1980).

20. See Daniel Bell, *The Cultural Contradictions of Capitalism*; Joseph Schumpeter, *Capitalism, Socialism and Democracy*; and Fred Hirsch, "The Ideological Underlay of Inflation," in *Political Economy of Inflation*, ed. Hirsch and Goldthorpe, pp. 263–284.

21. See Suzanne Berger and Michael Piore, *Dualism and Discontinuity in Industrial Societies* (New York: Cambridge University Press, 1980), p. 69 ff.

22. See Ingar Svennilson, *Growth and Stagnation in the European Economy* (Geneva: Economic Commission for Europe, 1954); Joseph Schumpeter, *The Theory of Economic Development* (New York: Oxford University Press, 1961); and John Cornwall, *Modern Capitalism: Its Growth and Transformation* (Oxford: Martin, Robertson and Co., 1977). Certain important qualifications apply to Cornwall's model at certain stages of development: In less developed nations the key emphasis that Cornwall gives the manufacturing sector, as a means to achieve the take-off stage to industrialization, can also result in growing unemployment and a failure in agricultural and domestic market development. Cornwall also neglects an important exogenous variable, namely the country's effort to borrow or develop technology, which is not insignificant in a theory driven by technical progress.

23. See N. Kaldor, *Strategic Factors in Economic Development* (Ithaca, NY: Cornell University Press, 1967); and N. Kaldor, "Economic Growth and the Verdoorn Law: A Comment of Mr. Rowthorn's Article," *Economic Journal* (December 1975).

24. Kenneth Arrow, "The Economic Implications of Learning by Doing," *Review of Economic Studies* (June 1962).

25. See Cornwall, pp. 152 ff.; and R. Minami, *The Turning Point in Economic Development: Japan's Experience* (Tokyo, 1973).

26. See Philippe Schmitter, "Interest Intermediation and Regime Governability in Western Europe and North America," in *Organizing Interests in Western Europe: Pluralism and the Transformation of Politics*, ed. Suzanne Berger (Cambridge, England: Cambridge University Press, 1981); P. Schmitter, "Still the Century of Corporatism," *Review of Politics* 36 (January 1974): 85–131; and Gerhard Lehmbruch, "Consociational Democracy, Class Conflict and the New Corporatism," in *Trends toward Corporatist Intermediation*, ed. Philippe Schmitter and Gerhard Lehmbruch (London: Sage, 1979), pp. 53–62.

27. See Chapter 7, "The Neocorporatist Nations" in Graham K. Wilson, *Business and Politics* (Chatham, NJ: Chatham House Publishers, 1985), pp. 103–113.

28. See, for example, Peter J. Katzenstein, "Capitalism in One Country? Switzerland in the International Economy," *International Organization* 35 (autumn 1980): 507–540. And, for a contrast of Switzerland as a form of "liberal corporatism" and Austria as an example of "social democratic corporatism," see P. Katzenstein, *Small States in World Markets: Industrial Policy in Europe* (Ithaca, NY: Cornell University Press, 1985).

29. See Manfred G. Schmidt, "The Politics of Labour Market Policy: Structural and Political Determinants of Rates of Unemployment in Industrial Nations," in *Managing Mixed Economies*, ed. Francis G. Castles, Franz Lehner, and Manfred G. Schmidt (volume 3 of *The Future of Party Government*, ed. Rudolf Wildenmann) (Berlin/New York: Walter De Gruyter, 1988), p. 6.
30. Karl P. Sauvant and Hajo Hasenpflug, *The New International Economic Order: Confrontation or Cooperation between North and South?* (Boulder, CO: Westview Press, 1977), p. 369.
31. Fahil Al-Chalabi, Deputy Secretary General of OPEC, "OPEC's View of the Second Oil Crisis," paper presented at the Johns Hopkins University, School of Advanced International Studies, Bologna Center, Bologna, Italy, June 2, 1980.
32. Matthew L. Wald, "After 20 Years, America's Foot Is Still On the Gas," *New York Times*, October 17, 1993.
33. James Tanner, "War-Ravaged Kuwait Rebounds into Ranks of Major Oil Nations," *Wall Street Journal*, January 28, 1994.
34. Fadhil J. Chalabi, "OPEC: An Obituary," *Foreign Policy*, no. 109 (winter 1997–98): 126–140. The comparative statistics above are from this source.
35. Youssef M. Ibrahim, "Cheap Oil Focuses Minds," *New York Times*, March 28, 1999.
36. See Part 2 of *Modern Inflation*. Also see Wilhelm Hankel, "Germany: Economic Nationalism in the International Economy," in *West Germany: A European and Global Power*, ed. Wilfred Kohl and Giorgio Basevi (Lexington, MA: D. C. Health, 1980), pp. 21–43.
37. See W. Hankel, *Prosperity Amidst Crisis: Austria's Economic Policy and the Energy Crunch* (Boulder, CO: Westview Press, 1980), p. 149. Originally published as *Prosperität in der Krise* (Vienna: Molden, 1979).
38. Katzenstein, "Capitalism in One Country?" p. 511.
39. Robert E. Norton, "The American Out to Save Poland," *Fortune* 121, no. 3 (January 1990): 129–134.
40. Juliet B. Schor, *The Overworked American: The Unexpected Decline of Leisure* (New York: Basic Books, 1992).
41. Philip Slater, *The Pursuit of Loneliness* (Boston, MA: Beacon Press, 1976). Also see David Shenk, *Data Smog: Surviving the Information Glut* (New York: HarperCollins, 1997).
42. Alan Bloom, *The Closing of the American Mind* (New York: Simon & Schuster, 1987). On the other hand, Swiss data indicates that open, direct democratic participation increases happiness. See "Happiness is a Warm Vote," *Economist* (April 17, 1999): 92.
43. See R. Isaak, "The Conservative Tradition of American Liberalism," *American Political Thinking: Readings from the Origins to the 21st Century* (Fort Worth, TX: Harcourt Brace, 1994), pp. 1–13.
44. The World Bank, *World Development Report 1997*, Table 3 (Washington D.C.: World Bank), p. 218.
45. David Cameron, "The Expansion of the Public Economy: A Comparative Analysis," *American Political Science Review* 72 (December 1978): 1243–1261.
46. Lecture by Fritz Scharpf on *Sozialdemokratische Krisenpolitik* in Europe at the University of Heidelberg, June 9, 1988.
47. "The Clinton Budget," *Wall Street Journal*, February 8, 1994, p. A12.
48. Philip G. Cerny, "Paradoxes of the Competition State: The Dynamics of Political Globalization," *Government and Opposition* 31, no. 3 (spring 1997): 267.

INDUSTRIAL POLICY,
"ECONOMIC MIRACLES,"
AND THE ENVIRONMENT

The material standard of living in the United States, as measured by GDP per capita, was 25 percent higher in 1997 than in the nearest G-7 economies, Japan and western Germany. With the other G-7 economies, the gap with the United States widens, reaching 45 percent for Britain. The difference comes from lower job creation, lower productivity, or both.
> —William Lewis, McKinsey Global Institute, Wall Street Journal (5/21/98)

To achieve competitive success, firms from the nation must possess a competitive advantage in the form of either lower costs or differentiated products that command premium prices.... We must explain why a nation provides an environment in which firms improve and innovate and continue to do so.... The behavior required to create and ... to sustain competitive advantage is an unnatural act in many companies....
> —Michael Porter, The Competitive Advantage of Nations (1990)

Looking backward, future historians will see the twentieth century as a century of niche competition and the twenty-first century as a century of head-to-head competition.
> —Lester Thurow, Head to Head (1992)

CONSIDER HOW QUICKLY THE WORLD ECONOMY CAN SHIFT: "THE COLD WAR IS OVER AND THE Japanese won," stated former U.S. Senator Paul Tsongas in his 1992 presidential campaign. By 1998 Japan was in its deepest recession and the worst financial crisis in an industrialized nation since World War II, while the U.S. economy was barely anticipating a slow-down from a record eight-year economic boom. The "economic miracle" economies of Southeast Asia that had experienced waves of double-digit growth suddenly found themselves deserted by investors and suffering from the environmental consequences of reckless growth—like an empty ransacked room after a wild party. The rain forests smoldered in record numbers from Indonesia to Brazil and thousands of barrels of oil spilled on the Nigerian coast as incentives for short-term economic gain and survival outstripped concerns about long-term environmental sustainability.

The cold war—focused on the Soviet threat—was the glue that held the German and Japanese allies in a position of permanent dependence in relation to the

United States. It also served to diffuse American economic strength for the sake of preserving military predominance. When such overwhelming military strength suddenly appeared superfluous with the collapse of the U.S.S.R., the dependence of allies upon the American security umbrella waned as well. The Gulf War against Iraq in 1990–1991 served more to underscore that America's security business was independent of European and Japanese concerns than anything else, despite the greater dependence of these allies upon foreign oil (witness Japan's slow response to joining the anti-Iraq coalition). The United States suddenly found itself specialized in an area with flawed comparative commercial advantages—military power—for to sell its high-tech weapons and planes in the short-term was to undermine American hegemony in the long run (although this has not stopped the support of the Clinton administration for conventional arms sales abroad). With some desperation, the Americans began a building down of their armed forces (until the reversal in 1999) and widespread industrial restructuring domestically, looking to Japanese and European commercial successes with wariness. Meanwhile, German and Japanese independence from the United States grew, epitomized by German reunification and the coining of a new Japanese term, *kenbei*, meaning dislike of the United States.[1]

From the perspective of collective learning, "the Big Three"—the United States, Japan, and Germany—have often fallen into the habit of trying to learn most from each other. Or, put another way, they see each other as the major competitors whose standards they have to meet, if not to surpass. That this habit is probably a myopic one that tends to blind the three major economic states of the industrialized North to breakthroughs in other nations will not, for the moment, concern us here. Rather, the focus will be upon the reasons for being so absorbed in trilateral competitiveness and the recipes of the Big Three for success. Each of these three countries is culturally complex enough to keep its two major opponents scratching their heads for years, trying to figure out what is really going on "over there." Indeed, these three major players in the world economy are so complicated to understand and to predict that it is no surprise that Northern industrialized countries become preoccupied with each other. So self-absorbed are they that they find little time left over to try to understand other cultures in depth—even though their long-term survival may depend upon it. Add the complications of German unification (which the Germans themselves have a hard time sorting out) and the interlocking of the German economy with other members of the European Union and it is not surprising that rich countries become bogged down trying to figure out the likely moves of their rich opponents.

Origins

In considering the origins of the differences in American, Japanese, and German competitiveness, keep in mind that, in terms of being *a unified nation-state*, the United States is the oldest (born in 1776). The centralized state of modern Japan dates from 1868 and the first unification of Germany from 1871 (with the second unification still in progress). Political stability, therefore, gives the United States one kind of competitive edge. However, this very stability is based on preserving a chaos of individualism through federalism and checks and balances that make any national reform or radical policy change extremely difficult (except in wartime). The United States is a liberal state in a postliberal era. Germany and Japan, on the other hand, have much longer cultural histories than does the United States, which gives them a basis for **communitarianism** or the cooperative group form of capitalism colored by *Gemeinschaft* (community) in Germany or the spirit of *wa* (harmony) in Japan. As Professor George Lodge of Harvard has noted, we are confronted with a competition between the individualistic, Anglo-Saxon form of capitalism of the United States versus the communitarian capitalisms of Japan and Germany.[2]

The events that have taken place since World War II are well known, so we can make a long story short. The United States and Britain won the war militarily and, therefore, were able to establish the Bretton Woods system, the embodiment of Anglo-American hegemony. However, by the late twentieth century, it appeared to many that Germany and Japan had won the peace economically. By occupying West Germany and Japan and greatly restricting the amount they could spend on the military, the United States forced its competitors to focus all their efforts on applied economic success or commercial business. The Germans and Japanese, in short, were *forced* to free-ride on the American security system and the Bretton Woods dollar system. They were also forced to rebuild their bombed-out factories and physical infrastructure totally, whereas the Americans and British made do with old plants that had not been bombed. And just in case this modernization and targeting did not do the trick to restore German and Japanese competitiveness, the Americans kicked in generous grants of economic aid (most notably, the Marshall Fund). In their moment of glory at the top of the heap militarily and economically, the Americans were tempted by **hubris**—the Greek concept of false pride in trying to do more than one can (which leads ultimately to downfall). As noted previously, had the Americans not given such great amounts of money away in the form of grants, the United States could now recall the loans with interest and help to eliminate its foreign debt problem. By 1990 the U.S. federal debt had climbed to 59 percent of Gross National Product (GNP), up from 34 percent in 1980. And interest payments on the debt climbed to almost 15 percent of federal income (from 9 percent) in the same time period.

Perhaps the American dislike of **savings** (or postponed consumption) stems from the belief that the United States will always remain "Number One" in the world (hubris with a capital H). But, whatever the motivation, the Americans refuse to save, compared to their Japanese and German competitors. If one takes the 1980–1988 period (up to the fall of the Berlin Wall), the net personal savings as a percent of disposable income was 5.5 percent for the Americans compared with 12.2 percent for the West Germans and 16.4 percent for the Japanese.[3] By 1993, the U.S. savings rate had fallen below 4 percent, despite what initially was referred to as an anemic, jobless recovery from recession. And by 1998 private indebtedness rose to record levels, giving the economy a "consumption" boost that used to come from government deficits in the 1980s (for the Federal deficit turned into a surplus).

Why does savings matter? Savings provides the capital for investment in new equipment and plants—for new infrastructure creating new jobs. Their high savings rate permitted the Japanese to have factories constantly modernized, usually keeping them under seven years on average. In comparison, American plants are generally older. Old plants plus low savings can add up to a significant competitive disadvantage. In terms of private and public investment in plants and equipment, research and development, infrastructure, and skills, the United States invests only one-half of what the Japanese invest and two-thirds of what the Europeans invest. Yet the paradox of the U.S. economic boom of the 1990s appeared to be that since the American GDP was 70 percent driven by consumption, as long as Americans kept spending more than they should, the economy stayed dynamic and the self-confidence led to entrepreneurial risk-taking and job-creating start-ups. Venture capital remained abundant.

In contrast, the savings mentality, fostered in both the German and Japanese cultures, is a cheap way to productivity. To increase productivity it is often cheaper and easier to reduce the inputs through savings than to increase the outputs with greater effort or technological innovation. Germans always think of savings first. They are brought up to be thrifty. As in the Japanese case, the experience of war fought on their soil taught them the meaning of scarcity and the necessity of savings. In theory, the Americans are at a competitive disadvantage with these opponents in not having had to fight a war on their own soil since the Civil War.[4] Wartime destruction and the scarcity of raw materials also taught the Japanese and Germans to rely upon their wits. In developed economies, productivity increases stem from value added to existing production processes. Indeed, the trend is toward increasing productivity through innovation in production processes more than through creating new products.[5]

The Japanese provide the clearest illustration here. After World War II they aimed to make the textile market more productive. But they gradually shifted to manufacturing, particularly to consumer electronics and automobiles. In all these cases, as an island economy the Japanese were obliged to import almost all of the raw materials (and often the technology) they required for production. So their competitiveness and productivity depended upon the value they added to these imported resources in terms of production and management processes, design, and adaptation to global markets. Their economic survival depended on adapting quickly to the outside global economy, collectively learning how to transform imported materials into manufactured goods that consumers wanted. Typically, they started at the low-price ends of the markets they targeted, aiming for increases in market share rather than short-term profitability. This strategy also shored up their full-employment objective. Once they captured a large share of the market, their costs went down because of **economies of scale** (that is the lowering of production costs because of being able to operate on a large scale). This increased their competitiveness and made it difficult for others to meet their price. Then they increased the quality of the products and perfected the efficiency of their production processes, permitting them to go up-scale in product (i.e., from small cars to luxury family automobiles). This had the virtue of permitting them to make more money on fewer products, so that external tariff penalties imposed by others (such as the United States) had little effect on the bottom line.

INDUSTRIAL POLICY AS A KEY TO COMPETITIVENESS

JAPANESE TARGETING

It was no accident that the Japanese were able to target certain promising industries or markets for collective development at the exclusion of others, therefore reducing national "opportunity costs." In common with the Germans and French and in contrast with the United States, the Japanese have a feudal heritage, which accustoms them to accept the hierarchy of their society and the legitimacy of elite institutions. After World War II, the Japanese were determined to catch up with the West economically, no matter what the short-term social and economic sacrifices might be for individual citizens or consumers. The bureaucratic governmental elite, which has much greater social status in Japan (and France) than in the United States, led this passionate battle for economic growth. It began with long-range plans for modernization in the nineteenth century. After World War II these efforts culminated in the cooperation between the prestigious Finance Ministry and Ministry of International Trade and Industry (MITI), which aimed to create a Japanese environment conducive to the cultivation of world-class competitors among private companies in key economic sectors.[6]

The divisions of MITI mimic the major trade associations and become the basis for sharing out quotas of business. These trade associations and major corporations, in turn, all belong to the *Keidandren*, the Federation of Economic Organizations, which is organized in a way that mirrors the divisions at MITI. Highly educated personnel go back and forth between these organizations much as they do between Pentagon posts and major defense industry management positions in the United States.

There is a great thirst for knowledge and a social obligation to collect information in these bureaucracies—data on world market trends, the timing and nature of technological breakthroughs, and the reasons for the success of key industrial leaders. The purpose is to overlap sources of information so that industrial decision-makers are saturated with it. Together with the intelligence arms of the major **keiretsu** or cartel networks of companies (based on long-term, cross-shareholding among members), the entire Japanese economic system is like a global octopus with arms spread everywhere to pick up information of strategic economic significance. Companies are rarely subsidized directly by the government. Rather, the aim is to give companies the financial incentives to consolidate and become competitive enough that there are several key players in each field critical for national economic competitiveness. It is a matter of creating conditions under which such competitiveness can thrive and become effectively targeted. By obtaining extraordinarily high market shares of key economic sectors—electronic products, heavy equipment, steel, and transportation—Japan not only achieved economies of scale but greatly increased the entry costs of would-be new competitors.

None of these key industries were based on natural resources (which Japan had to import—as opposed to the United States), but were manufacturing sectors in which Japanese success depended upon high value added.[7] This, in turn, increased the payoffs of investing in research and development and in the practical application of innovations discovered by others. As was the case with Germany, Japan benefited from having a large pool of trained engineers and a demanding educational structure that fostered applied, technological competitiveness (see Chapter 7). But while German scientists focused on basic research, inventing the fax machine in a Siemens AG lab, the Japanese stressed applied research—turning the fax into a marketable product.

Finally, Japanese elites have long-term vision. Japanese companies often have a 200-year plan. The aim is to be strategically positioned for the long term in order to keep employment high, market share constant or expanding, and to reduce opportunity costs. Social harmony based on government-business-labor cooperation and a company commitment to lifetime employment for over 20 percent of the full-time work force reinforce this strategy as well as the Japanese work ethic. Financing of firms is typically done on a ten-year basis in which the local or regional bank has representatives on the board of directors. This permits long-term planning, since firms do not rely on the annual support of stockholders for their financing—the system that forces managers of American companies to worry about how to return a profit *right now.*

These basic elements of the Japanese system remain intact despite the speculative financial run-up that grew from 1986–1991, only to collapse in the long recession in 1991–1998—the worst since World War II. In 1989, the central bank of Japan deliberately punctured the bubble of financial speculation at its peak by increasing discount rates to starve the money supply, thereby "normalizing" real estate prices.[8] With this "non-Japanese" financial speculation and excessive consumption wrung out of the system, Japan can be expected to come back competitively in the twenty-first century after its long "cold shower." The corruption in the Liberal Democratic Party, which governed since World War II until the mid-1990s, is also being attacked systematically and thereby reduced. This is symbolized by the party's loss of domination in parliament and by the economic reforms pushed through in 1998, providing $500,000 billion by the turn of the century to turn around the country's financial system. Earlier in the decade the change-oriented Prime Minister Morihiro Hosokawa headed a fragile coalition government symbolizing a social commitment to change, but political fragmentation prevented an effective follow-through—epitomizing the political stalemate in the Japanese system. Large companies downsized and reduced commitments to lifetime employment. Japan confronted global change and slowly adapted its political economy to new realities of global competitiveness. This positioning is symbolized by the annual percent of fixed investment as a percent of Gross Domestic Product (GDP) from 1988–1992: 32.7 percent in Japan compared to 21.3 percent in Europe (EU minus Luxembourg) and 15.1 percent in the United States.[9] But when the contagion from the Southeast Asian financial crisis hit in the late 1990s, it was clear that Japan had done too little too slowly and was swept down as it watched its heavy investments in its neighbors plummet and the crisis in its own financial system deepen. But Peter Drucker contends that the stubborn continuity of the Japanese bureaucratic elite have always put society ahead of the economy (in contrast with the United States) and that this elite dominance in ruling industrial society is the global norm, not the exceptional American rejection of being governed by the same established elite. Nevertheless, in a grossly overbanked society, the banking crisis may force the bureaucrats eventually to undo Japan's most distinctive economic organization, the *keiretsu*: the cluster of businesses around a major bank. This organization is a mutual support association and the members of a component company hold enough of each other's shares to assure that the *keiretsu* has effective control of ownership. But in coping with staggering market declines, the banks at the center have been forced to sell off shares to offset their huge losses.[10]

Contrast the depth of this fall with the 1980s when Japan represented the "entrepreneurial state," subsidizing key technology centers guided by MITI to bring together the "fusion technologies" of the future. Much of the funding was actually part of the proceeds from privatizing former Japanese government monopolies, which went into "industrial investment accounts" and from there to the technology centers. Germany, too, funded technology centers: Collective learning from each other's models has become critical for industrial competitiveness. But this form of state regulated learning often mitigated against a dynamic product market, such as that which drove the American boom of the 1990s. By aiming for the supercomputer market, MITI picked the wrong target in the 1980s and the state bureaucracy was too clumsy to shift to other targets quickly enough. The tradition of job security mitigated against new flexible job creation in both Japan and Europe, and by 1997 U.S. GDP per capita was 25 percent higher than GDP per capita in Japan or in the western states of Germany.[11]

GERMAN CONCENTRATION AND FOLLOW-THROUGH

The Japanese and Germans have a profound respect for each other's cultures despite significant differences in their industrial policies. Both cultures revere education. Both find waste distasteful, if not downright threatening to economic survival. Both have used order, efficiency, and collective learning to bring about post-World War II "economic miracles." Both benefit from taking a feudal, hierarchical past somewhat for granted as the basis of social stability from which to take calculated collective entrepreneurial risks. Both rely upon concentrations of big companies and financial institutions to lead the way in terms of global competitiveness. Neither culture likes to leave anything to chance. As noted earlier, Germany and Japan have both benefited from free-riding upon the liberalism of the United States in terms of financial and military security. And both struggled to get out of their deepest recessions since World War II in the 1990s with a sober sense of the need to sharpen collective competitiveness and to create jobs—with Germany emerging first but still with record unemployment and labor costs.

Despite the 1998 shift to the coalition government between the Social Democrats and the Green Party, Germany has a culture of conservatism. In a modern sense, it can be traced to Bismarck's Prussian "White Revolution," which united Germany in the 1870s by coopting working-class support through the establishment of worker disability and other forms of social security. Late industrialization gave the working class a greater political voice than in other nations because industrialization developed at the same time that the franchise (voting rights) expanded.[12] This was a "work-oriented" culture of strong unions, highly respected apprenticeship training (dating back to the feudal guilds), and an evolving system of codetermination in which management and workers cooperated to set long-term corporate policies in 50–50 percent participation schemes. Germany has a **social market economy** in which the government ensures the solidarity of the social contract through class-mitigating welfare measures (state-subsidized healthcare, pensions, unemployment and disability insurance, university tuition, labor advising and training, etc.), while leaving the private sector free to operate in the economic market. The social "maintenance base" is thus clearly separated from the freedom to take entrepreneurial risk (see Chapter 8). Government steering focuses on economic process (i.e., tax subsidies for new housing), not on economic results (i.e., rent control).[13] Political stability is furthered by a constitutional law limiting representation in the parliament to political parties that receive at least 5 percent of the vote.

Generally, German elites have been able to count on widespread social consensus on work-oriented policies, worker participation, and worker benefits at the bottom of society. This has permitted a consensus at the top in the form of support for large firms or cartels in such key economic sectors as pharmaceuticals and banks. Just as the allies failed after World War II break up the essence of the *zaibatsu* financial cliques (which were merely reincarnated by *sogoshosha* trading companies and the *keiretsu*), so they failed to break up the domination of the German economy by major companies. The domination of I. G. Farben (which produced gas-chamber poison and used slave labor from Auschwitz), for instance, was presumably broken up and replaced with the hegemony of Bayer, Hoechst, and BASF (yet Farben still survives).[14]. And German financial markets are dominated by three large commercial banks—Deutsche Bank, Dresdner Bank, and Commerzbank. State and economic tradition has assured Germany of the stability of industrial and financial concentration while a conservative, work-oriented culture and educational system have provided German business with predictable, systematic follow-through.

Unlike Japan and the United States, Germany's share of world exports has been higher than its share of the world economy represented by Gross National Product. It is a heavily export-dependent economy. Given high labor costs, due mainly to generous fringe benefits, Germany's competitiveness in exports has depended on increasingly higher levels of **product differentiation**, that is, updating products with technology and sophistication in specialized market niches. Germany's problem in competitiveness in the 1980s, however, was that the business areas in which Germany had traditionally been most successful were the areas in which it had recently been losing market share. This included world exports such as transport, chemicals, power generation and distribution, office equipment, and semiconductors and computers.[15] In new areas, like microelectronics, German patents shrank between 1987 and 1992 by more than one third while rising by almost one third in Japan and doubling in the United States. To shake up the complacency of the German system in order to make it hungry and competitive once more required a major crisis or historical change that would force it to restore its economic dynamism and to rethink its economic strategy: something like a second reunification, which, in fact, occurred in 1989.

GERMAN UNIFICATION: BUST OR BONANZA?

The debate over whether the financial mismanagement of German unification will lead to a "bust" or whether the addition of East to West Germany will become an economic "bonanza" is misplaced. German unification is an historical process that transcends the political and economic: It created a new context that brought Germany a number of social, economic, and political problems in the short run followed by greater power in the long run. Chancellor Helmut Kohl succeeded in reuniting Germany and in pushing through the Euro currency only to lose domestic support and the 1998 election because many Germans found the price of reunification to be much more expensive than promised and disliked giving up their stable German mark for a speculative currency experiment that took their one sure defense against inflation away from German control.

The political and economic reforms orchestrated by Gorbachev (see Chapter 10), which ended the cold war and broke apart the Soviet Union, provided a unique but narrow window of opportunity for Germany to reunify. In October 1989, Gorbachev visited orthodox Communist leader Erich Honecker for the fortieth celebration of the East German state. Just four months later, Gorbachev was asked to approve German reunification and accept a common German currency.

Specifically, Honecker fell soon after Gorbachev's visit because of widespread protests that the police were unable to contain. By November 1989, free travel was permitted for East German citizens and the Berlin Wall was opened. The Politburo had resigned and communist reformist Hans Modrow headed a transitional government until free elections could be held in the spring of 1990. Chancellor Helmut Kohl of West Germany proposed a ten-point German federation plan for integrating the two Germanies. This political initiative mobilized all other political factions in West Germany to offer their own reunification ideas so as not to be outmaneuvered before the December 1990 West German election. Kohl's plan was soon countered with a proposal by Modrow (with Gorbachev's approval) for a neutral, demilitarized united Germany without ties to either the NATO or Warsaw Pact alliances. Kohl and his Western allies turned down this proposal.

Meanwhile, over 2,000 East Germans per day were permanently migrating over the border to West Germany, leaving the East German economy (which already had a labor shortage before the exodus) in shambles. The East German currency fell like a rock. East German-made portable stereos in East Berlin, selling for twenty times the price of their better-made West German counterparts just a subway stop away, piled up on the shelves unsold. Color TV sets in spacious East German apartments cost a hundred times as much as the monthly (subsidized) rent. By February, warnings seeped out of the West German capital of the imminent financial collapse of East Germany. Elections had been moved up from May to March 18, 1990. And in a political move without the Bundesbank's approval, Chancellor Kohl proposed to substitute the West German mark for the East German currency, hoping this symbolic gesture would give East Germans confidence and would stem the tide of people coming into his country and putting severe strains on a social system already suffering from unemployment and a housing shortage. Despite the warnings of Karl Otto Pohl, president of the West German Bundesbank, that a rapid currency union would involve serious risks of rising inflation, higher interest rates, and deepening budget deficits, Chancellor Kohl's government went ahead with plans for monetary unification. Politics overwhelmed economics in the decision-making process.

Rather than taking the exchange rate between West German and East German marks that the economic markets called for at that time—between 1:4 and 1:5—as the basis for currency unification, the Kohl government decided upon 1:1.8 (taking the average of active and passive money). If one compares this sudden hardening of the East German mark with the much slower hardening process of the West German mark in terms of its dollar exchange rate since the end of the Bretton Woods system in 1973, the contrast is staggering. In 1973, one dollar was worth 3.66 German marks (DM). In 1993 one dollar was worth about 1.60 DM. As German economist Wilhelm Hankel pointed out, if one calculates the hardening—130 percent—and derives the annual average, one comes up with about 4.5 percent hardening per year. This gradual but consistent hardening of the DM permitted West Germany to keep inflation out of the domestic economy, but to keep its exports competitive in the global economy (keeping their rise in price typically just under the rise in the global inflation rate). But the West German-East German currency rate used had the effect of an overnight hardening of the East German mark of between 400 and 500 percent! Clearly the new price levels of East German goods (particularly given their lower quality) could not compete with the West German goods. Overnight the real, manufacturing market of former East Germany was devastated by this overvalued currency and became merely a consumer market for goods produced in West Germany.[16] The whole economy of the East German states was declassed: The people felt entirely dependent upon the western states of Germany to which many self-respecting young, skilled people fled, seeking truly productive jobs.

While relatively independent (with an inflation-fighting priority, like the U.S. Federal Reserve Bank), the Bundesbank was forced by law to carry out West German government policy. Pohl quickly adapted and became a leader in the monetary reform given certain prerequisites the West German government demanded: complete freedom of commercial activities, the recognition of private property, unlimited rights of investment and tax and price reforms, and East Germany's acceptance of the Federal Republic's Bundesbank as an autonomous institution for the securing of monetary stability.[17]

Higher inflation, higher interest rates, greater unemployment, larger public deficits, and higher taxes were inevitable in West Germany as East and West German monetary and economic integration proceeded. However, as the world's largest exporter, with a record trade surplus of $81 billion in 1989 (exceeding Japan's for the first time since the 1970s), the booming West German economy was well-positioned to take on the responsibilities of subsidizing the East German economy and integration process. Many West German banks and industries, such as Siemens (electronics), Zeiss (optical equipment), Dresdner Bank, and Volkswagen had already revived ties with East German firms with the market openings made possible under *perestroika* and were ready to expand East German operations. And East Germany ranked second only to the Soviet Union among the East bloc's industrial powers. Given the common language, culture, and even educational structures—such as the apprenticeship system—the long-term odds favored a reunified Germany becoming an economic powerhouse (with a population of some 78 million) rivaling the United States and Japan.

However, for some East Germans, such as novelist Christa Wolf, who were proud of the socialist cultural integrity of their own forty-year-old society and who believed that the creative destruction of capitalism would destroy this cultural integrity through the overbearing hegemony of West German business and government, these prospects were dark rather than bright. Social jealousy became pronounced as "the poor cousins" from the East experienced how far behind they were and as some of the established West Germans had second thoughts about overloaded social services, higher taxes, and increased competition for jobs and housing. The East Germans found it difficult to adjust to a social situation in which their apartments were not subsidized and in which work was not guaranteed as they had been used to under socialism.

Both the United States and the Soviet Union accepted the inevitability of German unification. Since the overwhelming majority of the East Germans polled supported reunification and both the Soviet Union and the United States had committed themselves to the "self-determination" of the East German people, they could do little but go along with the historical momentum. This momentum was, however, speeded up deliberately by Chancellor Helmut Kohl's foreign policy advisor, Horst Teltschik, who spoke of East Germany's imminent economic collapse in a press briefing before Kohl went to Moscow for talks. This stoked alarmist fears that could only accelerate the pace of union.

The United States shifted toward an ambiguous policy about Germany's future role in NATO in order to permit reunification to go through more easily. In February 1990, the foreign ministers of the four major powers (the United States, France, Britain, and the U.S.S.R.) agreed with the foreign ministers of the two Germanies at a meeting in Ottawa to a two-phase process of negotiating German unification. First, internal unification measures would be worked out by the two Germanies after East German elections; and, second, external security measures would be negotiated with the four Allies. The fall 1990 meeting of the thirty-five-nation Conference on Security and Cooperation in Europe then confirmed the conditions of the unification of the German state.

German unification represents a form of "quick-study" collective learning using external change and opportunity (Gorbachev's *perestroika* policy) to restructure an expanded maintenance base.[18] The stimulus of German unification, in turn, speeded up the process of European integration, led by the French who were fearful of being declassed and pushed to the periphery as Germany again became the major Central European power. The influence of the United States was threatened with decline in Europe as American troops were withdrawn and the cultural commonality of "Europe's Common House" found its own new integrity in differentiation from the American (and, to some extent, Anglo-Saxon) culture. In his book *Perestroika* (1987), Gorbachev spoke of this threat to European culture: "The threat emanates from an onslaught of 'mass culture' from across the Atlantic.... Indeed, one can only wonder that a deep, profoundly intelligent and inherently humane European culture is retreating to the background before the primitive revelry of violence and pornography and the flood of cheap feelings and low thoughts." French Eurocentric film policy in the 1993 GATT talks confirmed this perception of the threat of Anglo-Saxon (read "American") cultural hegemony (see Chapter 3). Similarly, in the 1990s, unemployed German youth in the East German states became mobilized in right-wing, ethnocentric group action against foreigners. This movement was financed by right-wing groups in West German states who feared being declassed by thousands of immigrants pouring into Germany.

Globally, Anglo-American hegemony succeeded so well in creating prosperity that it subsidized European and Pacific Rim countercultures that undermine some of its assumptions while pragmatically adapting others. Liberalism brings out postliberal reactions. Increasing global multipolarity in economic power breeds multicultural renaissance and the protectionism this implies in terms of preserving cultural identities from the creative destruction of world capitalism.[19]

In the postunification era, Germany has discovered that increasing productivity alone does not make for competitiveness if wage (and fringe benefit) increases outstrip the growth in productivity. After Japan and Portugal, Germany posted the biggest productivity gains (adjusted for inflation) between 1980 and 1993: 2.8 percent annually. In contrast, the United States and France were at the bottom of the list, and in Britain productivity actually declined. It is true that in most countries wages increased faster than productivity. But in the United States and Japan, wages and productivity have moved in unison.[20]

By paying salaries in semiannual bonuses, Japan has been able to keep wage increases in line with what is going on in the real economy. **Wages**, which economist Lester Thurow defined as "bribes paid individuals to sacrifice an hour of leisure," reflect the German mark's external value. Both wages and real interest rates soared at the time of German unification. Export growth slumped. Imports poured in. These trends reflect the significant resources needed to modernize the eastern German states, leading to a large German current account deficit. This rebuilding of the eastern states will take years. When German interest rates go up faster than world market prices, the profit margins of German companies are squeezed. Since these companies rely upon domestic financing, their costs of capital go up. Therefore, although Germany was second only to the United States in terms of exports in the early 1990s, the Germans came under increasing pressure as domestic inflationary pressures and union militancy threatened to undermine German competitiveness. The heavy cost of subsidies flowing to the Eastern states (through a 7.5 percent solidarity tax on all taxpayers in former Western Germany) began to take its toll. Between 1990 and 1998 more than $625 billion had been transferred from the west to the eastern states, financed in part by social security charges that rose from 35.5 percent of wages in 1991 to 42.3 percent in 1998.[21] Chancellor Helmut Kohl became more preoccupied with foreign affairs, particularly with pushing through the Euro currency, than with the domestic restructuring the economy required. He paid for it by losing the 1998 election to Social Democrat Gerhard Schröder, whose campaign focused on the key domestic concern: an 11 percent unemployment rate (which Kohl had failed to cut in half as he promised) in which there were twice as many without jobs in the Eastern German states as in the West. Indeed, as the twentieth century came to a close, Harvard economist Robert Barro forecast that productivity in the East, stymied by government wage intervention, would reach only 68 to 76 percent of the West's by 2030. By that date there will almost be as many people over sixty-four as between ages fifteen and sixty-four—a higher percent than any other industrialized country except Japan (where the number of workers under thirty will decline 25 percent by 2010). So even if unemployment falls to 9.7 percent by 2003 as the Organization of Economic Cooperation and Development projects, the increasing old age pension drag will combine with the "catch-up" problem in the East to put a heavy burden on the engine of German competitiveness.[22]

While the coalition between the Social Democrats and the Green environmentalist party did push forward a program of so-called ecology tax reform on energy that would permit a slight reduction in social security charges, this may be too little too late for German competitiveness and too tepid to do much for the environment. Increased wage costs have made German businesses reluctant to hire and 2.5 million jobs were eliminated between 1991 and 1998, with some 4 million people unemployed. New pressures were put on a social security system in an aging population that extended generous pension benefits to 15.5 million people in the eastern states. A sort of "reform fatigue" set in as Europeans who had cut deficits for the sake of qualifying for the Euro began to show resistance, electing center-left politicians promising to bring back social benefits undone for the sake of creating a European Central Bank with a strong currency. The German government mimicked the French in the late 1990s, calling for lower interest rates to stimulate demand, while Wim Duisenberg, President of the European Central Bank, independent of the politicians, resisted these pressures as long as possible in order to insure that the Euro would be born a stable and attractive child.

THE INDUSTRIAL POLICY DILEMMA OF THE UNITED STATES

Unlike Japan and Germany, the United States has no feudal heritage and no natural inclination to accept hierarchies of authority and status. Whether or not dogmatic liberalism is all that Americans know (as historian Louis Hartz argued), it *is* probably true that most Americans agree with the proposition that that government governs best which governs least.

The greatest political and economic advantage of the United States is the stability of its constitutional framework. When things go wrong in the world, money and people flood into the United States—the last bastion of political stability, individual freedom, and government-protected capitalism. Private property is sacrosanct, the very extension of individual freedom as Americans understand it.

But the greatest advantage of the United States may, paradoxically, become at times the greatest obstacle to social change in order to adapt collectively to new demands of the world economy. For if the stability of individual freedom and private property are sacred, everything else comes in a distant second, from social ethics to collective economic competitiveness to educational excellence to ecological survival. This is the dilemma of industrial policy in America.[23] More specifically, it was the particular dilemma of the administration of Bill Clinton.

The industrial policy debate has gone on in the United States since its founding. "Money is the vital principle of the body politic," said Alexander Hamilton, a founding father and the first secretary of the treasury. But Thomas Jefferson, founding father, author of the Declaration of Independence (1776), and the third American president, said "The care of human life and happiness, and not their destruction, is the first and only legitimate object of good government." Hamilton stood for a strong, centralized federal government steered by a financial aristocracy that strove for economic and financial power for the United States. In his "Report on Manufactures," Hamilton suggested the use of government subsidies and tariffs for industries in order to compete with the British. Jefferson, on the other hand, opposed the conservative, Federalist position of Hamilton and advocated a populist, decentralized form of agrarian democracy.

Although Jefferson initially appeared to win ideologically, ultimately Hamilton's ideas have prevailed (consider the dominance today of big business, the chairman of the Federal Reserve and the Treasury Secretary). The competitive dynamism within the U.S. economy is in part due to the American refusal to decide clearly between these conceptions of Hamilton and Jefferson. While America avoided the mercantilism represented at the time by countries such as Spain, as business historian Thomas McCraw noted, "it did exhibit for 150 years after the Revolution a pronounced tendency towards protectionism, mostly through the device of the tariff." During the late nineteenth century, giant industrial monopolies emerged (see Chapter 4). These monopolies were later somewhat deterred by largely ineffective antitrust legislation.

The major thrust of industrial policy was aimed to shore up national defense. From the Congressional approval to purchase muskets from inventor Eli Whitney at the end of the eighteenth century, to the tremendous subsidies for sophisticated technologies and weapons in World War II, to the skyrocketing defense budget of President Ronald Reagan (which helped to break the back of the Soviet empire), Americans have appeared to accept state subsidies for defense industries ("Pentagon Inc.") as part and parcel of becoming a powerful nation in the world. Hamilton would have smiled in agreement.

Adam Smith, on the other hand, would have had his doubts. Since World War II, myriads of American school children have been taught the virtues of free markets and economic processes in contrast to the statist economics of socialist systems. But the historical part about protectionism, subsidies, and cartels is usually touched on lightly, if at all. Great industrial powers, such as Britain and the United States, typically begin to propagate their classical economic liberalism after they establish an industrial base that is globally competitive.[24] After they establish an efficient maintenance base they benefit most from open markets around the world in which to launch their entrepreneurial expansion.

The American government's problem in the post-cold-war era was how to get the public to back a centralized industrial policy that was not based on defense, or Pentagon, Inc. The solution of the Clinton administration was initially to focus on **managed trade**, or government intervention to steer trade relations with other countries toward the national interest, or at least to avoid unequal tariff trade-offs. The opposite of this philosophy is the laissez-faire liberal approach of Michael Boskin, chairman of President George Bush's Council of Economic Advisers, to whom is attributed the statement: "It does not make any difference whether a country makes computer chips or potato chips."[25] This assumes a world market in equilibrium where the costs of capital, labor, and physical plant are equal everywhere and workers are free to move from low-wage areas to higher ones to equalize things.

But in her book *Who's Bashing Whom?: Trade Conflict in High Technology Industries*, Clinton's first chairperson of the Council of Economic Advisers, Laura D'Andrea Tyson, argues that it matters a great deal who is making what and where they are making it. Increasing returns from economies of scale, efficiencies from interacting learning curves, benefits from targeted external linkages, and technological spillovers "are not the stuff of perfect competition and market optimality." The key to competitiveness is for governments to help create "a virtuous cycle of economic growth, innovation, and learning by doing" (see Chapter 8). Big auto makers can pay high wages only due to great economies of scale. Productivity rises as new technology spills over from semiconductor machine tool makers to chip manufacturers. Lacking a strong machine-tool industry, the United States risks becoming dependent upon Japanese chip makers and the business groups that control them. While investments in research and development (R & D) typically bring returns of between 35 and 60 percent higher than those from investments in plants and equipment, companies alone are afraid to take the risk since it is uncertain who exactly will get the returns from R & D investment. Yet economies that tap into abnormally high returns from capital and labor will have higher incomes than those that do not.

The shift from Bush to Clinton, in short, was a shift from an industrial policy that was officially laissez-faire liberal with implicit centralized industrial planning for defense to a policy of postliberal economic intervention that explicitly subsidized technologies and training vital for U.S. competitiveness in high-tech industries, including defense. But this ideal focus on high-tech competitiveness and training was largely eclipsed by government interventions for universal healthcare, welfare reform, and criminal containment, not to mention legislative limits on spending in order to bring down the huge budget deficit or the war in Kosovo.

In the decade-and-a-half following World War II, the United States had all the advantages: an unscathed industrial plant, a prosperous population, a backlog of large technological investments because of the war, a hunger to work, and a desire to restore peaceful harmony. American productivity overwhelmed that of other countries. However, by the late 1960s, trade gaps were emerging, despite a falling dollar. Inflation was headed up. By the early 1970s, wage levels were stalemated or declining in real (inflation-adjusted) terms. Many of the fifty largest export firms depended on natural resources (including agriculture), as opposed to the "value-added" manufacturing focus of the emerging Japanese and German economies.[26] The proportion of American-made goods subject to international competition leaped from 20 to 80 percent between 1972 and 1982! Semiconductor and computer firms became complacent after a Pentagon, Inc. subsidized environment helped them to start up.

Perhaps the best example is the fall from competitiveness of IBM, which lost market share to the point it could no longer control the introduction of new innovations as it once could. By 1985 it had become clear that consumers had moved away from its mainframe computer business. Yet it took three years for IBM to shift gears and slowly to react.[27] Its downsizing and decentralization oriented toward customers in different markets is illustrative of America's transition from a manufacturing economy to a service and information economy, and from complacency to aggressive, niche-specific competitiveness. As IBM's Robert Logan said in Brussels in 1992: "It used to be said that 'The big eat the small.' Today the motto has become 'The fast eat the slow.'" What is required is collective learning turned on high speed.[28]

A second case of complacency and decline in American competitiveness is the semiconductor industry. In the late 1970s, the semiconductor industry, based in Silicon Valley, California, represented all that people thought was ideal in

American economic liberalism: fresh, innovative thinking, future-oriented entrepreneurship, long-term, risk-oriented companies not seeking government hand-outs but wealth and independence. At that time, 85 percent of the semiconductors in Japan came from America. But by 1983, with the help of their government bureaucracies and financing, Japanese semiconductor companies were spending more on new facilities than were U.S. firms. Everything was downhill from there, epitomized by a MITI-steered shortage of 256-kilobyte DRAM chips in the late 1980s that jacked up the prices much as the OPEC cartel had done with oil. High-tech U.S. firms had become totally dependent upon the Japanese DRAMS. The 1986 Semiconductor Agreement between the United States and Japan, which gave the United States a 20 percent share of the domestic Japanese semiconductor market, underscored this trend, while helping to turn it around.

Government policy shaped the microelectronics industry from the beginning—starting with the United States in World War II and the cold war with the Pentagon Inc. advantage, then shifting to the Japanese steered by MITI, and tilting in the 1990s to government-subsidized East Asian producers, particularly Korea.[29] American firms had cut down drastically in semiconductor production, since they could not make sufficient short-term profits, threatening to set up a situation of long-term American dependence. But then the pay-offs of the semiconductor agreement took hold, and starting in 1992, the U.S. semiconductor industry rebounded sharply.

There is the danger that **downsizing** (reducing the number of employees and noncore related businesses) is but a one-shot booster of productivity. As Americans watched the slowdown in global economic growth in industrialized countries from 4.4 percent in 1988 to 3.3 percent in 1989 to 2.6 percent in 1990 to 0.9 percent in 1991 and 1.7 percent in 1992, it is little wonder that they went in for downsizing and radical restructuring.[30] But the side effects in the United States (as elsewhere in the world) included not only potential dependence on foreign producers but also rising job turnovers, crime, ethnic hatred, religious extremism, and nationalism. American banks were reluctant to lend money even when interest rates fell. The infrastructure was exposed as inadequate to support the high-tech communications necessary for global competitiveness.[31] American teenagers scored near the bottom in math and science tests in comparison with other industrialized countries.[32] The very social fabric that underpinned the economy seemed to be coming apart. For example, in his 1994 State of the Union Address, President Bill Clinton spoke of the "stunning and simultaneous breakdown of community, family, and work—the heart and soul of civilized society." (The slaughter by teenagers in a high school in Littleton, Colorado in 1999 is a case in point.) American companies merged with others for competitive strength and set up joint ventures with key competitors and suppliers abroad.[33] They became mean and lean and their manufacturing productivity rose.[34] Clinton's aim was to maintain this corporate competitiveness through managed trade in order to stimulate job creation at home, while simultaneously introducing legislation to buffer the domestic social costs—in healthcare, welfare, criminal activity, and job training. And Congress and Ross Perot helped to persuade him to attack the American budget deficit as well, which amounted to $255 billion by 1994.

American liberalism seemed to have met its postliberal match. However, the diffusion of objectives on the part of the Clinton administration leaves one uncertain as to whether the payoffs from these many pursuits will ever catch up with the costs. The "follow-up" is uncertain. This is illustrated by the lack of specific targeting in Vice President Albert Gore's advocacy of government funding for an "information superhighway" throughout the United States. This superhighway would provide two-way communication on multiple channels, thereby guaranteeing both rich and poor access to a service that does not yet exist and which they may or may not use.[35] The thrust of telecommunications mergers came to monopolize the structure of this market access before the "virtual reality" even came into being. *The new competitive trend is to reinvent social reality for markets of the future that do not yet exist.*[36]

THE "LIMELIGHT EFFECT" OF U.S. ECONOMIC DYNAMISM AND THE BACKLASH

The clout of American elites is reinforced by the **limelight effect**—the tendency of other people in the world to mimic American trends once the focus is concentrated on success emanating from the United States—for better or for worse. High tech, deregulation, entrepreneurship, management training, and revolutions in telecommunication and financial services illustrate the demonstration power of the American economy. The limelight effect is the epitome of soft power—the attractiveness of pull, enhanced by the strength of American marketing techniques. A low-tech example is McDonald's, known as a fast-food chain (but more accurately it is an astute real estate franchise business). Singapore's government encouraged families to have birthday celebrations in McDonald's restaurants to stimulate meetings for future spouses and to increase an appetite for consumption in an effort to mimic the consumption-driven dynamism of the American economy. While Europeans (notably poor at job creation) often put down jobs at McDonalds as being of low quality, a new McDonald's is created in the world every eighteen hours; in order to obtain a job in the franchise in Zurich one must speak three languages fluently, and the price of a "Big Mac" has become an international indicator of purchasing power parity in *The Economist*. Yet the backlash against the soft cultural power of McDonalds has been significant, culminating in the longest trial in British history. In this "McLibel" suit, McDonalds brought a libel suit against an organization called London Green Peace in 1990 for a pamphlet the group distributed claiming that McDonalds uses bad meat, encourages the felling of rain forests to grow crops for the cattle, exploits children, depresses wages, and is guilty of cruelty to animals. While the franchise was cleared of all but the last three charges (after spending $16 million in legal fees) and created 6,000 more outlets around the world during the three years duration of the trial, the anti-McDonalds pamphlet is now on the Internet (under "McSpotlight") and has been read by some 16 million people.[37] At the high tech end, Microsoft and Intel create prototypes of twenty-first century competitiveness of which most countries can only dream: Software and its storage in monopolized microchips may be the ultimate form of soft power. These companies set the global standards for their economic sectors. And Hollywood dominates the global film industry to such an extent that the Europeans have felt obligated to restrict the market share of non-European (read American) films to 50 percent in the European Union to keep Euro soft power from going really soft.

As German journalist Josef Jaffe notes, in terms of the soft power game, the United States is in a class of its own: "On that table, China, Russia, Japan, and even Western Europe cannot hope to match the pile of chips the United States holds. People are risking death on the high seas to get into the United States, not China. There are not too many who want to go for an M.B.A. at Moscow University, or dress and dance like the Japanese."[38] Whereas earlier there was a much greater flow of people and capital out of the United States than coming in, this trend appears to be reversing. From being the world's greatest creditor, since 1997 the net U.S. foreign debt was more than $1 trillion, increasing at an annual rate of 15 to 20 percent (with Japan owning some $300 billion and China $50 billion in U.S. treasury bonds). And by the early 1990s, instead (as previously) of many more Americans going abroad than foreigners coming here, the outflows and inflows were equal.

For better or for worse, the world is still reeling from the political and economic impact of the Thatcher and Reagan ideological revolutions, a reversion to Adam Smith. Once the Cold War enemy—the Soviet Union—self-destructed, American hegemony's main target became to maximize the logical outcome of its resurrected liberal economic creed—commercial success. The wave of global privatization not only freed up new markets but lowered prices as competition flourished. The Clinton administration appointed an investment banker, Robert Rubin, as treasury secretary and used the power of diplomacy, French-style, to maximize American economic interests and exports. Alan Greenspan was kept as head of the Federal Reserve, which assured monetary stability and preemptive attacks on even the possibility of a rise in inflation. By 1999 the United States was nine years into an economic boom with low unemployment, high productivity growth, and moderate inflation. The federal government budget had been transformed from deep deficits to a surplus (see Figure 9-1 on page 248). And the stable chaos of the American domestic market permitted the entrepreneurial freedom for private firms to restructure, down-size, and take creative risks in high tech, telecommunications, and financial services, thus setting an international standard of job creation and competitiveness that took other countries by storm. The New York and NASDAQ stock exchanges became the global standards and helped to make the top fifth of Americans in income disproportionately rich.

And while many of the bottom 80 percent of the American population were psychologically lifted by the American economic boom and lower unemployment rate—to the point of taking on debt and pushing the consumer bankruptcy rate to an all-time high (4.4 percent) in 1997, many lost their jobs in the restructuring. New jobs are often temporary, paying less than former jobs.[39] Such trends lead to what social scientists call a decline in social capital, which

Figure 9-1   Federal Government Budget (in Billions of U.S. $)

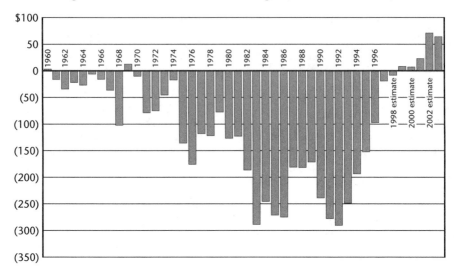

Source: Office of Management and Budget, Executive Office of the President of the United States

is reinforced by the decline in participation in community volunteer organizations. The backlash to American economic hegemony, which benefits the top 20 percent the most, is surfacing within the United States as well as without. Partly this is because of the development of the United States as a truly multicultural society of competing ethnic groups, leading to cultural conflicts. President Clinton fostered the theme of diversity more than national unity. And as the United States enters the second phase of hegemony in which it is no longer really necessary to impose its will militarily abroad to gain influence as economic, political, and cultural influence flows to it at home, the home front is in social, cultural, and educational disarray. Political scientist Samuel Huntington argues that given domestic forces pushing toward heterogeneity, diversity, multiculturalism, and ethnic and racial division, the United States may not be able to effectively define its "national interests" without a significant enemy to oppose. Indeed, multinational corporate policies and cultural *diasporas*—immigrant cultural groups like American Jews supporting Israel and Chinese immigrants sending direct investment from the United States to China—may be defining U.S. foreign policy as much as the U.S. State Department does.[40] Both within public (state) and private (corporate) organizations, a model of coping with change is needed that will help identify the glue necessary to hold a culture's integrity together, on the one hand, and to specify the risks and efforts necessary to adapt this core to the changing world economy for the sake of economic and political survival, on the other hand. And the emerging economies, such as those in Asia, give us a cautionary tale of what happens if such risks get out of balance.

"ECONOMIC MIRACLES" AND THEIR OPPORTUNITY COSTS

If we first consider for a moment what was labeled as "an economic miracle" in the past fifty years in terms of industrial policy and other factors, it is then easier to assess the "opportunity costs" environmentally, financially, socially, and politically of such rapid waves of economic growth. Then we can come back to the question: If economic growth is put on high speed before all other priorities, does it inevitably lead to bank melt-downs and social and environmental catastrophes as we experienced in the late 1990s in Asia?

Economic miracles are made, not born. National economic achievements that appear to deviate from the laws of nature or so to transcend those laws as to seem that they are brought about through some superhuman agency are "miracles" mainly in the perception of the beholder.

Such perceptions became fixated upon certain countries in the second half of the twentieth century, largely due to the reversal of depressed circumstances of nations that lost World War II (such as Germany and Japan) or due to being classified as developing or "Third World" (such as the "four little dragons" of East Asia). To be perceived to be an "economic miracle" it helps to start in a relatively "down-and-out" position from which it is much easier to double or treble economic growth. But even if economic "miracles" are not really miracles after all but a lucky mix of external and internal factors that come together in a surprising synergy, one would like to be able to look behind such achievement to see how it was accomplished in different cultural contexts.

The collective learning process coordinating external opportunity with domestic factors has been neglected in earlier analysis of economic development. Conventional economists typically identify links between the macro and the micro as "exogenous variables." Accordingly, collective learning is often put in the box of "education" or "literacy," a sideshow of domestic policy; while in reality, given propitious conditions, it may be the whole game (see Chapter 7). Groups and organizations targeted for learning that facilitates applied economic objectives are more apt to become extraordinary economic performers than those distracted by other objectives and perceptions.

IDENTIFYING "ECONOMIC MIRACLES"

An "economic miracle" seems to start from a disadvantageous situation of wartime destruction, poverty, or structural dependence and then rise like a phoenix from the ashes. But which indicators are useful in knowing an "economic miracle" when one sees one?

The first criterion used here to sort out "economic miracles" was unusually high rates of positive annual growth of Gross Domestic Product (GDP), that is, at least 8.8 percent each year over a period of at least three years. Given the perception of Chile as a "miracle country" (see *Wall Street Journal*, January 25, 1993), Chile's "first wave" 8.8 percent annual GDP growth rate was used as a minimal benchmark (GDP growth in Chile was 9.8 percent for 1977, 8.4 percent for 1978, and 8.3 percent for 1979—averaging 8.8 percent). And to discern which of the miracles had the potential to recur, Chile's average investment of 16.7 percent of GDP for the three years of its miracle wave was used as a benchmark (investment as percent of GDP for Chile was 14.4 percent in 1977, 17.8 percent in 1978, and 17.8 percent in 1979—averaging 16.7 percent). While the initial miracle wave of many countries seems largely to be caused by a surge of economic "inputs," without plowing a good share of the capital spawned by this growth into investment in plant and equipment and future job creation, an "economic miracle" is not apt to last long enough to be identified as such or to spill over into future "miracle waves." Such miracle waves are usually characterized by significant increases in exports and imports. Two kinds of economic miracles can be identified using the criteria above: (1) "miracles" perceived as such because their volume of trade during their miracle waves was at least of the benchmark, Chile ($2.933 billion in exports and $3.490 billion in imports)—registered in **bold** type below; and (2) "hidden miracles" with less trade volume than Chile's during its miracle wave.[41]

"Economic miracles" characterized by *one wave* of outstanding annual economic growth and significant investment between 1950 and 1993 included **West Germany** (1950–1952), Spain (1961–1963), Malta (1973–1979), **Malaysia** (1988–1991), **Chile** (1977–1979),Venezuela (1954–1956), **Iraq** (1975–1980), Iran (1965–1972), **Brazil** (1971–1974), the Dominican Republic (1969–1973), Libya (1961–1969), Syria (1974–1976), Egypt (1975–1977), Belize (1987–1990), Paraguay (1977–1980), Suriname (1975–1977), Solomon Islands (1976–1979), Cameroon (1978–1981), Cape Verde (1978–1981), Congo (1979–1982), Gabon (1971–1976), Lesotho (1976–1978), Nigeria (1968–1971), Rwanda (1967–1970), Sudan (1974–1977), and Zambia (1964–1967). Those countries in the 1950 to 1993 time frame that had *two waves* of outstanding growth were **Thailand** (1976–1978, 1988–1990), **Japan** (1959–1961, 1966–1970), **China** (1963–1966, 1983–1985), **Hong Kong** (1962–1965, 1976–1981), **Taiwan** (1963–1973, 1976–1978), **South Korea** (1976–1978, 1986–1988), Botswana (1969–1974, 1978–1981),Israel (1954–1957, 1961–1965), and Oman (1974–1978, 1981–1985).

Finally, economic miracle countries in the past four decades characterized by *three or more waves* by GDP growth and investment include **Singapore** (1966–1973, 1979–1981, 1987–1990), and the Maldives (1976–1979, 1983–1985, 1988–1990).

By demystifying these "economic miracle" countries and pinning down their growth cycles and commonalities, other nations can perceive them as merely high economic achievers at certain historical moments (versus "miracles") and collectively learn from them how to attain such achievement and what the opportunity costs are apt to be.

Some influential economic miracle countries stand out. Among "one wave" miracles, West Germany started the 1950s with a 29.4 percent annual GDP increase, dropping the next year to 18.3 percent increase with annual increases in the subsequent five years being 8.8 percent, 8.3 percent, 7.7 percent, 12.0 percent, and 7.2 percent respectively. Japan's multiwave performance in terms of annual GDP growth was the most impressive of all: It began the 1950s with a 26.6 percent increase, slipping to 19.7 percent growth in 1951 followed by an uninterrupted exceptional GDP annual growth rate averaging 9.4 percent for the next twenty-two years! No wonder the Japanese model was to prove to be so influential for all other would-be economic miracle countries (particularly in Asia)! Thus, Taiwan began a two-decade spurt of annual GDP growth in 1952 with 10.9 percent, averaging 9.2 percent from 1953 through 1973, and with growth spurts in the late 1970s and late 1980s.

EXTERNAL FACTORS

The utility of annual GDP growth increases as an indicator of economic miracles is borne out when one compares high points and low points. In the post World War II era, many of the miracle countries had concentrations of high growth at the beginning of the 1950s, fed by the liquidity of U.S. loans, grants, and investments and shielded by the hegemony of U.S. military security. Commercial applications of technology provided by the war and abundant supplies of labor at moderate cost also played a role, not to mention the demand stimulated by postwar consumption. This "wave of global economic growth" was consolidated and driven to high levels of intensity as individual country miracle growth waves interacted in terms of trade and modeling, causing a kind of growth contagion. In contrast, the period immediately following the quadrupling of oil prices by OPEC in 1973 was one of slowdown in growth rates as industrial costs went up and a widespread recession of 1974–1975 set in (consolidated by reactionary, tight monetary policies on the part of industrialized countries when central banks, unfortunately, all overreacted at once bringing the national business cycles down in sync).

External factors helping to set up national opportunities for economic miracles include the following: *war devastation* (providing the necessity for immediate reconstruction with highly motivated (hungry), low-paid labor, *threat from a neighbor* (i.e., containing Stalin's U.S.S.R. as the motive for the Marshall plan, the efforts of Asian countries to counter the residual effects of Japanese occupation, etc), *colonialism as a source of stimulation and learning* (i.e., nations occupied by Japan or England mimicking the behavior of the occupiers whom they sought to replace), *superpower grants and loans* (the U.S. liquidity provided through the Marshall Fund, etc., after the war and in the 1990s through mutual fund investments in East Asia), *foreign direct investment* (i.e., United States in Europe after the war, expatriate Chinese in China and other Asian countries in the 1980s and 1990s), *transfer of technology and management skills from others* (from the United States to Europe and Japan after the war, from Japan to the East Asian "dragons" in the 1970s and 1980s), *easy access to world markets* (the free trade ideology behind the Bretton Woods institutions in the postwar period, resurrected through GATT tariff rounds).[42] However, these types of external factors alone do not provide the necessary elements for a national economic miracle. Critical internal factors are part of the mix.

INTERNAL FACTORS

While not all of the internal factors below may be present in all economic miracles, most of them reappear with enough frequency that they must be taken seriously by those who would bring about new "miracles" (or keep old ones going):[43]

- postauthoritarian unity and political stability (Germany, Japan, South Korea, Taiwan, Singapore, Chile, China, etc.)
- cultural homogeneity (Germany, Japan, South Korea, Taiwan, etc.)
- nationalism and pride in independence (all miracle countries)
- sources of cheap (skilled) labor (Germany, Japan, South Korea, China, etc.)
- high literacy and learning rates (Germany, Japan, S. Korea, Singapore, Taiwan, Hong Kong, etc.)
- high status bureaucracy (Japan, S. Korea, Singapore, etc.)
- currency reform or stable money: an effective banking & credit system (Germany)
- entrepreneurial chances (Germany, Japan, Hong Kong, Singapore, S. Korea, Taiwan, Malaysia, etc.)
- efficient agriculture (Germany, Japan, S. Korea, China, etc.)
- high investment rates as percent of GDP (Germany, Japan, Thailand, Hong Kong, Singapore,etc.)
- government targeted firm subsidies/protection (all)
- government regulation/subsidy for savings rate: sacrifice (Japan, Germany, Singapore, S. Korea, Taiwan, etc.)
- government modernization of infrastructure (all)
- government population controls (China, Singapore, etc.)
- import substitutions (Japan, S. Korea, etc.)
- export subsidies (Japan, S. Korea, Singapore, Taiwan, etc.)
- attempts to limit range of class or income gaps (China, Germany, S. Korea, Japan, Malaysia, etc.)
- education and training reforms (Japan, S. Korea, Singapore, Taiwan, Germany, etc.)
- government-targeted R&D subsidy (Japan, S. Korea, Singapore, Taiwan, China, etc.)
- government-run firms (China, S. Korea, etc.)
- alliances with foreign multinational firms (all)
- privatization (Germany, Japan, Taiwan, S. Korea, China, etc.)
- "hunger" or vitality of people (drive) (Germany, Japan, S. Korea, China, etc.)

While most of these internal factors are fairly transparent, "postauthoritarian unity and political stability" requires clarification. Many of the more prominent economic miracles, such as Germany, Japan, and most recently, China, were outgrowths of "postauthoritarian" structures of the past still in place, though hidden from view, providing a taken-for-granted stability and unity from which concentrated economic growth strategies could be launched. Economist Mancur Olson stressed the break-up of established distributional coalitions or dominant interest groups due to these authoritarian-to-postauthoritarian transitions, freeing up social structures for entrepreneurship and extraordinary economic efforts.[44] But Olson oversimplifies. At least as important as the break-up of the old is the residual structure of the old that still remains, providing a kind of underground stability that goes unquestioned while people scramble for economic advantages up above. Thus, the large concentrated German banking and chemical companies provided a traditional structural basis of stability despite failed efforts of the American occupiers to break up such concentrations of power. The long-time "one party" democracy of Japan provided the unity and stability that often steered dynamic creative people away from electoral politics (where the outcome was all too certain) to the field of commercial economic risk-taking. Similarly, the Japanese occupation of South Korea limited Korean political activities and steered their efforts into learning from the Japanese institutionally and economically in order to try to beat them on the economic battlefield. What is at stake here is not just shaking up the system with the postauthoritarian liberation, but the channeling of mass perceptions into pure economic targets, leading the fruits of growth to be plowed back into the economic infrastructure as investment in order to set the stage for future waves of growth. All societies have their collective learning processes but only some position and target these processes to achieve extraordinary economic achievement, concentrating their "inputs" into waves high enough to make a global impression.

COLLECTIVE LEARNING AND THE LOGIC OF PERCEPTION

Recent work on the logic of perception suggests that at any historical moment in time people treat a given set of perceptions as if it were a funnel: Ultimately the perceptions are "worked down" to a stable loop or repeating pattern of meaning.[45] After a while this pattern becomes habitual and a group of people come to see things in the same way even if this perceptual world happens to become inconsistent with what is going on in the world economy.

Societies in a postauthoritarian phase limit the perceptual options of their peoples, steering their "funneling" behavior into habitual "schemata" or prototypes of meaning that operate like "branding irons" upon social reality. Should these schemata happen to all be targeted toward economic growth and productivity at an optimum meeting point of the external and internal factors listed above, an "economic miracle" in terms of annual GDP growth and investment is likely to result. Recall that collective learning is the social learning process of distinguishing these "legitimate" patterns or schemata of adaptive behavior within an organization in order to manage change without losing cultural integrity. The cultural tradition or funneling pattern that steers collective learning in Japan, for example, is characterized by a "tight" cluster of neo-Confucian hierarchical schemata in which commitment to life-long education opens the people to a dynamic receptivity to new learning, setting them up for continuous economic and cultural development. And this cultural pattern typifies those "neo-Confucian" East Asian countries that learned much from Japan as well—South Korea, Singapore, Taiwan, and Hong Kong—despite distinctive differences in each case. Germany is characterized by cultural schemata focusing on a "work-oriented" process of socialization, "order," and apprenticeship. And the United States, in contrast, has a cultural tradition of "loose" laissez-faire individualism, socializing immigrants into American values and civil legal arrangements rather than training them either for hands-on work or for commitment to life-long learning for its own sake.

The continuing debate as to whether or not the economic miracles of East Asia are depressed by or rather fostered by their neo-Confucian heritage is answered by the collective learning thesis within the postauthoritarian context. On the one hand, the thirst for learning and patience with hierarchies of authority are fostered by the Confucian cultural heritage—the traditional context. On the other hand, the gradual liberation from this tradition (i.e., through the collective learning from American or Japanese models) provides individual motivation for dynamic collective entrepreneurial risk taking, Schumpeter's "creative destruction." The traditional cultural context is the Yin, the targeted collective learning or adapting to trends in the global economy, the Yang: Both are integral parts of the dynamism of Asian economies. If the liberation from tradition goes too far, Schumpeter's prediction may kick in: The capitalist process of creative destruction succeeds only to do itself in, leading the economic miracles inevitably to self-destruct as they tear up the institutional rationality and efficiency that permitted them to succeed in the first place. This threat of capitalism self-destructing helps to explain the tenacity of the judicial system in Singapore in upholding its conservative laws even when foreigners are involved. And it explains why the leadership of Malaysia goes out of the way to distinguish its path from typical western development, advocating a consistent hold upon Asian tradition.

At any one time a nation or group of people can only cope with a certain number of incoming perceptions at once and traditional culture helps to sort out these numerous bits, delimiting what is considered "legitimate" in terms of the dominant cultural schemata. If the society is too open there may be too many alternatives, splitting up and polarizing the process of collective learning and making it difficult to maintain a consistent standard of economic and educational competitiveness over time. Anglo-Saxon cultures are often cited as cases in point. On the other hand, if the society is too closed, there is not room for the flexibility, creativity, and entrepreneurial risk without which economic miracles cannot blossom—such as the authoritarian regime of Mao in China. A postauthoritarian regime holds in the number of alternatives, as it were, to maintain a controllable "loose-tight" mix of schemata or prototypes of meaning that enable collective learning to be targeted upon economic growth and productivity. If the looseness comes at the right tempo, a slow but building liberation from traditional authoritarian constraints, there is enough stability and predictability to attract foreign investment. And if postauthoritarian perceptions must be funneled into a stable, reappearing loop or pattern, why not target inputs into a virtuous cycle of economic dynamism and competitiveness? Of course, at a later stage of development continued extraordinary economic growth (or multiwave achievement) depends on efficiency gains stemming from painful policy choices.

STEPS TOWARD "ECONOMIC MIRACLES"

Comparing the past economic miracles we have identified, one can ask: Without which essential steps could these miracles not have occurred? Or, more precisely, what blueprint can be proposed for engineering a miracle based on what these miracles had in common?

1. The essence of an economic miracle is to catch a wave of global economic growth and let it lift your country from a trough to a peak.

2. Catching the wave usually involves free-riding on the coattails of a major economic power in terms of capital and technology transfer and modeling some of your institutions and innovations after theirs.

3. Traditional cultural schemata have to be translated into a process of "continuous structural conversion": A collective thirst for new technological adaptation and economic reform become second nature in order to increase efficiencies in the domestic infrastructure and to continually differentiate exports from their competition.

4. Social and political stability must be sufficiently maintained to attract foreign portfolio and direct investment. Efforts to limit the ratio between highest and lowest wage earners further this objective.

5. Initially, self-sufficiency must remain a constant goal—first in agriculture, then in social psychology, and finally economically (often involving population control), aiming for a collective sense of agency and autonomy seeking strong regional ties to aid in this effort.

6. Government incentives should be used to force a high domestic rate of savings, capital which is then redirected to update the infrastructure, transportation, housing, education, and training. Such inputs alone largely explain the emergence of economic miracles.

7. Peg the currency's value to that of a major international reserve currency for the sake of stability and then at propitious moments devalue or revalue it for the purposes of stimulating economic development and export growth. When the currency becomes overvalued for international political reasons, encourage firms to make direct and portfolio investments in strategic countries abroad to maximize the investment clout of the currency. When devaluing, permit interest rates to rise high in banks at home in order to increase savings and then devalue suddenly and extremely (preferably for a brief phase) to stimulate exports. However, long-term ability to keep the foreign investment one attracts depends on transparency in the banking and financial regulatory systems.

8. Government institutions should become semiharmonious information targeting networks that serve both to create an environment in which the country's vital industries can compete globally and to tilt efforts of entrepreneurs towards the most fruitful target sectors—the strategic industrial clusters of national comparative and competitive advantage. Long-term sustainability and ecological risk-reduction depends on the degree to which government subsidies go to environmentally oriented start-ups ("green-green businesses") or *ecopreneurship*.

9. Transfer security costs to others as much as possible through global or regional alliances: Pick the umbrella with the most freedom and flexibility.

10. Establish alliances or blocs with key trading partners, permitting manufacturing to take place where labor is skilled but labor cost is lower.

11. Once an economic miracle is established, the cozy complacency of citizens who benefit from its prosperity must constantly be interrupted in order to increase efficiency at home and to spawn wealth-generating, risk-taking entrepreneurs. To avoid overreliance upon taxes, forced saving, and subsidies to multinational companies: (a) constantly update the educational and technological skills of the workforce and encourage a commitment to life-time learning; (b) subsidize cutting-edge research and development, particularly in sustainable industries, and (c) use regional alliances as sources of new vitality, technological innovation, and collective motivation, as well as semi-closed markets for your goods.

12. Push an economic agenda of sustainable global growth at international institutions aiming for recurrent global waves of economic growth in order to keep economic miracles going, employment rising, and foreign investment flowing.

OPPORTUNITY COSTS AND SUSTAINABLE DEVELOPMENT*

All blueprints have opportunity costs, and since prescriptions for economic growth involve extremes at times, these costs in human terms can be extremely high (as the crises in Thailand, Indonesia, and Russia in 1997–1999 illustrated). This is the fine print on the medication that tells you to consult your physician before accidentally overdosing. For example, export growth based upon weapons or drugs is not only immoral but can destroy the social fabric of society. Nigeria's oil-based economic wave of 1968–1971 surfaced in 1998 with an oil spill one-sixth the size of the giant Exxon Valdez spill in Alaska and a rising polarization between the West's richest corporations and millions of the world's poorest people.[46] Thailand's heavy reliance on sex services as a major "export" can produce an inadvertent mass suicide at home in an era of AIDS. And industrialization at the expense of rain forests in Indonesia and Brazil can maximize short-term growth and survival at the expense of long-term deterioration of the air, land, and water on which future generations must depend.[47] In deliberately limiting its economic growth, including the number of tourists who may visit each year, Bhutan may have discovered moderate growth recipes that make for happy campers. "The key to Bhutan's success on its path of sustainable development seems to lie in its readiness to implement policies with long-term effects (and often without quick pay-offs), and to carefully build a system of new values and to alter present ones, but without the destruction of good and beneficial values inherent in the traditional social and cultural structure."[48] Extreme growth targets can undermine sustainable development. On the other hand, two of the most influential miracle countries, Germany and Japan, have become world leaders in developing pollution control devices.

Spending time in the "miracle" countries is the only way to know if the opportunity costs of extraordinary economic growth are worth the trade-offs in potential pollution, social disintegration, and corruption. Development recipes must

---

Sustainable development was defined by the Brundtland Commission as follows: "Humanity has the ability to make development sustainable—to ensure that it meets the needs of the present without compromising the ability of future generations to meet their own needs." Cf. World Commission on Environment and Development, *Our Common Future*. (Oxford: Oxford University Press, 1987), p.8.

not only be adapted to specific cultures but negative side-effects must be anticipated and countered before growth models are initiated. The best solution is to build these strategies for the deterrence of negative side effects into the growth recipes from the outset and to aim for "green growth" that will not merely provide short-term jobs but sustainable development for coming generations. Setting up attractive financial opportunities with high interest rates, for example, can attract a flood of foreign capital that the existing banking and financial systems may not be able to digest. If the banks become inefficient and corrupt and lose legitimacy, the foreign capital can leave faster than it came, pushing the nation into a deep systemic crisis (see Chapter 11). Economic miracles are made and not born. But this merely underscores that human beings are responsible for their domestic and global consequences. In *Green Logic* (1999) I argue that the only legitimate, ethical state subsidies for the private sector should go to green start-up businesses in order to create environmentally sustainable jobs. It is not sufficient just to make existing firms environmentally responsible: A social and cultural process of transformation is required in order to stimulate "ecopreneurs" to create "green-green businesses" or new environmentally oriented firms that contribute to a sustainable world one would want to leave to one's grandchildren.[49]

QUESTIONS FOR THOUGHT

1. "... the United States, Japan and Germany ... have fallen into the habit of trying to learn most from each other." Try to identify main characteristics that distinguish "the Big Three" from one another. Also pay close attention to historical and cultural issues as well as to their implications for economic behavior.

2. Why is "the entire Japanese economic system ... like a global octopus with arms spread everywhere to pick up information"? How is this achieved?

3. Give a brief description of Germany's "collective conservatism," drawing parallels to Japanese culture wherever possible and considering explicitly the characteristics of Germany's social market economy.

4. Prove that "German unification represents a form of 'quick study' collective learning ... using external change and opportunity ... to restructure an expanded maintenance base" by summarizing the benchmarks of the reunification process. What were the opportunity costs for Helmut Kohl? The German economy?

5. Taking the industrial policies of Japan and Germany into consideration, why did the Clinton administration think the time seemed ripe for the United States to follow a more "centralized" industrial policy not based on defense or Pentagon, Inc.? Evaluate Clinton's policy of "managed trade" as well as IBM's Robert Logan's motto, "The fast eat the slow." Where do Microsoft and Intel fit in?

6. Spontaneously list all the factors you can think of that go into the making of "an economic miracle." Now put numbers in front of them to indicate the order of priority in terms of importance. Then compare your results with the lists of internal and external factors in the text.

7. Which deterrent factors have to be built in to an economic growth plan for

a nation to prevent it from either melting down financially or from destroying itself environmentally? What does "speed" have to do with it? What does "sustainable development" signify? "Ecopreneurship"?

NOTES

1. See S. Ishihara, *The Japan That Can Say No* (New York: Simon & Schuster, 1991); see also, Kishore Mahbubani, "Japan Adrift," *Foreign Policy*, no. 88 (fall 1992): 126–144.

2. George C. Lodge, *Perestroika for America* (Boston, MA: Harvard Business School Press, 1991), pp. 15–16. Also see Charles Hampden-Turner and Alfons Trompenaars, *The Seven Cultures of Capitalism* (New York: Currency/Doubleday, 1993).

3. Nathaniel Nash, "Persuading Americans to Save," *New York Times*, December 17, 1989. Notable is the continuous decline of U.S. personal savings from 1973, when it was 10 percent.

4. Economist Mancur Olson makes this case in, perhaps, the most extreme terms, arguing that the West German and Japanese "economic miracles" were largely due to the effects of totalitarian governments and foreign occupiers who broke up the old distributional coalitions in power and paved the way for growth, so that free and stable social systems were established. See Olson's *The Rise and Decline of Nations: Economic Growth, Stagflation, and Social Rigidities* (New Haven, CT: Yale University Press, 1982), Chapter 4.

5. As economist Lester Thurow puts it: "In the twenty-first century sustainable competitive advantage will come much more out of new process technologies and much less out of new product technologies. Reverse engineering has become an art form.... What used to be primary (inventing new products) becomes secondary, and what used to be secondary (inventing and perfecting new processes) becomes primary." Cf: L. Thurow, *Head to Head: The Coming Economic Battle Among Japan, Europe, and America* (New York: William Morrow and Co., 1992), p. 45.

6. See Chalmers Johnson, *MITI and the Japanese Miracle* (Stanford, CA: Stanford University Press, 1982); T. J. Pempel, *Policy and Politics in Japan: Creative Conservatism* (Philadelphia, PA: Temple University Press, 1982); and Ezra Vogel, *Japan and Number One: Lessons for America* (Cambridge, MA: Harvard University Press, 1979). Vogel writes: "MITI's aim is not to reduce competition among Japanese companies but to create the strongest possible companies with the greatest competitive potential" (p. 72).

7. See Michael Porter, *The Competitive Advantage of Nations* (New York: The Free Press, 1990), pp. 384–421.

8. See Daniel Burstein, *Turning the Tables: A Machiavellian Strategy for Dealing with Japan* (New York: Simon & Schuster, 1993), p. 38.

9. Statistics from "The World Economy in Charts," *Fortune*, July 26, 1993, 92.

10. Peter Drucker, "In Defense of Japanese Bureaucracy," *Foreign Affairs* 76, no. 5: 68–80.

11. William Lewis, "McKinsey Global Institute," *Wall Street Journal*, May 21, 1998.

12. See R. Isaak, "Germany: Economic Powerhouse or Stalemate?" *Challenge* (September–October 1992): 41–46. Also see Thomas Janoski, *The Political Economy of Unemployment: Active Labor Market Policy in West Germany and the United States* (Berkeley, CA: University of California Press, 1990), pp. 9–33.

13. See "West Germany: A Social Market Economy," Chapter 2 in R. Isaak, *European Politics: Political Economy and Polity Making in Western Democracies* (New York: St. Martin's Press, 1980), pp. 27–62. See also Klaus Peter Krause, "In Search of the Meaning of 'Social' in a Social-Market Economy" (originally in German in the *Frankfurter Allgemeine Zeitung*, October 8, 1988), *German Tribune*, no. 1344, October 23, 1988, p. 7.

14. See Edmund L. Andrews, "I. G. Farben: A Lingering Relic of the Nazi Years," *New York Times*, May 2, 1999.

15. Porter, *The Competitive Advantage*, pp. 355–382.

16. Wilhelm Hankel, *Die sieben Todsünden der Vereingigung* (Berlin: Siedler, 1993), pp. 22–23.

17. Ferdinand Protzman, "Bonn's Point Man on Currency," *New York Times*, February 12, 1990.

18. The growing literature on the process of German unification includes: Smyser, *The Economy of United Germany* (New York: St. Martin's Press, 1992); Konrad H. Jarausch, *The Rush to German Unity* (New York: Oxford University Press, 1993); Elizabeth Pond, *Beyond the Wall: Germany's Road to Unification* (Washington, D.C.: Brookings Institution/Twentieth Century Fund, 1993); and Peter H. Merkl, *German Unification in the European Context* (University Park, PA: Pennsylvania State University Press, 1993).

19. On cultural clashes resulting from this inevitable change, see Samuel Huntington, "The Clash of Civilizations?" *Foreign Affairs* (summer 1993); and Robert D. Kaplan, "The Coming Anarchy," *Atlantic Monthly* (February 1994): 44–76.

20. Statistics above are from "Unification Has Weakened Germany's International Competitiveness," *Trends: Economy, Politics, Financial Markets* (Frankfurt: Dresdner Bank, August 1993), pp. 3–7.

21. Roger Cohen, "Germany's New Face," *New York Times*, October 25, 1998.

22. See John Vinocur, "Downsizing German Politics, *Foreign Affairs* 77, no. 5 (September/October 1998): 10–16.

23. See "The Conservative Tradition of Liberalism," Introduction to R. Isaak, *American Political Thinking: Readings from the Origins to the 21st Century* (Fort Worth, TX: Harcourt Brace, 1994).

24. See James Fallows, "How the World Works," *Atlantic Monthly* (December 1993): 61–87.

25. The interpretation of this statement is indebted to Lester Thurow, "Free Market Fallacies," *Foreign Policy*, no. 92 (fall 1993): 187–191.

26. Porter, *The Competitive Advantage*, pp. 284–301.

27. See David Evans, "IBM Rediscovers Its Customers," *Canadian Business* (November 1990): 37–48.

28. On Pace University MBA International Field Study trip to IBM in Brussels, May 7, 1992.

29. Summary of a history of the semiconductor industry published in 1992 by the Semiconductor Industry Association as cited by James Fallows in "Looking at the Sun," *Atlantic Monthly* (November 1993): 90. The article by Fallows illustrates that the Japanese success in semiconductors and American failure cannot be explained by the economic rules of Anglo-American liberalism. But, by the same token, his logic may have a hard time explaining the strong recovery of the U.S. semiconductor industry since 1992. See also Larry Bridwell and Marc Richard, "The Semiconductor Industry in the 21st Century: A Global Analysis Using Michael Porter's Industry Related Clusters," *Competitiveness Review*, no. 1 (1998): 24–36.

30. Statistics are from Leonard Silk, "Dangers of Slow Growth," *Foreign Affairs* 72, no. 1 (1992): 167–182.

31. See Joan C. Szabo, "Our Crumbling Infrastructure," *Nation's Business* (August 1989): 16–24.

32. For example, the mathematics test scores of thirteen-year-olds in the United States in 1991 were lower than the students in many of the countries testing comprehensive education (only Spain, Slovenia, and Jordan had lower scores). International Assessment of Educational Progress: 1991 Statistics, National Center for Educational Studies, *Digest of Education*, 1993, Table 390, p. 415. Also see Kenneth J. Travers and Ian Westbury, "The IEA Study of Mathematics I: Analysis of Mathematics Curricula," *Supplement* (Urbana College of Education of Illinois University Study for International Association for the Evaluation of Educational Achievement, 1989), pp. 115 and 121; and "International Science Report Card from the *Second* IEA *Study*" (U.S. Teachers College, Columbia University, 1988), pp. 2–3. Also see David Kearns, "The Education Gap," *Institutional Investor* (December 1989).

33. See Lynn K. Mytelka, ed., *Strategic Partnerships and the World Economy* (Rutherford, NJ: Fairleigh Dickinson University Press, 1991); and Martin Starr, *Global Corporate Alliances and the Competitive Edge* (Westport, CT: Quorum Books, 1991).

34. The U.S. productivity growth rate averaged 4 percent annually in manufacturing in the 1980s. But for Japan, the comparable productivity growth rate was 5.7 percent. Cf.: Keizai Koho Center, *Japan: A Comparison*, 1991, p. 70.

35. See "America's Information Highway: A Hitch-hiker's Guide," *The Economist* (December 25, 1993–January 7, 1994): 35–38.

36. See Tracy Goss, Richard Pascale, and Anthony Athos, "The Reinvention Roller Coaster: Risking the Present for a Powerful Future," *Harvard Business Review* (November–December 1993): 97–108; Ikujiro Nonaka, "The Knowledge-Creating Company," *Harvard Business Review* (November–December 1991): especially 96–97; and William H. Davidow and Michael S. Malone, *The Virtual Corporation: Structuring and Revitalizing the Corporation for the 21st Century* (New York: HarperCollins, 1992).

37. "McLibel," Report on 60 *Minutes*, CBS, December 28, 1997.

38. Josef Joffe, "How America Does It," *Foreign Affairs* 76, no. 5 (September/October 1997): 24. "Soft power" was first introduced by Harvard political scientist Joseph S. Nye.

39. See Lendol Caldor, *Financing the American Dream* (Princeton, NJ: Princeton University Press, 1998).

40. Samuel P. Huntington, "The Erosion of American National Interests," *Foreign Affairs* 76, no. 5 (September/October 1997): 38–40.

41. For the tables and full statistics of these various types of miracle waves over the past fifty years, see R. Isaak, "Making Economic Miracles: Explaining Extraordinary National Economic Achievement," *American Economist* (spring 1997). Statistics compiled from IMF, the World Bank, UN, & *The Economist*.

42. See Ezra Vogel, *The Four Little Dragons: The Spread of Industrialization in East Asia* (Cambridge, MA: Harvard University Press, 1991); Jung-en Woo, *Race to the Swift: State and Finance in Korean Industrialization* (New York: Columbia University Press, 1991); and J. Woronoff, *Asia's Miracle Economics* (New York: M. E. Sharpe, 1986).

43. See, for example, Paul Krugman, "The Myth of Asia's Miracle," *Foreign Affairs* (November/December 1994). And Gary Gereffi and Donald L. Wyman, *Manufacturing Miracles: Paths of Industrialization in Latin America and East Asia* (Princeton, NJ: Princeton University Press, 1990).

44. Mancur Olson, *The Rise and Decline of Nations* (New Haven, CT: Yale University Press, 1982).

45. See Edward de Bono, *Water Logic* (London: Penguin, 1994).

46. Roger Cohen, "High Claims in Spill Betray Depth of Nigerian Poverty," *New York Times*, September 20, 1998.

47. See Diana Jean Schemo, "Rising Fires Renew Threat to Amazon," *New York Times*, November 2, 1997.

48. Alexander Keck, "The Case of Bhutan: The Sustainable Development Process of a National Economy Under a Policy of Collective Learning," MBA *Papers of Distinction* 14, no. 1, The Center for Applied Research, Pace University (New York: Pace University, June 1996), p. 29. See also World Bank, *World Development Report: Knowledge for Development* (New York: Oxford University Press, 1999).

49. See R. Isaak, *Green Logic: Ecopreneurship, Theory and Ethics* (Hartford, CT: Kumarian Press, 1999). Originally published by Greenleaf Publishers of Sheffield, England (1998). Also see E. von Weizsacker, A. Lovins, and L. H. Lovins, *Factor Four: Doubling Wealth, Halving Resource Use* (the New Report to the Club of Rome). London: Earthscan Publications, 1997; Lester Brown et al., eds., *State of the World* (New York: W. W. Norton, 1999); and Amory B. Lovins, L. Hunter Lovins, and Paul Hawken, "A Road Map for Natural Capitalism," *Harvard Business Review* (May–June 1999): 145–158.

POST-SOCIALIST TRANSITIONS

Better to return and make a net than to go down to the stream and merely wish for fish.
—Chinese Proverb

Through eight governments in nine years, ranging from Christian nationalists to ex-Communists, Poland has kept to the same basic path of Western reform that has made it a viable and valuable partner for world powers.
—Daniel Michaels, Central European Economic Review (1998)

Social capital can be transmuted, so to speak, into financial capital. In novelist Amy Tan's Joy Luck Club, a group of mah-jong playing friends evolves into a joint investment association. China's extraordinary growth over the last decade has depended less on formal institutions than on guanxi (personal connections) to underpin contracts and to channel savings and investment.
—Robert D. Putnam (1993)

ONCE UPON A TIME THERE WAS A WORLD MORE OR LESS DIVIDED INTO BLACK STATES AND RED states—the capitalists and the socialists (or would-be communists). The conflict between them occurred in a world economic market in which the capitalist states attempted to "contain" the progress and power of the communist (or socialist) states. This was the cold-war "containment" doctrine of former U.S. Ambassador to the Soviet Union, George Kennan.

Then, in 1989, the Berlin Wall came down—symbolically dividing these states. The Soviet Union disintegrated into numerous ethnic regional political units declaring independence.

Communism collapsed as an ideology, along with the capitalists' cold-war doctrine of containment. Presumably, "capitalism" had won the cold war. However, the dominant result was an increasingly global world market in which states per se *seemed* to fall into the background in terms of importance. The cold-war rationale for the legitimacy of states was gone.

Governments were forced to look to economic self-sufficiency and competitiveness, underlaid by domestic security and cultural integrity, for a new rationale for their existence. But most of them were financially, if not intellectually, indebted to cold-war militarism in their industrial and economic structures and were not prepared for this sudden sea change in geopolitics. They needed radical restructuring but found themselves swamped with habits of the past. Domestic weaknesses, swept under the carpet when the focus was on cold-war enemies abroad or communist ideologues at home, were brutally exposed: The emperor seemed to have no clothes, undermining state **legitimacy**—that deference to elites produced by force and awe.

In the post–cold-war world, "East-West" relations became part of North-South relations—the interdependent network between developed ("North") and developing ("South") nation-states and regions. Although one might identify Cuba, North Korea, and the People's Republic of China as exceptions to this rule, given their socialist governments, the political economies of these states can be better explained in a North-South context of global economic competitiveness than in the old East-West framework. At the beginning of the twenty-first century, only two contexts matter economically: North-North relations (between competitive, developed, industrialized states) and North-South relations. For the Northern countries, "North-North" relations are always on the front burner, given their domestic self-absorption with economic growth, unemployment, and social security.[1]

One reason for this self-preoccupation among the rich is the widespread economic incompetence of their political leaders and political parties. The victory of the capitalists over the communists in the cold war disguised economic mediocrity of performance in the "victorious" industrialized states. The administrations of Presidents Reagan and Bush won the cold war with defense and technological budgets that put the country in a permanent debt and capital-importing position. It was an expensive victory. Chancellor Helmut Kohl correctly seized the historical moment to reunify Germany. However, he made economic promises and established monetary and fiscal policies that effectively mortgaged the future of German citizens for years to come.[2] The rest of the world initially subsidized German reunification through the high-interest-rate regime the Germans imposed in trying to contain the domestic inflation caused by their deficit spending on the Eastern German states. Thus, "victorious" politicians from the North on the level of short-term geopolitics served up long-term macroeconomic "black holes" with which future generations would have to cope. The intellectual shield of Anglo-American superiority that dominated the West was thrown into question at the very moment it was declared officially to have predominated.[3] "Post–cold-war economics" involved first and foremost a return to an understanding of the following:

1. economic liberalization
2. basic macroeconomic principles
3. recipes for "privatizing" former state-run industries and institutions

Secondly, but possibly of greater long-term significance, post–cold-war economics was concerned with the global expansion of massive unemployment stemming from radical restructuring and political efforts to manage this joblessness. Such unemployment makes scandals among powerful elites in industrial societies intolerable, bringing down governments, as well as chief executive officers of major corporations.

The cold-war era of two superpower blocs after World War II was as much an historical aberration as was the incredible global economic growth of the 1950s and 1960s. In the post–cold-war era we may return to the slower "normal" rates of economic growth in industrialized countries (after the U.S. boom of the 1990s is over) and of diverse multicultural conflict in a multipolar world.[4] In order to understand these transformations, let us first go back briefly to the origins of the cold war, beginning with the revolution of Lenin in 1919 and the emergence of Stalin's model of political economy.

ORIGINS

"Imperialism is capitalism at that state of development in which the domination of monopoly and finance capital has taken shape, in which the export of capital has acquired pronounced importance, in which the division of the world by international trusts has begun, and in which the partition of all the territory of the earth by the greatest capitalist countries has been completed."[5] So wrote Lenin in 1916 in *Imperialism, the Highest Stage of Capitalism.*

A year later he took over the Bolshevik Revolution, establishing the Soviet Union on the Marxist-Leninist principle of leadership by an elite, vanguard party dictatorship of the proletariat and peasantry for the sake of a revolutionary society. The Communist Party assumed total political control, nationalizing industry, organizing the Soviet Youth Movement (Komsomol), proclaiming atheism, making marriage unnecessary, and totally redirecting education. According to Lenin, although the political process decides "what is to be done," state structure specifies "who can do what to whom" (*kto/kovo*) in the state and the economy. Convinced that England and Germany had reached the point of capitalist concentration when their disintegration would begin, according to his theory of imperialism, Lenin instructed the Comintern—a network of communist parties directed secretly by the Soviet Communist Party—to help speed up this process.

While a number of Western intellectuals were attracted by the Russian experiment, the overwhelming majority of Americans and Western Europeans feared the "Red Terror." Diplomatic relations were broken off with the Soviet Union, which was soon isolated in the world community. By 1920 neither the nationalization of factories nor Marxian economic principles helped salvage a Soviet economy that was in desperate shape. Lenin realized that his country could not afford to put through revolutionary principles at home and simultaneously expand the communist movement into world revolution. Ever the pragmatist, Lenin announced the principle of taking one step backward in order to take two steps forward and postponed the global revolutionary effort. He announced the New Economic Policy, which denationalized industries, praised native millionaires, and invited foreign investment. The West was relieved, believing that the Soviet Union had matured into a normal player in the game of nations. A Soviet nonaggression and mutual trade pact was signed with Germany in 1922 at Rapallo.

But then Lenin died in 1924 and was replaced by Communist Party strong-man Joseph Stalin, who advocated "socialism in one country," based upon a demanding Five-Year Plan. Industry was nationalized and agriculture was collectivized in the 1930s. Stalin believed that the Soviet Union had to build up its economic and political power in order to become a fortress for future world revolution, and he used whatever authoritarian means necessary to crush political opponents, such as Leon Trotsky, who advocated simultaneous world revolution.

THE STALINIST MODEL: COLLECTIVE LEARNING THROUGH SHORTAGES

Stalin argued that in a period of rapid national modernization, the Soviet Union must exist in peaceful coexistence with the rest of the world, avoiding war and seeking trade until Russia became a great military-industrial power. Moreover, he stressed the total subordination of agriculture to the rapid development of heavy industry, using whatever authoritarian methods were required by the state. Although the Eastern bloc countries did not always subordinate agriculture to heavy industry, the basic structures of the East European hegemony of the U.S.S.R. largely mimicked the **Stalinist model** (with the exception of Yugoslavia, which had a market-type socialism and was only in the shadow of Soviet hegemony). Some studies suggest that the domestic structure of East European states was so similar that it was not a determining variable in accounting for the different economic strategies these states adopted in the 1970s and 1980s.[6] The heritage of the Stalinist model in Eastern Europe must be understood in order to assess the meaning of specific national economic reforms that depart from this model. The institutions of Soviet hegemony and similar status as small-resource or capital-poor economic systems in the world economy reinforced this commonality.

Apart from the state ownership of the means of production, the key difference between communist and capitalist economic mechanisms is that communist systems rely on direct controls in the allocation of resources, whereas for most purposes capitalist systems depend on markets.* Until the revolutionary reforms of the late 1980s, the central planning authority established output goals for major commodities of Eastern nations, including individual input targets for firms or groups of companies and supply plans specifying where the enterprises were to obtain their nonlabor, material inputs, and to whom they were to ship their outputs. The coordination problems in such a regional, collective system of centralized planning were staggering, not to mention the adjustments that eventually had to be made if errors or misjudgments emerged in the planning process (which was inevitable). Given the high priority allocated in socialist systems to full employment (what some call "overfull" employment), plans tend to

---

*Exceptions to this in the United States include government interventions of the Federal Reserve (Central) Bank in the money markets and of the Pentagon in the government procurement contract markets.

be drawn too tightly (with few margins for error for lack of productivity) and projected output targets cannot be achieved with the proscribed inputs. Demand is chronically greater than supply, much as with the case of inflation in free-market economies.[7]

Because there is a lack of markets for land and capital in Stalinist political economies, rent, interest, and profits are not accurately accounted for, and the pricing system for commodities is called "irrational" by Western economists.[8] This is partly because direct controls rather than decentralized markets are used in resource allocation with all the errors and inertia of bureaucratic administration. Specifically, both ministries and enterprises are evaluated on the basis of output performance over time according to the central plan, thus motivating managers of ministries and enterprises to conceal from their superiors both capacity and overorder inputs and to avoid new technology. The Stalinist model is also characterized by *commodity inconvertibility*, meaning that foreigners are not permitted to spend either their own currency or the native currency on commodities within the socialist state (i.e., intermediate products like coal or machinery, not consumer products purchased by tourists and embassies). Commodity inconvertibility had the effect of stimulating rigid bilateralism in foreign trade between countries within the socialist bloc. Each socialist country had to keep a balance in trade with every other socialist nation, for to run a surplus would have raised the problem of how to spend it given the restrictions of the Stalinist structure. Thus the Stalinist model dampened interbloc socialist trade, although it had no such effect on East-West trade where the socialist countries were in hot pursuit of "hard" (convertible) Western currencies.

Uncertainties involved in expanding the Stalinist nation's trade rendered it more vulnerable to shortages given unpredictable downturns, leading socialist planners into a behavioral pattern of trade aversion, dampening growth.[9] The Stalinist model overemphasizes maintenance strategy by rewarding risk-reduction rather than entrepreneurial growth. Resource shortages and bureaucratic bottlenecks determine economic polity, not prices. And single-party elites, not producers and consumers, create and manage the shortages.[10]

Stalinist economies result in chronic hard currency deficits. The full employment policy drives managers to protect firms rather than letting weak enterprises go bankrupt, reducing their competitiveness through a permanent "greenhouse" treatment or "tenure." Full employment policy yields a seller's market, for there is always surplus demand given endemic shortages. Goods are distributed according to a central plan rather than sold, and "salesmanship" is so unnecessary as to be irrelevant. Tariffs on international goods are redundant given centralized state control and planning, although they can work as implicit quotas discriminating against countries that do not have "most-favored-nation status."[11] The lack of practice or irrelevance of "selling" leads to poor packaging, poor product quality, and a difficulty in adapting products to fit the consumers in specific foreign markets, stifling international competitiveness.

POST-STALINIST ECONOMIC GROWTH AND STRATEGIES

Economics is the study of collective choice among alternative uses of scarce resources. Scarcity is the mother of economic value. By rewarding risk-reduction and permitting shortages to determine economic policy, the Stalinist model made scarcity permanent and shortages inevitable. The global transformation toward a post–cold-war economy reversed these assumptions, making supply or surplus capacity inevitable as everyone sought to produce many of the same things anticipating market demand that might or might not arise. One illustration is the transition from the reliance of East European "satellite" states upon the Soviet Union for trade to the breakup of the Soviet Union and the subsequent decline in Russian demand for East European goods. In the process, the **Comecon**, or **Council for Mutual Economic Assistance (CMEA)**, formed in 1949 to assist in the economic development of Bulgaria, East Germany, Poland, Rumania, U.S.S.R., Czechoslovakia, Hungary, and Albania, disintegrated at the end of the 1980s after some significant initial "Eastern bloc" successes.

While Stalin was alive, the Soviet Union used its centralized power to redirect East European trade from the West to the U.S.S.R. (the Soviet share of East European trade rising from 25 percent in 1947 to 82 percent in 1954). Soviet extractions from its East European "satellites" included $1 billion each from Rumania and Hungary in goods, 6.5 million tons of coal from Poland, and so on. The value of this extraction by the Soviet Union has been estimated to equal the value of Marshall Plan aid given by the United States for West European reconstruction.[12]

After Stalin's death, Soviet leaders realized they had reached a point of diminishing returns in extractions from their CMEA allies and would have to invest in their growth or subsidize them in the future. Some of this investment had already been made in the form of "mixed" companies founded in the East bloc with some of the extracted wealth. But these had caused great local resentment, given Soviet control and the disproportionate share of the proceeds that flowed back to the Soviet Union. Some refer to this as the "ghettoization" of Eastern Europe.[13]

The Soviet Union was motivated by the Eastern European riots of 1953 to cancel debts and extend credits—as long as the CMEA allies continued to buy Soviet goods. This shift resulted in economic growth in the Comecon countries outstripping the national income growth in the European Common Market between 1950 and 1980 (7 percent for CMEA excluding the U.S.S.R. versus 5 percent for the EEC).[14] Thus the Soviets managed to have their hegemonic ghettoization and a pattern of dependent economic development in the East bloc too.[15]

Within the CMEA countries, different foreign policy and economic strategies evolved despite the similarities in domestic structure. For example, there was a sharp break even among the most Stalinist of East European states—Rumania and East Germany—in 1968 when Rumania established official diplomatic relations with West Germany without informing any of its East bloc allies. For the quarter of a century before his violent overthrow in 1989 Nicolae Ceausescu, Secretary General of the Rumanian Communist Party, was able to use a conservative version of the Stalinist model at home to give him the leeway to take independent foreign policy stands—as France did within the NATO alliance (without the Stalinist model at home, of course). This was the first step to the success of Chancellor Willy Brandt's *Ost-politik* of the 1970s, in which West Germany tacitly recognized World War II boundaries in exchange for political and economic cooperation with Comecon countries.[16] Given the desire of the West German people for unification with East Germany, the state strategy of West Germany was always different from that of any other NATO member country, tilting heavily toward détente and economic, if not political, integration with East European states.

COCOM AND TECHNOLOGY TRANSFER

West Germany's unique position geopolitically between East and West was underscored by the controversy in the early 1980s concerning a West German contract to build a West Europe-Soviet gas pipeline. Anticipated to fill one-third of West Germany's energy needs, the United States feared that the West Germans would become too energy dependent upon the Soviet Union and that the West European, Japanese, and U.S. firms subcontracted in the project would transfer technology with national-security risks in the process.

The Reagan administration prohibited American firms from participating in the project and appealed to the principles of the **Coordinating Committee on Multilateral Export Controls (Cocom)** as a basis for stopping Japan and European NATO allies from exporting to the U.S.S.R. as well. The United States, Japan, and all members of the NATO alliance except Iceland are members of Cocom, an organization set up in the cold war atmosphere of 1949 (operating out of a wing of the U.S. consulate in Paris) that coordinates a list of strategic technology prohibited for export to communist or other high security risk countries. However, led by West Germany, the Europeans and Japanese refused to prevent their companies from participating in the gas pipeline project, and the American government was forced to back down and let its firms participate or face the economic costs of losing business to international competitors.[17]

In 1984, the tables were turned when West Germany and France complained about American trade liberalization with the People's Republic of China.[18] Cocom members often circumvent the restrictions by exporting technological goods (such as digital computers) to countries where they are legal and then reexporting them to countries on "the blacklist." Such efforts cause great strains between governments and businesses within NATO countries. Difficulties in coordination emerge because the export controls in the United States are more stringent than the Cocom list and stricter than the domestic controls of other NATO countries (particularly Germany). In the late 1980s the U.S. government protested the sale of technologies and chemicals that enabled Libya to construct a chemical weapons plant: American export restrictions (coordinated by the State, Defense, Energy, and Commerce departments) kept American firms from being involved in such sales, while European countries had looser restrictions, letting such sales sift through. It is difficult to prohibit other countries from selling the elements of potential chemical weapons plants when the United States has stockpiled so many chemical weapons itself. By 1990 the Russian-American détente, the transformation of Eastern Europe, and pressures from the business community led the Bush administration to ease up on Cocom restrictions on high-tech sales to Eastern Europe.

Technology transfer refers to the movement of knowledge or techniques that contribute to the production process across national borders. In a high-tech/high-information, service-sector-dominated age, Benjamin Franklin's principle of sharing all knowledge and techniques with all human beings for the benefit of mankind is a notion considered naive, if not archaic, by leaders of modern nation-states. So technology gaps grow between countries of the North and the South, increasing the gaps in economic production and growth.[19] Often the countries of the East bloc were twice discriminated against: as economic members of the South and as strategic risks of the East.

INTERPRETATIONS

PERESTROIKA, THE DEMOCRATIZATION OF RUSSIA, AND THE "VIRTUAL ECONOMY"

Perestroika (restructuring) and related political and economic reforms announced by Mikhail Gorbachev in the late 1980s represented the most innovative domestic and foreign policy changes in the Soviet Union since the death of Lenin. These ideas did not spring spontaneously from the head of one man, but were carefully developed by a reformist team who patiently kept their blueprints in the drawer until the timing was ripe. Such planning evolved in recognition of the failure of a stalemated socialist economy. The 5 percent annual average growth rate in the GNP in the late 1960s fell to 2 percent by the late 1970s and approached zero growth in the late 1980s.[20]

While the U.S.S.R.'s structural economic problems were obvious by the late 1970s, many Western observers clearly did not take their consequences into account until the turnover of a series of aging Soviet leaders in the 1980s. A dark joke circulating in the U.S.S.R. symbolized the ossification which the Soviet political economy had come to represent: In answer to the question—What is the difference between a crocodile and the Politburo?—came the reply: The former has forty teeth and four legs, while in the latter the numbers are reversed.

Failures were rampant in the political as well as the economic system. Although the share of the GNP claimed by defense spending had reached 15 to 25 percent (compared to 1 percent in Japan, 3 percent in West Germany, and 6 to 7 percent in the United States), Soviet security policy could not prevent a Cessna 172 piloted by a young West German from landing in Red Square or the Afghan rebels from defeating the Soviet army. Moreover, flaws in the Soviet healthcare system had actually led to *reductions* in average life expectancy, unlike any other industrial nation.[21] Poor harvests entailed billions of dollars of purchases of grain and food from the West. And since some 80 percent of Soviet export earnings came from the sale of primary energy, when the price of oil unexpectedly dropped and the dollar exchange rate (in which most energy is priced) plummeted, the U.S.S.R. was suddenly faced with shortfall in annual earnings of hard currency exports of between $8 billion and $10 billion.[22] Since Soviet policy was not to import more than it exports to avoid difficulties with obtaining hard currency for exchange, Soviet trade volume with the West sank about 40 percent. The technological gap between the Soviet Union and leading Western European countries was great, not to mention the gap with Japan and the United States, whose technology in a number of sectors was significantly ahead of that of the Europeans.

Gorbachev was elected Secretary General of the Communist Party of the Soviet Union at the beginning of 1985. There are three key concepts that made up the core of the reforms Gorbachev advocated: *glasnost* (openness), *perestroika* (restructuring), and *uskorenie* (acceleration). The first two of these became among the best-known foreign-language terms in the world.[23] Gorbachev used these notions as the basis of what he called "the new thinking."[24]

Perestroika was a strategy of decentralization that aimed to increase the personal responsibility of key managers in Soviet economic organizations and to make them more easily accessible to those in the region they serviced. A number of the top economic administrators were dismissed when Gorbachev came to power—particularly hard-liners whom he wanted to replace with people who understood his new thinking. But given this philosophy of increased personal responsibility for what goes wrong in the system, there was more turnover of personnel in economic organizations than in the past, when party loyalty and seniority often led to what amounted to lifetime tenure. Moreover, these shifts shook up the complacency of managers of large corporations from abroad who quietly counted upon their "old buddy" ties with comrades in the national bureaucracy, who were now replaced or who often had to share authority with newly created regional economic institutions. These economic institutions, in turn, were expected to become "independently operating economic entities" with flexibility and the power to make entrepreneurial decisions. Business firms that operated successfully were no longer to be penalized by having profits skimmed off or by having their production quotas increased. Typically in Stalinesque economies managers with political clout measured success by their ability to reduce their production quotas, giving their workers a better working life.

However, according to the same logic, subsidies would not necessarily be forthcoming for firms that failed: Bankruptcy became a threat that led to efficiency. Russian citizens were disconcerted by the possibility of losing a job in a state that used to guarantee them employment. Functional and regional decentralization moved quickly in some sectors. By 1988, 170 Soviet firms were authorized to make business deals directly with foreign partners in contrast to the old "foreign trade monopoly" system of having all deals go through the Foreign Trade Ministry.

The ultimate models of *perestroika* were supposed to be joint ventures with foreigners that attract capital, transfer technological and organizational know-how, teach Russian managers sales marketing skills, and illustrate day-to-day operations (*glasnost*) as well as the more rapid pace of Western business (*uskorenie*). From the time the Joint Venture Act came into force in January 1987 to March 1988, thirty joint venture deals were approved with Western partners.

But in the early 1990s, the dissolution of the Soviet Union picked up speed. Gorbachev lost power and stepped down. The rise of Boris Yeltsin as the only elected president of Russia and his push for economic liberalism led to political and economic turmoil and rampant inflation. The traditionalists in the Russian parliament revolted. Yeltsin dissolved the parliament, calling for new elections. But the major winner in the elections of December 1993 was ultranationalist Vladimir Zhirinovsky, whose mislabeled "Liberal Democratic Party" overwhelmed Yeltsin's allies, symbolizing conservative resistance to economic reforms and socioeconomic dislocations.[25] Voters, however, approved Yeltsin's constitution, which increased presidential power. The social trends culminating in these election results served to deter foreign investment as the Gross Domestic Product shrank by double-digits annually from 1992–1994, making mass unemployment inevitable. Resources and power shifted to corrupt allegiances who positioned their banks and private firms to benefit from quick stock market rises (based often on high interest paying bonds or debt certificates) until the Russian currency collapsed in 1998. Some 40 percent of banks and financial institutions were run by oligarchs or the Russian mafia who identified capitalism with corruption and with getting as much cash as possible to a safe haven outside the country: This was "crony capitalism" with a vengeance.

The Russian financial collapse was based on a large budget deficit and an inability to service the debt—particularly debt denominated in short-term dollar liabilities. But beneath the surface the problems were deeper. The Russians had fooled themselves into believing in what Professors Clifford Gaddy and Barry Ickes have called a "virtual economy"—a pretense that the economy was much larger than it actually was, permitting a larger government and expenditures than Russia could afford. It was an economy in which no one paid in cash if they could avoid it (70 percent of business was done by barter), in which taxes were systematically underpaid, workers were often not paid, and manufacturing facilities usually took value from the economy rather than adding value to it. As the Karpov commission reported in 1997: "An economy is emerging where prices are charged which no one pays in cash; where no one pays anything on time; where huge mutual debts are created that also can't be paid off in reasonable period of time; where wages are declared and not paid; and so on. [This leads to] illusory or 'virtual' earnings, which in turn lead to unpaid, or 'virtual' fiscal obligations, and nonmarket, or 'virtual' prices." Gaddy and Ickes conclude that the Russians developed a "virtual economy"—a present-need oriented house of cards that no one wanted to question since everyone would lose if the system collapsed—as, in fact, it did in 1998.[26] But the Russian people seem not to be thinking of any replacement for the virtual economy with which they have so identified. And the Western illusion of "reforming" such a pretension appears to be twice removed from reality.

Of course some large investment banks, such as Goldman, Sachs, and Company, based in the United States, saw Russia as a vehicle for easy money and helped to set the Russians up for a fall with false financial expectations. In June of 1998, for example, Goldman flew in former president George Bush (paying him $100,000) to entertain Russia's former prime minister in the House of Unions in Moscow in order to discuss deals on the side. As a result, Goldman helped the Russian government raise money by selling $1.25 billion in bonds and later arranged a complex deal to exchange short-term Russian debt for long-term Russian debt, in order to give the Russians room to breathe. By late August the Russian government stopped paying much of what it owed on its debt, threatening to default totally unless it received more capital from the IMF. The holders of Russian bonds found themselves with worthless paper. And Goldman Sachs, which had earned tens of millions of dollars in fees and protected hundreds of millions it had at stake in Russia, escaped virtually unscathed.[27]

Even previous to the collapse, German companies invested much more in Poland and the former Czechoslovakia than in Russia.[28] The main reasons were the chronic lack of hard currencies (appreciation tending convertible money) held by Russian customers, excessive Russian bureaucracy, legal uncertainties concerning private property, and the unclear jurisdiction of governmental authorities. The process by which the former East bloc satellites such as Poland and Czechoslovakia positioned themselves for this investment is an instructive lesson in collective learning.

EAST BLOC REVOLUTION

Philosopher Søren Kierkegaard told the story of a flock of geese kept in a wire cage by a farmer. One day one of the geese looked up and saw there was no top, telling the others excitedly: "Look, there is no top, we may leave and become free!" Few listened or turned their heads to the sky. So he flew away alone. When it became clear that Gorbachev would not use force to put down revolutionary change in his Eastern European satellites in 1989, one Eastern European people after another looked up and saw they were free to express themselves and to throw over their keepers. The top was off the cage and the birds just started to fly.[29]

The politico-economic revolutions in the Eastern bloc are examples *par excellence* of collective learning: One group mimicked another, revolting in domino series until not a single Communist Party monopoly was left standing intact. Within the first six months of 1990, all the nations of East Europe held free elections in one form or another. Actually, the 1989–1990 transformation was just the beginning of a collective learning process in which Eastern Europeans started to unlearn forty years of obedience to Communist one-party rule, of job security in state-run enterprises, and of working along as opposed to working hard, given the absence of meaningful individual economic incentives. The revolutions brought widespread social uncertainty, skyrocketing inflation, devalued currencies, rising unemployment, and lack of confidence that newly elected leaders, who often had little experience, could manage the politico-economic crises.

An underground joke in the formerly communist nations indicates the paradoxes of their economic development. In responding to the question "What is communism?" came the reply: "Communism is the longest and most painful route from capitalism to capitalism." Since all of the East bloc countries were scrambling at once to adopt the liberal assumptions of Western capitalist democracy, it was clear that not all of them would be equally successful in attracting foreign investment.

From 1989 to 1994, foreigners invested more than $10 billion in the twenty-two successor states of the Comecon. Germany and the United States were the heaviest investors. Over half of all **foreign direct investment (FDI)** (that is, the establishing or expanding of corporate operations in a foreign country) in Central and Eastern Europe went to Hungary in this period, attracted by political stability and clear guidelines concerning private property. The Czech Republic nearly rivaled Hungary as a magnet of foreign direct investment, given the credibility of its stringent reforms even after the traumatic split up of Czechoslovakia into two separate nations, the Czech Republic and Slovakia. But let us turn to the country coming in a distant third in terms of direct foreign investment—Poland.[30]

LIBERALIZATION AND PRIVATIZATION IN POLAND

Even though Poland, by late 1993, was the only reformed East bloc country experiencing positive economic growth, it received less foreign investment than Romania on a per capita basis (although a greater absolute amount). An unresolved debt hangover and frequent changes in government explain the difficulty Poland had in attracting funds. By the end of 1992, in terms of registered foreign direct investment into Poland, the United States was responsible for 40 percent, Italy for 25 percent, Germany 15 percent, and France 7 percent. Whereas government approval for such foreign investment is unnecessary in Hungary, in Poland it is necessary for investments in defense, real estate, sea- and airports, wholesale trade, and legal services.[31] Government red-tape deters foreign investment.

The coming and going of governments as Poland tried to move from political liberalization to economic liberalization made for an image of uncertainty. For example, when the Italian steel manufacturer Lucchini signed a letter of intent to purchase a majority share of Huta Warzawa, a state-owned Polish steel company, in 1991, the Polish industry minister resigned the day before the Italians first sought government approval, and two months later the prime minister offered to resign the second time approval was requested.[32] Such delays discourage investors.

In 1989 the formerly outlawed Solidarity union movement began the transition into governmental power, initiating the economic reforms. The goal was to position Poland to join the prosperous European Common Market, now called the European Union. But this requires the adoption of some 7,000 legal regulations and the **harmonization** (or matching) of national monetary and tax policies with those of the "Euro-club."

A key post–cold-war strategy of developing states is to position themselves to join a regional economic bloc made up mainly of developed states. In order to be asked to join, they try to learn from the developed states as models, mimicking their behavior—until they are slowed down by a cultural or political reaction at home stemming from threats to traditional perceptions of collective integrity.

By initially deciding to model its political and economic reforms after post-war European states to the west, Poland hoped to cut the costs of experimentation and gain early membership in the Common Market. As Deputy Prime Minister Leszek Balcerowicz described the Polish view of collective learning: "Poland is too poor to experiment. We will therefore follow working models. Let the rich countries experiment if they want."[33]

Poland has problems typical of most of the East bloc countries: an economy skewed toward the heavy industrialized sector and dominated by state-owned companies; underdevelopment of light industry, the service sector, the distribution and financial networks; plus an archaic agricultural system. Harvard economist Jeffrey Sachs (who advised Polish reformers) identifies three stages in Poland's economic reforms:[34]

1. *Economic liberalization*—legal and administrative transformation to recognize the right to hold private property and to bring in market competition. This represents reaching for classical economic liberalism.

2. *Macroeconomic stabilization*—controlling *inflation* (or more money chasing fewer goods; a rise in the general level of prices) by limiting budget deficits, containing growth in the money supply, and setting up a stable, uniform basis for the exchange of a convertible currency. This represents a maintenance strategy to establish economic equilibrium both in *fiscal policy* (the relationship between government spending and taxes or income) and *monetary policy* (the government's policy of controlling the money supply, interest rates, and convertible exchange rates).

3. *Privatization*—transferring state property to private hands. This represents an entrepreneurial strategy of taking risks for the sake of growth and development beyond the maintenance base of fiscal policy and monetary policy. The limits to privatization, of course, represent limits in the acceptance of classical economic liberalism.

Unlike many other economic reform plans in East Europe, the Polish strategy was to reach these three stages in reform as quickly as possible. The rationale, as Jeffrey Sachs points out, is the same one that would apply if the British decided to shift from left-hand-side drive to right-hand-side drive on their roads: Should the change be gradually introduced by first just putting trucks on the other side of the road, letting the other vehicles drive on the same side as usual?

The Poles went for the "Big Bang" tempo of radical change, pushing through liberalization and stabilization all at once on January 1, 1990, followed six months later with privatization—the most difficult of the three stages given the massive restructuring and attitude changes required. As Sachs notes, if the Poles chose to privatize at the same rate as the British under the policies of Prime Minister Margaret Thatcher—five firms per year during the 1980s—it would take several hundred years to privatize the some 3,000 Polish industrial firms owned by the state![35]

Polish privatization succeeded most markedly in small retail businesses, as well as in the trucking, construction, and small industrial sectors. But things have gone much more slowly in the large industrial sector, where the plan (fashionable in Eastern Europe) was to distribute a certain number of shares freely to the citizens; since there was not yet a stock market in the Western sense, it was hard to evaluate the consequences.

Early on, Polish economic reforms appeared successful as exports surged in 1990 and 1991. But imports surged too, as consumer-starved Poles bought Western goods. Prices shot up. On average, though, consumption was somewhat higher than before the reforms. However, of the $25 billion of aid pledged to Poland by the twenty-four richest nations of the West by 1993, little got to the Poles: Advisors got some, some was never sent (due to "risks" in helping small businesses), and much went to benefit the donors rather than the donee. Unemployment exploded, particularly in the small farming and large industrial sectors. Since the reform philosophy behind privatization made it harder to subsidize firms in the private sector than in the former publicly owned firms, the legitimacy of the government came under constant pressure by thousands of displaced people. Disenchantment was so great that those representing the communists were reelected in 1993 as people sought to recover the integrity of their lost past.

Paradoxically, privatization increases growth and the range of choice in society, while imposing losses on beneficiaries in terms of jobs and social security.[36] The shift from publicly to privately produced goods and services is the key to competitive liberalization economically, but it results in political and cultural attempts to recover lost social status and security.

In February 1995 Poland's coalition government named a former communist Jozef Oleksy as premier with the approval of President Lech Walesa. By 1995 inflation was still high at 22 percent, although down from 32 percent in 1994. Unemployment remained high at almost 16 percent in 1995. By 1996 the annual growth rate had reached 7 percent (up from 5 percent in 1994) and the country joined the OECD. The private sector accounted for over 60 percent of GDP. The government aimed to meet the Maastricht convergence criteria for the European Monetary System by 2000. Claiming to be the fastest growing economy in Europe, Poland wanted to become a full member of the EU by 2000.[37] However, contagion from the Asian financial crisis and Russian meltdown (not to mention the war in Kosovo) threatened to reduce the growth in foreign investment that stoked this hope, throwing open the timing of Poland's turn-of-the-century goals.

But "socialist resistance" to globalization for the sake of national development was not limited to Poland and Eastern Europe. In February 1997, thousands of Albanian investors gathered to demand reimbursement of most of their life savings lost in the collapse of Albanian pyramid investment schemes—speculative capitalism run amok. A month later the Albanian president called for the resignation of the government, a national state of emergency was declared, and many Albanians fled to Italy.

And consider the "socialist market economy" being developed by the Chinese. The Clinton administration took China so seriously that demands for human rights were put on the back burner in order to come to better terms with what could become the world's next geopolitical superpower, if not a key partner for American trade (and source of future U.S. jobs).

CHINA: FROM ECONOMIC REFORMS TO POTENTIAL SUPERPOWER?

Ending 1993 with an annual economic growth rate of 13 percent, factory output up 23 percent, and exploding retail sales, China appeared to have succeeded not only in its economic reforms, which began with a shift to free markets in 1978, but in becoming a potential superpower.[38] When the World Bank decided to reorder the economic size of nations in terms of **purchasing power parity** (the ability of average people in a nation to buy the same basket of goods in their own currency), China was ranked number three (despite a per capita income of only about $380). And China could pass both number two (Japan) and number one (the United States) in the twenty-first century. But in order to become "Number One" in purchasing power parity, China will have to move beyond economic liberalization to consolidate its maintenance base with macroeconomic stability and successfully privatize its firms without provoking a destabilizing political revolution. To assess its future chances, let us look briefly at Chinese post-World War II economic development.

Unlike the Polish case, the People's Republic of China was not constrained in its *economic* experiments with the possible hegemonic intervention by a superpower (although there were times in its political revolution when Chinese leaders no doubt were concerned with a Soviet invasion as the Chinese turned radically to their own route to socialism). After his victory in the civil war and his establishment of the People's Republic of China in 1949, Mao Zedong turned first to the Stalinist model as a basis for Chinese modernization: politicization of the economy by the state and an emphasis upon heavy industry. However, by 1956 widespread famines in China had convinced Mao that the Stalinist model was not appropriate. In the Hundred Flowers Campaign, Mao emphasized the importance of agriculture as well as light industry. After the Revolution, control had been Mao's concern. Now it turned to feeding his people and creating a stable agricultural system. People, not machines, were his priority, he announced (he had more of them, after all). And modernization of the rural areas became primary, not the Soviet stress on urban centers.[39] Mao initiated the Great Leap Forward, which in many ways established the triumph of the Maoist approach over Soviet modes.[40] Mao's strategy was to concentrate on organizing the agricultural and light-industrial sectors without diverting material capital from heavy industry. Attention was paid to producing fertilizer, improving seeds, and developing irrigation and farm equipment.

But in opposition to some of the Chinese elite who argued for the necessity of material incentives, Mao denounced capitalist tendencies that developed among small producers as in agriculture. He sacrificed economic progress for the sake of his goal, which was the internationalization of communist values through social education. He incited the Cultural Revolution of 1966, sending university students throughout China to spread his ideological doctrine, arresting capitalists, and sending intellectuals out to work the fields. Pragmatist Deng Xiaoping, a former friend of Mao's in the leadership, was made a waiter.

Economic growth slowed in China and party unity was undermined as the political struggle between economic-growth-oriented technocrats and Maoist social revolutionaries polarized opinions in the society. Two years after Mao's death in 1976, following a period of understated "de-Maoification," Chinese leaders launched an ambitious investment program in industry and agriculture, depending upon imported technologies and loans from abroad. The self-sufficient maintenance base of agriculture established by Mao became the launching pad for a series of market-oriented political and economic reforms that shook the socialist camp and impressed the industrialized West. China's annual average GNP growth rate went from 5.5 percent in the 1971–1975 period to 6.1 percent between 1976 and 1980, to top 9 percent throughout the 1980s.[41]

However, problems arose due to some consequences of the reforms: imbalances in industrial supplies, deterioration of consumption, higher state deficits, and inflation. In 1979 the Chinese took a step backward—called the policy of readjustment—in order to go ahead later with their major economic reform plans. Incentives in the farming sector were improved, permitting part of the farmland collectively owned by a state production team to be assigned to specific individuals, families, or groups. They, in turn, could keep the proceeds from any surplus production in excess of the contracted quota that went to the production team.

The distinction between "readjustment" and "reform" faded as more innovations were carefully introduced. Industrial firms were given more freedom in their production and marketing decisions and their managers became responsible for profits and losses. Bonuses and fringe benefits (such as company housing) could be used as incentives. And managers of such state-owned companies could sell or barter surplus products (after meeting their production quotas) and borrow funds from banks.

Beginning in 1981 government-approved small businesses were permitted to be opened in urban areas in fields like repairs, restaurants, or retailing. These entrepreneurs could hire one or two workers, or up to five apprentices in the case of skilled craftspeople. In 1984 a large private company was allowed to operate outside the state-planning system for the first time as a pilot experiment—the Minsheng Shipping Company.[42] As the largest Chinese conglomerate before the Revolution one has a sense here of the "restoration of an old maintenance base" to give it a better chance to succeed in an extremely competitive world economy— much as large German firms reemerged after a superficial effort at breaking them up after World War II or the Japanese *zaibatsu* (financial cliques) were reborn in their postwar reincarnation as *sogoshosha* or trading companies. Political economic managers in times of structural stalemate, attempting to breathe new life into their national economies, try taking calculated entrepreneurial risks in support of the maintenance of old industrial champions from the past. Such maintenance-entrepreneurial strategy mixes are used as pilot experiments to recreate past success in new, competitive organizational forms.

The collective learning strategy of the Chinese government before the 1989 rebellion was to call on capitalists of former times to apply their skills to economic productivity. Thus the son of the founder of the Minsheng Shipping Company was put in charge of the company. Stockholders shared in profits and losses and paid taxes to the government on the company's profits. And the manager was free to hire and fire workers at will and to set business targets without interference by centralized planning. The experiment proved successful and served as a model that was repeated in other regions.[43]

Similarly, in 1978, Zhao Ziyang, first secretary of the Communist Party in Sichuan Province, permitted six factories to keep a part of their profits for reinvestment in plant or distribution to the workers. Productive workers could be given bonuses and lazy ones punished. Within two years this pilot experiment spread to 6,600 enterprises, producing 45 percent of China's industrial output.[44] Such carefully planned and targeted pilot experiments in entrepreneurship could help to transform China into one of the world's great competitive nations in the twenty-first century.[45] Or, to paraphrase Mao, little sparks can set off forest fires. But fires have a way of suddenly springing out of control....

To superimpose entrepreneurial market mechanisms on top of a Stalinesque centralized and controlled economy results in contradictions, confusion, and corruption. As permission to fire workers in China spread, state budget deficits escalated, since the commitment to full employment must remain the top priority in a socialist state. Some entrepreneurs were obnoxiously successful, raising questions about the state's ability to keep the range of competitive inequalities in check. Workers learned to go after larger bonuses as a value rather than to produce or meet production targets as a social obligation above all others. Managers of refrigerator plants were subsidized with bonuses for producing a surplus much beyond the existing demand on the market, while less expensive items not as favorably targeted were underproduced although they were badly needed.

Such economic distortions and widespread corruption on the part of selfish individuals led Chinese leaders to retrench and restore centralized planning where it had lapsed in the late 1980s. This retrenchment delayed plans to free prices of most goods and services, reimposed price controls that had been lifted, cancelled construction projects, and brought Beijing more actively back into managing the economy. Some feared that the retrenchment would slow down the initiative of restructuring in the Chinese economy. Others thought the double-digit inflation rate, panic buying in anticipation of shortages, and reckless capital spending called for a reining in of the forces released by the decentralizing reforms.[46]

But typical of China's multiphase policies, while some reforms were being pragmatically cut back, other forms of restructuring were being introduced, such as the transfer of home ownership from the state to private individuals. The pragmatism of China's reformist program is caught in the aphorism of the leader Deng Xiaoping: "It doesn't matter whether a cat is black or white; it matters only whether it can catch mice." And one new "mouse-trap" that China was experimenting with was the introduction of a more widespread stock market system. In 1988 the Communist Party adopted a plan to turn state-owned companies into stock-issuing enterprises. And stock markets were set up in Beijing, Shenyang, and Shanghai, which mostly operated as do Western bond markets, paying a fixed interest rate and not bringing ownership rights to shareholders. Initially, the stock system spread quite rapidly with between 7,000 and 10,000 firms having issued shares by 1989, one company on Hong Kong's border even trading stock to foreigners.[47] But then came the great democratic revolt and repression of 1989.

CAPITALIST REFORM MINUS DEMOCRACY
EQUALS RAISED EXPECTATIONS AND REBELLION

In *The Old Regime and the French Revolution* (1856) Alexis de Tocqueville wrote that it is not always when things are going from bad to worse that revolutions break out, but rather when an oppressive rule over a long period without protest suddenly finds the government relaxing its pressure. So it was in the People's Republic of China. Deng thought capitalist reforms without political liberalization would modernize the Chinese state without difficulty. Even with economic growth and personal incomes expanding, the people found their raised expectations frustrated by inflation, political corruption, and the lack of freedom of speech. Resentment built up over market-oriented reforms near the coast by those in state-run firms inland.

In April of 1989, thousands of students, later joined by workers, marched through the capital of Beijing demanding more democracy and an end to government corruption. Defying a ban on public protests, they camped in Tiananmen Square, set up tents, and began a hunger strike. In the middle of this, Mikhail Gorbachev, on a state visit to China, arrived to formally reconcile the antagonism between the two communist countries. Both the demonstrators and the government initially showed great restraint toward each other until a government split between hard-liners and those sympathetic with the students was resolved by the victory of the hard-liners. In early June, the hard-liners ordered troops from outlying parts of China who were unfamiliar with the meaning of the protests to come in and take over the center of Beijing with force. Hundreds of people were killed or wounded by soldiers and tanks. Deng (fearing that another student cultural revolution would do him in again) and hard-liner Prime Minister Li Peng consolidated their power. Intellectuals and leaders of the democratic rebellion were imprisoned.

Initially, the government crackdown damaged the infrastructure in Chinese cities, raised great feelings of uncertainty, and caused a mass exodus of foreigners. The American government, among others, halted weapons and technology transfer to China and was openly critical of human rights violations. But the Chinese regime ignored these criticisms and proceeded with targeted economic reforms combined with political repression.

In 1990, the government permitted foreign development of land, the Shanghai stock exchange opened, and foreign banks resumed lending to China. During the next two years, the government eliminated export subsidies, attempting to qualify for membership in the General Agreement on Tariffs and Trade (GATT). Tariffs were lowered on a number of goods and price controls were restricted to a handful of basic necessities. By 1993, the Chinese strategy paid off as the Chinese economy grew at an inflation-adjusted rate of 12.8 percent and the Clinton administration renewed China's most-favored-nation trade status. (This was done on an annual basis, presumably pending "progress" on human rights.) While industrial output had increased six-fold compared to the late 1970s, the free market in China seemed almost out of control as acceptance of capitalism was often considered synonymous with corruption and crime rates rose as fast as economic growth.[48] The prices of property and stock skyrocketed and inflation ballooned. Deng praised moneymaking: Government measures to curb corruption should not discourage enthusiasm for economic growth. The regime's strategy appeared to be to give the people the economic hope of becoming rich to distract them from the Western temptation of becoming liberated politically. A "socialist market economy" resulted in short-term success, even though foreign observers worried about the Chinese economy "overheating." Foreigners failed to appreciate the existing stocks of social capital, the embedded community trust, norms, and networks that facilitate collective learning, and the accurate targeting of local entrepreneurship.[49]

The Chinese are moving through the basic three stages of post–cold-war liberal economics we have identified: economic liberalization, macroeconomic stability, and privatization. But their development is distinguished by their unique culture and geographic and demographic circumstances. The vast area of the country encouraged the Chinese government to target economic liberalization in certain "pilot areas," particularly regions near Hong Kong (such as Guangdong) and the coasts, where free-market behavior is most advanced. Macroeconomic stabilization has been extremely difficult since China has more of a society or civilization than a "state" in the Western sense.[50] This complicates the centralized control of the money supply by a "central bank." The risk of hyperinflation is thus built into the system, making it easier to stimulate economic growth than to slow down such stimulation when the economy threatens to become "too hot." In 1994, economic growth slowed sharply as inflation stayed high. Finally, privatization is being gradually introduced in targeting particular sectors and "pilot companies." For example, the Shougang Corporation, a steel producer, developed a unique Shougang Contract System personally approved by Deng.

The **Shougang Contract System** involves: the firm contracting with the state, defining the limits of privatization; internal contracts within the firm; salary increases tied to individual contributions; company policies decided upon democratically by workers and staff, and a shareholding system in which a certain percentage of the profits are remitted to the state. The hard negotiations in the system concern how much of the profits should be paid annually to the state. Such gradual privatization experiments in the large industrial sector permit the Chinese to maintain a sense of state control and "profit-sharing," while still providing autonomy and motivation. Shougang Corporation's productivity and profitability increased significantly since the introduction of the contract system and the company expanded from iron and steel to seventeen other sectors, including electronics, finance, shipbuilding, and tourism. By 1994, the Shougang Corporation was made up of twelve large companies with some 158 large- and medium-sized factories, 57 domestic affiliates, and 61 joint ventures with both Chinese and foreign partners.[51] About half of industrial output can be attributed to state enterprises. However, they usually lose money and tend to grow only with subsidies from Beijing.

In February 1997 Deng Xiaoping died. His successor, Jiang Zemin, managed the recovery of Hong Kong from the British as a Special Administrative Region of China in July. China's state council placed the two major stock exchanges under the China Securities Regulatory Commission, creating a more centrally controlled exchange to stabilize share prices. Jiang announced the sale of many state-owned businesses (increasing the rate of privatization). By 1998 the state employed only 18 percent of the work force, compared with more than 90 percent in 1978 (which included peasants in communes then).[52]

At the beginning of the Chinese reforms the debt-to-equity ratio for state-owned enterprises was about 10 percent. But due to heavy increases in borrowing, by 1995 the debt-to-equity of all state-owned firms (commercial and manufacturing) was over 500 percent! From 1978 until 1998, outstanding credit for all financial institutions went from 190 billion to 7.5 trillion *renminbi*. In the same period, outstanding credit almost doubled as a percentage of GDP from 53 percent to 100 percent. This rapid rise in debt recalls the situations in South Korea and Thailand before they were hit by the financial crisis of 1997: How was China able to ward off the contagion for so long? There are a number of reasons—many, paradoxically, having to do with China still being behind in modern economic development. The currency, for example, is not convertible for capital account transactions. If Chinese savers become worried about their currency they cannot withdraw it and exchange it for assets denominated in foreign currencies. Also, nonresidents are not permitted to purchase most stocks ("A" shares) bought and sold on the Shanghai and Shenzhen stock markets. Rather they must buy the "B" shares denominated and priced for foreigners. Hence, if foreign investors turn sour on "B" shares, there is no adverse effect upon the Chinese currency. And since the currency is not convertible, neither foreign nor Chinese speculators can act if they feel the *renminbi* is overvalued and likely to depreciate. Most foreign investment is in the form of long-term direct investment rather than short-term portfolio investment. The Chinese have built an economic wall around their society that buffers them to an extent from the contagion of financial meltdown abroad.[53]

No wall, of course, can keep out globalization indefinitely—particularly when China's large export industries are in sync with the global economy. By 1998 the Chinese economy had slowed down. The 8 percent growth rate targeted by the government as necessary to keep the unemployment rate in socially stable limits seemed like a dream. Waves of cheap imports from other Asian countries in crisis flooded the country. Capital was leaving (to the tune of $20 billion in 1997). The government erected protectionist measures to hold off devaluation as long as possible; it cracked down on unauthorized currency trading, subsidized prices in steelmaking, petrochemicals, cars and televisions, and put up barriers to imports and foreign investment that threatened local industries.[54] A $1 trillion public works program was aimed at growing the economy at century's end to keep up demand and economic growth for the 1.2 billion population that has a per capital income of about $350 per year. There is a strategy of shifting business from foreign companies to Chinese firms: China State Power stopped importing small-scale power-generation equipment—a significant loss to Siemens and General Electric. But Chinese government efforts to consolidate industries Japanese style met with resistance. The effort to reduce the 120 auto manufacturers established in the 1980s was countered by strong willed provincial and local governments who wanted to maintain a presence in what they consider to be a pillar industry in the society, even though such small companies cannot benefit from economies of scale. However, the government was able to close the Guangdong International Trust and Investment Corporation, a large investment company drowning in debt. Nevertheless, these efforts to manage change were but a prelude to more closings and higher unemployment following the decline of the Shanghai real estate market and increasing overcapacity throughout the nation as the global deflationary storm seeped through the Chinese wall.

IMPLICATIONS

LEARNING PRINCIPLES: POSITIVE TRANSPARENCY AND AGENCY

In terms of collective learning, the Chinese elite observed the disintegration of the Soviet Union and its depressing economic consequences and decided to go their own way. They assumed that economic liberalization could proceed without significant political liberalization. That this strategy largely succeeded despite the massive political repression of the democratic revolt of 1989 is due in large part to an astute policy of creating economic hope by praising the virtues of wealth and opening opportunities for entrepreneurship. This is a **policy of positive transparency:** the reporting of facts in a context of hope that makes it imaginable that they can be changed, improved upon, and learned from in order to better the life chances of the people.[55]

Contrast this Chinese policy, for a moment, with the inadvertent **policy of negative transparency** from which the communities in the former Soviet Union suffered: Suddenly, centralized barriers to information flow were stripped away, exposing overwhelming levels of hidden pollution, sickness, inflation, and social and economic underdevelopment. Overnight, the people in Russia were shocked to learn that birth defects among newborns were rising at almost the same sharp rate as the population growth was falling and that the number of mothers dying during pregnancy and childbirth was ten times higher in Russia than in developed countries. The same policy of negative transparency stunned the Russian people when they learned that the number of children born out of wedlock had risen to 15 percent. In the United States, the rate is above 25 percent and shocks no one![56]

The policy of negative transparency blocks collective learning with *future shock*—the sense of being overwhelmed with change, rather than stimulating positive collective action to adapt and to improve. Collective learning builds on strength, not weakness. If the only news you hear is bad news, it is difficult to focus on your strength and to motivate others. Individuals overwhelmed with dismal facts presented in a negative context perceive themselves to be powerless. The incentives to learn are missing. The staggering environmental, social, and economic problems of a society must be faced but in a context of positive transparency that gives them hope and a framework in which specific actions can be seen to lead to concrete improvement. Collective learning that results in positive economic change depends on a **sense of agency**—the belief that individual action makes a critical difference.

Psychologist M. Brewster Smith put it this way: "Some people more than others seem to be in charge of their lives—to be Agents or "Origins" of personal causation rather than Pawns. The unprecedented human situation with its headlong trends toward multiple disaster sets a high premium upon Agency, upon the rearing of people who will not passively take these trends for granted."[57]

Such a sense of agency can best be fostered collectively in the long run with a grassroots democratic organization that views the local community as Jack McCall does in his *Small Town Survival Manual*—as a bucket where much may be poured into the top but the bucket never overflows until the leaks are plugged in the bottom in order to *keep money and jobs at home* that otherwise leak out. McCall, a local American government consultant who saved many small rural towns in the United States from going bankrupt, suggests the following steps to accomplish this survival plan: (1) Do a survey of what people in the local community and immediate region want; (2) Specialize in what customers want, using any comparative advantage at hand; (3) Add value to products, processes, and raw materials

to satisfy the needs identified by the people, using import substitution and training to increase the quality of jobs and products created in the community; (4)
Improve the aesthetics of where you live and work; (5) Bring out the local cultural heritage, involving everyone with enthusiasm and community spirit.[58] To the extent such community endeavors involve environmentally oriented start-ups, I
have argued in *Green Logic* that federal and international governmental agencies
should provide seed money. A grassroots policy of transparency and collective
learning should be a positive sustainable process that creates a healthy community for one's grandchildren.[59]

A policy of positive transparency increases the sense of agency by giving dependent communities the self-confidence to become more independent and self-
sufficient. The neoclassical recipes ala Jeffrey Sachs summed up here—economic
liberalization, macroeconomic stability, and privatization—are keys to such independence in the post–cold-war world economy. But Sachs typically pushed all
of these policies at the same time in a form of "shock therapy": controlling inflation, cutting subsidies to state industries, freeing up price controls so that prices
follow the market, and so on. And some countries that were "Sachsed," such as
Poland and Russia (where government elites hired the Harvard economics professor as a key advisor) discovered that despite positive initial economic results,
a cultural and political reaction set in, an understandable resistance to being
shocked by so much change at once. Sachs's fast-fix tempo worked well when
first tried in Bolivia, rapidly reducing the inflation rate of 24,000 percent per year
in the mid-1980s. But Polish and Russian resistance to radical neoclassical economic therapy was underestimated, leading the Polish to bring back hard-line
communists and the Russians to bring back right-wing nationalist extremists.
U.S. Deputy Secretary of State Strobe Talbott, Clinton's key advisor on Russia, argued that Russia needed "less shock and more therapy," consolidating support for
Yeltsin.[60] Too many people were thrown out of work and dislocated from social security and the traditional cultural context.

By 1994, Yeltsin's two-year proliberalism economic reform movement was
over. His proreform cabinet ministers resigned under pressure from right-wing
members of parliament. The reforms brought down the inflation rate from 2000
percent in 1992 to about 900 percent in 1993. The antireformist consolidation
served to stabilize the Russian government in the short term but at the price of
increasing inflation, as more rubles were printed and state-sponsored corruption
spread. Sachs protested the idea that Russia had ever really had a "shock therapy" at all, given an inflation rate that never fell below 20 percent per month and
given that only five privatized firms were declared bankrupt in 1993. He accused
the West of making the Russian problem worse by promising $28 billion in aid,
while only putting $4 billion on the table.[61] Upon resigning as an advisor to Yeltsin
in 1994, Sachs sharply criticized the IMF for pushing Russia to cut its deficit without providing any noninflationary means to finance part of it.[62]

One month after $4.8 billion was belatedly dispersed to Russia by the IMF in
July 1998 (of $11 billion approved for continued reforms), the Russian government

and central bank abandoned their commitment to a broadly stable exchange rate, unilaterally froze some of the nation's external and internal debt and started the meltdown of the Russian currency and financial markets that threw the country into economic chaos and political uncertainty. The absence of positive transparency came home to roost in a regime dominated by corrupt oligarchs. By granting widespread tax exemptions to its friends, failing to pursue tax evaders aggressively, and running up debt by not carrying through with the fiscal discipline required for reforms, the Russians lost credibility on Western financial markets that may take years to restore.[63]

The post–cold-war economic order has become a postliberal order in which each cultural unit first seeks the wealth and liberation promised by neoclassical economic recipes only to back off at some point in movements of resistance for the sake of political autonomy and cultural integrity. In this process, world capital flows clearly play a critical role, as illustrated in the next chapter.

Questions for Thought

1. Characterize the former Stalinist-communist economic model by interrelating the following key terms: *allocation of resources, output goals, full ("overfull") employment, inflation, pricing system, marketing.*
Why were managers inclined to "avoid new technology"? Why was risk-reduction rewarded?

2. Describe the reform concept launched by Gorbachev, using his own terms and illustrating it in the framework of economic development in the post-Stalin era.

3. Explain the three stages of liberal economic reform identified by Jeffrey Sachs and their "Big Bang" implementation in Poland after January 1, 1990.

4. Show how Mao, Zhao Ziyang, and Deng Xiaoping followed through on a multiphase economic policy, at times even taking "one step backward in order to take two steps forward."

5. Evaluate the psychological elements expressed in the policies of positive/negative transparency in their effect on the success of economic reforms in the former U.S.S.R. and in China. Why do you think Poland has been relatively successful? Give examples in your country of "the sense of agency."

6. What recipes or strategies can you recall from the chapter for creating a sustainable local community that survives economically without losing its cultural integrity despite the pressures of globalization?

Notes

1. For an example of the self-preoccupation of the industrialized countries of the North (resulting here in an overly positive assessment of Europe), see Lester Thurow, *Head to Head: The Coming Economic Battle among Japan, Europe and America*

(New York: William Morrow and Co., 1992). And see Jeffrey Frieden and Barry Eichengreen, eds., *Forging an Integrated Europe* (Ann Arbor, MI: University of Michigan Press, 1997).

2. See Wilhelm Hankel, *Die sieben Todsünden der Vereinigung: Wege aus dem Wirtschaftsdesaster* (Berlin: Siedler Verlag, 1993). For a more positive view, see W. R. Smyser, *The Economy of United Germany: Colossus at the Crossroads* (New York: St. Martin's Press, 1992). And Richard Deeg, *Finance Capitalism Unveiled: Banks and the German Political Economy* (Ann Arbor, MI: University of Michigan Press, 1998).

3. See, for instance, Christopher Layne and Benjamin C. Schwarz, "The Perils of Stability," *New York Times*, October 3, 1993, in which they suggest that "By linking America's prosperity to international economic interdependence and using our military commitments to secure that interdependence, U.S. strategy oddly conforms to the Marxist interpretation of American foreign policy." Also see Robert Pahre, *Leading Questions: How Hegemony Affects the International Political Economy* (Ann Arbor, MI: University of Michigan Press, 1999) in which Pahre finds that a leading state harms others when it has many allies, but is good for the international economy when it lacks allies.

4. See Samuel P. Huntington, "The Clash of Civilizations," *Foreign Affairs* (summer 1993), in which he argues that future conflicts in world politics will be dominated not by ideology or economics but by the clash of civilizations, and particularly Western civilization against the rest (which could, of course, be interpreted as an ideological viewpoint in itself).

5. V. I. Lenin, *Selected Works* 2 (Moscow: Lenin Institute, 1963–1969): 709. For a summary of Lenin's development, see "Lenin: Elites, Imperialism and Revolution," Chapter 2 in R. Isaak, *Individuals and World Politics*, 2nd ed. (Belmont, CA: Duxbury Press of Wadsworth Publishing Co., 1981).

6. Ellen Comisso and Laura Tyson, "Preface" to special issue on "Power, Purpose and Collective Choice: Economic Strategy in Socialist States," *International Organization* 40, no. 2 (spring 1986): 189.

7. Franklyn D. Holzman and Robert Legvold, "The Economics and Politics of East-West Relations," in *World Politics and International Economics*, ed. C. Fred Bergsten and Lawrence B. Krause (Washington, D.C.: The Brookings Institution, 1975), p. 284. On "over-full" employment planning, see Franklyn D. Holzman, "Overfull Employment Planning, Input-Output, and the Soviet Economic Reforms," *Soviet Studies* 22 (October 1970): 255–261.

8. See Ludwig von Mises, "Economic Calculation in the Socialist Commonwealth," in *Collectivist Economic Planning*, ed. F. A. Hayek (London: Routledge & Kegan Paul, Ltd., 1935), pp. 87–130.

9. Holzman and Legvold, "East-West Relations," pp. 285–286.

10. See Janos Kornai, *Economics of Shortage*, 2 vols. (Amsterdam: North Holland, 1980); and Paul R. Gregory, "The Stalinist Command Economy," *The Annals* 507 (January 1990): 18–25.

11. Holzman and Legvold, "East-West Relations," pp. 286–287.

12. Glen Alden Smith, *Soviet Foreign Trade* (New York: Praeger, 1973), pp. 81–83.

13. Edward Weisband, Robert Rosh, and Scott Rosenthal, "Dual Ghettos and Dependent Development: The Economic Consequences of Superpower Hegemony in Eastern Europe and Latin America," paper presented at the Annual Meeting of the International Studies Association, Atlanta, Georgia, March 27–30, 1984.

14. J. Wilcyznski, *The Economies of Socialism*, 4th ed. (New York: George Allen and Unwin Press, 1982), p. 53.

15. Weisband et al., p. 17.

16. R. A. Isaak, "International Integration and Foreign Policy Decision-making," an unpublished doctoral dissertation (New York University, 1971), pp. 232–242.

17. See D. A. Loeber and A. P. Friedland, "Soviet Imports of Industrial Installations under Compensation Agreements: West Europe's Siberian Pipeline Revisited," *Columbia Journal of World Business* 18, no. 4 (winter 1983): 51–62. One observer has noted that the key rule operative in Cocom is that "In America everything is banned that is not expressly permitted, while in most of Europe the opposite is true." See Jurgen Klotz, "Not Everyone Believes Cocom Can Stop Technology Transfer to East Bloc," *The German Tribune*, no. 1289 (September 1987): 7.

18. Frederick Kempe and Eduardo Lachica, "Cocom Feuds over Trade to East Bloc," *Wall Street Journal*, July 17, 1984, p. 27.

19. See UNCTAD Secretariat, report of the Secretariat, *Towards the Technological Transformation of Developing Countries* (New York: United Nations, 1979); and Bruce R. Guile and Harvey Brooks, eds., *Technology and Global Industry: Companies and Nations in the World Economy* (Washington, D.C.: National Academy Press, 1987).

20. Statistics from the CIA *Handbook of Economic Statistics*; *International Institute Strategic Studies: The Military Balance*. 1988–1989; OECD *Economic Outlook, December* 1988 as reported in the *Wall Street Journal*, January 23, 1989.

21. Graham T. Allison, Jr., "Testing Gorbachev," *Foreign Affairs* 67, no. 1 (fall 1988): 20. For an analysis of the stalemated Soviet economy, see Marshall I. Goldman, *U.S.S.R. in Crisis: The Failure of an Economic System* (New York: W. W. Norton, 1983).

22. Axel Lebahn, *Politische und wirtschaftliche Auswirkungen der Perestrojka auf die Sowjetunion sowie auf ihre Beziehungen zu Osteuropa und zum Westen, Aussenpolitik*, Jg. 39, no. 11 (1988): 114.

23. Ibid., p. 109.

24. See Mikhail Gorbachev, *Perestroika: New Thinking for Our Country and the World* (New York: Harper & Row, 1987).

25. See, for example, Elisabeth Runfien, "Signs Grow of Cabinet Shake-Up, Retreat From Reforms in Russia: Postelection Decisions Are Counter to Austerity, Privatization Policies," *Wall Street Journal*, December 20, 1993, p. A8. And see "Institutes: Russian Economy Continues to Decline," *The Week in Germany* (New York: The German Information Center), May 13, 1994.

26. Clifford Gaddy & Barry Ickes, "Russia's Virtual Economy," *Foreign Affairs* 77, no. 5 (September/October 1998): 56.

27. Joseph Kahn and Timothy L. O'Brien, "For Russia and Its U.S. Bankers, Match Wasn't Made in Heaven," *New York Times*, October 18, 1998.

28. "Poll: Lack of Hard Currency Hinders German-Russian Business Deals," *The Week in Germany* (November 26,1993): 5.

29. For background on the Eastern European events, see Hoyt Gimlin, "Balkanization of Eastern Europe (Again)," *Congressional Quarterly Research Reports* 2, no. 17 (November 3, 1989): 618–630; and "East of Eden: A Survey of Eastern Europe," *The Economist* (August 12, 1989): 11ff.

30. The statistics above are from "Eastern Europe: Foreign Investment—A Harbinger of Economic Recovery," *Trends: Economy, Politics and Financial Markets* (Frankfurt: Dresdner Bank, August 1993): 13–17. See also *Central European Economic Review* 6, no. 9, *Wall Street Journal Europe*, November 1998.

31. Ibid., *Trends: Economy, Politics and Financial Markets*, pp. 14, 17.

32. Gail E. Schares, "Eastern Europe Tries to Stoke up Its Fire Sale," *Business Week*, October 21, 1991, 52.

33. Cited in Jeffrey Sachs, "The Economic Transformation of Eastern Europe: The Case of Poland," *American Economist* 36, no. 2 (fall 1992): 4.

34. Sachs, p. 5ff.

35. Ibid., p. 6. On the disappearance of aid to Poland, see Barry Newman, "Disappearing Act: West Pledged Billions of Aid to Poland—Where Did It All Go?" *Wall Street Journal*, February 23, 1994.

36. I am grateful to Alexander Keck of Pace University and the University of Heidelberg for this particular formulation of the dilemma. The following illustrate the trade-offs involved in the process of privatization: Raymond Vernon, *The Promise of Privatization* (New York: Council on Foreign Relations, 1988); John Vickers, *The Politics of Privatization in Western Europe* (London: Totowa, 1989); Dennis Gayle, *Privatization and Deregulation in Global Perspective* (New York: Quorum Books, 1990); Hans Blommestein, *Methodes de privatisation des grandes entreprises* (Paris: Centre pour la cooperation avec les economies europeenes en transition, 1993); Steve Hanke, ed., *Privatization and Development* (San Francisco, CA: The International Center for Economic Growth, 1987); Kevin R. McDonald, "Why Privatization Is Not Enough," *Harvard Business Review* (May–June 1993): 49–59; Sandra Wilson, "The Private Sector and Local Authorities, OECD *Observer* (October/November 1992): 25–28; Ira Lieberman, "Why Is Privatization Currently a Major Issue?" *Columbia Journal of World Business* (spring 1993): 9–17; "Why Jobs Come Last," *The Economist* (April 25, 1992): 63–64; David Rudnick, "The Pains of Going Private," *Euromoney Supplement*(May 1993): 21–23; and John Odling-Smee, "What Went Wrong in Russia?" *Central European Economic Review, Wall Street Journal Europe* 6, no. 9, November, 1998, p. 6.
37. See, e.g., J. K. Bielecki, "Country Profile—Poland 1996," European Bank for Reconstruction and Development, 1996 (http://www.kprm.gov.pl/mszdpi/eurobank/eurob1.html); and Daniel Michaels, "Poland Breaks Out," *Central European Economic Review* 6, no. 9, *Wall Street Journal Europe*, November 1998, pp. 14–17.
38. "Cracking the China Market," *Wall Street Journal*, December 10, 1993, RI.
39. See "Mao: Charisma, Limited Warfare and Modernization," Chapter 3 in Isaak, *Individuals and World Politics*, pp. 44–61.
40. Benjamin Schwartz, "China's Developmental Experience 1949–1972," in *China's Developmental Experience*, ed. Michel Oksenberg (New York: Praeger, 1973), p.22. Also see Michel Oksenberg, "Policy Making under Mao Tse-tung 1949–1968," *Comparative Politics* 3, no. 3 (1971): 323–360.
41. *Wall Street Journal*, January 23, 1989, p. A8.
42. Haitani, "Market and Planning," pp. 359–60.
43. See Vigor Fung, "China Allows the Rebirth of Some Private Corporations," *Wall Street Journal*, August 10, 1984, p. 22.
44. "China Walks the Edge of the Capitalist Road," *Business Week*, October 18, 1982, 80–86.
45. See Dwight H. Perkins, *China—Asia's Next Economic Giant* (Seattle, WA: University of Washington Press, 1986); and N. J. Wang, *China's Modernization and Transnational Corporations* (Lexington, MA: D. C. Heath and Co., 1984).
46. Nicholas Kristof, "China's Big Lurch Backward Theory Is Now Seen as Study in Pragmatism," *New York Times*, January 3, 1989.
47. Nicholas Kristof, "Selling China on a 'Public' Privatization," *New York Times*, January 8, 1989. On events leading up to the 1989 policy reversal, see John P. Burns, "China's Governance: Political Reform in a Turbulent Environment," *The China Quarterly* (Special Issue: *The People's Republic of China after 40 Years*) (September 1989): 481–518.
48. "Cracking the China Market," R2ff.
49. On social capital, see Robert D. Putnam, "The Prosperous Community: Social Capital and Economic Growth," *The American Prospect* (spring 1993): 35–42.
50. See, for example, Jonathan D. Spence, *The Search for Modern China* (New York: W. W. Norton, 1990); and Ezra Vogel, *One Step Ahead in China: Guangdong under Reform* (Cambridge, MA: Harvard University Press, 1989).
51. The data on the Shougang Contract System comes from Rong-pin Kang, "The Shougang Contract Management Responsibility System: Effects, Practices and Thoughts" (Beijing: Institute for International Business, Shougang Research and Development Co., 1993). Also see "China Economy Slows, Challenging Investors," *Wall Street Journal*, May 16, 1994.

52. David M. Lampton, "China: Think Again," *Foreign Policy*, no. 110 (spring 1998): 23. Also see *China 2020: Development Challenges in the New Century* (Washington, D.C.: World Bank, 1997).
53. Nicholas Lardy, "China and the Asian Contagion," *Foreign Affairs* 77, no. 4 (July/August 1998): 78–88.
54. "China Builds a Wall—But Will It Hold?" *Business Week*, October 12, 1998, 124. See also, Nicholas Lardy, *China in the World Economy* (Washington, D.C.: Institute for International Economics, 1994).
55. R. Isaak, "Developing Country Recipes for Collective Learning, Economic Development & Global Environmental Responsibility," (p. 7), a paper first presented at the International Environmental Institutions Research Seminar at Harvard's Center for Science and International Affairs, December 11, 1992, revised for presentation at the 1993 annual International Studies Association Convention in Acapulco, March 27, 1993, and published as *Working Paper No. 116*, November 1993, by the Center for Applied Research, Pace University, 1 Pace Plaza, New York, NY 10032. Also see R. Isaak, "What Is To Be Done?" concluding chapter in *Green Logic: Ecopreneurship, Theory and Ethics* (West Hartford, CT: Kumarian Press, 1999).
56. Statistics from the *New York Times*, October 4, 1992.
57. M. Brewster Smith, "On Self-Actualization: A Transambivalent Examination of a Focal Theme in Maslow's Psychology," *Journal of Humanistic Psychology* 13, no. 2 (1973): 17–33.
58. Jack McCall, *Small Town Survival Manual* (Columbia, MO: University of Missouri, 1988).
59. R. Isaak, *Green Logic: Ecopreneurship, Theory and Ethics* (West Hartford, CT: Kumarian Press, 1999).
60. Carla Anne Robbins, "Talbott's Abiding Passion for Russia Shapes His Career and Clinton Administration's Policy," *Wall Street Journal*, January 7, 1994.
61. Interview with Jeffrey Sachs on the MacNeil-Lehrer Newshour, public television (Channel 13), New York City, January 21, 1994. Sachs forecast in this interview that Russia was moving toward incoherence, hyperinflation, huge budget deficits, and extensive corruption through black markets. He was pessimistic about Russia's willingness to adopt the necessary therapies of moving to print less money and stopping subsidies for firms.
62. Jeffrey Sachs, "The Reformers' Tragedy," *New York Times*, January 23, 1994, Op-Ed.
63. John Odling-Smee, "What Went Wrong in Russia?" *Central European Economic Review*, *Wall Street Journal Europe* 6, no. 9, November 1998, p. 6.

BUSINESS CYCLES
AND CAPITAL FLOWS

The faster capital works, the less of it you need.
—Stan Davis and Christopher Meyer, 1998

In advanced industrial economies the waves of the business cycle may be becoming more like ripples.
—Steven Weber, 1997

While the typical recession in industrial economies involves a drop in output of just 2 percent, recessions in Latin America, the Middle East, and sub-Saharan Africa are respectively three, four, and six times more severe.
—Ricardo Housmann, 1997

The failure of the IMF to include any proposals for debt rescheduling in its programs was the equivalent of Homer writing The Iliad without mentioning Helen.
—David Hale, Zurich Group, 1998

THE BRETTON WOODS SYSTEM HAS UNRAVELED, BUT NOT DISAPPEARED. GLOBAL CAPITAL FLOWS outstrip trade flows, smoothing out business cycles in the industrialized countries. At the same time the Asian crisis of the late 1990s spilled over into an emerging markets crisis, pushing international institutions to their limits in terms of short-term lending. Financial uncertainties and competitiveness sparked an unprecedented wave of mergers between large firms both domestically and internationally. With "casino capitalism" spinning at full tilt, the question becomes: How can seemingly unpredictable economic change be "managed" globally without the promise of bailing out speculative investors from investments that go sour in areas of the world where capital is badly needed? This chapter attempts to take apart some of these trends in business cycles, mergers, capital flows, and ad hoc "management" of global economic change by overwhelmed institutions. One way to comprehend these economic shifts is to start with the conventional view of business cycles and then to describe how globalization has served to "dampen" them in industrialized countries while intensifying them in emerging economies.

ORIGINS

SHORT-TERM, INTERMEDIATE, AND LONG-TERM BUSINESS CYCLES

The rumored death of the business cycle turned out to be premature. But like many forecasts of mortality at the end of the twentieth century, life-extending changes due to technology somewhat transformed the phenomenon in question making it harder to characterize. Let us start at the beginning.

During the late stage of the manufacturing-based U.S. economy of the 1950s and 1960s, a short-term business cycle was identified as mapping out a repetitive pattern of boom and bust. This classic cycle was characterized by four stages: (1) *expansion*—business activity picks up and the economy grows, leading to a (2) *peak*—an overheated economy sparks inflation, which results in a raising of interest rates; (3) *recession* results from the higher interest rates, diminishing business activity causing the economy to contract; finally a (4) *trough* is reached and inflation goes down along with interest rates, stimulating the beginning of another economic expansion.

In everyday usage, the concept of **business cycle** refers to three- to eight-year patterns of rising and falling economic activity, of expansion and recession, peaks and troughs. However, many economists have found these short-term fluctuating modes of behavior alone to be insufficient to explain and predict business patterns. Therefore, they have combined short-term "business cycles" with intermediate-term (fifteen to twenty-five years) "long-swing" investment (or Kuznets) cycles, and long-term or "long-wave" (forty-five to sixty years) **Kondratieff cycles**. Some have used such cycles, together with power transitions, to anticipate wars between states.[1] (See Figure 11-1.)

Expansionary economic phases can be viewed as part of a **syntropic process**, a building up of production, employment, incomes, stock market prices, and construction. Periods of recession or decline, on the other hand, may be seen as a form of **entropic process**, of obsolescence and disintegration. Business or corporate survival depends on anticipating syntropic and entropic shifts in the economy, at least in terms of the key sectors upon which the lifeblood or cash flow of the business depends. But such economic forecasting is precarious. It depends on where one is standing and on whether one is preoccupied with short-term, intermediate-term, or long-term cycles when analyzing change.

Consider the interconnection between short-term and intermediate-term cycles. Harvard economist Alvin Hansen concluded that from 1795 to 1937 in the American economy there were seventeen cycles of an average duration of 8.35 years. One to two minor peaks occur regularly between the major peaks of these eight-year cycles, each minor cycle lasting less than half the duration of the major or "normal" business cycles. However, in looking at the key sector of building construction, Hansen noted that the cycle in this area averaged between seventeen or eighteen years in length, or about twice the length of the normal business cycle. He concluded: "American experience indicates that with a high degree of regularity every other major business boom coincides roughly with a

Figure 11-1   American Business-Cycle Experience (Percent of Long-Term Trend)

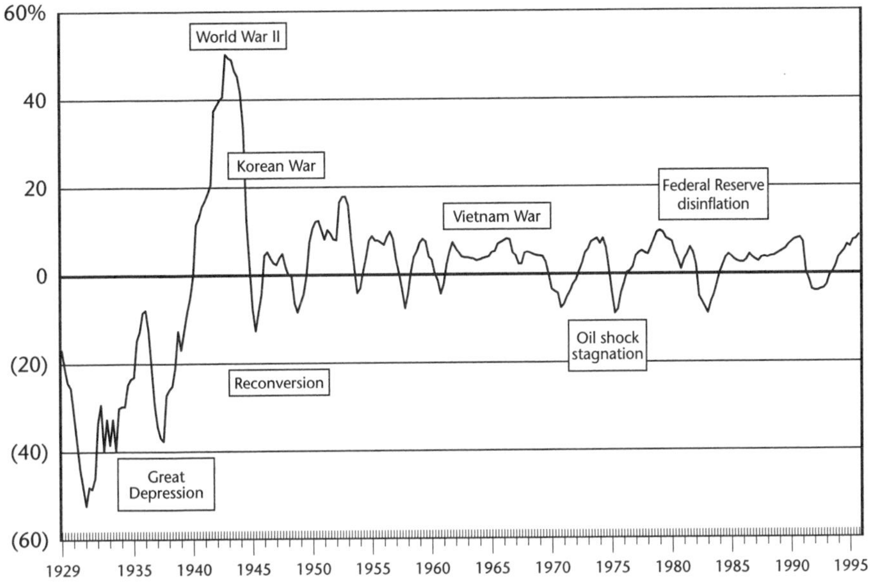

Source: Campbell R. McConnell and Stanley L. Brue, *Macro Economics,* 13th ed. McGraw-Hill Inc., 1996, pp. 144–145.

boom in building construction, while the succeeding major cycle recovery is forced to buck up against a building slump.... [T]he depressions which have fallen in the interval of the construction downswing are typically deep and long. And the succeeding recovery is held back and retarded by the unfavorable depressional influence from the slump in the building industry."[2]

In illustrating the interconnectedness of short-term business cycles and **intermediate-term Kuznets cycles** (referring to the 1971 Nobel economist Simon Kuznets, who discovered them in 1930), Hansen makes clear that a corporate strategy dependent upon the building construction sector would most likely come to grief if it failed to consider the perspective of the intermediate-term cycle; if it focused, for example, only upon short-term cycles. But what about the opposite danger? It is also possible to go wrong in strategic planning by unduly stressing long-term cycles lasting half a century or so at the expense of neglecting short-term fluctuations.

Russian economist Nikolai D. Kondratieff fathered the concept of the long-wave cycle in capitalist economies of some fifty years in length. (Kondratieff died later in one of Stalin's concentration camps.)[3] This iconoclast discovered two-and-a-half cycles in a series of price, wage, interest rate, and value-affected data, with troughs in 1790, 1844–1851, and 1890–1896; and peaks at 1810–1817, 1870–1875, and 1914–1920. Although production data do not always fit well into Kondratieff s framework, the "idealized" Kondratieff

Wave approximates the actual behavior of U.S. wholesale prices closely enough to suggest to long-wave observers that the American economy is overdue to descend into a depression.[4]

Objections can be raised to long-wave forecasts of a probable depression. First, a preoccupation with entropic processes of long-wave decline may blind the forecaster to counter-cyclical syntropic processes of economic growth and technological innovation. These positive developments may balance out the entropic processes sufficiently to keep what might have become a depression within the bounds of what may be a series of limited recessions. The long-wave model may also suffer from what Karl Popper called the "poverty of historicism" by basing future projections upon past behavior, whereas we can never know what people in the future will know and therefore cannot predict what their options will be. Another objection to the long-wave depression thesis is that it could become a negative self-fulfilling prophecy, having a **reverse Pygmalion effect**—increasing the odds of extraordinarily bad economic outcomes by projecting such negative expectations. The difficulty for the strategist who overemphasizes the long wave is the tendency to miss the healthy trees by taking a distant view of the dark forest: Not all sectors decline in any particular recession. The astute entrepreneur may be far better off looking for hidden positive opportunities in familiar territory in a situation of economic turbulence.

Otherwise he or she may go bankrupt by accepting fatalistic, cyclical determinism and waiting for a decade or more to pass in order to catch the next long wave as it begins to make its "inevitable" ascent. For example, by ignoring market cycle timing and by focusing on specific company situations he knew from interviewing or personal experience, Peter Lynch was able to maintain the highest average returns for his Fidelity Magellan Fund portfolio of stocks throughout the 1970s and 1980s, transforming it into the largest American mutual fund (see Lynch's One Up on Wall Street). The long-term wave recalls the material determinism against which Benedetto Croce warned us two years after the onset of the Great Depression of 1929: "The sterility of matter will not bring forth and cause to blossom either morals or religion or poetry or philosophy, and not even economics itself, which requires the glow of life, keen intelligence, and eagerness."[5]

The short-term business cycle has been transformed in the past twenty years as the industrialized economies have shifted from manufacturing to the service sector, and globalization and technological development have radically shortened reaction times and raised demand expectations for sophisticated products and services. The U.S. economy, for example, is no longer dominated by manufacturing, construction, and housing as it was in the 1950s. Gavin Cameron has characterized economic growth in the information age as a shift from physical capital to "weightless output"—such as computer software, financial products, telecommunications, the Internet, entertainment, and management consulting. Such goods accounted for some 23 percent of U.S. GDP between 1987 and 1994 and are often infinitely expansible, or capable of being

Figure 11-2   1997 Top Mergers and Acquisitions

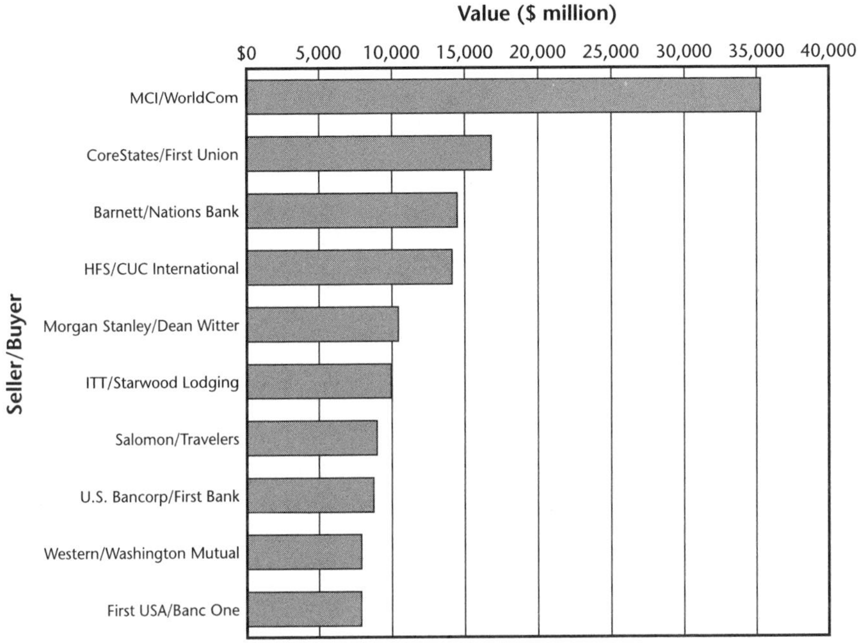

Source: Houlihan Lokey's Mergerstat www.mergerstat.com

used by many people at the same time.[6] In 1997 the top mergers and acquisitions in terms of value were in the "soft" telecommunications, banking, financial services, management consulting, and insurance sectors (see Figure 11-2).

This new "weightless" economy is less sensitive to interest rates in comparison with the manufacturing-dominated economy, which thrived when rates were low and credit was cheap. The service-based economy is more sensitive to the rise and fall of labor costs than to changes in interest rates. Deregulation, technological efficiency, and globalization resulted in a proliferation of multiple independent subeconomies, each with its own business cycle. This diffusion appears to have contributed to a smoothing out of the overall business cycle, making the highs less high and the lows less low. This overall cycle has become longer and more resistant to recession. Rather than the U.S. average three to four years of economic expansion before recession kicked in, there has been only one short recession in the past seventeen years.[7]

In the post-World War II period, economist Victor Zarnowitz demonstrated that the expansions of U.S. business cycles have become longer but more variable in length, while the contractions have become shorter but more uniform in length. The long expansion of the 1990s was characterized by a notable lack of inflationary pressures. Neither low unemployment nor high capacity utilization sparked inflation as they did in the past. In fact, in real terms, U.S. wages fell or only negligibly increased for the last decade and a half. And although capacity utilization theoretically was supposed to stimulate inflation when it reached 81–82 percent, it has remained above that level in the United States since 1994, and still producer and consumer price levels have not spiked upwards. Thus the normal business cycle, while not dead, has been dampened in its extremes due to the effects of the globalization of production, changes in finance, the shift toward service jobs and temporary employment, counter-cyclical government policy, the impact of emerging markets, and the consequences of information technology. As political economist Stephen Weber argued, "These six factors tend to reduce transaction costs, make supply and demand more fluid, compensate for production imbalances and smooth out growth and adjustment.[8]

THE POLITICS OF BUSINESS CYCLES

The smoothing out or dampening of business cycles in industrialized countries such as the United States has political implications domestically and globally. Power flows to elected officials who reign over stable, expanding markets, and capital flows to these markets seeking shelter from volatility and uncertainty elsewhere.

Bill Clinton's reelection in 1996 was not unrelated to the American economic boom, and the money flowing into the flourishing U.S. stock market from abroad was just another indicator of this positive sense of self-fulfilling prophecy. Indeed, American political management of the business cycle as a priority has served to assure American hegemony in the world. The "collective learning" by others in mimicking the business systems and stock markets of the United States are just natural outcomes of this "limelight effect," as others ape the successes of the world's only superpower. Anti-Americanism and terrorism are, of course, the flip sides of this American dominance (accentuated by the war in Kosovo). And there are domestic ideological consequences as well, as political economist Mark Rupert notes: "In place of the kinder, gentler liberalism that was hegemonic during the postwar decades—which John Ruggie has called "embedded liberalism"—we now find instead a hard-edged liberalism that strives to focus the violence of market forces directly upon working people through policies that emphasize fiscal retrenchment, containment of inflation and "flexible labor markets" in a context of rigorous global competition.[9]

In the past, the relationship between politics and business cycles has been equally pronounced. Business cycle theory typically focuses on cyclical responses to external shocks. The most pronounced examples are the economic forerunners to the two world wars. Germany and the United States tilted heavily toward protectionism at the end of the nineteenth century, stimulating depression and the conflicts that would culminate in World War I. The Great Depression similarly prepared the groundwork for World War II as trade nearly collapsed and competitive monetary blocs emerged. The "oil shocks" of the

1970s led not only to subsequent recessions but to the creation of the Group of Seven (G-7) in 1975 and the European Monetary System (precursor of the European Monetary Union) in 1979.

When asked in 1982 why he predicted a world economic recovery in 1984, given the global recession and widespread pessimism about the economic future, William W. Crouse, president of the Latin American Region on Health Care Group, answered: "Because a number of major countries have elections in 1984 and the economy picks up before elections."[10]

In Western democracies, the dependence of corporate planning upon governmental policies takes on a certain wavelike form that usually follows the pattern of national elections. In an analysis of electoral-economic cycles in twenty-seven countries between 1961 and 1972, political scientist Edward Tufte discovered that in nineteen of them, short-run accelerations in real disposable income per capita were more likely to occur in election years than in years without elections. Tufte concluded: "The politicians' economic theory of election outcomes gives great weight to economic events in the months before the election; thus the politicians' strategy is to turn on the spigot surely and swiftly and fill the trough so that it counts with the electorate."[11] Upswings in real disposable income per capita are highly correlated with greater electoral support for incumbents.

By using instruments of economic policy like tax cuts, money creation, and transfer payments, politicians up for reelection can stimulate spending, economic growth, and job creation in the months before the election. Managers of multinational corporations seeking to maximize corporate interests and to buffer themselves against unfavorable change can systematically use their "international election portfolio" to take advantage of these spurts of economic growth, spending, and credit availability. And they can lower their vulnerability in the off-years between elections. Higher volatility in emerging market democracies magnifies the importance of electoral economic cycle taxation and spending, even more than in more stable industrialized democracies. The greater the volatility, the larger the boom must be in order to impress voters that it was the result of political management and not mere chance.[12]

Of course these general electoral-economic cycle schedules are often counterbalanced by government incompetence in the management of macroeconomic tools for its own interest. Such government incompetence has become more apparent as changes in the global economy narrow the options of state economic policymakers—such as the rise of OPEC and the Euro-credit market. In the late 1970s, President Jimmy Carter perfectly mistimed the recession his economic advisors had been coordinating, believing that Americans would stop spending once they anticipated hard times ahead, while in fact they kept spending out of an accurate sense that Carter's anti-inflation policy would prove ineffective in the short term and that dollars should be used up before they lost even more value. Thus, the belated recession preceding the 1980 presidential election was timed to the advantage not of the incumbent, as it should have been, but of the challenger, Ronald Reagan. President Reagan, however, initially appeared to be equally unable to manage the electoral-economic cycle. Waging an excessive battle against inflation, which resulted in record-high interest rates, the recessionary effect overwhelmed the stimulation provided by general tax cuts and tax advantages for high-income investors. This dampened the electoral chances of Reagan's fellow Republicans up for election in the fall of 1982 who had been promised an economic recovery in time to lift their sinking boats. The Reagan recovery followed, but at a high cost in federal deficits pushed up by Keynesian defense spending. The overemphasis on anti-inflation policy through tight money and high interest rates caused the international value of the dollar to rise to such an extent that the resulting U.S. trade deficit brought about a "structural recession" in 1981, which could no longer be easily arrested by short-term economic levers.

President George Bush complacently overestimated the electorate's willingness to believe in an economic recovery that was actually in progress, resulting in Bush's loss to Clinton in 1992. When Clinton was first elected he used the operational motto "It's the economy, Stupid!" This suggested that he understood like few before him the importance of the business cycle for his electoral chances. Carefully cultivating the interests of big business as he moved to the center of the political spectrum, coopting many of the economic issues of the Republican Party and naming an investment banker as his treasury secretary, Clinton appeared at times to become one with the business cycle, steering policy for the sake of a booming stock market in which 50 percent of American families had some sort of direct or indirect stake. At times Clinton seemed willing to export almost anything that moved and to embrace Calvin Coolidge's statement that "The business of America is business," despite his relatively liberal stance on social issues. When the Asian crisis of 1997 hit, capital flowed to a booming United States and to Europe, attracted by the fleeting promise of stability due to the united effort to form a single Euro currency.

GLOBAL PATTERNS OF CAPITAL FLOW

In the second half of the twentieth century there were distinctive shifts in patterns of the global flow of financial capital. Whereas before the Second World War there was little public foreign aid to other countries to speak of, in the first twenty-five years of the Bretton Woods regime after the war, *public* foreign aid dominated capital flows between the North and the South. Developing countries depend on economic growth, open markets, and stable investment stemming from the North. The developed countries, particularly the United States, provided the liquidity. But in the 1970s and early 1980s *private* commercial banks played an increasingly important role in financing public works and private industrial development in developing countries. This pattern, however, was interrupted by the debt crisis described in Chapter 5. In the late 1980s and early 1990s, commercial lending to credit-worthy developing countries resumed. But public financial flows abroad met with political resistance at home (see Chapter 2). The dominant shift in funding was to international stock mutual funds led by large institutional investors in developed countries. While such portfolio investment mitigated the trend a decade earlier, in which more money flowed from South to North than North to South, it came at a price: The poorest of the poor countries received little of this investment and within the newly industrializing countries, only those firms and sectors with brand names or with the highest short-term growth potential were targeted for support.

As direct and portfolio investment settled in the emerging markets, the domestic labor markets in the developed countries felt downward wage pressures. Not only had union strength declined with the shift of the OECD economies from manufacturing to the service sector, with union membership losing more than 6 percent each year in the 1980s in these countries, but companies used this "labor flexibility" to focus on hiring temporary rather than full-time workers, further undermining the bargaining power of labor. The smoothing out of business cycles due to the lowering of potential wage inflation had the effect of redistributing power from the have-nots to the haves.

The development of sophisticated technology not only reduced the need for full-time workers, but changed how firms treated human capital. Just as technology made it possible to keep just enough inventory for immediate needs and drove companies to use capital equipment up as fast as possible before it became obsolete, part-time workers were given systems to work on with built-in training or software (reducing training costs) and were often treated as if they were as expendable as any other factors of production. The euphoria of high job creation rates in the United States, for example, is often short-term: One is constantly being turned over, job security is a daily preoccupation, and long-term planning is hopelessly complicated. Chairman of the Federal Reserve Alan Greenspan relies on these very motivations to keep inflation down, believing workers put a premium on job security out of fear of job obsolescence and are willing to tie pay to performance, reducing the potential demand for wage increases. Moreover, according to Greenspan, heavy investment in computers and other technologies is boosting productivity growth above the trend of recent decades, which, together with globalization, permits companies to shift production easily around the world and head off inflationary bottlenecks from capacity shortages.[13]

The effect of financial flows was even more pronounced in the labor markets of the developing countries than in the United States, particularly in the aftermaths of the debt crisis of the 1980s and the Asian crisis of the 1990s. Following the debt crisis, direct and portfolio investment followed a "flight to quality": The industrial countries' share of net capital flows increased from 57 percent in 1980–1982 to 73 percent in 1983–1986, and then up to 85 percent in 1987–1990. Within the developing world, there was a shift to countries that were believed at the time to be the best credit risks—to the Asian emerging markets (which increased their share of the financial resources going to nonindustrial nations from 22 percent in 1980–1982 to 37 percent in 1987–1990). But in the early 1990s there were other significant shifts. Capital flowing to industrialized countries peaked in 1990 and then fell from 85 percent to 83 percent. And the absolute value of capital inflows to Latin America doubled (the percentage share rising from 24 percent to 34 percent), with the main loser being Sub-Saharan Africa (falling from 21 percent to 12 percent of total capital inflows.[14]

The next major shifts occurred after the Mexican devaluation in 1995 when foreign direct investment soared by 40 percent overall and 65 percent of all direct foreign investment went to Asia in 1995. The following year a record net inflow of capital went into emerging markets.[15]

Compared to $34 billion in private capital that flowed to developing countries in 1987, $256 billion flowed there in 1997. But what goes in quickly can leave just as quickly. The Asian crisis struck in 1997–1998 and capital fled the emerging markets in 1997–1998 into the United States and industrialized Europe. For example, the five Asian economies hit worst (South Korea, Indonesia, Thailand, Malaysia, and the Philippines) received $93 billion in private capital in 1996 only to see an overall outflow of $12 billion in 1997—a $105 billion shift equal to 11 percent of their combined GNP.[16] While developing countries received a record $256 billion of private capital in 1997, according to the World Bank, capital flows fell sharply after the Asian financial dam broke. The breakdown of the Russian economy, the worst Japanese recession since World War II, and devaluations in Brazil, Mexico, and Venezuela in 1998 merely intensified this trend as capital sought safe havens in the most stable industrialized countries. Even the capital markets of Canada were under pressure. Merrill Lynch announced a global credit crunch, anticipating a broad deflationary slowdown worldwide.[17]

INTERPRETATIONS AND IMPLICATIONS

THE LEARNING CONTAGION OF STOCK MARKET AND FINANCIAL MERGERS

Global capital flows are typified by "collective learning"—sporting the euphemism "contagion"—in the sense that when managers of institutional investment hear of negative economic news, such as a devaluation in a country from a colleague, they react ("learn") sooner rather than later. They shift their portfolio investments out of that country before they can harm the "performance ratings" that keep their stock mutual funds in business. This form of "collective learning" can have perverse effects: A mere unsubstantiated rumor can lead to large shifts of investment actually bringing about a devaluation that might otherwise have been unnecessary—a negative self-fulfilling prophecy.

Waves of mass collective learning become contagious as evident in other forms: Companies merge because competitors have just become bigger and presumably stronger by merging. Even stock markets merge in order to compete with other stock markets. Globalization has so increased the tempo of trans-actions in the world economy that managers feel pressured to act sponta-neously before they have had time to evaluate the effects of their behavior, on the assumption that their clients will forgive them for acting too soon more eas-ily than for reacting too late. Corporate managers often calculate that take-overs are the fastest way to build revenue and profits, particularly in a time of booming markets when it is easy to issue stock.

In the United States alone, the record volume of mergers between com-panies in 1996 of $626 billion was topped by nearly 50 percent when mergers and acquisitions reached $919 billion in 1997. Worldcom's offer of $36.5 billion to acquire the MCI Communications Corporation epitomizes this trend in the telecommunications industry—the leading sector for mergers and acquisitions in 1997 ($90 billion in total announced values). The runner-up sectors for that year in U.S. mergers were commercial banking ($75 billion), investment firms ($58 billion), hotels and casinos ($46 billion), and utilities ($42 billion). Some economists suggest that such merger and acquisition activity occurs in the late stage of expansion in a business cycle, just before contraction starts to set in. Indeed, as Figure 4-1 (on page 119) illustrates, while the value of mergers and acquisitions in the United States continued to increase in 1998, the quan-tity declined sharply.

When this huge merger wave began in the 1980s, Martin Lipton, of the law firm Wachtell, Lipton, invented a "poison pill" or "flip-over" to prevent some-one from acquiring a firm: This took the form of a written contractual clause giv-ing the shareholders of an acquired firm the right to buy shares in the new combined entity at a large discount (for example, 50 percent), diluting any gain to the bidder. The motive was to protect shareholders against offers that were too low. The poison pill became so popular that it became routine. But the negative implication is that incompetent managers can protect themselves from being taken over through this means. The rules of "casino capitalism" be-came increasingly complex.

The fast merger activity gave the impression that investors were placing bets on fantasy growth potential and synergies that might emerge in the future rather than investing in concrete assets or businesses that they understand. Masses of people increasingly invest in a blur of products and services, which management consultants Stan Davis and Christopher Meyer refer to as *offers*: Offers are "productized" services and "servicized" products.[18] People are in-vesting in intangibles and gambling on the interconnectivity of companies to bring in profits from a whole that is more than the sum of its parts.

If you combine massive listings of these intangibles together and give them short acronyms as labels, you have the essence of what today is referred to as a *stock market*. There are tangible things produced by many of the compa-nies listed on a stock exchange. But most investors buying shares treat the companies as if they were intangible offers, rarely understanding what is real-ly behind the labels. And stock exchanges themselves have been merging to consolidate against competition from other stock exchanges; not only did the American stock exchange combine with NASDAQ to better compete with the New York Stock Exchange, but the London and Frankfurt stock exchanges merged in 1998 in order to better compete with the Americans.

From the viewpoint of political economy, the British and Germans united without the French in order to maintain the classical liberal economic principles that they wanted to govern the merger. Meanwhile, the French protested bitterly at being declassed and left on the sidelines, arguing that the Germans had abused their position as headquarters for the emerging European Central Bank as a launching pad for this merger. In response to the complaint by Jean-Francois Theodore, the president of the Paris stock exchange, that the London-Frankfurt exchange axis treated the rest of Europe's markets like second-class citizens, the Germans made the French an offer that only added insult to injury: Paris could join the alliance as a junior partner with a 20 percent stake compared to 40 percent each for Frankfurt and London. In angry response Theodore proposed an alliance of the French stock exchange with those of Milan, Madrid, and the Benelux countries. The only problem was that his presumed alliance partners were not keen on the idea. The French, never to be underestimated diplomatically, simultaneously explored links with the New York Stock Exchange. But neither the New York Stock Exchange or the second largest Nasdaq stock market were anxious to seal a deal that would cut out a link with London or Frankfurt. In terms of stock market capitalization as of 1998, London's (just over $2 trillion) was almost twice the size of Germany's (just over $1 trillion), which was larger than that of France (under $1 trillion).[19]

MORAL HAZARD VERSUS THE HAZARD OF BEING MORAL

Given the "Social Darwinist" mergers typifying casino capitalism, it is little wonder that the lender of last resort—officially the IMF—found itself up against the limit of its resources when a crisis unfolded involving emerging countries. The purses behind the IMF, after all, were those same industrialized countries trying to outposition each other in the merger sweepstakes while simultaneously cutting their budget deficits, in part to make themselves more attractive for foreign capital. While the business cycles seemed to smooth out to mere ripples in the industrialized countries, the same could not be said for emerging economies. The United States experienced an unprecedented nine-year stock market boom in the 1990s and policymakers debated as to whether a 2.5 or 3.5 percent growth rate would be best for continued stability of financial markets. In the same period, in a mere four years the growth rate in Argentina went from a positive 7 percent to a negative 4 percent and back to a positive 8 percent, while the growth rate fell over 20 percent in various Eastern European nations and Russia in the early 1990s. The spill-over from the Asian crisis of 1997–1998 to Latin America and transitional economies in Eastern Europe, particularly Russia, threatened the IMF with bankruptcy.

U.S. Treasury Secretary Robert Rubin's strategy to win more funding from the U.S. Congress for the IMF ($14 billion in 1998) was to come out firmly against the risk of *moral hazard*—the danger of promising to bail out speculative investors who plough money into high risk situations figuring that the countries would be too important to fail and the IMF or U.S. Treasury would ultimately guarantee them from losing their money.

The world economy was suddenly confronted in 1998 with a global credit crunch and once more with the dilemma John Maynard Keynes faced at Bretton Woods: how to organize international institutions that could provide enough liquidity to head off global deflation, if not depression, while simultaneously maintaining a credible, stable global money and credit system with insurance instruments for crises. Credibility or credit? That was the question: how to provide liquidity with appropriate conditionality that would assure future striving toward credit-worthiness....

Three main schools of thought emerged during the global financial crises of 1997–1998: (1) the classical, conservative free-market school advocating the elimination of the IMF and promoting free capital flows as complementary to free trade flows for the sake of global economic growth; (2) the status quo liberal reformist school represented by the U.S. Treasury Department and the IMF; and (3) the radical restructuring school demanding a new world financial institution or Board of Overseers to establish and enforce universal bank and credit lending standards and monitoring of performance.

The Free Market School   The ultimate case for the classical free market school was made by former U.S. Secretary of State George Shultz, former Secretary of Treasury William Simon, and former chairman of Citicorp/Citibank, Walter Wriston, in 1998. They argued that the IMF overplayed its hand in the Asian crisis and that the expectation of massive IMF intervention "spurred a global meltdown of financial markets." The Asian bailout of between $118 and $160 billion was set up by the $30 billion IMF bailout of Mexico in 1995, leading governments and lenders to anticipate that they would be rescued but not the people, who always have to suffer from the IMF-mandated austerity measures. Without the promise of the bailout, lenders would presumably not have been as likely to make bad loans and investors would have been more cautious, knowing that they would have to share the pain of their own risks (the moral hazard argument). The U.S. Congress, therefore, should grant no new money to the IMF, and abolish it since the organization is "ineffective, unnecessary and obsolete."[20]

The assumption of the classical laissez-faire approach is that transparent free markets will reward good investments and punish bad ones, rationally directing capital to where it is most efficient for world economic growth. Safety nets built in by the IMF, on the other hand, muck up this rationality, and involve perverse incentives raising the moral hazard of giving private speculators some assurance that their bad bets will be covered with public bail-outs. Just as states should leave business to the markets domestically, international capital flows should be left to the international markets with the least government intervention possible.

The Liberal Reformist School   The liberal reformist school seeks to head off radical institutional change, arguing that while the IMF and other international institutions have their weaknesses, they should not be eradicated nor replaced, but reformed for the challenges presented by the globalized economy. They argue, in short, for the status quo plus. Two key spokesmen for this position were Stanley Fischer, first deputy managing director of the IMF, and Robert Rubin, U.S. treasury secretary in the Clinton administration.

While Fisher did not deny that the IMF failed to see the worst of the Asian crisis coming, he advocated five reforms to make the IMF and emerging economies more effective in crisis management in the future: (1) More timely, accurate and comprehensive data must be provided to the IMF, particularly greater transparency concerning forward transactions by central banks; (2) enhance effectiveness of IMF surveillance and transparency to ensure country exchange rate regimes are consistent with other policies and sustainable capital inflows; (3) strengthen domestic financial systems by ensuring compliance with the twenty-five core standards of the Basle Committee on Banking Supervision of 1997; (4) encourage countries to adopt international standards in bankruptcy codes, securities training, and corporate governance, including accounting; (5) sequence liberalization in opening countries' capital accounts rather than either pervasive capital controls or a rush to full liberalization.[21] Moreover, Fischer denied that the availability of IMF programs encourages reckless behavior by countries: "For most investors in the Asian crisis countries, that must have seemed like a bitter joke."[22]

Backing up Fischer's position are a number of factors. The IMF has no legal power to extend guarantees and there is, therefore, no assurance that the institution will intervene in every balance-of-payments crisis. There is little evidence that the 1995 Mexican bailout produced an Asian lending boom, but merely that capital flows to Asia did not fall as sharply since the area was perceived to be much more creditworthy. Nor do IMF actions prevent losses: $40 billion in investments were wiped out in Mexico even though the United States and IMF headed off default by the Mexican government. IMF "conditionality" terms are harsh to the point of sometimes being counterproductive, so governments do not see IMF bailouts as a an attractive alternative if they can avoid it. Lacking enforcement power, the IMF cannot seize assets or force any country into bankruptcy court. And as indicated in Chapter 2, the cozy guarantees made by Asian governments to reckless banks precipitated the financial crisis.[23]

Treasury Secretary Robert Rubin called for an effort to "modernise the architecture of the international financial markets" while largely going along with the thrust of Fischer's suggestions. Stating that "We won't spend a nickel to help a bank or an investor," Rubin clearly voiced concern about moral hazards.

In a so-called "G-22" meeting (the G-7 industrialized countries plus the fifteen most important emerging economies) before the annual conference of the IMF and World Bank in October of 1998, President Clinton proposed a reform plan for the IMF to give it the power and resources to intervene early and proactively before a serious devaluation occurred, rather than waiting with too little too late. Some of these reforms were subsequently adopted and applied with some success in Brazil.

The Radical Restructuring School   Referring to the liberal reformist school as "the Wall Street-Treasury" complex (as in the former "military-industrial complex"), economist Jagdish Bhagwati argued that this view identifies the interest of Wall Street with the good of the world and misapplies the virtues of free market ideology in trade to support the unregulated mobility of global capital flows. The supposed enormous benefits of the free flow of capital across borders are not persuasive, according to Bhagwati, while the costs are becoming more apparent as the "mad money" system is driven more by volatile financial markets than by governments.[24] Political economist Dani Rodik examined capital liberalization in 100 countries between 1975 and 1989 in terms of growth, investment, inflation, per capita income, and educational levels and found that capital mobility had no significant impact on counties' economic fortunes.[25] The quality of evidence for or against capital mobility is, indeed, weak: No statistical distinction is usually made between liberalizing foreign direct investment (seen as good for growth by most economists) and panic-prone portfolio investment, which often tends to come and to leave too quickly.[26]

However, the roller-coaster effects of fast-moving capital flows have led to calls for a radical restructuring of international financial institutions from experts who have benefited enough from these waves to know. George Soros, who made a fortune in speculating against the British pound, argued that "international capital movements need to be supervised and the allocation of credit regulated" and called for establishing an "International Credit Insurance Corporation" to guarantee private sector loans up to a certain amount for a modest fee while providing that countries must submit a complete financial statement of their situation in order to qualify. A less controversial expert, Wall Street economist Henry Kaufmann, proposed setting up a Board of Overseers of Major International Institutions and Markets to set minimum capital requirements for institutions, coordinate uniform standards for lending and accounting, and to monitor performance. Those not meeting the criteria would be limited in their ability to borrow, lend, or sell.[27]

Elsewhere I have suggested that the Bank for International Settlements (BIS) could become the embryo for a World Central Bank by becoming "a transparency shop" specializing in technical functions such as the transparency of international accounting standards, banking and investment firm regulations, and other tasks too time-consuming or bothersome for the IMF, World Bank, Federal Reserve Bank, or European Central Bank.[28]

Although national resistance for the sake of protecting state sovereignty can be expected to such proposals, some sort of board may be needed to head off the trend to use the IMF as lender of first resort rather than last resort in crisis situations. In this inevitable restructuring of international institutions, long-term environmental sustainability is as important to consider as short-term liquidity. One could build in a prerequisite that only governments who target their subsidies for the private sector toward green entrepreneurship or environmentally and socially responsible start-up companies qualify for any long-term credits.[29] Such a criterion could complement the suggestion for the IMF to condition its assistance on countries' penalizing all lenders of foreign currency in the event IMF intervention is required, and having each country require that creditors automatically lose some of their principal when their debt matures and is not extended.[30] The ultimate solution may point toward the suggestion of German economist Wilhelm Hankel that a world central bank indeed be created to monitor currency and banking credit systems. Without regulations by such a central institution, the developed countries will continue to be overbanked and the developing countries underbanked.[31]

At issue is not merely creating an international system that forces banks and speculative investors to suffer the pain of their losses due to "moral hazard." Rather, new and stable sources of liquidity are necessary to keep economic growth and job-creation going worldwide in an era of global deflation—backed by an institution that functions globally as well as the Federal Reserve Bank does nationally in the United States. The moral issue is environmentally sustainable job creation for millions of unemployed people who suffer the existential losses of casino capitalism and of global business cycles that hit the developing countries the hardest.

Questions for Thought

1. Compare short-term, middle-term, and long-term business cycles and try to explain why short-term cycles have appeared to become more moderate in the developed countries. How does the construction cycle illustrate the importance of knowing the cycle particular to the specific economic sector in which you work?

2. Why is the emerging "weightless economy" less sensitive to interest rates? Why do mergers and acquisitions seem to be concentrated heavily in these "soft" sectors?

3. How might you interpret the issues of the 2000 American presidential election in terms of the politics of business cycles?

4. Describe the evolution in shifts in global patterns of capital flow since the middle of the twentieth century. What are the implications of the shift to the dominance of the private sector for global social justice?

5. Explain why the "learning contagion" of stock market shifts and financial mergers occurs. Is the hegemony of the Federal Reserve in combination with a U.S. Treasury Department run like an investment bank a viable long-term solution?

6. Compare and contrast the proposed solutions of the free-market school, the liberal reformist school, and the radical restructuring school of thought to the dilemma of moral hazard. Why are environmental sustainability and the formation of a world central bank both apt to be pushed off of the political agenda of established elites?

NOTES

1. See "Special Issue: The Economic Foundations of War," *International Studies Quarterly* 27, no. 4 (December 1983), particularly the article by Raimo Yayrynen: 389–418.

2. Alvin H. Hansen, *Fiscal Policy and Business Cycles* (New York: W. W. Norton, 1941), pp. 18–24.

3. Alekandr Solzhenitsyn, *The Gulag Archipelago* (New York: Harper & Row, 1974), p. 50 fn.

4. N. D. Kondratieff, "The Long Waves in Economics Life," *Review of Economic Statistics* 17 (November 1935). Also see George Garvy, "Kondratieff's Theory of Long Cycles," *Review of Economic Statistics* 25 (November 1943); and W. W. Rostow, "Kondratieff, Schumpeter, and Kuznets: Trend Periods Revisited," *Journal of Economic History* 35, no. 4 (December 1975). Also see W. W. Rostow, *Why the Poor Get Richer and the Rich Slow Down* (Austin, TX: University of Texas Press, 1980), Chapter 1 and 2. See also Jay W. Forrester, "A Great Depression Ahead?" *The Futurist* (December 1978): 379–385.

5. Benedetto Croce, *History of Europe in the Nineteenth Century* (New York: Harcourt, Brace and World, 1963, originally published in 1933), p. 37.

6. Gavin Cameron, "Economic Growth in the Information Age: From Physical Capital to Weightless Economy," *Journal of International Affairs* (New York) 51, no. 2 (spring 1998): 447–471.

7. Randy Merk, "The Evolution of the Business Cycle," *American Century, Investor Perspective* (Third Quarter 1997): 4. See also John M. Wells, "Business Cycles, Seasonal Cycles, and Common Trends," *Journal of Macroeconomics* 19, no. 3 (summer 1997): 443ff. And Danny Quah, "One Business Cycle and One Trend from (Many), Many Disaggregates," *European Economic Review* 1997 38, no. 3–4: 605–609.

8. Steven Weber, "The End of the Business Cycle?" *Foreign Affairs* 76, no. 4 (July/August 1997): 70.

9. Mark Rupert, "Contesting Hegemony: Americanism and Far-Right Ideologies of Globalization," in *Constituting International Political Economy*, ed. Kurth Burch and Robert A. Denemark (Boulder, CO: Lynne Rienner Publishers, 1997), p.114. For the *absence* of U.S. hegemony in twentieth century painting, see Michael Kimmelman, "A Century of Art: Just How American Was It?" *New York Times*, April 18, 1999.

10. William Crouse, "Future Trends in International Business," Panel at conference on The Increasing Internationalization of Business, Pace University, White Plains, New York, March 6, 1982.

11. Edward Tufte, *Political Control of the Economy* (Princeton, NJ: Princeton University Press, 1978), pp. 10–11.

12. Ricardo Hausmann, "Will Volatility Kill Market Democracy?" *Foreign Policy*, no. 108 (fall 1997): 60.

13. Dean Foust, "Alan Greenspan: An Unlikely Guru," *Business Week*, August 31, 1998, 70.

14. Stephany Griffith-Jones and Barbara Stallings, "New Global Financial Trends: Implications for Development," *Journal of Interamerican Studies and World Affairs* 37, no. 3 (fall 1995): 59.

15. International Monetary Fund, "International Capital Markets: Developments," *Prospects and Key Policy Issues* (Washington, D.C.: IMF, September 1997): 1.

16. "Towards A New Financial System: The Perils of Global Capital," *The Economist*, April 11, 1998, 52.

17. Merrill Lynch, "The Global Credit Crunch," August 24, 1998.

18. Stan Davis and Christopher Meyer, *Blur: The Speed of Change in the Connected Economy* (Reading, MA: Addison-Wesley, 1998), p. 22.

19. "What About Others?" *The Economist*, July 25, 1998, 75–76.

20. George Shultz, William Simon, and Walter Wriston, "Who Needs the IMF?" *Wall Street Journal*, February 3, 1998, Op-Ed.

21. Stanley Fischer, "IMF and Crisis Prevention," *Financial Times*, March 10, 1998, p. 12.

22. Kevin Muehring, "Myths of Moral Hazard," *Institutional Investor* (New York) 32, no. 4 (April 1998): 37.

23. Ibid, pp. 33–39.

24. Jagdish Bhagwati, "The Capital Myth," *Foreign Affairs* 77, no. 3: 7–12; and Susan Strange, *Mad Money: When Markets Outgrow Governments* (Ann Arbor, MI: University of Michigan Press, 1998).

25. Dani Rodik, "Should the IMF Pursue Capital-Account Convertibility? *Essay in International Finance*, no. 207 (Princeton, NJ: Princeton University, 1998).

26. "Capital Controversies," *The Economist*, May 23, 1998, 72.

27. Richard Haass and Robert Litan, "Globalization and Its Discontents," *Foreign Affairs* 77, no. 3 (May/June 1998): 2–6.

28. Robert Isaak, "A World Central Bank: To Be or Not to Be?" In Wilhelm Nölling, Karl Albrecht Schachtscheider, and Joachim Starbatty, *Währungsunion und Weltwirtschaft* (Stuttgart: Lucius and Lucius, 1999), pp. 255–264.

29. Robert Isaak, *Green Logic: Ecopreneurship, Theory and Ethics* (Sheffield, U.K.: Greenleaf Publishers, 1998); U.S. edition (West Hartford, CT: Kumarian Press, 1999).

30. Haass and Litan, p. 5.

31. Wilhelm Hankel, *Das grosse Geld-Theater: Uber DM, Dollar, Rubel und Ecu* (Stuttgart: Deutsche Verlags-Anstalt, 1995). As Hankel pointed out in personal correspondence (2/12/99) with the author, the dream of a world central bank goes back to the last chapter of A *Treatise on Money* (1930) of John Maynard Keynes who also saw the potential in the Bank for International Settlements to become a central bank of central banks with a supranational unit of account.

GLOBALIZATION AND RESISTANCE

These fragments are the disjecta membra [scattered parts] of an elusive, coveted and vaguely scented knowledge.

—Guido Ceronetti

In social manipulation our tools are people, and people learn, and they acquire habits which are more subtle and pervasive than the tricks which the blueprinter teaches them.

—Gregory Bateson, *Social Planning and the Concept of Deutero-Learning* (1972)

The open world economy—whatever the rhetoric of businessmen and economists—is a political construct, neither natural nor self-sustaining. Globalization—which entails not simply the opening of markets but also societies—has been a product of American foreign policy over 50 years.

—Fareed Zakaria, *Our Hollow Hegemony* (1998)

AT THE END OF THE TWENTIETH CENTURY, GLOBALIZATION LED TO A CONTAGION OF FINANCIAL meltdown as the Asian crisis spread to other emerging economies and then threatened the industrialized nations with its deflationary impact. This panic or contagious behavior of bankers and investors withdrawing money can be seen as one negative mode of "collective learning," as individuals moved in a herdlike fashion to avoid perceived risk. A collective learning approach to international political economy assumes that a people's investment, competitive behavior, and sense of reciprocity (if not fair play) are not just individual or abstract phenomena. Rather they result from a social learning pattern with a specific organizational context and cultural pattern. We learn not just from the teacher but from the milieu in the classroom. Our values are shaped not just by the ends or objects obtained by those to whom we grant deference, but by the rules of the game or means that our political leaders, bankers, and corporate managers use to get to their ends.

Malaysia's imposition of controls on capital flows constituted an angry protest against dependence on the whims of speculative foreign investors in the 1990s— a symbolic effort to preserve some sense of cultural integrity and political sovereignty from turbulent financial storms resulting from the globalization of the world's financial markets, technology, and sources of information. Or, to take another example that counters the advocacy of globalization for the sake of economic growth before all else, the Swedes would not be so generous with foreign aid and willing to sacrifice great ranges of personal income if the neocorporatist culture of their society did not place equality of economic opportunity before individual self-aggrandizement.

This book started with the analogy of a tale by O. Henry. The political authority of a society broke down not because of the economic asymmetry or inequality itself but because of the collective learning by the people when foreign goods were introduced in a situation of high demand and structured scarcity. The inequality was the fuel; but the recognition that desired goods were being arbitrarily withheld was the match. The book ends with a similar moral: While capitalist models of political economy may win in the short and medium term as means to maximize economic growth, standards of living, and individual freedom, the legitimacy of elites in such societies will be undermined to the extent wealth gaps or ratios between high and low incomes become too extreme. Or, as Lord Overstone put it, "No warning can save a people determined to grow suddenly rich." Aristotle argued that stable democracy requires a large middle class. Extremes of wealth and poverty and of economic opportunity undermine the legitimacy of democratic societies and the stability of global political economic systems. We live in a era in which Americans and Europeans spend $17 billion a year on pet food—$4 billion more than the estimated annual additional total needed to provide basic health and nutrition for everyone in the world. Meanwhile, the average African household at the end of the twentieth century consumed 20 percent less than it did twenty-five years before.

If an undemocratic world economy is envisioned as one large, potential democratic society, extremes of rich and poor and blatantly unequal economic opportunities in different nations undermine the legitimacy of the existing world order, destabilizing it. Thus the Asian money crisis at the end of the twentieth century was no accident: It was a perceived crisis of legitimacy, a psychological and political crisis as much as it was a financial and economic one. And transnational terrorism that recurrently makes itself apparent is motivated, in part, by a sense of poor minority cultures being declassed and marginalized by the existing capitalist system: The rules appear to be heavily loaded not only against one's self but against one's people. While this general diagnosis of the consequences of extreme inequality seems obvious, effective political economic recipes to do something about the situation are not.

DEFINING THE SITUATION

International political economy is the study of the politics behind the economic relations among peoples and nations in order to assess their relative wealth and power. Anglo-American ideology structured the institutional context of international economic exchanges during the nineteenth and twentieth centuries through a *pax Britannica* followed by a *pax Americana*. The socialist antithesis to this hegemony—whether in its Soviet or Chinese or nonaligned manifestations—failed. However, the cold war struggles during the twentieth century did serve to undermine the legitimacy and financial soundness of the Anglo-American order. Great Britain was already financially crippled by the end of World War II. But U.S. military spending, hyped up to fever pitch during that war, led the way to push the Americans into becoming the world's greatest national debtor (four times that of Brazil) in absolute terms by the end of the 1980s. This was mitigated only by the fact that the U.S. debt was in its own currency and that currency happened still to be the world's key reserve currency. That the foreign debt of the United States grew to over $1 trillion by the end of the twentieth century, while the European Union countries were able to avoid foreign debt, may be a precursor to a future shift in economic power. Significantly, at the end of the 1990s the Europeans were logging in balance of payments surpluses while the United States was carrying hundreds of billions of dollars in annual balance of payments deficits. The Americans ended the twentieth century attempting to run hegemony on the cheap. As editor of *Foreign Affairs* Fareed Zakaria put it: "Washington has enjoyed playing the part of sole superpower.... But it has not wanted to pay the bills in political capital, energy, attention or dollars."[1]

As the USSR and United States discovered they could no longer afford their strategic arms race, the bipolar world became increasingly multipolar. International change became increasingly unpredictable: The greater the number of major players, the greater the uncertainty in global outcomes. Not only did a number of other nations obtain nuclear weapons, but Japan, Western Europe, and newly industrializing countries became world-class economic competitors in a number of fields. Ideologically, First, Third, and Fourth Worlds proliferated. Second (socialist) Worlds diminished. And within these "Worlds" the trend was toward disintegration within states for the sake of the ethnic autonomy of small, self-contained units. Those used to viewing world affairs with binoculars now were looking through a kaleidoscope. With the spread of multipolarity—militarily, technologically, economically, and ideologically—the primacy of global logic was countered with ethnic revolts. But the old, industrialized countries increased their arms sales to feed the frenzy of local and regional conflicts away from home. The inequality between nations and peoples became more pronounced as technological developments and socioeconomic change accelerated both the tempo of life and the collective adaptations necessary to remain internationally competitive. Globalization—constantly pushed by a U.S. foreign policy advocating open markets—became more transparent: Finance, markets, technology, information flows, transportation, institutions and product standardization were integrated throughout the world. And hand in hand with globalization came fragmentation into local and regional groups, as many peoples and regions fell further behind the dominant trends, often resisting to protect the integrity of what was left of their traditional culture and way of being.

The cultural perception of what globalization means depends on where one is standing. For most Americans, globalization means "trade," particularly in the context of the raising or lowering of their living standards. However, two-way trade in goods and services makes up less than 30 percent of the U.S. economy. From the structuralist perspective globalization may be interpreted as merely an astute marketing gimmick on the part of the financial media to win acceptance for an international revolution in global finance. The value of total financial assets increased two and a half times faster than the aggregate Gross Domestic Product of all rich industrial economies since 1980, while the volume of trading in currencies, bonds, and equities increased five times faster.[2] For other countries, like Brazil, for example, globalization means the spread of the destructive liberal economic model of the North industrialized nations to the Third World, thereby forcing the South to mimic not merely the growth strategies but the ecological destruction of the North. While there is apparent consensus in favor of sustainable development by North and South alike, there is a striking absence of political initiatives to transform the economic, social, and political institutions that are responsible for the contemporary style of economic development resulting from globalization.[3] The watered-down standards on green-house gas emissions of the 1997 Kyoto protocol, which may or may not be enforced, demonstrate the difficulty.

Globalization would integrate and homogenize us all, but everyone does not want to be integrated and force-fed values they did not select themselves. A salient example is the Northern League's utopian movement to secede in Northern Italy and create a new state, "Patania." Globalization results in a democratic deficit.

Not only do transnational value and idea flows undermine indigenous cultural loyalties: "freed trade" that goes global creates new jobs that demand new skills while destroying old jobs, training routines, traditions, and psychological groundings. Production structures are increasingly aimed at production for regional or global markets. Financial structures widen their sights and aim for short-term returns on investment globally more than regionally or locally. The concept of retaining promising jobs, investments, or emotional stakes in one's locality has become an anachronism. Mobility is everything; loyalty to one community makes one vulnerable. Anticipating change in order to outposition it and to be less vulnerable, people are motivated to travel frequently to some other place: Economic growth stimulates only to dislocate. Those who refuse to move, travel, or restructure are passed by economically and slip into a shadow economy on the periphery of development. Globalization targets only to marginalize.

The accelerating rates of technological change and mobility of capital are the engines of globalization. These accelerations have resulted in three dilemmas related to the decline of the power of the state, according to political economist Susan Strange: (1) National and global market economies need a lender of last resort to give confidence to banks and financial markets and to apply Keynesian logic in economic downturns, but neither former hegemonial states nor international organizations can be counted on any longer to fulfill these tasks; (2) greatly empowered multinational corporations are motivated to destroy and pollute the earth, while states are handicapped in their efforts at countervailing power and regulation due to principles of sovereignty in international law; and (3) the shift of power from states to corporations has created international and nonstate authorities that are not accountable, and are often not transparent, thus creating a democratic deficit in all globalized countries.[4]

Meanwhile, as the twentieth century came to a close most of the world's people experienced economic recession—a sort of great unwinding of the promises of the post-cold-war economic era. Stable political regimes became an increasingly important factor in attracting foreign capital: Americans could much more easily export their casino capitalism than they could the conservative liberal framework that gave their political system predictability even as their president underwent impeachment hearings. The political stability, in turn, gave American entrepreneurs, small and large, a taken-for-granted springboard or maintenance base for their risk-taking: The GDP of California was greater than the GNP of China; the GDP of New York larger than the GNP of Canada; and the GDP of Alabama topped the GNP of Israel.[5] The Europeans attempted to use the founding of the Euro currency to the same effect, but without clear consensus on domestic political ground rules or a natural, individualistic risk-provoking culture independent of the state. The primacy put upon effectively managing economic risk became paramount in both rich countries and poor.

THE MAINTENANCE THESIS: MANAGING ECONOMIC RISK

The more dependent a country is, the more its managers usually seek control and stability. Or at least they strive for the appearance of equilibrium, which keeps them in power and makes their domestic situation seem predictable enough to outsiders to attract foreign aid and investment. Managers in wealthier or more independent countries, in contrast, can take this equilibrium or maintenance base for granted, using it as a springboard for entrepreneurial risk and technological innovation. Financial credit, too, flows more automatically to stable collectivities to support their risks.

Many managers in such a well-maintained milieu, however, do not take advantage of this dynamic management potential inherent in their privileged position. They prefer to minimize risks for the sake of preserving a comfortable routine and a status quo friendly to their interests, falling into a maintenance syndrome. Thus, there are distinctive but understandable conservative tendencies on the part of managers in both rich and poor countries to embrace stability and to optimize existing balances of power rather than to make policies aimed at radical change or long-term risk to adjust to the competitiveness required in the rapidly changing global economy. The maintenance base is a boundaried social system or organization oriented toward internal stability, security, efficiency, and risk-reduction. The "inside" perspective of the maintenance base contrasts with the "outside" efforts at entrepreneurial innovation, risk-taking, adaptation, and effectiveness in terms of changing external markets in the global environment. Effective collective learning in the world economy involves going from the inside out once the efficiency of the maintenance base can be taken for granted and can help to target entrepreneurial risks in new global markets. To become too preoccupied within the maintenance base is to be soon passed by as global competitors aggressively pursue new global opportunities from their home bases.

On the other hand, to diffuse oneself in too many risk-taking ventures at once, at the expense of neglecting the maintenance base, is similar to having too many irons in the fire, or to attacking with too many figures at once in a chess game without backing them up with protection. All risks need not be hedged, but they need to be collectively thought through. Risk-taking must be targeted after careful positioning and followed up. Extraordinary economic success over time demands a flexible yet tightly coordinated institutional infrastructure capable of backing up collective entrepreneurial targeting.

In the late twentieth century, economic advantages initially went to nations with a feudal, hierarchical tradition and taken-for-granted maintenance base of order that experienced an entrepreneurial break from this order. Typically their security needs were covered by others and they found ready access to finance and technology in a growing world economy: West Germany, Japan and South Korea, for example. The past hierarchical traditions of these countries underscored the importance of education and respect for those older and wiser with more experience. Consensus-building cultural schemata such as "shame" (in Japan) and "order" (in Germany) steered collective learning. A deep-seated social consensus at the maintenance base permitted such societies to concentrate their collective energies on adapting to opportunities and innovations abroad. However, when the world economy shifted from a focus on manufacturing to services, this very solidarity blocked creativity and flexibility in finance and technology. Indeed, in feudal societies of the past, the elites, whose landed status and legitimacy were displaced by modernization and democracy, attempted to recover their status through entrepreneurial efforts, thus bringing new economic life to the maintenance base of their countries as well as to their families. Recall the cases of the Balinese aristocracy, the samurai of Japan, or, more recently, the restoration of the Minsheng Shipping Company family as the first large private company allowed to operate outside the state-planning system in the People's Republic of China. The resurrection of large German firms after World War II and the reincarnation of the Japanese *zaibatsu* as *sogoshosha* in postwar Japan are other cases in point. In times of economic crisis or structural stalemate, political economy managers call on the support of old elites and successful economic organizations of the past, taking calculated entrepreneurial risks to breathe new life into their national economies.

Whereas nations with "industrialized" feudal or hierarchical pasts often represent tight ships of order in the international chaos of global political economy, the United States represents the maintenance of domestic disorder or chaos for the sake of individual freedom and dynamic markets. This stable chaos keeps the

Americans from being "ordered" around by hierarchical authorities and stimulates innovative creativity, as people cast off relationships, careers, businesses, homes, and lifestyles like unfashionable clothing in a restless, nonstop environment of mobility. Small wonder that savings rates are low, consumption high, markets innovative, and debt mushrooming in a country whose basic behavioral ground rules are freedom of action and the individual desire to freely choose to do well that which others in the society tell them is fashionable or appropriate. The possibility of exporting this consumer-led, democratic chaos of innovative mobility to other countries is limited by cultural resistance and tradition, despite American foreign policy efforts to transform them. The absence of a feudal experience in American history sets the nation apart from many others, making it as hard for Americans to understand those with feudal pasts as it is for citizens of countries with former feudal ties to understand a nation without them. It should come as no surprise that the United States became the dynamic source of global innovation, security, and credit in the twentieth century for other nations constrained by feudal/hierarchical pasts and defeats, given the different resource bases and cultural heritages.

SPEED LIMITS AND INFORMATION OVERLOAD:
ACCELERATION VERSUS RETARDATION

The tempo of socioeconomic and technological change speeded up intensely in the atomic century in which the response time for the presidents of Russia and the United States to decide whether or not a surprise nuclear attack signaled on the radar was real was cut to less than ten minutes. Peoples all over the earth found themselves future-shocked and overloaded with information. The Russian scientist Pavlov discovered that animals could be driven crazy if given too much stimulation or choice. The tempo of socioeconomic change threatens to have this Pavlovian effect upon the human animal. There are clear limits to how much information a human being or group of human beings can absorb and how fast human beings can be asked to think or to move without making irrational choices or breaking down.

In a high-tech, high-information global economy, information becomes power—but not just any information. The key to collective learning for economic and political effectiveness is to slow down the information flow, analyze it, select only the critical data for a clearly defined purpose, focus attention, and act on this targeted information, getting as much feedback as quickly as possible once action has been taken. Significant information is that "ah ha" phenomenon that radically changes how we see the world and that shakes us out of old routines or beliefs. Such a meaningful "information storm" (brainstorm) or breakthrough causes the socialist to realize one cannot stimulate economic growth without creating explicitly unequal material incentives, or causes the capitalist to see that the social control of violence or maintenance of social harmony depends

on explicit limitations upon human freedom and upon extreme income disparities. Clearly it is more comfortable to maintain conventional worldviews without
having such information-storm breakdowns (or lighting ups). But the tempo of
global economic change and the pervasiveness of international communications
guarantee that data overloads and information storms are inevitable for those
who continue to function as fully rational human beings capable of learning, leading to what Federal Reserve Chairman Alan Greenspan calls "the increased productivity of mistakes."

Speed control is perhaps the most underestimated phenomenon in international political economy. Speeding up and slowing down are equally important
strategic concepts, which can be used simultaneously in different sectors. Gorbachev tried desperately to get the Russian people to accept the concept of *uskorenie* (acceleration) in order to bring collective learning up to speed in furthering
his *perestroika* (restructuring) program. But the integrity of the Russian soul depends upon an extensive view of time, as eternal patience for the sake of eternal
values. The unhurried pace of life, which was the charm of Russian culture in the
nineteenth century (the Chekhov cachet), became a stumbling block for first Gorbachev's and then Yeltsin's desire for acceleration. Local ethnic communities
want autonomy for their cultural way of life first, distrusting state-sponsored programs of modernization. German Chancellor Helmut Kohl sped up the pace of German unification in February 1990 in order to outmaneuver the domestic political
opposition and to present the world with a fait accompli. He then paid the political price by losing the election in 1998, partly due to the high economic cost of
unification and his failure to halve the level of unemployment as he promised
(the cost of too much slowness?). President Carlos Salinas de Gortari of Mexico
did all he could to push NAFTA through quickly in 1993. The peso devaluation crisis followed a year later (the cost of too much speed?) And Prime Minister Mahathir Mohamad of Malaysia used state financial disincentives to slow down
speculative stock investment into his economy in 1994, which threatened to raise
the inflation rate. In 1998 he limited foreign investment and blocked foreign capital from leaving the country for a year.

On another front, no insignificant part of the success of the Japanese political economy in the post-World War II era was its ability to slow down the decision-making process by use of *nemawashi*, or the informal shaking down of ideas
among those who will be affected by them in order to prepare the ground or consensus for effective innovation. This slowing down process permits each individual in the company to make suggestions and point out weaknesses before a change
becomes official, refining and targeting adaptations before they are instituted, and
getting everyone on board before innovation is launched. The downside of the
slowness, of course, was reflected in the overdelayed political reaction to the Japanese recession of the 1990s: The elite wanted a social and political consensus to precede economic reforms in a context of fragmented political interest groups.

Nevertheless, such a slowing-down-in-order-to-follow-through-with-all-on-
board process might be one some American elites could learn from. The traditional

U.S. chief executive officer typically rams changes down the throats of subordinates in memos from the top of the hierarchy, thus putting his status on the line before the flaws are removed or before the soil has been properly prepared for change among his subordinates. On the other hand, in the same organization there are no doubt individuals who have to be motivated to accelerate their work processes—indeed, people whose slowness may be a hidden protest against the arbitrary authority represented by impulsive orders from the top. Take a positive example of the use of *strategic retardation* (or slowing down): During the 1987 stock market crash, the head of the New York Stock Exchange prohibited computer programming for a few hours, requiring brokers to make buy or sell orders by hand. Slowing down the system meant that it did not have to be shut down, cooling off panic. In 1997, the IMF tried much less successfully to slow down the spreading Asian financial panic by injecting too little capital too late and with conditions attached to funding that typically stifled growth rather than increasing it. By 1998, the G-7 financial elite (led by the Clinton administration) recognized the difficulty and agreed to an emergency IMF credit line of billions of dollars to make loans to countries threatened by financial meltdown before it could take hold, in order to slow down the process.

The international manager must use a deliberate policy of retardation not only as a cooling off device, but also to focus attention upon the quality of results. On the other hand, the strategy of acceleration speeds up the process of change by identifying with it and positioning oneself on the cutting edge (as did Yeltsin in riding the Russian transformation) or pushing through fait accompli policy (such as German unification by Kohl).[6]

COLLECTIVE LEARNING AND CULTURAL RESISTANCE

Information overload implies that collective learning is most effective when it is arbitrarily delimited and targeted but in a way that breeds consensus and high morale rather than polarization and resistance. If knowledge is the orderly loss of information, the critical prerequisite to collective learning is to create a consensus upon the criteria for sorting the wheat from the chaff. Ideology is only an abstract and imperfect criterion in this regard as those who tried to apply the Stalinist model of political economy discovered. What we are dealing with here is a dynamic link between the micro and macro levels of analysis, which enables groups of people to learn things efficiently and to apply them effectively in the context of a rapidly changing global economy. Cultural schemata or prototypes of learning consolidate "legitimate" information.

Collective learning is social learning with a specific organizational context and cultural gestalt: It is a process of differentiating legitimate patterns of adaptive behavior to manage environmental change without losing cultural integrity. The concept gets beyond the overly psychological notion of social learning theory—the result of reciprocal interactions among person (cognition), behavior, and environmental situation. Collective learning accepts these elements of social learning theory, and particularly its assumption that individuals can learn from others vicariously or from modeling their own behavior after others whom they have observed. But collective learning emphasizes the collective gestalt or organizational pattern that delimits the schemata for learning or for resistance to change. Such a collective gestalt or cultural context presupposes the legitimacy of specific learning models, structures, and paradigms, and the exclusion of others.* It emphasizes deutero-learning or how people learn learnings, what they pick up from the learning process and milieu, not just the content of learning.

For example, in Bulgaria during the cold-war era, the successful manager of the state-owned company was traditionally the one with enough clout with his superiors in the party hierarchy to get a reduction in the annual production quota for his factory, even though this behavior contradicts the functional purpose of the enterprise. The socialist manager learned that lower quotas were easier to reach, meaning bonuses for himself and his workers. Less work also means more free time and a higher quality of life. The collective schemata in such a political economy encouraged the most "successful" individuals to reduce their output—a learning pattern picked up fast but not exactly a recipe for increasing international competitiveness.

To take another example, the American worker is often stimulated to dance the Olsonian rag: Behavior is guided by the assumption that the interests of one's self and one's own small group are different from the interests of the larger organization. The worker quickly learns to maximize his or her own personal interests, income, and job prospects regardless of the costs to the organization or firm since, in any case, he or she will cut and run and take a job soon with another firm. The critical cultural schemata are short-term, self-interest maximization, and "learning by burning." The job mobility built into the cultural context of the system means that large organizations get left holding the bills for the opportunity costs left behind by workers whom they have trained and nurtured.

The Japanese and, to some extent Europeans, reduced such opportunity costs by assuring core workers of formal or informal lifetime job security. This breeds an atmosphere of trust and social community in the organizational and cultural context, which often serves to nip labor disputes in the bud and encourages management to invest in lifetime training programs for workers who may be with them a lifetime. However, the drawback in this motivational milieu is that once again the worker will catch on to the real rules behind the formal commitments: Lifetime security may dampen the enthusiasm for extraordinary achievement or taking innovative risks. In a culture like the Japanese, "where the nail that sticks up gets hit," consensus can mean complacent followership and deter creativity. Even the remarkably effective Japanese quality circles (modeled originally on W. Edward Deming's criterion of quality being the reduction of variation) may best serve the

---

*The following are four influential types of collective learning: (1) reduction of error within a rigid frame; (2) open, synergistic networking based on trust; (3) radical quantum leaps for technological breakthroughs; and (4) striving for absolute excellence beyond all existing benchmarks.

function of improving processes already in place by cutting costs, reducing hazards, and eliminating defects, rather than nurturing the "antisystem" mentality that leads to creative, technological breakthroughs.

Finding the "right people" for creative breakthroughs presupposes a cultural as well as a functional selection that may leave the majority outside the system or that could even systematically discriminate against the most successful individuals. A person who believes that *Ogni mattina io rinasco* (Each morning, I am born anew) may have to work for himself or herself to find a superior willing to put up with this first principle. Yet firmly held first principles are essential to individual and cultural integrity. A person with "character" is one willing to fight the fashionable trends or repressive laws even to the death, if necessary, for some higher value. Antigone thus insisted on the right to bury her brother, despite the law forbidding it. And Lech Walesa, the leader of the once-outlawed Solidarity trade union in Poland, took his stand so firmly and persistently that by 1989 the Polish government reversed itself and opened talks with him, recognizing Solidarity's right to exist, and Solidarity moved front and center into government power.

Throughout Eastern Europe there is a caldron of national movements to defend the cultural and political rights of autonomy for ethnic minorities. Cultural resistance to collective learning patterns directed from party officials and government leaders may be the key to the existential integrity of many peoples, even though their struggles have high collective costs. Collective adaptation for economic gain is not the ultimate end of human existence.

The successful national manager of a political economy must "read" the unmovable schemata of resistance scattered throughout the culture and give those marginal people of integrity a legitimate part in the process of collective economic transformation or watch desired reforms die of inertia. The extreme conservative reactions to the "shock therapy" economic reforms in Russia and Poland are telling illustrations of resistance to threats to traditional cultural integrity. So are the foreign capital controls of Malaysia and Hong Kong after the Asian financial crisis of 1997–1998.

THE PARAMETERS OF INTERNATIONAL POLITICAL ECONOMY

As a field, the divisions between some of the elements of international political economy—the state, the multinational corporation, the international organization, foreign economic policy, and domestic economic policy—tend to break down as the global economic change speeds up. But the attention paid to specific dilemmas and relationships between collective power and wealth in global context differentiates the field from others.

Within the United States, the field of international political economy derived from the split between security and economic specializations within academic international relations in 1973, particularly as interpreted by Charles

Kindleberger's "hegemony stability thesis" (see Chapter 1) and the concept of "liberal imperialism" of David Calleo and Benjamin Rowland. Recently, this heavy attention traditionally paid to hegemony or domination has shifted toward the social processes that constitute or create relations between power and wealth. The collective learning approach used here might be best understood as a middle-range theoretical focus in this effort by international political economists to comprehend how the politics of international economic relations are socially constructed.[7] And key to these social processes are belief systems that support or inhibit strategies of organizational adaption to global economic change.

CLOSURE VERSUS AMBIVALENT BELIEF SYSTEMS

Effective collective political economy strategies depend on anticipating the tendency of the human mind toward closure and countering it, or unlocking it, before it is too late. Collective organizational efforts can take on a life of their own and continue to the point of self-destruction unless they are derailed or side-tracked. An example of this "edge effect" gone mad, the momentum for the sake of aesthetic completion regardless of human consequences, is the World War II Manhattan Project that developed the atomic bomb in the United States. Participants in the project found that they were so caught up in the collective learning process after three years of night-and-day struggle to achieve the breakthrough that even though they knew Nazi Germany had surrendered they had to continue to completion. The result was dropping two atomic bombs on Japan. Once "group think" gets rolling and is stimulated with patriotism, money, honor, status, and wartime frenzy, the temptation for closure becomes almost irresistible.

Moreover, closure is often a much more attractive political style in a highly uncertain world situation than an ambivalent belief system. Stalin knew this. So did Mao Tse-tung. President Ronald Reagan benefited from this effect in the simplicity of his creed, although thankfully he turned out to be a pragmatic compromiser in practice. People want their great communicators to have simple, firmly held beliefs. Closure, in short.

Not that all closure is necessarily a bad thing. If one considers the successful modern cases in transforming authoritarian state-controlled economies to market-oriented, democratic economies, one often finds a moment of closure in historical time in which things are suddenly reversed, the price system decontrolled. Such was the case in the spring of 1948 in West Germany when the Reichsmark was almost without value, long lines surrounded stores, and black markets proliferated. German Economic Minister Ludwig Erhard, with the cooperation of the American occupation forces (in Operation Bird Dog), obtained a few wagonloads of paper money printed in the United States and declared "the Currency Reform" overnight. Each German citizen was at first permitted to receive forty new Deutsche Marks (DM) in a 1:1 exchange for the next to worthless Reichsmark. No one was to receive either more nor less than forty DM. A little later, each citizen was permitted to receive

twenty more. Thus began the Social Market Economy and West German economic miracle. And all done with a simple act of closure.*

Other forms of closure, however, may be incompatible with collective adaptation either for the sake of international competitiveness or for the sake of more
widespread economic opportunity or social justice. "Negative closure," for example, closes off the opportunity of becoming a U.S. Senator unless one has already been elected to that office and happens to have raised an average of more
than $4 million. The closure of thinking against truly democratic election financ-
ing in the United States is turning a democracy quickly into an oligarchy with over
90 percent of those elected to the Senate and House of Representatives typically being incumbents. Or the closure of unions that refuse to compromise with
management, even given the greater competitiveness and flexibility of workers
abroad in the same industry. Or the closure of management in not granting the
union workers meaningful lifetime pension and health benefits. Or the closure of
protectionism bills passed in the legislature to put such managers and workers
in a "greenhouse" until they use their time to become competitive.

But with the exceptions of infant industries, short-term import substitution,
strategic and high-tech sectors, the greenhouse strategy often backfires in its collective learning effects. By putting their electronics companies in a state-subsidized greenhouse program, the French in the 1950s, for example, encouraged
managers and workers alike to believe the comfortable support would go on forever. So they grew complacent and when the subsidies were withdrawn the French
electronics industry went into a major crisis: It could not compete in real terms
on the world market. And East Germans, used to guaranteed jobs and subsidized
housing under the closure of a Communist Party state until the fall of 1989, found
the "cold shower" of market uncertainty and competition painful as they joined
the West German collective learning process in the reunification of the 1990s.
Closure, in short, can lull one into thinking uncertainty and risk have been licked
and that one has it permanently made (despite the positive sense of social security
that this provides). Closure is usually too comfortable to work for long.

The opposite of closure is targeted, strategic openness. This is the essence of
the open-synergistic type of collective learning. As composer John Cage put it in
A Year From Monday (1967): "In music it was hopeless to think in terms of the old
structure (tonality), to do things following old methods (counterpoint, harmony),
to use the old materials (orchestra instruments). We started from scratch: sound,
silence, time, activity. In society, no amount of doctoring up economics/politics
will help. Begin again, assuming abundance, unemployment, a field situation,
multiplicity, unpredictability, immediacy, the possibility of participation." Not

---

*Of course it must be recalled that this currency reform was done under a military government that
could force the people who lost their savings to swallow it—not exactly a democratic recipe. Poland's
1990 "shock therapy" policy of removing price controls while keeping wage controls, ending subsidies for goods and services, privatizing state-owned companies, postponing foreign debt repayment,
and getting aid from the World Bank, IMF, and friendly governments bordered on short-term closure. But the people soon grew tired of sacrifices and voted to bring hard-line communists back into
power (see Chapter 10).

the cynical closure of Stalin nor the naive openness of democratic reformist ideology of the 1960s, but a yin/yang rhythm between the closure of necessary semi-control and targeting and the openness of spontaneous innovation and options for widening participation. The end of the twentieth century brought the realization of the systemness of the global economy, an in-house Keynesian system where international demand and supply can be stimulated or depressed with consequences for everyone on the earth.

MODELS AND MODELING

The twentieth century ended with the Era of the Nonautomatic Pilot Experiment. The scientific method and techniques of social learning spread throughout the globe, including the notions of vicarious learning, modeling, and the pilot experiment. What characterizes the economic organizational models that succeeded? On the national level these include the Japanese and the Swedish political economies during certain decades after World War II. In high tech, finance, and entrepreneurship, the American model predominated. On the regional or international level, early OPEC and the European Union come to mind. None of these political economy organizations succeeded overnight and all are imperfect still today (note the Japanese recession, the Swedish austerity policy, and the ups and downs of OPEC and the EU). All have in common a long history of frustrated consensus-building.

In the twentieth century, progressive business leaders led the way to the formation of the European Economic Community, which could not, however, have been born without the cold, strategic calculations of French and German leaders when they joined forces in the European Coal and Steel Community. A history of collective action, a striving for homogeneity to the point of a strategy of cultural exclusion, geopolitical strategic calculation, members with economic clout, and leadership by both business and government leaders are behind the success of the European Common Market—not to mention a benign American hegemony that not only let the bloc form, but helped to finance it. The 1989 expansion of the European Union (EU) nations to include six European Free Trade Association (EFTA) countries in a "European Economic Zone" provided a model for accepting Eastern European countries (such as Poland and Hungary) into a European bloc without having to admit them immediately to the more exclusive EC club. The Euro currency is perhaps the ultimate collective integration experiment, hoping to unite the members of the European Union club politically through a none too subtle "spill-over" effect from monetary integration. But if the Euro's value continues to decline against the dollar, as it did when launched in 1999, it could lead to EU disintegration.

OPEC, too, represented a coming together of members with economic clout (based on oil), a strategy of exclusion, hard strategic calculations, and an assumption that American hegemony would not stand in their way. And OPEC, too, created loose joint ventures with other oil producing nations to expand its influence—but found its power diluted over time as alternative energy supplies and conservation strategies countered its market domination. The timing of both the European integration and OPEC ventures was astute. The leaders' political sophistication suggests that such timing was no accident. Both were no doubt motivated to some extent by the desire for regional independence from the influence of the American hegemon. Other commodity cartels inspired by the OPEC model were based on more diffuse membership, a less scarce or demanded commodity (bauxite, bananas, and copper), and inappropriate timing, and were not successful. The prerequisites for successful economic organizations (such as market share, organizational leadership, consensus, and timing) must be studied before they can be applied effectively as models.

Both the Japanese and Swedish models represent deep-rooted traditions of neocorporatist consensus (the Japanese "without labor" and Sweden often almost labor-dominated), homogeneous populations, small states, and geographical locations on the periphery of American hegemony (that is, more protected by it than contributing to it). The literacy rate of both countries is high, and both are committed to maintaining a high level of intelligent participation by citizens in the economy (although the Japanese tendency to exclude women versus the Swedish tendency to include them is notable). Very little is left to chance when it comes to organizational networks in these countries. Control over population growth is a similar characteristic. The extreme hierarchical nature of influence and information processing distinguishes Japan from the extreme focus upon egalitarianism, particularly when it comes to economic opportunity, present in Sweden. Both countries have maintained legitimate roles for traditional, noble families, who are expected to contribute in the form of public service. Both cultures stress limiting the range of incomes between those earning the most and those earning the least as a principle necessary for social harmony and consensus (in marked contrast with the United States). Both target the industries they specialize in with great care, and both use government institutions and subsidies extensively in this task. They strive for international competitiveness while preserving the integrity of their national cultures, social commitments, and some modicum of security at home. And both suffered from the challenges of globalization in the 1990s (with Japan sinking into its deepest post-World War II recession, forcing a painful reexamination of its traditions in terms of their suitability for service sector competitiveness in such fields as finance and software, having found those traditions well-suited for competitiveness in manufacturing and electronic hardware).

In terms of modeling, one must also highlight the reliance on the strategy of the pilot experiment in the former socialist bloc—the capitalist zones and privatized factories near Hong Kong in the People's Republic of China, the experiments with stock markets in Hungary and China, and so forth. The initial aim in these cases appeared to be to graft market mechanisms on an outdated Stalinesque economic structure in order to make the political economy more competitive, attract Western hard currency and technology, and still not lose their integrity.

Given the ability of China to transcend the Stalinist focus on heavy industry and to become self-sufficient in agriculture, its success in its economic reforms compared with the Russian republics seemed inevitable, even given China's 1989 authoritarian crackdown. The Chinese have fostered economic growth by carefully targeting key industries in strategic regions for pilot experiments that are designed to serve as models or "signals" for the rest of the country should they succeed. Similarly, the East Asian NICs initially learned from Japan as their "model" (see Chapter 9).

One problem here is that it may always be more motivating to be part of a pilot experiment than to be a secondary copy of someone else's experiment, making the initial experiments more successful than their clones. On the other hand, to the extent bugs are worked out, going second may be better than going first (as Japan illustrated to the West in many industries). But whether or not any other country or region will be able to operate its treasury department as if it were an investment bank coordinated with the sophisticated management of its key world reserve currency by its central bank, as the United States did in the 1990s, is debatable.

Inequalities are necessary for economic purposes. What we have learned from "postliberal" successes is that such inequalities should be targeted for the overall strategic economic benefit of the nation.

STRATEGIES, CYCLES, AND PRINCIPLES

The success of political economy models in terms of economic growth depends on the ability of their managers to adapt them, using appropriate strategic mixes at opportune moments in short-term, medium-term, and long-term business cycles. The key strategies associated with the maintenance model used in this book are the defeatist, the free-rider, the maintenance, and the entrepreneurial. One reason so few successful economic models emerge from developing countries is that the global economy is structured to give them a choice between the least desirable of these two strategies: the defeatist and the free-rider. This is one reason managers in developing countries dream of being able to pursue a maintenance strategy—that is, they dream of being able to keep control of a self-sustaining system of equilibrium in which economic growth keeps up with the business cycle and the nation does not fall further behind. So if a country such as Mexico opts for a free-rider strategy in taking on as much debt as it can (as it did in the 1970s under the advice of the Cambridge School), one must understand this decision as one of the few choices realistically available to Mexico at the time. Bolivia's suspension of payments on its international debt in the 1980s was another free-rider variation, as was Russia's in 1998. But, as we have noted, entrepreneurship can spring from free-rider "boosts" under the right circumstances.

The dilemma of advanced industrialized countries is markedly different. They can more or less take the maintenance of their existing political economy and its legitimacy for granted and have a choice between different risk-portfolios or entrepreneurial strategies—depending on whether they prefer maximizing the objectives of economic growth and job creation, or prefer the objectives of more equal distribution of economic opportunities and increasing the quality of life for those in the present generation. To a certain extent these are future versus past and savings/investment versus consumption trade-offs from the economist's viewpoint. But the cases of Sweden and Germany illustrated that for fairly long periods (between periodic maintenance base restructurings for efficiency) it is possible for political economies to have their cake and eat it too (at least as long as the American protector protects).

No matter where one stands on these issues, they can be described in terms of maintenance-entrepreneurial (*maintenpreneurial*) strategy mixes. The economic threat to advanced industrial countries is more apt to come from risk-aversion or risk-shy behavior (or the *maintenance syndrome*) than it is from overdoing entrepreneurial risk-taking. A case in point is the failure of West European countries to develop their own microchips in time to compete with the Japanese and Americans in the microelectronics business globally, making them dependent for some time to come on foreign chips. We can conclude that the optimum strategy is a maintenance-entrepreneurial mix heavily loaded toward the entrepreneurial if the tempo of socioeconomic and technological change continues at a rapid rate.

The cycles that all managers must face, whether in the public or private sector, are short-term, medium-term, and long-term. Since political economy strategies depend on future assumptions concerning global economic growth or recession, energy prices, exchange rates, and so forth, competent managers of international economic change must master the global cycles that will affect all their decisions; and they must pay particular attention to the medium-term cycles specific to their own industry or national comparative advantage. One must decide whether to side with those who believe the twenty-first century will begin with a bust—or with a boom—or with a wash between bust and boom. The depression scenarios tend to highlight a gap between existing technological developments and the commercial ability to apply and sell these technologies, or a scarcity of liquidity given a global debt-load meltdown, or both.

From the collective learning perspective, the information-overload, risk-shy maintenance thesis suggests that there are definite limits to the ability of people globally to absorb existing technology (i.e., until people start throwing out computers every year like an old-fashioned pair of shoes). But the markets tend to discount this absorption problem well in advance, giving Silicon Valley its own private recessions (as in 1984) without necessarily contributing to a massive cyclical downturn.

The boom hypothesis has its own flaws, but perhaps not so many as the depression scenario. The optimists accurately forecast that the world's public and private financial institutions would ease the global debt crisis by informally writing off most of the developing country loans from the 1970s through longer terms and lower interest rates. They also argue that although the disinflationary trend may reverse, the rise of inflation will be gradual, thus providing the perfect elixir for global economic growth—stable growth with increasing liquidity. The baby-boom generation will spark consumption growth in the United States as illustrated by low savings rates and optimistic stock market speculation. International peace is presumed to break out after a settlement in Kosovo, giving the stability argument further plausibility. But there are some drawbacks to this rosy scenario when one considers the Asian financial meltdown in the late 1990s and when one looks at specific sectors of the global economy (leaving the overcapacity possibility in technology aside). If peace really succeeds, fewer weapons would be produced and sold, dampening these parts of the economy in those countries specializing in the weapons business. (With high-flying conventional weapons sales and a reversal toward higher U.S. defense spending this seems unlikely.) With well over half of the aerospace military market in the world, the U.S. economy could be struck hard with readjustment problems, followed by European countries. (This, however, optimistically assumes that the United States and Europe put peace before economic growth). The 1990s decline in commodities prices worldwide from oil to wheat to copper limited the capacity of commodity-based countries to purchase manufactured goods from others (although the reversal toward increased oil prices at century's end suggests that the price of commodities could turn around).

When one descends from the level of the long-term, Kondratieff boom-or-bust genre of cycle projections (fifty years) to middle-range Kuznets cycles (fifteen to twenty-five years) or short-term "business cycles" (seven to nine years), the need for the manager of global economic change to be up-to-date in key sectors becomes even more compelling. If the manager should have corporate or national stakes in the global construction business, for example, it becomes important to know that the Hansen/Kuznets cycle projects that every other short-term business cycle will be a real boom in the construction cycle in the United States. And the alternating recessions are apt to be particularly deep when they coincide with the construction slump (the construction cycle being seventeen to eighteen years in length, about twice the length of the normal business cycle). When the manager anticipates a short- to medium-term recession coming on in a specific sector, he or she should adopt a maintenance strategy of consolidation or efficiency cutbacks, while an anticipation of boom might well trigger a higher risk, entrepreneurial strategy of expansion. Another option is to ignore market timing altogether, like Peter Lynch, manager of the most successful (long-term) stock mutual fund, Fidelity Magellan, and to invest only in concrete situations with which one is very familiar. This systematic, close-to-the-ground entrepreneurial strategy permits one to gain from economies of scale (as one's investment portfolio becomes ever larger). Simultaneously, one maintains quality by reducing variations through limiting oneself to industries one knows, and one experiences higher growth than average macro-investment cycle returns by focusing on the micromanagement of undervalued situations. To the extent governments subsidize any such investments, I have argued in *Green Logic* (1998) that they should be oriented toward environmentally responsible companies, preferably green start-ups (since more jobs are created through small companies). For there is no ethical rationale for governments using tax money to support industries that destroy the environment of the world one's grandchildren will inherit.

Since public managers are responsible for forecasting levels of unemployment and for encouraging workers to shift from areas of low demand to areas of growing demand, such sector-specific short- to medium-term economic cycle research and micro-management analysis becomes invaluable to them as well. The economic aim of collective learning is to restructure the maintenance base of the organization or state with efficiency, cultural integrity, and equal participation, in order to position and target the collectivity for sustainable entrepreneurial niches and export-oriented growth.

These objectives are also in the interest of the G-7 nations who still have the primary responsibility for coordinating a system of global financial and monetary stability in which capital and trade flows support economic growth worldwide. Short of the unlikely possibility that a world central bank will be created, the key developed countries will have to continue to support and restructure the IMF, World Bank, BIS, and WTO and other existing international institutions to assure a stable global system of capital and trade flows. To legitimize this long-term with peoples who have to make sacrifices, if it is sustainable in terms of environmental responsibility as well as short-term financial responsiveness, the global system will gain in credibility for societies who believe that more than economics is at stake in globalization. The new economic architecture of the twenty-first century can be created progressively to take advantage of this opportunity, or become another short-term gesture of hollow hegemony in which ambitious rhetoric fails to follow through in the necessary transformation of the system of global economic management.

NOTES

1. Fareed Zakaria, "Our Hollow Hegemony: Why Foreign Policy Can't Be Left to the Market," *New York Times Magazine*, November 1, 1998, 80.
2. Saskia Sassen, *Losing Control? Sovereignty in an Age of Globalization* (New York: Columbia University Press, 1996), p. 40.
3. See Robert P. Guimraes, "O Desafio Politico Desenvolvimento Sustenado," *Lua Nova, Revista de Cultura e Politica*, nr. 35 (1995): 117. And, for a "northern" view: Richard Cooper, "Toward a Real Global Warming Treaty," *Foreign Affairs* 77, no. 2 (March/April 1998): 66–79; versus: R. Isaak, *Green Logic* (West Hartford, CT: Kumarian Press, 1999).
4. Susan Strange, "The Erosion of the State," *Current History* 96, no. 613 (November 1997): 365–369.
5. Professor Ray Lopez of the Lubin School, Pace University, provided these statistics compiled from *The Statistical Abstracts* (GDP) and Professor Warren Keegan's world GNP data (Global Strategy Institute, Pace University Press, New York).
6. See R. Isaak, "Politics in Public Sector Reform: A Collective Learning Perspective," in *Stand und Perspektiven der Öffentlichen Betriebswirtschaftslehre (The Status and Perspective of Public Sector Management)*, ed. Dietmar Bräunig and Dorothea Greiling (Berlin, 1999).
7. See Kurt Burch and Robert A. Denemark, eds., *Constituting International Political Economy* (Boulder, CO: Lynne Rienner, 1997).

GLOSSARY

absolute advantage   In trade, if one country can produce an item better and/or more cheaply than another.

absolute poverty   Conditions of deprivation that fall below any rational definition of human decency (as defined by Robert McNamara).

absorptive capacity   The extent to which a nation can absorb the products of another nation; limiting factors would be, for example, the degree of satiation or the stage of development.

ACP nations   The African, Caribbean, and Pacific states.

adaptive organizations   Organizations that react to daily changes as they come up, using maintenance strategies to keep stability, rather than anticipating the future in order to keep up with the cutting edge of innovation.

APEC   Asia Pacific Economic Cooperation; founded in 1989 as a consultative forum made up of Australia, Canada, Japan, the Republic of Korea, New Zealand, and the United States, plus the ASEAN nations (Brunei, Indonesia, Malaysia, the Philippines, Singapore, Thailand), and later joined by China, Hong Kong, and Taiwan; aims at trade liberalization and cooperation on issues such as investment regulations, technology transfer, telecommunications, and energy.

balance-of-payments deficit (difficulties)   For example, if more payments by domestic residents have been paid out than received from foreigners, or if more goods (in value) have been imported than exported. (BOP surplus = more exports than imports.)

Black Friday   Stock market crash on October 29, 1929; beginning of the Great Depression. (October 19, 1987, was the crash of 1987, or Black Monday.)

Bretton Woods system   Monetary system referring to the charter negotiated in 1944 in Bretton Woods, NH, which established the IMF and the World Bank, with the U.S. dollar as anchor, freely convertible into gold at any time; this monetary system was fundamentally aimed at avoiding the competitive exchange rate devaluations and "beggar-thy-neighbor" policies that led to the breakdown of the international monetary system in the 1930s following the Great Depression.

business cycle (short-term cycle)   Three- to eight-year patterns of rising and falling economic activity, of expansion and recession, peaks and troughs. Many economists have found these short-term, fluctuating modes of behavior alone to be insufficient to explain and predict business patterns; therefore, they have combined short-term "business cycles" with intermediate-term (fifteen to twenty-five years) "long-swing" investment (or Kuznets) cycles, and long-term or "long-wave" (forty-five to sixty years) Kondratieff cycles.

Cambridge school Neo-Marxist economics; created a "reverse debt trap" (mainly South American countries) by increasing the loans from foreign banks to such an extent that they had them by their loans, meaning, they were eventually too big to fail.

class Refers to how much you have got of what your society considers it important to get.

Cocom Coordinating Committee on Multilateral Export Controls; organization set up in the cold-war atmosphere of 1949 that coordinates a list of strategic technology prohibited for export to communist countries. Members are the United States, Japan, and all NATO members except Iceland.

codetermination Management and workers cooperate to set long-term corporate policies in 50–50 percent participation schemes.

collective learning Social learning process of distinguishing legitimate patterns of adaptive behavior within an organization in order to manage environmental change without losing cultural integrity.

Comecon (CMEA) Council for Mutual Economic Assistance—Eastern Bloc alliance.

communitarianism American theory that stresses the priority of "thickly constituted selves" (with a sense of duty and long-term commitment) loyal to specific communities; cooperative group form of capitalism colored by *Gemeinschaft* (community) in Germany or the spirit of *wa* (harmony) in Japan, as opposed to individualistic Anglo-Saxon form of capitalism.

comparative advantage The rationale that even if a country has an absolute advantage in producing two goods (i.e., produces them both cheaper than another country) it may still be more efficient—and therefore pay off for *both*—to trade and to each specialize in the one good with a relative advantage: A country has a relative/comparative advantage in a good if, for the production of one unit of that good, it has to give up less of the other good's production than the trading partner. That means it has lower opportunity costs (expressed in the other good's possible output with the factors used) for this good than the other country. For maximum efficiency, it is therefore important not to look at absolute costs of production but to compare each country's cost ratio to the other's (David Ricardo).

concessional financial assistance Either outright grants or soft-loans of the IDA.

corporatism A belief in political representation through functional, occupation-related institutions, not geographically defined electoral units.

creative destruction Process in which the new incessantly drives out the old. (Joseph Schumpeter's definition of capitalism.)

current account deficit The total export of goods and services that is less than the total import of goods and services (part of the balance of payments).

debt trap From the radical or neo-Marxist perspective; foreign aid is a tool for imperialism and social control, aiming to undermine the independence of developing countries (Cheryl Payer).

dependence A situation in which the economy of certain countries is conditioned by the development and expansion of another economy to which the former is subjected.

dependency theory Theory that arose in the mid 1960s, picking up Marx's theory of capitalist imperialism and the concern for the domestic distribution of wealth. Whereas the Marxist-Leninist thesis of capitalist imperialism suggests the necessity of foreign aid as part of the process of inevitable capitalist development, dependency theory argues that dependency causes underdevelopment and is apt to be critical of aid (Theotonio Dos Santos).

deutero-learning Comparison of how different groups of people learn how to learn.

development Spontaneous economic change within a nation not forced upon it from without; goes beyond mere growth, production; design of something new, distinctive (Joseph Schumpeter).

downsizing Reducing the number of employees and non-core related businesses.

dualism/dual economy Winning sectors attract resources from others left behind: Operates at many levels during all phases of a nation's economic development. The new drives out the old at an ever-increasing tempo, setting the state up for either vicious or virtuous circles.

dynamic economy of scale Involves continuous reductions in unit costs and increases in productivity attributable to continuous increases in output of a corporation, industry, or economy over time ("learning economies").

Earth Increment Chapter 33 of the Agenda 21 (UNCED 1992): shift levels of official development assistance from 0.35 percent to 1.0 percent of GNP.

economic liberalism Minimal state interference in the economy and maximum reliance upon the market (Adam Smith); predominant in Anglo-Saxon cultures.

economic miracle Perception of national economic achievement that appears to transcend the laws of nature as if brought about by some superhuman agency.

economic nationalism Mercantilism/statism/protectionism; spotlights the economic and power interests of a single nation-state in competition with all others, viewing the world economy as a zero-sum game in which that not gained by the state will necessarily be lost to other competitive states.

economics The study of collective choice among alternative uses of scarce resources.

economy of scale Lowering of production costs because of being able to operate on a large scale.

ECU European Currency Unit; unit of account for European central banks to calculate and display the exchange ratios between different EMS states; predecessor of the EURO as the future currency of the European Monetary Union, launched in 1999.

EEC European Economic Community.

EFTA European Free Trade Association; formed as second European bloc; originally made up of Britain, Austria, Denmark, Norway, Portugal, Sweden, Switzerland, but most eventually joined EU.

elites Those in superior social or political positions.

EMS, EMU European Monetary System, European Monetary Union.

Engel's law At different levels of income people have an elasticity of demand that differs; refers especially to the demand for food (or basic agricultural goods) that will decrease relative to the increase in income.

entrepreneur/promoter As opposed to maintenance manager/trustee; driven by the perception of opportunity; value-driven, often team-oriented; relies on performance-based, flat, informal modes of organization.

entrepreneurial risk Stresses effectiveness, risk-taking, export growth, and customer and niche creation in the external area of domestic and global markets; focus is on entrepreneurial "breakpoints" or developmental "takeoff points."

entropic process Process of obsolescence and disintegration (e.g., in periods of recession or decline).

entropy Disintegration and diffusion of energies (e.g., burning of fossil energies).

ethnocentrism Belief in the primacy/superiority of one's own people or way of life.

EU European Union (1993) emerging from ECSC (European Coal and Steel Community) 1952; European Common Market/European Economic Community (EEC) 1957 (Treaty of Rome); European Economic Area (EEA); European Association Accords (EAA).

Eurodollar   Dollar outside the United States.

Euromoney (off-shore banking system)   Mainly dollars outside the United States (e.g., put in European bank accounts). The volume started to grow in the late 1960s and increased tremendously in the 1970s during the OPEC oil crisis; it has led to some dilution of U.S. financial power.

external debt   Defined by the World Bank as the sum of portfolio investments and long-term capital inflows by nonresidents; the key category that causes the United States to be called the "world's largest debtor nation."

extraterritoriality   Exemption from the jurisdiction of local law; for example, after Perry's opening of Japanese ports in 1854, foreign trade interests began to invade Japan and demand that while the citizens of their countries resided in Japan they should be governed by their own laws rather than Japanese laws.

fascism   Right-wing reaction to socialism.

fixed exchange rates   Within a fixed exchange rate system, currencies trade at a fixed exchange ratio. If balance of payment imbalances occur and individual currencies become appreciation/depreciation tending, the involved countries' central banks have to intervene/interfere (e.g., buy up weak currencies [take them out of the market] to strengthen demand, or reduce excess supply, so their price [exchange ratio] does not go down).

flexible (floating) exchange rates   Any one country's currency is worth whatever people think it is worth at a particular moment; its price is therefore determined by the market's supply and demand.

foreign direct investment (FDI)   Establishing or expanding of corporate operations in a foreign country.

free-riding   The act of free-riding upon collective or public goods without paying the fair share (taking advantage of others' involvement—often occurring with public goods and in larger groups).

G3, G5, G7; Group of Three/Five/Seven   Group of major industrial nations: G3 = Germany, Japan, United States; G5 = G3 + Britain and France; G7 = G5 + Canada and Italy.

GATT (ITO/WTO)   General Agreement on Tariffs and Trade (International Trade Organization/World Trade Organization).

globalization   The integration of finance, markets, technology, information flows, transportation, institutions, and product standardization throughout the world.

Greater China strategy   Let other Asian countries be the pilot tests for China's long-term positioning.

GSP   Generalized System of Preferences; exceptions within international free trade granted to developing countries.

hard/soft currencies   Appreciation/depreciation-tending convertible money.

harmonization   Attempt by former eastern bloc countries (especially Poland) to match the national monetary and tax policies with those of the "Euro-club."

Heckscher-Ohlin-Samuelson theorem (HOS)   Refinement of Ricardian theory of comparative advantage to explain trade patterns within less restrictive models (e.g., Ricardo is based on assumption of labor as only input), based mainly on the observation that different countries are disproportionally favored with certain factors. According to Hechscher and Ohlin, international trade will lead to a country's specialization in those products that use the factor intensively in which it has a particular abundance. Central is the effect of international trade on factor prices. Samuelson later extended the HO-theorem into the thesis, that adaptations will eventually lead to an equalization of factor prices internationally, which presumably eliminates the need for factor migration.

hegemony/hegemon   Domination; a state or organization that dominates others in its region or in the world.

hubris　Greek concept of false pride in trying to do more than one can (which leads ultimately to downfall).

ideology　"falling in love with ideas that further a certain group's or state's concrete interests"; action-oriented nests of ideas or worldviews, serving to shore up the legitimacy of elites in power.

IMF　International Monetary Fund.

import substitution　Policy of systematically encouraging the domestic production of goods that used to be imported: aim is economic self-sufficiency.

indexation　Automatic, indexed hikes in industrial wages linked to inflation or rises in consumer prices.

industrial policy　State coordination with national business networks.

inflation　More money chasing fewer goods (leading to higher prices).

interdependence　The mutual dependency of developed and developing countries (Gunnar Myrdal).

intermediate technology　Developing countries should not aim for insatiable big business model of capitalist Westernization but wisely accept the limits of nature and the earth's resources and utilize intermediate technologies targeted for their own unique capacities and situation (E. F. Schumacher).

International Development Association (IDA)　Soft loan window of the World Bank, created as part of the World Bank Group in order to provide loans to developing countries on a more liberal basis than usually allowed within WB guidelines (e.g., fifty-year loans, some of them interest free, repayments starting only after a few years, and in local currency if convertible).

International Finance Corporation (IFC)　World Bank Group formed in 1956 to provide risk-capital for markets and to stimulate the international flow of capital (normally seven- to twelve-year period).

International Monetary Fund (IMF)　Institution founded to provide international liquidity and short-term credit to alleviate (short-term) balance-of-payments difficulties of its member nations ("conditionality" to establish strict conditions for the IMF loans—austerity measures, etc). Stabilizing institution governed by the Executive Board (elected directors) and the Board of Governors, made up of governors of each nation with voting power proportionate to subscription quotas in the fund (usually headed by European).

International political economy　The study of the politics behind the economic relations among peoples and nations in order to assess their relative wealth and power.

Just-in-time delivery/production　Originally a Japanese concept; just in time delivery of parts to the point of assembly by a few, well-trained suppliers; reduces the costs of storing inventory. Furthermore, the high percentage of workers in teams increases productivity and reduces defects.

keiretsu　Japanese cartel networks of companies—based on long-term, cross-shareholding among members.

Kondratieff cycle (long-wave cycle)　About fifty years in length; the "idealized" Kondratieff wave approximates the actual behavior of U.S. wholesale prices closely enough to suggest to long-wave theorists that the U.S. economy may soon enter a depression.

Kuznets cycle (intermediate-term cycles)　Intermediate term cycles (e.g., in the key sector of building construction).

Learning 1, 2, 3, 4　Learning 1: reduction of error within a rigid frame; Learning 2: open synergistic networking based on trust; Learning 3: radical quantum leaps for technological breakthroughs; Learning 4: striving for absolute excellence beyond all existing benchmarks.

learning organizations   Organizations that can transform themselves by anticipating change, discovering new ways of creating products and services: They have learned how to learn (Richard Hodgetts and Fred Luthans).

legal-rational society   Made up of contractual community relations (work prescribed by legal contracts), specific role structures (specialization rather than jack-of-all-trades), and achievement-oriented modes of social and political authority.

legitimacy   Deference to elites produced by force and awe.

liberalism   Maximization of individual interest and freedom (especially economic profit); rather than focusing on the state, the liberal stresses the market.

life chances   Implies a competitive struggle for survival among individuals or types of people (Max Weber); the odds of fulfilling the full range of human possibilities given the individual's social ties and options (Ralf Dahrendof).

limelight effect   Tendency of other people to mimic U.S. trends once the focus is concentrated upon success emanating from the United States.

liquidity   "Lifeblood that keeps the pieces of the world economy moving"; currency, money.

locomotive theory   One country expecting major spill-over effects from another country's (i.e., the locomotive) expansionary policies on its own economy; the main advantage lies in not having to deal with the typical trade-off of balance of payment and budget deficits. (The United States pursued such a strategy for a long time, somehow pressuring Germany and Japan into performing a stimulative policy for the sake of the U.S. economy.)

Lomé Convention   In 1975, the EEC signed the first Lomé Convention with forty-six developing countries from Africa, the Caribbean, and the Pacific (the ACP nations) to stabilize their export earnings and to make EEC capital and technical assistance available to them through a Center for Industrial Development.

Maastricht Treaty   Important treaty for European architecture, adopted in 1993. Mainly covers the steps toward EMU (single European currency); however, also includes the goals of common justice, security policies, and the common market.

maquiladoras   Mexican plants (strategically positioned) just below the U.S. border that assemble imported foreign (U.S.) parts for immediate re-export.

maintenance base   Maximizes efficiency, stability, and risk reduction inside the organization/institution (in contrast to entrepreneurial risk).

maintenance manager/trustee   Driven by resources currently controlled, tends toward formalized, promotion-oriented hierarchy in organization and is security-driven.

managed trade   Government intervention to steer trade relations with other countries toward the national interest, or at least to avoid unequal tariff trade-offs.

Marxism   Spotlights the contradictions in the capitalist system that emerge from individuals rationally maximizing their personal interest without regard for the overall consequences for social equity and community well-being.

mercantilism   See *economic nationalism.*

metropoles   Metropolitan centers of large, developed economies.

MITI   Japan; Ministry of International Trade and Industry; aimed to create a Japanese environment conducive to the cultivation of world-class competitors among private companies in key economic sectors.

Modern World System   The modern world can only be understood as a global system with a single division of labor and multiple culturals systems forming a international hierarchy in the ceaseless struggle of states and classes divided into core, periphery, and semi-periphery; extends Leninist interpretation of Marxism (Frank Baran and Immanual Wallerstein).

monetarism Argues that only monetary policy can influence the course of the GNP; declares money supply to be the most important factor in a nation's economic policy. The main link to economic activity is the dependence of the households' willingness to spend on the accessibility of liquidity or credit, which depends on monetary policy—spending will be higher with loose monetary policy, meaning higher supply of liquidity at lower rates (e.g., Milton Friedman).

Most Favored Nation (MFN) treatment Commits all parties to conduct trade on the basis of nondiscrimination (see *nondiscrimination*).

multilateral/bilateral aid negotiations NIEO assumed that the bargaining leverage of developing countries is greater in multilateral aid negotiations where norms and rules are more clear than they would in bilateral negotiations (between two states).

multinational corporation (MNC) Refers to a company owned by stockholders in several countries that is also based in two countries, but MNCs are often based and owned in only one country, with manufacturing facilities in two or more other countries that repatriate profits that are not invested (often called *transnational corporations*).

NAFTA North American Free Trade Agreement; started January 1994, creating a free trade bloc consisting of Canada, the United States, and Mexico.

neoclassical theory With respect to trade, each country should specialize in goods with comparative advantage, therefore minimizing opportunity cost and maximizing efficiency, which neoclassicists see guaranteed through a free trade system, interpreted as a positive sum, cooperative game; represents a form of economic Social Darwinism; the need for protection is only seen in sheltering infant industries (short-term) to free efficiency potentials; "liberalism modernized" (Smith, Ricardo, Heckscher, Ohlin, Samuelson).

neocorporatism Another interpretation of successful capitalist economies since World War II that stresses not the underlying economic factors of production, labor cost, inflation, investment, and learning-by-doing but the institutional relationships among major business, labor, and governmental interest groups, which are conducive to harmonious collective management and equity in representation by various levels of workers in society.

neomercantilism Policies of export-oriented growth in order to increase a country's structural surpluses.

neorealism Rooted in the power precepts of Machiavelli and the nationalistic economic policies of mercantilism; therefore, balance of payments surplus, for example, interpreted as control. Ultimate goal is striving for hegemony.

New International Economic Order (NIEO) Demanded by developing countries with the objective of making the basic needs of developing countries a priority; not only by improving the standards of living, but also by allowing a greater Third-World participation and effectiveness.

"new thinking" Gorbachev advocated three key concepts in his reforms (i.e., his "new thinking") beginning in 1985: *glasnost* (openness), *perestroika* (restructuring), and *uskorenie* (acceleration).

NICs Newly Industrialized Countries; most upwardly mobile of the developing countries (e.g., South Korea, Singapore, Taiwan).

nondiscrimination Once foreign goods cross the border into another GATT/WTO country, they are to be treated as domestic goods in terms of equal rights of competition.

nontariff trade barriers Quotas, customs, export subsidies, "voluntary restraints," domestic standards and rules.

OECD Organization for Economic Cooperation and Development; often referred to as "the rich men's club."

oligarchy System of government in which power is invested in a few, whether one is speaking of a domestic or international system of government.

oligopolistic industry   Industry controlled by a few sellers.

oligopoly   A system controlled by a few major powers.

OPEC   Organization of Petroleum Exporting Countries.

opportunity cost   Cost incurred as the result of foreclosing other sources of profit.

pax Americana/pax Britannica   A world peace system dominated by the United States after World War II, replacing the world peace system steered by Britain in the nineteenth century.

perestroika   Strategy of decentralization that aimed to increase the personal responsibility of key managers in Soviet economic organizations and to make them more easily accessible to those in the region which they serviced.

Plaza-Louvre Accords   The G3 agreed in the Plaza-Louvre Accords of 1987 to set target zones of plus/minus 12 percent for the mark/dollar and yen/dollar exchange rates. The agreement has helped to keep the dollar within narrower ranges than before (which has been an important factor for the stability of the EMS).

policy of negative transparency   The stripping away of centralized barriers to information, overwhelming people with news of pollution, sickness, crime, inflation, and underdevelopment.

policy of positive transparency   The reporting of facts in a context of hope, which makes it imaginable that things can be changed, improved upon, and learned from in order to better the life chances of the people.

politea   Aristotle's ideal form of a balanced, democratic-aristocratic state.

political economy   The collective capacity of a state or multinational organization to structure payoffs for effective learning or adaptation in the global system (or the study of learning by paying if such adaptation is blocked).

positioning   The "name of the game" in political economics. Countries try to position themselves in the world economy to be able to take advantage of changes and innovation. The starting position is very important: The rich countries focus on maintaining their position whereas developing or generally poorer countries seek to improve their position.

positive-sum/cooperative game   Cooperation will lead to a greater mutual payoff; "new pie is baked," as opposed to the assumption of zero-sum game, where the ultimate goal is to achieve the greatest share of fixed (existing) pie.

post–cold-war economics   Concerned with the global expansion of massive unemployment and creating growth through economic liberalization, macroeconomic stability, and privatization of former state-run industries and institutions.

postmodern sensibility of globalization   No-nonsense disenchantment in which actors from the state, market, and cultural spheres are caught playing a permanent game of catch-up, pushing their businesses across national borders ever faster only to undermine more systematically the integrity of their home communities.

power   The social capacity to satisfy human needs or wants relative to competitors (always increasing or diminishing).

principal supplier rule   Trade negotiations begin bilaterally with requests for tariff reductions made by the exporter of the largest volume of that product to the market of a second country.

principle of transparency   All producers and their governments should be aware of existing trade barriers.

product differentiation   Updating products with technology and sophistication in specialized market niches.

product life-cycle theory/neotechnologist school Focuses on four stages: the introductory stage (innovation), the growth stage, the maturity stage, and the phase of decline.

productivity Measure of how much output is produced per unit of input.

programmed aid: structural adjustment Basic institutional economic adaptation to world economic change (targeted by Lomé conventions).

public/collective good Good that is not reduced for use by other potential consumers, even after consumption by an individual, household, company, or state (e.g., a road, a sidewalk, the ocean, air); access can't be denied.

purchasing power parity Real exchange rate is 1, meaning that the same basket of goods can be purchased in either country, either in the home country with the home currency or, after exchanging it into foreign currency, in that foreign country.

Pygmalion effect Positive self-fulfilling prophecy.

rational choice perspective Assumes individuals will use all information to maximize their own interests rationally, minimizing their costs in contributing to public goods from which all benefit.

reciprocity Countries reduce tariffs in exchange for reciprocal reductions from other countries.

regime Principle, norm, or decision-making procedure around which actor expectations converge.

reserve currency A currency individuals and governments are willing to hold their wealth in (originally gold; later, for most countries, dollars).

reverse Pygmalion effect Negative self-fulfilling prophecy (e.g., increasing the odds of extraordinarily bad economic outcomes by projecting negative expectations).

savings Postponed consumption.

schema Prototype of meaning in a specific culture (indigenous) used for processing information and "branding" it with particular interpretations.

security Aiming for "unconditional viability." A party, organization, or nation is considered to be secure if it cannot be absorbed as an independent source of decisions (Kenneth Boulding).

sense of agency The belief that individual action makes a critical difference (positive self-determination).

Shougang Contract System Part of the Chinese economic reforms; gradual privatization through contracting, with remaining influence of the state.

social capital Embedded community trust, norms, and networks that facilitate collective learning and the accurate targeting of local entrepreneurship.

Social Darwinism "Only the strongest survive": In economic Social Darwinism, the strongest in each sector force the weak out of business (if the weak want to survive, they have to find a better niche for themselves).

social learning theory The theory that individuals can learn from others by *modeling* their behavior; the result of reciprocal interactions among people, their behavior, and the environmental situation.

social market economy Government assures the solidarity of the social contract through class-mitigating welfare measures, while leaving the private sector free to operate in the economic market; social maintenance base is thus clearly separated from the freedom to take entrepreneurial risk.

socialism A socioeconomic and political system in which private property is abolished and the means of production—capital and land—are publically owned for the interests of all. For Karl Marx, socialism was a transitory stage on the way from capitalism to the ideal, classless society—communism. For Louis Hartz, socialism was interpreted as a left-wing rebellion against feudalism.

soft power   Cultural and economic power that rests on pull, not on push, on acceptance, not on conquest.

sogoshosha   Japanese trading companies (still remaining even after break up of *zaibatsus*), most of which utilize a strategy aimed at securing sources of basic raw materials and maintaining a world market share. These companies serve big and small organizations, and gather foreign marketing intelligence from all over the world, sift through the information, and target it for the right company at the right place at the right time.

Special Drawing Rights (SDRs)   Units of account that can be transferred between the IMF and national central banks to help resolve balance-of-payment problems.

Stalinist model   Collective learning through shortages; characterized by commodity inconvertibility. The Stalinist model overemphasizes maintenance strategy by rewarding risk-reduction rather than entrepreneurial growth. Resource shortages and bureaucratic bottlenecks determine economic policy, not prices. Single-party elites, not producers and consumers, create and manage the shortages.

state quota   The government outlay as a percentage of the GNP.

static economy of scale   Reduction of unit costs as output over a given production period goes up (typically stemming from increases in plant, firm, or industry size).

status   How much others think you have got or the degree of deference others give to you based on how you got the goods or go about getting them.

strategic behavior   Refers to patterns of individual or collective behavior *after* it has occurred; "because of" motive, as opposed to "in-order-to" motive.

strategy   Intentional plan for the future, a cognitive design that can be both personal and organizational.

structural assets   At least five primary structures make up the maintenance base of each state (or multinational organization) in the world economy, which together determine its competitive structural position and relative independence or dependence: security structure, money and credit structure, knowledge structure, production structure, and value structure.

structuralism   Theory that the world economy is structured against those countries that depend on the production of primary commodities for their economic survival (unequal, asymmetrical system of trade); a trade gap growth between the center (developed countries) and the periphery (developing countries) (Prebisch-Singer).

sunk costs   Material and psychic costs of change.

sustainable development/sustainability   A development that is long-term and equitable and is therefore aimed at preserving resources for future generations (e.g., trees can only be cut if at the same time new ones are planted), as well as assisting and including poorer regions (redistribution, to some extent).

syntropic process   Expansionary economic phases can be viewed as part of a syntropic process, a building up of production, employment, incomes, stock market prices, and construction (versus entropic processes—recession or decline).

syntropy   The coming together of energies into a new order; "creation" of energies (e.g., photosynthesis).

technological society   Technologically exploitable knowledge undermines both traditional cultural norms and the social cooperation made possible by the legal-rational framework. Humans are overwhelmed and dominated by the so-called apolitics of scientific technique and expertise.

technology   Derives from the Greek word *techne*, meaning skill or craft, combined with "ology"—organized, systematic, purposeful knowledge.

technology transfer   Refers to the movement of knowledge or techniques that contribute to the production process across national borders.

terms of trade   Refers to exact exchange rate at a particular historical moment of one good or service in terms of another; usually used in a broader context: A country's purchasing power (in international trade, its potential to import) based on its export revenues (inverse real exchange rate).

trade bloc   An organized group of nations of limited membership that attempts to create a buffer zone of import, export, and protectionist strategies to maximize the collective economic benefits of its members at the expense of those outside the bloc (e.g., NAFTA, EU, MERCOSUR).

traditional society   Based on affective or prerational community relationships (blood ties), diffuse role structures (jack-of-all-trades), and ascriptive notions of social and political authority. (One of Weber's three ideal types of authority patterns: traditional, legal-rational, and charismatic social realities.)

transnational corporation   Corporation based and owned in only one country, with manufacturing facilities in two or more other countries that repatriate profits that are not invested.

UNCED   1992; UN Conference on Environment and Development, also called the Earth Summit, held in Rio de Janeiro, Brazil, to discuss topics such as hunger, poverty, illiteracy, and links to ecological and economical consequences. Several accords were signed, such as the Climate Protection Convention or the famous Agenda 21 for a sustainable development, as well as commissions such as the CSD (Commission for Sustainable Development) for their implementation. In 1997, Kyoto hosted the five-year follow-up conference, which was aiming at a more specific plan for the implementation of the climate goals (they came up with 5 to 7 percent below previous levels).

UNCTAD   United Nations Conference on Trade and Development (the "poor nations' pressure group"); originally stemmed from Group of 77; organized to promote the interests of the countries disadvantaged by the asymmetrical or unequal world trading system, and first headed by structuralist Raúl Prebisch.

UNIDO   United Nations Industrial Development Organization, established in 1966 to help the developing countries in the private industrial sector; UNIDO uses its Industrial & Technology Bank to help nations with marketing and capital financing strategies as well as its Special Industrial Services program (SIS) that provides special assistance through, for example, fellowship programs for technological and managerial training for key personnel.

unipolar versus multipolar global system   Hegemonic global system dominated by one power versus oligopolistic system controlled by a few major powers.

Verdoorn's law   The stress on the growth of output in determining the rate of growth of productivity rather than the level of output determining the average level of productivity (with productivity growth resulting from a learning process).

vicious circle   Sluggish productivity, which leads to difficulties in exports, problems in the balance of payments, lower productivity growth, excessive wage increases, and a decline in competitiveness in world markets. A vicious circle strategy involves devaluing the currency in order to stimulate export sales in the short term by making them cheaper; but this has the effect of increasing inflation at home, thus causing workers to demand higher wages to match rising living costs, driving up the costs of production, and making exports less competitive until the government intervenes with another devaluation to start the circle anew.

virtual organization   Collective learning network that can almost instantaneously produce and deliver products or services at any time, in any place, and in any variety to satisfy a specific customer.

wage Bribe paid to individuals to sacrifice an hour of leisure (as defined by Lester Thurow).

Weberian ideal types Characteristic typifications of particular categories of behavior. Corporate behavior patterns usually draw from more than one type, and sometimes from all of them.

World Bank/International Bank for Reconstruction and Development (IBRD) Complementary to the IMF's short-term assistance, the World Bank's major function has been to stimulate the flow of capital into long-term investment across national boundaries. Shortly after foundation the priorities shifted from reconstruction (then taken care of by, for example, the Marshall Plan) to development; loans are targeted for specific viable economic projects (typically to build up infrastructure as prerequisite to industrialization).

world-class organization An organization that creates global standards, positions itself socially to dominate soft power, and commands the greatest resources across borders. These organizations are guided by cosmopolitan managers with the latest concepts or knowledge, the greatest competence and up-to-date technological sophistication, and the best connections with other influential technological and economic elites throughout the world. (See "Learning 4.")

WTO World Trade Organization; went into effect in 1995. The WTO not only replaces and embraces the rules of the GATT but also takes over permanent organizational and monitoring functions through its own councils and secretaries housed in the headquarters in Geneva, Switzerland.

zaibatsu Financial clique of Japanese corporate groups stemming from the Meji Restoration of 1868, usually made up of manufacturing facilities, a bank, and a marketing organization (*sogoshosha*). The twentieth-century tradition of the *zaibatsu* was to have a holding company at the top directly controlling the specialized firms in the *zaibatsu* group (forbidden and dispersed during occupation following World War II).

SELECTED BIBLIOGRAPHY

Agmon, Tamir. *Political Economy and Risk in World Financial Markets*. Lexington, MA: Lexington Books, 1986.

Albert, Michel. *Capitalism Contre Capitalism*. Paris: Edition de Seuil, 1991.

Amin, S. *Imperialism and Unequal Development*. New York: Monthly Review Press, 1988.

Anderson, James E. *The Relative Inefficiency of Quotas*. Cambridge, MA: MIT Press, 1988.

Argylis, Chris. *On Organizational Learning*. Oxford: Blackwell, 1992.

Ayres, Robert U., ed. *Eco-restructuring: Implications for Sustainable Development*. Tokyo: The United Nations, 1998.

Balassa, B., ed. *Newly Industrializing Countries in the World Economy*. New York: Pergamon Press, 1981.

Bandura, Albert. *Social Learning Theory*. Englewood Cliffs, NJ: Prentice Hall, 1977.

Barthelme, Donald. "The Rise of Capitalism." *Sadness*, 143–148. New York: Farrar, Straus and Giroux, 1972.

Bates, R. H. *Rural Response to Industrialization: A Study of Village in Zambia*. New Haven, CT: Yale University Press, 1976.

Bates, Robert A., ed. *Toward a Political Economy of Development: A Rational Choice Perspective*. Berkeley, CA: University California Press, 1988.

Bateson, Gregory. *Steps to an Ecology of Mind*. New York: Ballantine Books, 1975.

Bauer, P. T. *Equality, the Third World, and Economic Delusion*. Cambridge, MA: Harvard University Press, 1977.

Becker, J. F. *Marxian Political Economy: An Outline*. Cambridge, MA: Cambridge University Press, 1977.

Bélanger, J., et al., eds. *Being Local Worldwide: ABB and the Challenge of Global Management*. Ithaca, NY: Cornell University Press, 1999.

Bell, Daniel. *The Cultural Contradictions of Capitalism*. New York: Basic Books, 1982.

Berger, Suzanne, and Michael Plore. *Dualism and Discontinuity in Industrial Societies*. New York: Cambridge University Press, 1980.

Bergsten, Fred, ed. *Global Economic Imbalances*. Washington, D.C.: Institute for International Economics, 1986.

Bhagwati, Jagdish. *New International Economic Order: The North-South Debate*. Cambridge, MA: MIT Press, 1977.

———. *The World Trading System at Risk*. Princeton, NJ: Princeton University Press, 1991.

Billet, Bret L. *Investment Behavior of Multinational Corporations in Developing Areas: Comparing the Development Assistance Committee, Japanese, and American Corporations*. New Brunswick, NJ: Transaction Publishers, 1991.

Block, F. L. *Origins of International Economic Disorder: Study of United States International Monetary Policy*. Berkeley, CA: University of California Press, 1979.

Boulding, Kenneth E. *Conflict and Defense: A General Theory*. New York: Harper & Row, 1962.
———. *Economy Love and Fear*. Belmont, CA: Wadsworth Publishing Co., 1973.
———. *The Image: Knowledge in Life and Society*. Ann Arbor, MI: University of Michigan Press, 1956.
Bradford, Colin I., and William H. Branson, eds. *Trade and Structural Change in Pacific Asia*. Chicago, IL: University of Chicago Press, 1987.
Brandt, Willy, et al. *North-South: A Program for Survival*. Cambridge, MA: MIT Press, 1980.
Braudel, F. *Capitalism and Material Life*. New York: Harper & Row, 1973.
———. *The Structures of Everyday Life: The Limits of the Possible*. London: Collins, 1981.
Brown, Lester, et al. *The State of the World 1999*. New York: W. W. Norton, 1999.
Brown, Michael Barratt. *The Economics of Imperialism*. London: Penguin Press, 1974.
Buchanan, J. M., and G. Tulloch. *Calculus of Consent: Logical Foundations of Constitutional Democracy*. Ann Arbor, MI: University of Michigan Press, 1962.
Burch, Kurt, and Robert Denemark, eds. *Constituting International Political Economy*. Boulder, CO: Lynne Rienner, 1997.
Calleo, David, and Benjamin Rowland. *America and the World Political Economy: Atlantic Dreams and National Reality*. Bloomington, IN: Indiana University Press, 1973.
Caporaso, J. A., and D. P. Levine. *Theories of Political Economy*. Cambridge, MA: Cambridge University Press, 1992.
Castaneda, J., and E. Hett. *El Economismo Dependentista*. Mexico City: Siglo XXI, 1978.
Casten, Thomas. *Turning Off the Heat*. Amherst, NY: Prometheus Books, 1998.
Chase, R., E. Hill, and Paul Kennedy. *The Pivotal States*. New York: W. W. Norton, 1999.
Chenery, H. B., M. S. Ahluwalia, C. Bell, J. H. Duloy, and R. Jolly. *Redistribution with Growth: Policies to Improve Income Distribution in Developing Countries in the Context of Economic Growth*. London: Oxford University Press, 1974.
Chilcote, R. H., ed. *Dependency and Marxism: Towards a Resolution of the Debate*. Boulder, CO: Westview Press, 1982.
Cohen, S. S., and J. Zysman. *Manufacturing Matters: The Myth of the Post-Industrial Economy*. New York: Basic Books, 1987.
Conway, Gordon. *The Doubly Green Revolution: Food for All in the 21st Century*. New York: Penguin Books, 1997.
Cornwall, John. *Modern Capitalism: Its Growth and Transformation*. Oxford: Martin Robertson and Co., Ltd., 1977.
Cox, Robert. *Production, Power and World Order: Social Forces in the Making of History*. New York: Columbia University Press, 1987.
Crane, George T., and Abla Amawi. *The Theoretical Evolution of International Political Economy: A Reader*. New York: Oxford University Press, 1997.
Dahrendorf, Ralf. *Lebenschancen*. Frankfurt: Suhrkamp Verlag, 1979.
Davidow, William H., and Michael S. Malone. *The Virtual Corporation: Structuring and Revitalizing the Corporation for the 21st Century*. New York: HarperCollins, 1992.
Deming, W. Edwards. *Quality, Productivity and Competitive Position*. Cambridge, MA: MIT Center for Advanced Engineering Study, 1982.
Denison, E. F. *Accounting for United States Economic Growth, 1929–1969*. Washington, D.C.: Brookings Institution, 1974.
Deo, Som. *Multinational Corporations and the Third World*. Columbia, MO: South Asia Books, 1986.
Deresky, Helen. *International Management: Managing across Borders and Cultures*. New York: HarperCollins Publishers, 1994.
De Silva, S. B. D. *The Political Economy of Underdevelopment*. London: Routledge Chapman & Hall, 1982.
Dicken, Peter. *Global Shift*. New York: The Guilford Press, 1992.
Douthwaite, Richard. *The Growth Illusion*. Tulsa, OK: Council Oak Books, 1993.
Drucker, Peter. *Innovation and Entrepreneurship*. New York: Harper & Row, 1985.
———. *Post-Capitalist Society*. New York: Harper Collins, 1993.
Duchene, Francois, and Geoffrey Shepherd. *Managing Industrial Change in Europe*. London: Francis Printer, 1987.
Eichhorn, Peter, ed. *Okosoziale Marktwirtschaft*. Wiesbaden: Gabler Verlag, 1995.
Engwall, L., and V. Zamagni, *Management Education in Historical Perspective*. Manchester: Manchester University Press, 1998.

Faber, Malte, and John Proops. *Evolution, Time, Production and the Environment.* 2nd edition. Berlin: Springer-Verlag, 1994.

Frank, Andre. *Crisis in the World Economy.* New York: Holmes and Meier Publishers, 1980.

Frey, Bruno. *International Political Economics.* Oxford: Basil Blackwell, 1986.

Friedman, Thomas. *The Lexus and the Olive Tree.* New York: Farrar, Straus and Giroux, 1999.

Frohlich, N., and J. A. Oppenheimer. *Modern Political Economy.* Englewood Cliffs, NJ: Prentice Hall, 1978.

Frydman, Roman, Cheryl Gray, and Andrzej Rapaczynski, eds. *Corporate Governance in Central Europe and Russia: Insiders and the State.* Budapest: Central European University Press, 1998.

Galtung, J. *The True Worlds: A Transnational Perspective.* New York: Free Press, 1980.

Gardner, Richard. *Sterling-Dollar Diplomacy in Current Perspective: The Origins and Prospects of Our International Economic Order.* New York: Columbia University Press, 1980.

Garten, Jeffrey. *The Big Ten: The Big Emerging Markets and How They Will Change Our Lives.* New York: Basic Books, 1997.

Geiger, Theodore. *The Future of the International System: The United States and the World Political Economy.* Boston, MA: George, Allen & Unwin, 1988.

Geogescu-Roegen, Nicholas. *The Entropy Law and the Economic Process.* Cambridge, MA: Harvard University Press, 1971.

Gertz, Clifford. *Peddlers and Princes: Social Development and Economies in Two Indonesian Towns.* Chicago, IL: University of Chicago Press, 1963.

Ghosh, Prapid K. *Multi-National Corporations and Third World Development.* Westport, CT: Greenwood Press, 1984.

Gilpin, Robert. *The Political Economy of International Relations.* Princeton, NJ: Princeton University Press, 1987.

Glick, Reuven, ed. *Managing Capital Flows and Exchange Rates: Lessons from the Pacific Basin.* New York: Cambridge University Press, 1998.

Goldstein, Judith, and Robert Keohane, eds. *Ideas and Foreign Policy.* Ithaca, NY: Cornell University Press, 1993.

Gourevitch, Peter. *Politics in Hard Times: Comparative Responses to International Economic Crisis.* Ithaca, NY: Cornell University Press, 1986.

Gowa, Joanne. *Allies, Adversaries, and International Trade.* Princeton, NJ: Princeton University Press, 1996.

Gunberg, L. *Failed Multinational Ventures: The Political Economy of International Divestments.* Lexington, MA: D.C. Heath, 1981.

Hagen, Everett. *On the Theory of Social Change.* London: Tavistock Publications, 1964.

Hall, Edward. *Beyond Culture.* Garden City, NY: Anchor Press, 1976.

Hampden-Turner, Charles, and Alfons Trompenaars. *The Seven Cultures of Capitalism.* New York: Currency/Doubleday, 1993.

Hampden-Turner, Charles. *Gentlemen and Tradesmen: The Values of Economic Catastrophe.* London: Routledge Chapman & Hall, 1984.

Hancock, Graham. *Lords of Poverty.* New York: Atlantic Monthly Press, 1989.

Hankel, Wilhelm, W. Nölling, and K. Schachtschneider, *Die Euro-Klage.* Hamburg: Rororo Aktuell, 1998.

Hankel, Wilhelm. *Die sieben Todesunden der Vereinigung.* Berlin: Siedler Verlag, 1993.

Hankel, Wilhelm, and Robert Isaak. *Modern Inflation: Its Economics and Its Politics.* Lanham, MD: University Press of America, 1983. German version: *Die moderne Inflation* Köln: Bund-Verlag, 1981.

Hankel, Wilhelm. *Weltwirtschaft.* Duesseldorf: Econ Verlag, 1977.

Hansen, Roger D., ed. *The Global Negotiation and Beyond: Toward North-South Accommodation in the 1980s.* Austin, TX: Lyndon B. Johnson School of Public Affairs, 1981.

Hardin, Garret, and J. Baden, eds. *Managing the Commons.* San Francisco, CA: W. H. Freeman & Co., 1977.

Hayek, F. A. *Monetary Nationalism and International Stability.* New York: Macmillan, 1937.

Herman, B., and K. Sharma, eds. *International Finance and Developing Countries in a Year of Crisis.* Tokyo: United Nations University Press, 1998.

Hirsch, Fred. *Social Limits to Growth.* Cambridge, MA: Harvard University Press, 1976.

Hirsch, Fred, and John Goldthorpe, eds. *The Political Economy of Inflation.* Cambridge, MA: Harvard University Press, 1978.

Hirschmann, Albert O. *National Power and the Structure of Foreign Trade.* Berkeley and Los Angeles, CA: University of California Press, 1980.

Hoecklin, Lisa. *Managing Cultural Differences: Strategies for Competitive Advantage.* Reading, MA: Addison-Wesley Publishing Co., 1995.

Hofstede, Geert H. *Cultures and Organizations.* New York: McGraw-Hill, 1991.

Hollis, W., and F. Lamond Tullis, eds. *An International Political Economy: International Economy Yearbook.* vol. 1, Boulder, CO: Westview Press, 1985.

Homer-Dixon, Thomas. *Environment, Scarcity and Violence.* Princeton, NJ: Princeton University Press, 1999.

Hopkins, Terence K., and Immanuel Wallerstein, eds. *Processes of the World-System.* Newbury Park, CA: Sage Publications, 1980.

Inoguchi, Takashi, and Daniel I. Okimoto. *The Political Economy of Japan.* Stanford, CA: Stanford University Press, 1988.

International Bank for Reconstruction and Development/World Bank. *World Development Report: Knowledge for Development 1998/99.* New York: Oxford University Press, 1999.

Isaak, Robert. *European Politics: Political Economy and Policymaking in Western Democracies.* NewYork: St. Martin's Press, 1980.

————, ed. *American Political Thinking.* Fort Worth, TX: Harcourt Brace, 1994.

————. *Green Logic: Ecopreneurship, Theory and Ethics.* West Hartford, CT: Kumarian Press, 1999. First published in Sheffield, U.K.: Greenleaf Publishing, 1998.

James, Harvey S., Jr., and Murray Weidenbaum. *Businesses Cross International Borders: Strategic Alliances and Their Alternatives.* Westport, CT: Praeger Publishers, 1993.

Janoski, Thomas. *The Political Economy of Unemployment. Active Labor Market Policy in West Germany and the United States.* Berkeley, CA: University of California Press, 1990.

Johnson, Chalmers. *MITI and the Japanese Miracle: The Growth of Industrial Policy, 1925–1975.* Stanford, CA: Stanford University Press, 1982.

Katzenstein, Peter J. *Small States in World Markets: Industrial Policy in Europe.* Ithaca, NY. Cornell University Press, 1985.

Kennedy, Paul. *Preparing for the 21st Century.* New York: Random House, 1993.

Keohane, Robert O. *International Institutions and State Power.* Boulder, CO: Westview Press, 1989.

————. *After Hegemony: Cooperation and Discord in the World Political Economy.* Princeton. NJ: Princeton University Press, 1984.

Keohane, Robert O., and Joseph S. Nye. *Power and Interdependence.* Boston, MA: Little Brown, 1977.

Keren, Michael, and Gur Ofer. *Trials of Transition: Economic Reform in the Former Communist Bloc.* Boulder, CO: Westview Press, 1992.

Keynes, John Maynard. *General Theory of Employment, Interest and Money.* New York: A Harbinger Book, 1965.

————. *Laissez-faire and Communism.* New York: New Republic, Inc., 1926.

Kim, Linsa. *Imitation to Innovation: The Dynamics of Korean Technological Learning.* Boston, MA: Harvard Business Review Press, 1997.

Kindleberger, Charles. *Power and Money: The Economics of International Politics and the Politics of International Economics.* New York: Basic Books, 1970.

————. *The World in Depression, 1929–1939.* Berkeley, CA: University of California Press, 1986.

Kornai Janos. *Economics of Shortage,* vol. 1. Amsterdam: North Holland, 1981.

Koves, Andras. *Central and East European Economies in Transition: The International Dimension.* Boulder, CO: Westview Press, 1992.

Krasner, Stephen D. *Structural Conflict: The Third World against Global Liberalism.* Berkeley, CA: University of California Press, 1985.

Kuznets, Simon. *Modern Economic Growth.* New Haven, CT: Yale University Press, 1966.

Li, Cheng. *Rediscovering China: Dynamics and Dilemmas of Reform.* Lanham: Rowman and Littlefield, 1997.

Lindblom, Charles. *Politics and Markets: The World's Political-Economic System.* New York: Basic Books, 1980.

Linder, Staffan B. *The Harried Leisure Class.* New York: Columbia University Press, 1970.

Lodge, Goerge C. *Perestroika for America.* Boston, MA: Harvard Business School Press, 1991.

Lutz, Ernst, and Julian Caldecott, eds. *Decentralization and Biodiversity Conservation*. Washington, D.C.: World Bank, 1996.

Makin, John H. *The Global Debt Crisis: America's Growing Involvement*. New York: Basic Books, 1984.

Mansell, Robin, and Uta Wehn. *Knowledge Societies: Information Technology for Sustainable Development*. New York: Oxford University Press, 1998.

Marris, Peter. *Loss and Change*. New York: Pantheon, 1974.

Martin, Hans Peter, and Harald Schumann. *Die Globalisierungsfalle*. Reinbeck: Rowohlt, 1998.

Marx, Karl, and Frederick Engels. *Communist Manifesto*. Chicago, IL: Charles H. Kerr, 1946.

Masuda, Yuji, ed. *Human-Centered Systems in the Global Economy*. London: Springer-Verlag, 1992.

McCall, Jack. *Small Town Survival Manual*. Columbia, MO: University of Missouri, 1988.

McClelland, David C. *Roots of Consciousness*. New York: D. VanNostrand, 1964.

McRobie, Goerge. *Small Is Possible*. New York: Harper & Row, 1981.

Michie, Jonathan, ed. *The Economics of Restructuring and Intervention*. Brookfield, VT: Edward Elgar, 1991.

Mill, J. S. *Principals of Political Economy*. New York: Penguin, 1986.

Milner, Helen. *Interests, Institutions and Information*. Princeton, NJ: Princeton University Press, 1997.

Moran, Theodore H. *Investing in Development: New Roles for Private Capital*. New Brunswick, NJ: Transaction Publishers, 1986.

Morgan, Gareth. *Riding the Waves of Change*. San Francisco, CA: Jossey-Bass, 1988.

Mundell, Robert A. *Monetary Theory: Inflation, Interest and Growth in the World Economy*. Pacific Palisades, CA: Goodyear Publishing Co., 1971.

Mytelka, Lynn, ed. *Strategic Partnerships and the World Economy*. Rutherford, NJ: Fairleigh Dickinson University, 1991.

Nohlen, Dieter, and Franz Nuscheler, eds. *Handbuch der Dritten Welt Band 2: Suedamerika: Unterentwicklung und Entwicklung*. Ludwigsberg, W. Germany: Hoffinan und Campes, 1985.

Nölling, Wilhelm, Karl Schachtschneider, and Joachim Starbatty, eds. *Währungsunion und Weltwirtschaff: Festschrift für Wilhelm Hankel*. Stuttgart: Lucius and Lucius, 1999.

O'Hanlon, Michael, and Carol Graham. *A Half Penny on the Federal Dollar: The Future of Development Aid*. Washington, D.C.: Brookings, 1997.

Ohlin, Bertil, Per Ove Hessleborn, and Wijman Per Magnus. *The International Allocation of Economic Activity*. New York: Holmes & Meier, 1978.

Olson, Mancur. *Logic of Collective Action: Public Goods and the Theory of Groups*. Cambridge, MA: Harvard University Press, 1971.

———. *The Rise and Decline of Nations: Economic Growth, Stagflation and Social Rigidities*. New Haven, CT: Yale University Press, 1982.

Packenham, Robert A. *Liberal America and the Third-World: Political Development Ideas in Foreign Aid and Social Science*. Princeton, NJ: Princeton University Press, 1987.

Polanyyi, K. *Great Transformation: The Political and Economic Origins of Our Time*. Boston, MA: Beacon Press, 1957.

Pollard, Robert A. *Political Economy of International Change*. New York: Columbia University Press, 1987.

Putnam, Robert D., and Nicholas Bayne. *Hanging Together. The Seven Power Summits*. Cambridge, MA: Harvard University Press, 1984.

Radice, H., ed. *International Firms and Modern Imperialism*. Harmondsworth, U.K.: Penguin, 1975.

Ravenhill, John. *Collective Clientelism; The Lomé Convention and North-South Relations*. New York: Columbia University Press, 1985.

Rawls, John. *Political Liberalism*. New York: Columbia University Press, 1993.

Ray, Debra J. *Development Economics*. Princeton, NJ: Princeton University Press, 1998.

Reich, Robert. *The Work of Nations*. New York: Alfred Knopf, 1991.

Ricardo, David. *Works and Correspondence of David Ricardo: Principals of Political Economy and Taxation*. London: Cambridge University Press, 1981.

Riddle, D. *Service-Led Growth: The Role of the Service Sector in World Development*. New York: Praeger, 1986.

Rodrik, Dani. *Has Globalization Gone Too Far?* Washington, D.C.: Institute for International Economics, 1997.

Rosecrance, Richard. *The Rise of the Trading State: Commerce and Conquest in the Modern World.* New York: Basic Books, 1987.

Rostow, W. W. *Stages of Economic Growth.* London: Cambridge University Press, 1971.

———. *Why the Poor Get Richer and the Rich Slow Down: Essays in the Marshallian Long Period.* Austin, TX: University of Texas Press, 1980.

Rothstein, Robert L. *Global Bargaining: UNCTAD and the Quest for a New International Economic Order.* Princeton, NJ: Princeton University Press, 1979.

Rowland, Benjamin, ed. *Balance of Power or Hegemony: The Interwar Monetary System.* New York: New York University Press, 1975.

Ruggie, John Gerard, ed. *The Antinomies of Interdependence. The Political Economy of International Change.* New York: Columbia University Press, 1983.

Sandler, Todd, ed. *The Theory and Structures of International Political Economy.* Boulder, CO: Westview Press, 1980.

Sassen, Saskia. *Losing Control? Sovereignty in an Age of Globalization.* New York: Columbia University Press, 1996.

Sauvant, Karl P., and Hajo Hasenpflug, eds. *The New International Economic Order: Confrontation or Cooperation between North and South.* Boulder, CO: Westview Press, 1977.

Schelling, Thomas C. *Micromotives and Macrobehaviour.* New York: W. W. Norton, 1978.

Schmidt-Bleek, Friedrich, and Paul Weaver. *Factor 10: Manifesto for a Sustainable Planet.* Sheffield, England: Greenleaf Publishers, 1999.

Schor, Juliet. *The Overworked American.* New York: Basic Books, 1992.

Schumacher, E. F. *Small Is Beautiful: Economics as if People Mattered.* New York: Harper & Row, 1975.

Schumpeter, Joseph. *The Theory of Economic Development: An Enquiry into Profits, Capital Interest and the Business Cycle.* Cambridge, MA: Harvard University Press, 1984.

Scott, James C. *Seeing Like a State: How Certain Schemes to Improve the Human Condition Have Failed.* New Haven, CT: Yale University Press, 1998.

Smith, Adam. *An Inquiry into the Nature and Causes of the Wealth of Nations.* New York: Modern Library, 1937.

Smith, Peter H. *The Challenge of Integration: Europe and the Americas.* New Brunswick, NJ: Transaction Publishers, 1993.

Smith, Tony. *The Pattern of Imperialism: The U.S., Great Britain, and the Late-Industrializing World Since 1815.* New York: Cambridge University Press, 1981.

Soros, George. *The Crisis of Global Capitalism: Open Society Endangered.* New York: Public Affairs, 1998.

Spiro, David. *The Hidden Hand of American Hegemony: Petrodollar Recycling and International Markets.* Ithaca, NY: Cornell University Press, 1999.

Strange, S. *Mad Money: When Markets Outgrow Governments.* Ann Arbor, MI: University of Michigan Press, 1999.

———. *States and Markets.* London: Pinter, 1986.

———. *Casino Capitalism.* Oxford: Blackwell, 1986.

———, ed. *Paths to International Economy.* London: George Allen & Unwin, 1984.

Strange, S., and R. Tooze, eds. *The International Politics of Surplus Capacity: Competition for Market Shares in the World Recession.* London: George Allen & Unwin, 1981.

Thomas, Vinod, Nalin Kishor, and Tamura Belt. *Embracing the Power of Knowledge for a Sustainable Development.* Washington, D.C.; The World Bank, 1997.

Thurow, Lester. *Head to Head: The Coming Economic Battle Among Japan, Europe, and America.* New York: William Morrow, 1992.

Triffin, Robert. *Gold and the Dollar Crisis: The Future of Convertibility.* New Haven, CT: Yale University Press, 1960.

Trompenaars, Fons, and Charles Hampden-Turner. *Riding the Waves of Culture.* 2nd ed. New York: McGraw-Hill, 1998.

Tsurumi, Yoshi. *Multinational Management: Business Strategy and Government Policy.* 2nd ed. Cambridge, MA: Ballinger, 1983.

Tucker, Robert W. *The Inequality of Nations.* New York: Basic Books, 1979.

Tufte, Edward R. *Political Control of the Economy.* Princeton, NJ: Princeton University Press, 1980.

Tyson, Laura D'Andrea. *Who's Bashing Whom?: Trade Conflict in High Technology Industries.* Washington, D.C.: Institute of International Economics, 1992.

United Nations. *World Economic and Social Survey 1998: Trends and Policies in the World Economy*. New York: United Nations, 1998.

Vernon, Raymond, ed. *Big Business and the State: Changing Relations in Western Europe*. Cambridge, MA: Harvard University Press, 1974.

——. *The Promise of Privatization: A Challenge for U.S. Foreign Policy*. New York: Council on Foreign Relations, 1988.

Vogel, Ezra. *The Four Little Dragons: The Spread of Industrialization in East Asia*. Cambridge, MA: Harvard University Press, 1991.

——. *One Step Ahead in China: Guangdong under Reform*. Cambridge, MA: Harvard University Press, 1989

Von Weiszacker, Ernst, Amory Lovins, and L. Hunt Lovins. *Factor Four: Doubling Wealth, Halving Resource Use*. London: Earthscan, 1997.

Wade, Robert. *Governing the Market: Economic Theory and the Role of Government in East Asian Industrialization*. Princeton, NJ: Princeton University Press, 1994.

Wallerstein, Immanuel. *The Capitalist World Economy*. Cambridge, MA: Cambridge University Press, 1979.

——, ed., *World Inequality: Origins and Perspectives on the World System*. Montreal: Black Rose Books, 1975.

Weber, Max. *Economy and Society: An Outline of Interpretive Sociology*. 2 vols. Berkeley, CA: University of California Press, 1978.

Weisband, Edward, ed. *Poverty Amidst Plenty: World Political Economy and Distributive Justice*. Boulder, CO: Westview Press, 1989.

Wicksell, Knut. *Lectures on Political Economy*. 2 vols. London: Routledge & Kegan Paul Ltd., 1934.

Wildenmann, Rudolf, ed. *The Future of Party Government, Vol. 3: Managing Mixed Economies*. Ed. Francis G. Castles, Franz Lehner, and Manfred G. Schmidt. New York/Berlin: Walter de Gruyter, 1988.

Wilkins, Mira. *The Maturing of Multinational Enterprise: American Business Abroad from 1914–1970*. Cambridge, MA: Harvard University Press, 1974.

World Resource Institute. *The Next Bottomline: Making Sustainable Development Tangible*. Washington, D.C.: World Resource Institute, 1998.

Yew, Lee Kuan. *The Singpore Story: Memoirs of Lee Kuan Yew*. Singapore: Simon & Schuster/Prentice Hall, 1998.

Young, Mary Emming, ed. *Early Childhood Development: Investing in the Future*. Amsterdam: Elsevier, 1997.

Young, Oran. *Governance in World Affairs*. Ithaca, NY: Cornell University Press, 1999.

Zamagni, Stefano. *Non profit come economia civile*. Bologna: Il Mulino, 1998.

Zysman, John. *Government, Markets and Growth: Financial Systems and the Politics of Industrial Change*. Ithaca, NY. Cornell University Press, 1983.

INDEX